"O'Neal is the real thing: An extraordinarily gifted actor who puts his considerable artistry to work in communicating the essential aspects of our shared humanity."

—WAYNE JOHNSON, SEATTLE TIMES

"Everyone who comes in contact with John O'Neal is changed for the better on the occasion. He works with all people with respect, humor and the quietest passion. It is difficult for people in our area to set aside time to renew a spiritual relationship to art and to history. Those who take the opportunity to do so with John O'Neal never forget it."

—LEILA GORDON, ARTS DIRECTOR
RESTON COMMUNITY CENTER, RESTON, VA

"O'Neal performs some brilliant acting turns to capture both the spirit of this mythic storyteller and the heart of his tales."

—MARILYN STASIO, NEW YORK POST

"There is magic to his art."

—SASHA ANAWALT, LOS ANGELES HERALD-EXAMINER

Don't Start Me
to Talking...

Don't Start Me to Talking...

Plays of Struggle and Liberation

THE SELECTED PLAYS OF

John O'Neal

Edited with Select Introductory Material
by Theresa Ripley Holden

THEATRE COMMUNICATIONS GROUP
NEW YORK
2016

Don't Start Me to Talking . . . Plays of Struggle and Liberation: The Selected Plays of John O'Neal is published by Theatre Communications Group, Inc., 520 8th Avenue, 24th Floor, New York, NY 10018-4156

The publication of *Don't Start Me to Talking . . . Plays of Struggle and Liberation: The Selected Plays of John O'Neal*, by John O'Neal, through TCG's Book Program, is made possible in part by the New York State Council on the Arts with the support of Governor Andrew Cuomo and the New York State Legislature.

TCG books are exclusively distributed to the book trade by Consortium Book Sales and Distribution.

Cataloging-in-Publication Data is on file at the Library of Congress, Washington, DC.

ISBN: 978-1-55936-419-5 (paperback)
ISBN: 978-1-55936-717-2 (ebook)

Cover design, book design and composition by Lisa Govan
Cover art by John Scott

First Edition, March 2016

Contents

CONTENTS

Acknowledgments

My gratitude goes out to all who helped to bring this book to fruition with their support and assistance in the writing and production of the plays contained in this book.

I would like to acknowledge the Free Southern Theater and all its members. My time spent with them greatly influenced my work as a playwright and actor.

Like theater, this book is the product of a collaborative process. I would like to thank my many collaborators: Thank you Theatre Communications Group for making this book happen; Michael and Theresa Holden who have been essential to much of my work in theater as well as in this book; Steve Kent, who directed most of the plays in this book.

And to the other artists whose work is included in this book, and with whom it has been my privilege to work: Dudley Cocke, Donna Porterfield and Ron Short of Roadside Theater; Naomi Newman of A Traveling Jewish Theatre; Rosalba Rolón of Pregones Theater; and Michael Keck, composer, musician and actor. Thank you all.

Also among my collaborators I count my family because of the love, support and inspiration they provided and continue to provide: My wife Bertha, whose support I have in all life's efforts; my daughter Wendi and my son William; and all my grandchildren.

I also extend a very heartfelt thank you to all of my many other collaborators too numerous to mention. I am grateful to all of you.

—JO

Over My Head
I See Freedom in the Air

A Foreword

By Charles Cobb

It is unfortunate that consideration of the mid-twentieth cen-
tury Southern Freedom Movement almost always ignores its
creativity in the arts. Poetry in particular accompanied movement politics. So, by way of introducing John O'Neal and this
book, I must introduce you to Black Art, particularly Black Art
as a part of Black Political Struggle.

I am an African-American writer and Student Nonviolent
Coordinating Committee (SNCC) veteran who believes that
our art has always been tied to our struggle. This is a centuries-
old truth of Black life. Beauty, after all, is part of what helps
us through despair, what reinforces resistance to oppression.
Who can doubt that? Perhaps more than any other group in
the United States, Black people have framed the ideas of freedom with words, song, dance, story and other media and forms
(some perhaps unknown). Black people have brought beauty
into the struggle for freedom and justice.

How could this not be so? For we are haunted, wrote
author and professor Jan Carew some years ago, by "ghosts in
our blood." So consider, for instance, these words of Sojourner

Truth, that continue to haunt me with their beauty and their relevance for today:

> I can remember when I was a little young girl, how my old mammy would sit out of doors in the evenings and look up at the stars and groan, and I would say, "Mammy what makes you groan so?" And she would say, "I am groaning to think of my poor children; they do not know where I be and I don't know where they be. I look up at the stars and they look up at the stars!"

Is this not poetry, although she is writing autobiographically of the slavery she remembered? To talk of slavery, as you must when discussing the Black world, Black life and the creative forces within it, is also to talk of the desire for freedom and freedom's struggle wherever and whenever you were born. As the old freedom song from The Southern Movement goes, "They say that freedom is a constant struggle."

Space does not permit a full exploration of this theme here, but I think the poet Eugene Redmond provides relevance for us today in understanding creativity in this manner as clearly as I have heard it stated: "Class and race, seen vividly, and devastatingly, during the reign of Hurricanes Katrina and Rita remain central to the theory and fact of African-American struggle and art." Or consider South African poet laureate Keorapetse "Willie" Kgositsile's take that embraces Black life on both sides of the Atlantic:

> There is only movement. Force. Creative power. The walk of a Sophiatown tsotsi or my Harlem brother on Lenox Avenue. Field Hollers. The blues. A Trane riff. Marvin Gaye or mbaqanga. Anguished happiness. Creative power, in whatever form it is released, moves like the dancer's muscles.

It is here within this tradition that we encounter John O'Neal and the importance of his work, some of which is found in the pages of this book. I am not going to summarize the book in this introduction, but I am compelled to point out that an important part of what has shaped his artistry is that the Free Southern Theater (FST) emerged from the dynamic of Mississippi's Freedom Movement in 1963 and was more than an effort to bring theater or performance to the South. The FST continued a very old tradition of struggle and was a conscious and determined effort to push forward recognition of the legitimacy, strength and voice of African-American life and experience. That creativity defined The Movement as much as protest is a point consistently missed by scholars and media analysts. But without understanding Movement creativity, which most often bubbles from the bottom up, understanding of The Movement is at best incomplete.

This is, in fact, something larger than "civil rights." As poet and Dillard University professor Jerry Ward once noted in conversation with literary critic Houston Baker: "In any literary history that we will write in the future, we will have to account for those writers and thinkers who were caught up in very active way(s) with SNCC. They moved across regions, and they too were agents of cross-fertilization and change."

At the time of the FST's founding (October 1963), John O'Neal was a Mississippi-based SNCC field secretary, who helped author the theater's founding prospectus of principles. What you see in this statement is a reflection of the organizing tradition that defined The Movement:

> Our fundamental objective is to stimulate creative and reflective thought among Negroes in Mississippi and other Southern states by the establishment of a legitimate theater, thereby providing the opportunity in the theater and the associated art forms. We theorize that within the Southern situation a theatrical form and style can be developed that is as unique to the Negro people as the origin of blues and jazz. A combination of art and social awareness can evolve into plays written for a Negro audience, which relate to the problems within the Negro himself, and within the Negro community.

The formality of the language does not obscure the fact that the newly formed theater was on an organizing mission. Its value was recognized not only by The Southern Movement. So one key point that helps introduce readers to the work contained in this book brings us to Jerry Ward's observation of the cross-fertilization that took place. Indeed, while The Southern Movement was the cutting edge of direct challenge to a white supremacist order, it spread the conversation about social change not only across the South but across the nation as well.

Charles Sherrod, SNCC's lead organizer in southwest Georgia in the 1960s, gives some insight into this conversation when speaking to a reporter in 1961, just after he had finished serving the thirty days of hard labor to which he had been sentenced in Rock Hill, South Carolina, for protesting segregation.

> You get ideas in jail. You talk with other young people you have never seen . . . Right away you recognize each other. People like yourself, getting out of the past. We're up all night sharing creativity, planning action. You learn the truth in prison. You learn wholeness. You find out the difference between being dead and alive.

Sherrod was twenty-two years old then. Shortly afterward he began an organizing project in southwest Georgia. He and his wife Shirley, still live and work there today.

This was a conversation, washing over us, North and South—not only about protest and jail, but also about words and music and a liberated Black existence in America—and it was being held by a whole generation of young Black folks, and carried us to a new level of Black consciousness. This was a generational exchange of political and cultural ideas.

The Junebug Jabbo Jones who appears in these pages emerged from a group of us who worked with SNCC and who had come off the Howard University campus where we had been heavily influenced by professor Sterling Brown, a master of the Black folk idiom. He showed us the wisdom contained in ordinary everyday Black life, and the power. We used it in our day-to-day life as SNCC organizers, often borrowing with pleasure or for political use the words and structure of language found in the Black life we encountered. Phrases that we passed among ourselves we gradually attributed to one figure: thus Junebug. We were pleased that John chose to develop this into a series of performances, for as Junebug would put it: "Mr. Say ain't nothin', Mr. Do is the man."

It is within this emerging consciousness that we find the nexus between The Black Arts Movement and The Southern Freedom Movement. Poet and activist Amiri Baraka, speaking of this at the 2010 conference held at Shaw University to commemorate the fiftieth anniversary of SNCC's founding, made an essential point about not only the Free Southern Theater or Civil Rights struggle or the Black Arts Repertory theater in New York: "We had to change the conversation." And that is exactly what happened with words and music as well as with political ideas and stances. Few things were more important to this change than the Free Southern Theater.

The FST died in 1980, giving birth to Junebug Productions, which continues to celebrate the legacy of SNCC, the FST and the Southern-based struggle for social justice and The Black Arts Movement.

Washington, DC
2015

Journalist and author Charles Cobb is a former SNCC field secretary. His latest book, *This Nonviolent Stuff'll Get You Killed: How Guns Made the Civil Rights Movement*, was published in 2014 by Basic Books in New York City.

Maybe These Young People Can Sit Me Down

A Foreword

By Steve Kent

John and I have worked together for almost three decades. For each of us it is our longest creative relationship. It began in a ROOTS meeting in Tennessee where I saw John perform an early version of *Don't Start Me to Talking* on a picnic bench in a camp dining room. It hasn't really ended yet.

What drew this straight black man who lived in New Orleans and this gay white guy from Los Angeles together is simply that we shared a worldview and a commitment to theater as a tool for progressive social change. We also shared a belief that the creative process should be available to everyone. We have lived together and created in the cities where the pieces were set— New Orleans, Chicago, San Antonio, Oakland, San Francisco. We have learned from each other, surprised each other, frustrated each other and fought passionately, but our friendship was never at stake. We were bonded by the work we knew we had to do, and we did this work best together.

Our creative relationship was a mutual mystery. There is a sequence in a documentary on our work by George King in which I am explaining to John some character work I wanted him to do. He got it and ran with it. Later, when I viewed the film, I couldn't imagine how John knew what I wanted him to do from what I saw myself demonstrating to him.

We always felt that the activities of the fictitious Junebug had to be consistent with actual history. In *Don't Start Me to Talking*, the penultimate story is set when Junebug is nineteen in 1950 and the last story is contemporary. The piece we were working on was about the 1960s and The Civil Rights Movement. We know Junebug was involved in The Movement but what was Junebug doing in the 1950s? It was a wonderful surprise to us when it became obvious that he had been a medic in the Korean War. His involvement in that war, and the issues about Black people and the military-industrial complex during World War II, Korea and Vietnam gave us the core of the third piece: *Ain't No Use in Going Home.*

We also felt that the characters should be consistent with each other. The large Tatum family, from which Junebug's best friend Po comes, are mentioned in Volume I and figure strongly in Volume II, as do the white oligarchs, the Whitten family.

We wanted our audiences to feel that these stories were "true" even if they didn't actually happen.

We were very open to each other. He was the writer and actor. I was the dramaturg and director, but who came up with what is impossible to trace. I know neither of us cared about that as long as the work was progressing well. Sometimes getting the pieces to where we wanted them to be would take years. As we liked to say: "We are not fast food!"

There were some basic tenets. It had to be cheap. It had to be portable. It had to be accessible. It had to be honest. It was based on stories of the people.

It was transformational in its nature. By this we meant that the conventions of the piece would use objects in a way that often changed their meaning: a ladder became a jail or a church or a locker; a plank became a porch or a table; a handkerchief became a book or a piece of intimate clothing—a process that makes direct use of the power of the audience's imagination. For example, John played Junebug who played many parts— sometimes as many as thirty in a single piece. We wanted the craft to be essentially invisible. Mostly, it had to be really good. If our theater was sloppy, people would probably think that our politics were too.

Our country is not good to artists. We are suspect. We are not respected unless we get rich. So we grow to ignore our second-rate status—after all we are not the point, our work is—and learn to live and work on very little. We have to subsidize ourselves. It may be said that we have to have jobs in order to do our work.

There are fewer and fewer of us still keeping on keeping on. It is simply too hard for most people. I am full of nostalgia and even grief for the passing of the alternative small-ensemble theater movement in the U.S. I remember the feeling of solidarity and support and shared vision that we used to experience as part of The Movements: Civil Rights, Anti-War, Women's and Gay Rights. But I am not despondent. Finally there seems to be stirring. There is something happening again. Maybe our experiences will be useful to those "coming up." That is why many of us have become teachers. We all would love to pass on the baton. As I sometimes hear, "Maybe these young people can sit me down."

Los Angeles
2015

Steve Kent is a director and dramaturg, who has worked with John O'Neal for more than thirty years, collaborating with O'Neal on major productions with A Traveling Jewish Theatre and Roadside Theater. He is currently Director of Theatre at the University of La Verne in Southern California.

A Personal Invitation

With My Mind Stayed on Freedom!
An Introduction

By John O'Neal

"Freedom Song" is adapted from a gospel music standard: "With My Mind Stayed on Jesus!" The Leader sings:

THE LEADER *(Sings)*:
It ain't no harm to keep your mind stayed on freedom!

THE CONGREGATION *(Sings)*:
It ain't no harm to keep your mind, stayed on freedom!
It ain't no harm to keep your mind, stayed on freedom!

Halle-u! . . . Halle-u! . . . Halle-u—u-u-u . . . Hau—jah!

(Second verse:)

THE LEADER *(Sings)*:
It ain't no harm to keep your mind . . .

THE CONGREGATION *(Sings)*:
Stayed on Freedom!
It ain't no harm to keep your mind, stayed on Freedom!
It ain't no harm to keep your mind, stayed on Freedom!

Halle-u! . . . Halle-u! . . . Halle-u—u-u-u . . . Hau—jah!

(Third verse:)

THE LEADER *(Sings)*:
    Walking and talking! . . .

THE CONGREGATION *(Sings)*:
    Walking and talking with my mind, stayed on Freedom!
    Walking and talking with my mind, stayed on Freedom!
    Walking and talking with my mind, stayed on Freedom!

    Halle-u! . . . Halle-u! . . . Halle-u—u-u-u . . . Hau—jah!

. . .

Summer 1948:

JOHN: My job that morning before school started was to help Pop-Paw, to patch the roof of *"Ma-Maw's* henhouse" in our shared back yard. I must have pestered him with two or three dozens of questions before, Pop-Paw's patience was worn down to a frazzle. He fixed me squarely in his field of vision, pulled himself to his full 6' 4" frame and said:

POP-PAW: "If you don't have anything worthwhile to say, Son . . . then for God's sake, don't waste anybody's time saying it! . . . It's better to be *quiet* and thought-*fool*, than to open your mouth and *prove* it!"

JOHN *(Now)*: Here I was—going on eight years old, about to go into the third grade! Ever since that hot day in August, I always *tried* to think carefully about what I had to say before I decided whether to say it or not.

    To this day when I need to write something, my mind jumps to Pop-Paw and me out there working on the roof of Ma-Maw's henhouse!

    It's one of the reasons that I prefer writing plays to writing sermons, which Pop-Paw favored or oratory which my dad favored. I prefer to work in a realm where the right to rewrite is a given! I remember the old theater saying, "Plays are not written, they are rewritten. Again and again and again and again . . ."

I hope that you enjoy reading these plays as much as I have enjoyed writing, producing, sometimes directing and sometimes performing in them and rewriting and rewriting them. And *re*writing them again and again. I also hope that they stimulate you to think about where we have come from to get to where we are in the stream of history *today* in the struggle for Freedom, Justice, and Equality in America and among all people in *The World*.

I also hope that you appreciate and pay careful attention to what the characters in these plays do and *don't do*, what they say and *don't* say as you read them. Would you have made the same choices if it were you? . . . I also hope these scripts give those for whom this is an introduction to this kind of "storytelling theater," "grist for your mill." I hope you come away with clear images of what happened in "the theater in your head." Your head is the best theater in town! AND it's the only place where it's always NOW! The actors in *your* theater are always subject to the *present moment's* decisions that you and the performers make and fail to make! Every time you revisit a play in your theater it may be or may not be the same as you remember or you may be surprised to discover some things are altogether different! Those are the best ones! What a wonderful world it is for us to live, work and play in!

Just remember, *you* are THE ACTIVE AGENT for the things you imagine. You are responsible for all the other things you do or don't do here, just as you are in all the other places you go.

Sometimes you might want to go back and read a section two or three times before you feel like you got it right! Don't worry! Take your time. You're the boss!

This collection contains four pieces for solo performance, two for duets and three plays written for small ensembles. The choices revealed by these scripts were dictated by the *economic, social* and *historical* circumstances extant at the time they were done and by the audiences of oppressed and exploited people who were working as hard as they can to improve the quality of life for themselves and others who were, and still are, similarly situated.

I call the plays in this book "Junebug Storytelling Plays." The idea is to write them to encourage vivid performances of the stories, so that audiences can perceive the points clearly yet feel the necessary emotive force/the heart of the experiences being recounted. There should be no doubt what the experiences *must* have been like for those who actually suffered the stories being shared. One of the plays included here, *Don't Start Me to Talking or I'll Tell Everything I Know: Sayings from the Life and Writings of Junebug Jabbo Jones Vol. I,* was the *last* play ever produced by the Free Southern Theater (the theater that I co-founded with Gilbert Moses and Doris Derby in 1963), and was the first play ever produced by Junebug Productions (the theater that I founded in 1980).

The "Junebug Jabbo Jones," (who is the inspiration for these plays) I learned of in SNCC entered the collective consciousness through the gates of Howard University sometime in the late 1950s. The fictional professor, "Dr. Junebug," invented by the students in their satirical tales about him left little ambiguity about who the arrogant, narrow-minded, self-centered, self-serving, pretentious fakes with faulty grammar were. But when the bad acting, stuffed shirt profs prevailed over the *serious* educators, one way students had of balancing accounts was to feature the bad actors in their funny stories. In no time, that "Junebug Jabbo Jones" became available to the world of literature at large.

Despite the strong anti-rural biases that run rampant through modern western culture, the longer the young SNCC cadres mocked, as they worked thanklessly in plantation fields and homes in the South, the less Junebug seemed like the critique of the narrow-minded professor, and more he seemed like the humble, grassroots people we most admired and sought to imitate. This is the "Junebug Jabbo Jones" that I most admire and seek to celebrate in my writing.

Although the plays in this book are fictional, they are each based in historical and social realities that I have witnessed and have taken great pains to insure the historical accuracy of. The stories collected here are presented as "praisesongs" for the courageous "grassroots leadership" that I have seen and with whom I have shared confidences in places where my own work has brought me, from southern Illinois, to the length and breadth of the Black Belt, to other communities that may or may not be named in the text or identified in the scripts. After all, the struggle of oppressed and exploited people is global and indivisible. The international struggle for social justice will continue until it's won!

I'm proud to be included among the thousands of Movement veterans who survive to tell their own stories of "The Movement!"

We made the decision to move toward small casts, simple sets and costumes, the *creative* use of music, empty space and rich, sensual *suggestions* on stage to evoke the presence of what is not actually there except in our imaginations. Where theatre space is scarce and going *to* the theatre is not a common social practice, touring productions were driven by the economic realities within whose terms our theater was obliged to function. We had very little money so we had to cut way back on more expensive things. We had to rely more on things that we had in relative abundance—like audiences who are accustomed to doing much more with much less.

My guess is that you're already a theater lover. After all, whether you bought it or not, you are holding this book and reading it right now! You already know that regardless of how large or small the company, no matter how large or small the role one does, theater is always a collaborative enterprise in which THE AUDIENCE *always, always, always! plays the most important AND the most creative roles!*

I deeply appreciate the opportunity to share this work and these ideas with you. I hope that it turns out to be as satisfying for you to *read* and think about these plays as it has been for me to write them and to collaborate on various productions of them, as you and I are collaborating now.

I hope this project serves each of us well.

Yours in the struggle to make the world a better place for all of us to live in.

Enjoy!

New Orleans
2015

John O'Neal, Junebug's Founder and Artistic Director for more than thirty years, co-founded the Free Southern Theater in 1963 as a cultural arm of The Southern Civil Rights Movement. In 2013, John retired as Artistic Director of Junebug Productions, but the company is still carrying on its work and mission in New Orleans.

A Historical Note

By Theresa Ripley Holden

John O'Neal began to write plays in 1960 while he was in college at Southern Illinois University and has continued to do so to this day. John has written or co-written numerous plays; nine of them are included in this collection. This book contains the plays that have been fully produced and have been performed across this country and internationally.

In the early years of Junebug, John began his longtime partnership with Steve Kent, who directed eight of the plays contained in this book. Then in 1983 John began a thirty-year partnership with Michael Holden and me to undertake the work of getting his plays presented across the country and internationally, of producing many of his plays and of partnering with John on the cultural organizing for the long-term community residencies that often accompanied the performances.

In 1963, John co-founded the Free Southern Theater and in 1980, from the ashes of the Free Southern Theater, he founded Junebug Productions as the organizational successor of the Free Southern Theater to carry on its mission and legacy. John's plays, like many plays, not only realize their artistry and meaning when performed, but his plays come alive, resonate and echo within the audience. His audience is hearing their stories lifted up. And, like the work of the Free Southern Theater, the effect of his plays did not stop at the curtain call; their stories rippled out into the community and the impact of the residency work that most often accompanied the performances is still felt today.

Austin
2015

Theresa Ripley Holden is a theater artist, professor, performing arts manager and organizer. She is the Co-Director of Holden & Arts Associates, a management company; and the Director of the Artist and Community Connection (ACC), both based in Austin, TX. Theresa served as Managing Director of Junebug Productions and produced many of John O'Neal's plays.

SECTION 1

The Junebug Jabbo Jones Plays

Volumes I–V

Storytelling: Plays and Our Imagination

A Note about the Junebug Jabbo Jones Plays

By Theresa Ripley Holden

All of the Junebug plays feature Junebug Jabbo Jones, the main character who is telling the audience the stories. The place is in the very theater where the performance is occurring, until Junebug "sets the next scene" for us, and takes us somewhere else. The time is the very time the performance is occurring, until Junebug brings us to another time. The stage is almost bare. An actor is playing the character of Junebug Jabbo Jones, an African-American, itinerate storyteller, who travels from town to town to tell stories about what he has seen and heard. He says he is a storyteller instead of a liar, because, he says, "A liar's somebody trying to cover things over, mainly for his own private benefit. But a storyteller, that's somebody trying to uncover things so everybody can get something good out of it." His stories are sometimes about his own life or the lives of the many, many characters he met along the way. The result of this simple storytelling style with little artifice, in the form of a play, allows the audience to more easily "hear" a truth for their lives; or, as Junebug would say, "Get some good out of it."

3

The character of Junebug Jabbo Jones, in all of the Junebug plays and in the other plays in this collection where Junebug appears, always wears the same outfit: old denim overalls, a blue work shirt, old high-top boots, a dull-colored sport coat, a red bandanna around his neck, a white handkerchief in his pocket, and a soft, well-worn wide-brimmed felt hat. His clothing is soft and worn, but very clean and tidy. He always carries his beautifully carved walking stick.

These stories carry us into the past, and present, sometimes within the same scene. When performed, these plays have an "improvisatory style" (although the scenes are all fully scripted). This style grants the audience license to imagine what is going on, to "see" the various settings, to "hear" the different voices of the many characters, all being played by one actor.

In performance, this makes the stories come alive in the minds of the audience, which often can be more powerful than fully realized stage settings and many actors. The same license of imagination is now granted to the reader of these plays.

Don't Start Me to Talking or I'll Tell Everything I Know

Sayings from the Life and Writings of
Junebug Jabbo Jones, Volume I

PRODUCTION AND PERFORMANCE HISTORY

Don't Start Me to Talking or I'll Tell Everything I Know: Sayings from the Life and Writings of Junebug Jabbo Jones was written by John O'Neal, with Ron Castine and Glenda Lindsay.

The play was brought to its final form through collaboration with Steve Kent in 1982. John O'Neal has played the leading role of Junebug Jabbo Jones in all the performances that have been done since its premiere in 1980 up to the present day.

The play premiered at the Provisional Theatre in Los Angeles, California, in 1982 under the direction of Steve Kent. Earlier versions of the play were presented as a work-in-progress by the Free Southern Theater in New Orleans, the Black Theater Alliance of New York and the Baltimore Theater Project. This early version was directed by Curtis King in 1980.

Don't Start Me to Talking or I'll Tell Everything I Know has been performed close to one thousand times across North America, and to date has visited large cities and small towns in forty-nine states, many provinces in Canada and six other countries. The play has been performed on the campuses of most major universities and colleges and at many smaller colleges throughout the U.S. It has been performed at hundreds of small and large community venues.

—*TRH*

Scene 1

I'm Who it Is Talking to You

A walking blues like Freddie King's "I'd Rather Be Blind" plays as pre-show music. The lighting should feel like a clearing in the swamp at four A.M.

The stage is set with two stepladders, each positioned at a forty-five-degree angle at center stage. One ladder is eight-feet high, the other is six-feet high. A plank of wood rests on the second wrung between the two ladders.

Junebug enters through the house with a boom box blaring the same walking blues of Freddie King. He wears his usual outfit: old denim overalls, a blue work shirt, old high-top boots, a dull-colored sport coat, a red bandanna around his neck, a white handkerchief in his pocket, and a soft, well-worn wide-brimmed felt hat. His clothing is soft and worn, but very clean and tidy. He holds his beautifully carved walking stick, and carries a canvas bag containing two camp stools, a canteen, a tin cup, a bottle of rubbing alcohol and other objects that he considers important.

When he arrives on stage he unpacks his bag, placing the boom box on the plank, one camp stool downstage right, the other down left, and the rubbing alcohol on the floor. He opens his canteen and pours himself a drink. Then he sprinkles the circumference of the playing area with his libation, restores the boom box to his shoulder, retrieves his walking stick and raises a toast to the audience. He turns off the boom box.

JUNEBUG: My granddaddy was a jack-leg Baptist preacher—maybe some of you all don't know what a "jack-leg" something or other is . . . hum-m-m-m. You ever seen a dog looking for somewhere to go? . . . 'til finally he gets somewhere. He stop and jack up his leg beside something, it could be a tree or a house or telephone pole or anything—it ain't necessarily no toilet but it'll do? Well, that's what a jack-leg something is—it ain't necessarily what you got to use it for but it'll do.

So, my granddaddy, on my mama's side, was a jack-leg Baptist preacher. He used to tell me things. One time he told me, "Son, takes three things to make a good speacher. Number one: you got to tell the people what you going to tell them. Number two: you got to tell the people. Number three: you got to back up and tell them what you done told them."

Now, you see me, I am a storyteller. I was *called* to be a storyteller. I say "storyteller" 'stead of *liar* 'cause it's a heap of difference 'tween a storyteller and a liar. A liar's somebody trying to cover things over, mainly for his own private benefit. But a storyteller, that somebody trying to uncover things so everybody can get something good out of it. So I'm a storyteller. A storyteller. It's a heap of good meaning to be found in a story if you got a mind to hear.

The meaning and the message to be found in the stories I'ma to tell this (evening): . . . see, right here I'm about to tell you *what I'm going to tell you* . . . A man with a devilish heart is the one most likely to aim his rump at a seat of power . . . I don't believe you all understood what I said. I going to tell it again. *A man with a devilish heart is the one most likely to aim his rump at a seat of power.* But then again you can lead a horse to water but you can't make him drink—

meaning by that ain't nobody can make you do anything you ain't already got a mind and heart set to do. Now that's the meaning and the message to be found in the stories I'ma tell, if you got a mind to hear . . . got a mind to hear.

Now, it's one more thing you need to know, 'fore I get started good and proper: I ain't the first one to carry the title of "Junebug Jabbo Jones," neither the only one to carry that name. The *first* Junebug started out life as a Negro slave. From the time that he was big enough to see straight, his maw knew, "This here is going to be one of them '*bad* niggers!'" That nigger was so bad as a child he would not take funk from a skunk. Right away his maw seen it wasn't half a chance for that boy to make a full-grown man 'fore the white folk would kill him! So when he made seven years old she got together with her auntie—which some people say could work roots—and they took him down to the river and made out like he got drowned down there. They mourned him, had a funeral and everything. They wore black clothes for three weeks! But, in actual fact, what they done was to take him off down in the Cypress Swamp and turned him over to Crazy Nigger Bill to raise.

Now Bill was so crazy he decided to he'd rather run off and live in the swamp by himself than to spend his life as a slave. That's how *crazy* Nigger Bill was.

See, Bill had belonged to what they used to call a "good master." A Baptist preacher, had taught Bill how to read and everything. He had every intention in his heart of making a preacher out of Bill.

Bill had to run off one night during a thunderstorm 'cause that preacher had a fit of rage when Bill showed him where it said in the Bible, "It's a sin 'fore God for a man to hold a slave or to be a slave. It's in The Book!"

That preacher got so mad at what Bill had showed him in that Bible that he went to grab himself a gun so's to shoot Bill with it. Bill seen him go for that gun so he took out running in that thunderstorm. The preacher had Bill lined up dead in his sights. Bill seen the preacher had the drop on him so he come up stark still, stretched out his hands in the air and hollered something loud in African. A bolt of lightning just as red as blood come down from the cloud, struck the barrel of that gun, sealed it up plumb shut, knocked that preacher down square on his butt and turned every hair on his body from jet black to silver white right on the spot!

Bill come back over there. Stood up over that preacher all sniveling up in the mud and rain, smiled—kinda sad like to himself—then turned around and walked off down in the Cypress Swamp. He stayed down yonder too.

From that night on, anytime you's to pass that white-haired preacher's house, *day or night*, you could see him. He'd be sitting up on the porch with four or five guns spread all around himself, 'side from that one that got sealed shut by that bolt of lightning. "I'm a kill 'air man who went down there in the Cypress Swamp to get at Bill 'fore I gets down there to get him . . ." but he ain't never gone down there. And he ain't never again stood astride a pulpit nor let his shadow fall across the face of an open Bible. It was a lots of people scared to go down in that swamp 'cause of Bill. They called him "Crazy" 'cause that's what the white folks called him. Some of them thought it was haunts down yonder but it wasn't no haunts 'cept for Old Crazy Bill and that first Junebug, that's all.

From the time he's seven years old 'til he made a full-grown man Junebug stayed down there with Old Bill. Many a time they would sit up all night long reading and studying together. Daytimes they'd spend studying how to get food and clothes out the swamp and how to make medicines out the plants and things down there and all kind of stuff.

Since they didn't have to spend all their time working like all the other slaves had to do, Old Crazy Bill and Junebug had plenty time to think. They seen what all was going on for fifty or sixty miles in 'air direction from that swamp.

They could see, in spite the fact it was some terrible conditions that most of the colored people lived up under, in most sections it was more of them than they had white folks. Ain't 'ike it is in here. Then again, there was a whole bunch of white folk that might as well's to have been black for all they could get out of life. If people could have just seen that it ain't no telling what might have happened.

Every now and then somebody could get so mad that they couldn't take no more and they would stand up for themselves. Lots of them would try to run away but they would put them old dogs in behind them and chase them down and catch them and beat them up real bad, maybe even kill them, unless that first Junebug and Bill would get to them first and hitch them up with somebody from the Underground Railroad.

They seen how people would make up funny sayings and songs to make the days go faster and make the loads seem lighter. They seen how people would put secret messages in their stories and songs. And they seen how people had a heap more power than they thought they had. Why between colored slaves and the poor white people, didn't hardly nothing get done around there unless they were the ones that did it. But everybody was so busy trying to keep their own heads from getting cracked that didn't nobody stand back to see the *big* picture, what was happening to everybody.

Well, sir, right there they seen where it was a job needed to be done. They knew it was a bunch of white folks that would have killed them for teaching people how to read or spreading news they did not want spread. But still and all, they said, "It's a job needs to be done and *we* the ones to do it. We *got* to do it!" So, soon's that first Junebug got big enough in years to travel out of that swamp on his own, he took to traveling 'round from plantation to plantation, living by his wits, collecting stories about people and the things they did and said. Then, so people could get a better picture about how they could get together to help change things, make things better, that first Junebug would tell people's stories. He would tell these over here what these over here been up to. That way those that was doing things to help gain their freedom would be made to feel support and encouragement, and them that wasn't doing all they could, or should would be uncovered, made to feel shame.

Whenever that first Junebug come by a person look like they might make a pretty good storyteller, he would start to talking to them on the sly. He would help them to figure out how they could run away. He'd take them down in the swamp, turn them over to Old Crazy Bill. Bill would train them how to make their figures, how to read and everything they needed to know to be a good storyteller. Before long it was a whole bunch of people traveling around just watching what people be saying, listening to what they was doing, and telling stories to whosoever wanted to hear, all of them doing it under the title of "Junebug Jabbo Jones."

Well, the way it turned out, it was my great, great . . . well, let me tell it to you like this. Take this right here for my granddaddy. *(Counting on the fingers of one hand)* And take this one for his granddaddy. Now go back and get the daddy before that, which that will make him my granddaddy four times removed . . . on my daddy's side. He's one of them first early-on Junebugs. Ever since him, it's come down to one son out of every one of his coming generations to take up this storytelling work.

See me? I'm just the son of this current generation in my family. It'll be another son in the generation after mine, and another son in the generation after his and another in the generation after that. As long as it's work to be done, it'll be a Junebug out here somewhere trying to help get the job done. I don't know, it might be one or two of them in here right now. We ain't got no sign. You see, that ain't my name, it's a *title* of a job I've got to do, like "King" or "Prince." They don't just have to be colored. And they definitely ain't all men.

Now, if this old Junebug you done stumbled up on today happens to tell your story, do you reckon it would be a story that would make our chests stand out, make us all feel proud; want to get in up behind you and help you along . . . or do you reckon that it would be the kind of story to make you feel shame, make you want to run away and hide your head before we find us a stick good enough to crack your skull with.

What you reckon?

Scene 2

In Them Old Cotton Fields Back Home . . .

JUNEBUG: My old home place is down a dog-leg branch from the twin oak trees on the New Caledonia Road between Seven Waters and Four Corners, which ain't too far from Magnolia which is about nine miles south and a little bit west from McComb which is the county seat of Pike County down in south Mississippi.

Hm-m, some of you may not know where that's at . . . You know where Jackson, Mississippi, is? Well, if that's Jackson, *(Pointing)* and I know y'all know about New Orleans? Well, if that's Jackson and that's New Orleans, then my home is right there.

I don't care what you heard about Mississippi, coming up we had us some good times but we had some bad times too.

I had this cousin named Lee Roy . . . which I reckon I still got him. Ain't heard of him to die. Matter of fact we used to call him "Lazy Lee Roy" 'cause he don't care nothing about no work. Aw, he'd take and count the dots on them dancing dice all night long. Take a pencil and paper and write down the numbers every time they roll and would stay up nights to study them figures. Give him a deck of cards he'll shuffle them up and make them march like soldiers, but that's about as close as he'd want to get to some work.

One time old Double-L, that's what we used to call him for "Lazy Lee Roy," old Double-L had won this big old stakebody truck in a game of cards—a 1937 Studebaker. He'd won it off a preacher from up around Tupelo. Being as he didn't care for no work he didn't have too much use for that truck so he'd let me borrow it anytime I took a mind to.

'Bout the only thing us colored people could do for cash money in Mississippi when I was coming up was work that cotton. It was a lot of work to be done, but if you needed to have straight up cash money, you had to hit that cotton patch. So I got together with a bunch of people and orga-

13

nized something like a union. We figured out what our time ought to have been worth and we'd tell everybody what that money was and wouldn't nobody work 'til we got that figure. That's how come we called it something like a union, wouldn't nobody work.

We was working on Colonel T. L. Whitten's plantation. Colonel Whitten was known to be one of the slickest planter's around them parts at the time. Between him and his brothers they had the biggest part of the land, they had the sawmill, the cotton gin, the feed-and-grain company, they had the bank up in McComb! I swear you couldn't pick up a clod of dirt around there and chunk it less'n it was to sprinkle on something them Whitten boys had something to do with.

All during the cotton-chopping season, we couldn't get nowhere with the Old Colonel. So that summer I borrowed Double-L's truck and drove all over the area organizing. I drove up to Jackson and most to New Orleans organizing, so when it come to cotton-picking time that fall I had it organized! It was organized tighter than Dick's hatband. I mean it was organized!

I told Dan Skinner—he's T. L.'s overseer—I told him what our figure was. I was surprised. Oh, I knew Dan well. His daddy used to work shares off a plot of land my daddy owned over on the other side of The Bottom. He stuck up closer than a tick to a hound dog behind my oldest brother, Abraham, 'til they got big enough to start chasing skirts. So I knew him well! But Old Dan, he still surprised me when he taken and rolled his chaw from one side of his jaw to the other and said, "*Pi-tuight!*, well all right Junebug, I reckon we can get up next to that."

I figured we's going to have to negotiate. But come sunup that next morning, it was a bunch of happy fellows out there in Whitten's cotton field snapping up that cotton.

Round 9:30 I hauled my first sack full of cotton up to the wagon. Old Dan Skinner weighed it. "*Pi-tuight!*, well, Junebug, you doing pretty good there, boy! You got yourself about eighty-five pounds there. *Pi-tuight!*"

Right away I knew something was wrong. I ain't picked me no eighty-five pounds of early-morning, dew-wet cotton since I's a boy ten or twelve years old. Not only did I have good speed in my hands and feet, I had studied that cotton. I seen where you'd come out ahead working two half rows at one time instead of a whole one. Say everybody else would start over here, I'd go way off yonder side and start over there. I'd run down and snap me up a half of a row right quick. Then on the far end of that field I squat down between that half of a row here and a whole row here and start to snap that cotton with either hand. On top of that, every ten or twelve feet I'd reach down and grab a handful of dirt and throw it up in that sack. I knew that something was definitely not right. I was good for four hundred pounds on a slow day. Hell! I had fifteen pounds worth of dirt up in there!

I told him, "Mr. Skinner, it must be something wrong with y'all's scale."

"*Pi-tuight!* You calling me a liar, boy?"

"Nawsuh. I ain't calling nobody a liar . . . not yet. I just think it's something wrong with y'all's scales."

They had some fifty-pound sacks of feed corn from their store up in town sitting on the wagon. I grabbed two of those fifty-pound sacks of feed corn, pitched them in a empty cotton sack and hitched them up to that scale. It run up to eighty-five pounds and quit.

"Now that you mention it, it do look like some lying's going on around here! Hey, fellows this looks like something we ought to take up with Colonel Whitten himself."

My daddy tells me that Colonel Whitten went for a hell of a man in his day. By the time I come to know him he was still mean but he'd been beat down by the alcohol that he'd done got used to leaning on. By the time we got to the Big House in Double-L's truck, Dan had done beat us up there. They was standing up there on the porch waiting for us.

"I understand that you boys are calling Mr. Skinner here a liar."

"Nawsuh. I ain't called nobody a straight-up liar, yet. I just said there's something wrong with the scales y'all got down there in the cotton patch. It looks like it's cutting out of about fifteen pounds out of every hundred we pick."

"How'd you come to figure that?"

"Well we taken two fifty-pound sacks a feed corn—from y'all's store up in town—and dropped them off in a empty cotton sack and hitched them up to the scale. She run up to eighty-five pounds and quit. Mr. Skinner said, 'It look like the Checker Board people cut y'all a short weight on that last order of feed corn y'all got at y'all's store.' Well, I told him, if that's a fact, it looks like it's a whole bunch of people be mighty proud to know that, 'cause that'll mean that they due a refund equal to fifteen pounds out of every hundred of feed corn been bought at y'all's store here lately."

The old man started weaving and wobbling trying to get from under the weight I's putting on him.

"By damn, Dan! I told you this weren't no proper way to deal with these nigras, I told you that! I ought to have knew better than to listen to the likes of you. You go around to the back door and tell Afrodite to send me my lemonade!" He'd done got to missing that alcohol he's used to leaning on. "I'll take this up with you later."

"As for you boys, I'm sorry that I let this POOR WHITE TRASH talk me into trying to cheat you all out of your money. I'm sorry about that, I'm truly sorry. But, if I was to pay you the price you're asking I couldn't make no money. If I can't make no money, I'd soon have to go out of business. And if I have to go out of business, it wouldn't be no time before you poor boys wouldn't have nowhere to work, and you know I wouldn't like that. So, Junebug, you go on and take these boys on back down to the cotton fields and pick that cotton. Get it nice and clean and, to show you that our hear' is in the right place, I will give, plumb-out flat-down give you a nice side of salt-cured pork for every man, woman or child on your crew. How about that, Junebug?"

"Nawsuh. We've done already talked it over and we've come to the mind, if we can't get our money we can't work."

"By damn, if you don't want to work, you get your lazy black butts off my property!"

"I don't know, White Folks, you might want to think that over. I don't believe you going to find nobody around these parts to work for no less. The longer you leave that cotton out in the field the more it's going to cost you to get it in."

"*Pi-tuight!* You want me to get your shotgun, Colonel?"

"By damn, Dan, will you be quiet! I'm sick plumb up to here of you trying to meddle in my business, don't you hear? Besides I don't need no shotgun to deal with these boys . . . *do I, Junebug.*"

"Nawsuh, you don't need no shotgun to deal with us boys. All you need is a little bit of money and a little bit of respect. Since it looks like you all are running short supply of both those things, we'll go on back down to the field and get our stuff and we'll leave. Yes, sir, we'll leave. But get where you want to get that cotton in just let us know, we'll be glad to come back and snap it up for you."

So we went on back down there and got our stuff together but before we left, we taken all the cotton that we'd already picked and poured it out on the ground.

It was way down in December before they was able to get that cotton in too. Ralph Tatum and his brother, Skinhead, had a terrible fire over on their place. Lost their old home place and everything in it, lost their barn, four or five cows and a registered breeding bull which it was the main thing they had counted on to make most of their money. They lost all of that. They's in a bad way after that fire. Between them they had 'bout fourteen children at the time. It was getting close to the holiday season and they come to us and told us, "We're sorry. We figure we going to have to get that cotton off the Whitten Plantation. We sorry."

I told them, "Well, all right." And that's what they done.

Scene 3

Every Shut-Eye Ain't Sleep

JUNEBUG: When I was eighteen years old it come my time to leave home. I didn't have no more money than it took to get a bus ticket to New Orleans but it was time to go so I left. My mama fixed me a shoe box full of fried chicken and biscuit bread. Having no more sense than a junebug in springtime 'cause I ate the whole thing before we even much as got to the state line, so when the bus pulled up to the bus station in New Orleans I was in a bad condition.

The weather was badder than a blister on a mailman's foot. It had been raining three days straight without stopping. They had a hurricane sitting out in the Gulf waiting to come in. It was bad! I didn't want to come down off that bus but the driver came back to me and said, "Come on, boy, you got to get off here. I'ma put this bus in the barn and get out of here. Come on now."

I didn't know they had no barns for buses but I come down off of that bus in all that bad weather. Thinking, "What I'm going to do now?!" Considering the fact of my problem, without no money; well, I did have a twenty-dollar gold piece in the sock of my left foot which my granddaddy gave me for good luck, he said his granddaddy had given it to him. It was said to be the first twenty dollars made by anybody in our family since the end of slavery. I'd have given up two arms and a leg 'fore I gave up that twenty-dollar gold piece so I was in a hard way for something to eat and somewhere to stay.

And considering the fact that I was already mad about having to ride the back of that old "Jim Crow" bus I made up my mind what I was going to do. "I'm going in this *white* waiting room to get me something to eat."

First, didn't nobody pay me too much mind. Despite the fact that it was way up in the morning before day it was a whole bunch of people sitting up in there. "Due to the hurricane I reckon." I had been sitting there for a while when this funny-talking lady came over to me. I finally figured out that she had come to take my order! This lady at the other end of the counter said, "You can't serve no nigras up in here, dahwling." They got in a cross-talk about first one thing and then another, 'til finally, somebody called the cops. This policeman came and said he was going to take me to jail. I tried to talk to him but he twisted my arm up behind my back and took me off and threw me in jail . . . Which that was the main thing I was counting on in the first place. Now I had a place to stay, something to eat while I waited out this hurricane.

They threw me in this cell next to this fellow they called "Sleepy." I swear, I was in that jail for near to two weeks and it wasn't nothing to happen while I was in there that Sleepy didn't know about as soon as it happened. He seemed to know things that he shouldn't have had a way of knowing unless somebody told him. Like he knew where I came from, knew this was my first time away from home, knew that I'd schemed up on a way to get these white people to throw me in jail and he knew that I had a twenty-dollar gold piece in the sock of my left foot. At first I thought it was something spooky going on, but it wasn't nothing spooky.

He just paid real good attention to things that most people didn't pay no mind to. He said he knew where I came from by listening to how I talk. And said that he could tell that I had a twenty-dollar gold piece in the sock of that left foot by the way I'd favor that foot when I'd walk, and by the fact that I'd never take the sock off of that foot unless I didn't think it was anybody looking.

Sleepy was something else! He was the one that told me, "Take it easy, Youngblood, before you let impatience make a fool out of you. Every shut-eye ain't sleep. Sometimes, Youngblood, a man with a grin and a handshake can be ten times more dangerous than a man with a stick and a gun. But a rabbit in a brier patch still has plenty of room to run. It takes a still hand to catch a fly. Every shut-eye ain't sleep."

Sleepy would say things like that to put a puzzlement on your brains. Sometimes I would sit up all night long trying to get a good understanding out of the things that Sleepy had told me.

When my time got short, Sleepy called me over to his cell. "Hey, Youngblood, come here. I got something to tell you. Come on, man! Look. I've got somewhere to go when I get out of here and I've got some stuff in a locker down at the bus station. I want you to go down there and get it for me. Keep it 'til I get ready for it."

"I don't know, Sleepy. I don't know anybody in this town. I don't know where I'm going to stay. I wouldn't know where to tell you to find me when you get ready for it."

"When I get ready for it I'll know where to put my hands on you."

"I don't know, Sleepy. If you think it's all right."

"It's all right! Look, it's some good stuff up in there. You're welcome to use any part of it as long as you take good care of it." And he gave me this key. We kept on talking for two or three days. Finally, the jailhouse man came and said, "Hey, boy! Get your stuff together. It's time for you to get out of here."

Sleepy rolled over on his bunk and said, "Remember, Youngblood, every good-bye ain't gone." Those were the last words I remember Sleepy to say to me while I was in that jailhouse. He had told me to go to this big fancy hotel down on St. Charles Avenue and ask for this fellow named "Jeff-the-Chef." I seen where to get from the jailhouse down to the hotel I had to go right by the Trailways Bus Station. So I decided to go in to find out what Sleepy had up in there. I found the lockers and looked up the one with the right number on it, made sure that no one was looking, got out the key that Sleepy gave and opened it up.

He had a little black satchel up in there. It looked like the kind doctors used to carry. He had some shoe-shine stuff packed up in there all neat and orderly. And it was some books . . . some on black history and . . . one about *Revolution in Africa*! I took Sleepy's bag and my stuff and got out of there.

When I walked into the kitchen of the Pontchartrain Hotel, this great big fellow walked over to me, took one look at Sleepy's bag in my hand and said, "Come on in here, Youngblood, and put your stuff down. Come on and get yourself something to eat."

He was talking my talk now. All that jailhouse food would do is fill you up so I was ready for some good food. And they had some good food in there! It had some funny names to it but it was good. Jeff brought a plate piled up high like this (*Shows a very high stack*) and set it down in front of me and I knocked that stuff out in no time flat. When I heard him coming back down there where I was at I grabbed the plate and started licking it like a little lost puppy. When Jeff seen me doing that he went and got me another whole plate of food, and said, "All right, Youngblood, eat now for the hunger that's to come."

After I cleaned that plate I started eyeing the "Mile High Pie" and thinking, "How am I going to get some of that?"

Jeff came back where I was and said, "Hurry up, Youngblood. You got to go to work in 'bout half an hour."

"Go to work"!

"Yeah. You got to change your clothes and go to work."

And that's how I come to get my first job. Shining shoes. It was the first paying job I'd ever had—aside from that cotton-picking work—and it was a good job too. I worked at that shoe-shine business for a good while and I don't remember a day I didn't make at least thirty dollars—and that was good money in them days. It wouldn't be bad money now if you could get it. I had been working at the Hotel Pontchartrain for about eighteen months when this white fellow—which everybody who came there was white besides those of us who worked there, it being during the time of segregation—anyway this guy who looked like a movie cowboy started coming in my shop real regular. Every time he came in there he had the same old foolishness on his mind. "Say, boy. You know where I can get me a *colored* gal? . . . You wouldn't know anything about a *white* woman would you?"

That man had plucked my last nerve. I made it up in my mind that the next time he came into my place of business with that foolishness, I's going to be the one put an end to it.

It couldn't have been more than a week or ten days later that I's sitting in there sucking on a hot cup of coffee. I had been up all night reading and studying the night before so I was trying to restorate my eyes. I heard that man head straight for Junebug's House of Divine Shine. "Oh Lord!"

No sooner than he put his bottom in the seat of the shoe-shine stand I ducked my head and started snoring over that hot coffee like I'd been sleeping for three weeks.

"Hey, boy!" I kept right on snoring. He reached down to shake me. I snored louder. He kicked me in the side with his pointy-toed boots. I jumped up and turned that hot coffee so it would spill over the middle of his brand-new white suit. He dodged trying to get out the way of that hot coffee and fell on the floor from the seat of that shoe-shine stand.

I jumped up, bucked my eyes and started scratching my head and other places where I wasn't itching. See, he already thought I was a fool so I was going to play the fool for him. I said, "Lord, have mercy! Is this whole world done come to an end while this poor old lazy darkie's down here sleeping?"

"Look what you done, nigger!"

"Lord, have mercy! We done had us an accident, ain't we, boss? Uhmpht-uhmp-uhmp! Here, let me help you up, boss." But before I reached to help him, I dug my hand down in a can of black-paste shoe polish, hid my hands behind my back spread thick globs of it over both of them, and grabbed by the elbows of his new suit and drug my hands down to his hands. When he saw what had happened he jerked back, fell back down on his butt and started cussing and fussing and talking in tongues!

Since he was so upset about being two-toned, I got bottle of black liquid polish and tried to make one color of him. He was some mad! He came up from there swinging. He hit me in the stomach and doubled me over. He straightened me up with the other hand. He was about to kick me in the place where it would hurt the most. I dodged and pushed him back with my foot. He slipped to his butt again. My hand came down on a can of dirty, soapy water. I splashed it in his eyes. "Oh-ohh! He can't see now."

See I knew I had lost my job now, so I figured I better
have a good time while I was doing it. I called that man
everything but a child of God. Did I beat him? I beat him so
bad! I beat him like Billy beat the drum.

I tell you what, I have lost many a good job in my lifetime
but I ain't never a job I enjoyed losing like I enjoyed losing
that one.

Big Boss man, can't you hear me when I call?
You ain't so big, you just tall that's all.

(Intermission.)

Scene 4

Senator Bilbo and Bessie Mae

JUNEBUG: Hope y'all don't mind I'm taking my shoes off. My feet
are killing me. If you do mind that just too bad I'm taking
them off anyway. I got a pain right here that goes through
to the bone. 'Far as I know it don't mean nothing though.

It's a natural fact though that some people can tell the
weather by the bunions on they feet or the rheumatism in
they joints and such. My daddy could read the hip on his left
side better than most people can read the *Farmer's Almanac.*

When Daddy was fourteen years old, Miz Bessie Mae
kicked him in the backside for getting out of place with her.
Miz Bessie was the regular plowing mule on the farm when
Daddy was coming up. They tell me Bessie would plow all
day long, long as they let Senator Bilbo graze near one end
of the field that she was working.

"Senator Bilbo" was the name my granddaddy give to this
cantankerous old jackass who wouldn't do 'nair lick of work
except for the fact that Bessie Mae had done fell in love with
him. Pop-Paw said he called him "Senator Bilbo" 'cause the

Bilbo they had in Washington didn't look no better and was about half as smart as that jackass was.

See when my daddy was a young man, they had this senator from the State of Mississippi name a Bilbo who was so hard on colored people you wouldn't believe it. Bilbo was the type of man who would get up right in the halls of Congress and say, "Excuse me, gentlemen, but they about to lynch a nigger back in my home district and I want to get back down there 'cause I wouldn't want to miss the party." That's the type of man he was.

Pop-Paw was not no mean man, but it's some mules that won't do a damn thing 'less you to beat them. Pop-Paw used to drive that mule to town every Saturday afternoon, I feel to believe that he did it just so he could beat up on that ornery jackass. Bilbo would get it in his mind to stop right in the middle of Main Street every doggone time. Pop-Paw, a deacon of the church, would start fussing and cussing and he would carry on something terrible. The more Pop-Paw would fuss the more that mule would just stand there.

After he'd got the biggest crowd he thought he was going to get, Pop-Paw would jump down from the wagon, grab a stick (which I believe he must have been carrying for this purpose), and he would beat that mule to a fare-thee-well. "You a no-good jackass, Senator Bilbo, you ain't no good! Your mammy weren't no good! Your grandmammy weren't no good! Senator Bilbo, you no-good jackass you! . . . "People used to come from all over town to watch Pop-Paw beat up and cuss on Senator Bilbo. The only thing the colored people loved more than seeing Pop-Paw beat up and cuss on Senator Bilbo was to watch Joe Louis beat up on a white man and get paid for it!

And old! He was old! My granddaddy had him for forty-seven years and he said that Bilbo looked to be full grown when he first come by him. So Senator Bilbo had to be more than fifty years old when he died—and he wouldn't have died then if he hadn't been so damn ornery.

Y'all remember Miz Bessie Mae? Well, she had some strange rules for a mule. It did not matter which side of

her you's to stand to rig her up as long as you did not get
in twixt her and Senator Bilbo wheresoever he happened
to be standing. This particular day, Daddy was ponderating
something serious in his mind when he come down to the
barn to rig her up and he misremembered Miz Bessie Mae's
rule. Daddy bent down to pick up a line and Bessie Mae
seen where he had got out of place with her. She wheeled
around, let him have it with both barrels!

Daddy was laid up for six weeks. Soon as he was able to
hobble around on a stick he come down to the barn. He
held old Bilbo responsible for the misery in his hip. "All
right you old sway-backed son-of-a-no-count jackass, you
going to work today if you don't never work no more!"
Daddy grabbed the mule collar off the wall, throwed it up
on Bilbo and got him rigged to the plow. But when Daddy
went to drive that old jackass out the barn. Bilbo grit whatever was left of his teeth and would not budge. Well, my
daddy was on the ornery side too. He said, "All right, you
no-good jackass you, ain't 'nair one of us going nowhere
'til you decide to do some work. They stood right like that
for three days and three nights. That jackass never moved a
muscle 'til he died.

After Bilbo died, Miz Bessie Mae would not eat, would
not drink a drop of water or nothing. She just took up
the spot where Bilbo had stood 'til she was dead too. At
least Bessie Mae had the good grace to keel over when she
expired. Bilbo had been so ornery that he dropped dead
standing up.

It weren't long after that that the real Senator Bilbo, up
in Washington, DC, got cancer of the mouth and throat
which served to be the cause of his dying too. They say before
he died he had a change of heart and apologized to all the
colored people for all the mean and nasty things that he
done to them while he was alive. 'Course you know it's a lots
of people have a change of heart when they feel the chill of
the midnight hour coming on.

It wasn't long after that that Daddy noticed every time
there come a change in the weather he could feel it in that

hip. 'Fore he passed, he got to where he could tell when it
was going rain four or five days from now. That's how come
I told you that some people can tell things by the misery in
their bodies, the rheumatism in they joints and such.

Me, all I know is that when I'm tired my feet hurt. When
I get hungry my stomach growls and when I get drunk, my
head starts to spinning before it starts to throbbing real
hard. Which that's the reason I don't drink too much. *(Takes
a nip from the canteen)* I only drink for medicinal purposes.
I got a little cold right now.

Scene 5

Down in the Boys' Gym

JUNEBUG: Back in the days, us boys had the habit of sneaking
out of study hall and meeting up down in the boys' gym.
In those days you had to sneak if you was going to smoke a
cigarette.

I won't lie to you, the main subject of conversation down
in the boys' gym was sex. I remember this one day, we was
down there blowing more smoke than a steam engine on
an uphill grade. They was all talking about what all they was
doing and who all they was doing it to. The way it turned
out, Percy Proctor, Doctor Proctor's youngest son, was the
one doing most of the talking.

Doctor Proctor was the only colored doctor they had in
that section of the state when I was coming up. They had
a couple of them up in Jackson, but you didn't go that far
for a doctor unless you was going to the hospital and didn't
nobody go to the hospital unless they was going to get cut
or thought they was going to die or both.

Since they had plenty of colored people down there in
south Mississippi at the time, Doctor Proctor was doing
quite well. True enough, sometimes he got paid with a

bushel of canned peaches or a couple of hens or something like that but still he done quite well. They had a two-car garage with two cars in it, and they had this great big old two-story brick house with six of these here columns just like the white folks.

Doc and Mrs. Proctor was very nice, but by the time Percy come along they had begun to get a little old—see Percy was an accident. And being old like that they couldn't take the right kind of care of the child so Percy come out kind of spoiled . . . well, the fact of the business was that Percy was plumb rotten.

To begin with he was not no pretty sight. If you didn't know him you might of thought there was something wrong with him. Don't get me wrong now, I ain't got nothing against ugly people, I ain't never had none in my family but I got good friends who could write books on the subject, and true enough, you can't judge a book by looking at the cover. Ugly is not so much a question of how you look on the out-side, it's what's inside that counts—but Percy! He's the type of fellow you can look at on the outside and see right away that his insides was damn near ruined. He had this great big old water-head and these little squeachy eyes that would not stand still so you could get a good look at them. He was kind of on the high yellow side so he's got this stringy brown hair which his head is too big for, so he looked like a little bald-headed man from the time he's about seven years old. It's unusual in a man of that high yellow complexion but the boy had lips that hung out like bumpers on a boxcar. And he was working them overtime that day.

The prettiest girl in town was Beulah Mae Cushenberry. She was Elder Cushenberry's daughter. Elder Cushenberry was the pastor down at the Holiness Church which they called themselves "The Saints of God." Certain times of the year, it wouldn't be nothing for them to have preach-ing and singing down there five or six nights a week. They nearly always had somebody playing piano and beating of the drums, right in the church house! And dance, Lord, I mean they could dance!

Normally, Beulah Mae was the shy quiet type of gal, but when the spirit got in her she would get happy and do that holiness dance. She would start to jiggle things I did not know had jiggle in them. Beulah Mae would start jiggling down one side of the church and there was this fellow named Billy Blue Black on the other side of the church would nearly always get the spirit about the same time. Beulah Mae would be jiggling down one side and Billy Blue be just dancing down the other side and Elder Cushenberry be up in the pulpit just singing and sweating, "Sweet Jesus! Sweet Jesus! Sweet Jesus!"

This other little guy be beating on the piano and shaking and trembling like he was having an epileptic seizure or something. How he's able to keep a tune on that thing at all is a mystery to me, but I swear that that piano would do everything but get up and walk, and some nights it'd look like it be trying to do that too. Everybody in the church be up on they feet just singing and shouting and clapping their tambourines, trying to get a good look at Beulah Mae and Billy Blue do the Holy Dance. All the time Elder Cushenberry be up in the pulpit just sweating and shouting, "Sweet Jesus! Sweet Jesus! Sweet Je-e-e-e-sus!"

It got to be big sport among us boys to meet up at the Holiness Church to see Beulah Mae do her dance . . . 'til Elder Cushenberry got wise. When a bunch of us would come to the church he'd make a big thing out of it: "I believe we have some sinners up in here! You boys, y'all come down front here. Amen! Bring them boys down front!"

They'd make us sit on the mourner's bench. When it came to a certain point in the service, we'd have to stand up and testify. We had to tell who we was, who our families was, how come we come to the Holiness Church, and how come we wanted to take the Lord as our personal savior. The truth be told, we didn't want to take nothing but a good look at Beulah Mae.

I remember one time Pap McKinney said, "I ain't going to testify. Nawsuh, I ain't got nothing to say." I betcha them saints sung and prayed on him for four hours straight without stopping:

So glad I got good religion,
So glad I got good religion,
So glad I got good religion,
My feet been taken from the miry clay.

That soon broke us up from trying to play church!

Still and all it wasn't no question that Beulah Mae was the finest woman in four counties. Neither was it no doubt that she was not giving it up. She was so nice, everybody respected her. Not so much because she wasn't giving it up, but because she was so nice.

On this particular day old liver-lipped Percy Proctor got to flapping his liver lips so fast that 'fore he knew what he had said, "Beulah Mae? She promised to give me some! Yeah, uh-huh! She promised it to me, this weekend!" Ain't nobody paid him no mind. Beulah Mae going to give it up, she could have a damn sight better than Percy Proctor.

Pap McKinney told him, "You so nasty and so ugly, a well-paid business lady'd have to put a gag in your mouth and a kroger sack over your head before she'd take your money!"

"Naw! She promised it to me! . . . Yeah, this weekend! . . . To prove it? . . . to prove it . . . all right, all right! I'm going to bring her drawers to school on next Monday morning!"

Nobody paid him a bit of attention. He was a natural-born liar and didn't have the sense enough to be embarrassed when he got caught in one. So nobody paid him 'nair bit of attention 'til that next Sunday afternoon, when the news come around that Beulah Mae and her daddy, Elder Cushenberry, had not been to church that Sunday morning. *They* didn't never miss church! That got the grapevine just a buzzing.

The next morning, which was the Monday morning, wasn't nobody late for school but Percy Proctor and Beulah Mae. Beulah Mae never did show up. But right after the bell for the first hour sounded, Percy come strolling in like a little banty rooster. Regardless of the fact it was a hot day late in May he had on a brand-new long-sleeved shirt. Now it's been raining all weekend long but my man, Percy's wearing these here dark sunglasses which covered up half his face.

He tried to speak to everybody, "Hey, Little Mama. What's happening, Little Papa?"

Didn't nobody hear a word the teacher said that day. Couldn't wait 'til the noon hour come. Everybody ganged up on Percy Proctor and marched him down to the boys' gym. By the time I got there it was so crowded I had to push and shove to get where I could see, and there's old Percy, puffing on a Lucky Strike cigarette and bragging about what he'd done to Beulah Mae. He held up a pair of white cotton drawers. He said they was Beulah Mae's bloomers. He passed them around so everybody could get a good look and tell that they had that Ivory Snow smell that Beulah Mae always had.

He pulled down the collar on his shirt and showed us these scratch marks on his neck and said, "It got so good to her she just had to scratch me! It was some of the best stuff I ever had!"

"It was probably the *only* stuff *you* ever had!" That's what Pap McKinney told him.

Percy just kept right on bragging, talking about first one thing and then the next, 'til finally . . . one by one, all the boys left out of the boys' gym. After while it wasn't nobody left down there but Percy Proctor, Billie Blue Black and myself.

Percy looked up and seen it wasn't nobody there but him and us and said, "Well, I guess I take my little stuff and get out of here."

Billie told him, "Wait a minute, nigger! If y'all was having such a good time, how come you have a black eye?"

"I ain't got no black eye."

"You lying, nigger!" Billie shook the glasses off of Percy's face. He jerked the sleeves up on his arms and seen all these scratch marks running up and down his arms and said, "Uh-huh. I guess that's a sign of pleasure too, huh?"

Billie got so mad. His eyes got real narrow and shiny red. The veins bulged out in his forehead and his neck, he was trembling like he's trying not to cry.

Percy was so scared! He opened his mouth like he was going to say something. Billie told him, "Hush your mouth, man! I'm tired of listening to your lies. But I'll tell you this.

If Beulah Mae is hurt in any way, I'm going to see to it that you pay!" He threw him down on the floor and tramped out the door with the cotton underwear in his hand.

I later come to find that he went straight to Elder Cushenberry's house.

"Sir, I . . . I want to marry Beulah Mae."

Elder, he wouldn't look at him. "I done found out, I got the devil sleeping in my own household. I prayed on it for three days and three nights, and the Lord told me I got to kick the devil out of my household, and, son, if you want to marry her it's between you and the devil and I ain't got nothing to do with it."

With that for a blessing, Billie Blue and Beulah Mae got married. They both dropped out of school and went to work. They moved in with Billie's grandmother, Miz Amy Black. She had a nice little place out on the edge of town. After about three or four months Beulah Mae started to get big and I reckon they got tired of listening at people laugh and giggle at them behind they backs so they moved over to a section in Greene County Alabama. Billie had some more kin people lived over there.

Percy, he finished out that year in school but that next summer, Doctor and Miz Proctor sent him off to one of them big fancy boarding schools up North. They made a lawyer out of him. Right now he's a judge in the juvenile court in Chicago, Illinois.

Billie? Like I said, him and Beulah Mae moved over to this section around Greene County, Alabama. The people over there elected him to serve a term as the first black sheriff they ever had in that section. He made a right good sheriff too. When it come down toward the end of his term the people come to him and said, "Hey, Billie, we got to get ourselves together to run so we can serve another term."

Billie said, "No. I appreciate your respect and consideration but I ain't going to run and serve no more 'til it get so that people that run and serve in office can spend more of their time doing the job they been elected to serve than they have to spend fighting all the big shots that have all the money. That's something we can all do. We don't need to be elected to nothing to do that."

Oh, Billie, him and Beulah, they had three fine children. All of them blue, black and shiny, just like Billie Blue.

Scene Six

Tommie Too-Tough Tucker

JUNEBUG: There's this guy in my hometown named Tommie Too-Tough Tucker. He was the radio 'far as the colored people was concerned.

This old radio we had at our house wouldn't get but one radio station, that was the one that come out of McComb. From five o'clock in the morning 'til ten-thirty at night that was a sure 'nuff white radio station, you could look at it and see it was a white radio station. But ten-thirty when Tommie Too-Tough got a hold of that radio, Lord, the whole town would start rocking.

On Saturday afternoons, right after the evening news, Tommie Too-Tough would change his name to "T. T. Tucker, Jr." and change the way his voice would come out to do this program he called "The Memorial Hour," which that was something I never could understand 'cause it wasn't nothing but a fifteen-minute program. Anyway, on the fifteen-minute Memorial Hour, Tommie would announce all the names of the people which had been funeralized by the colored undertaking parlor.

The program would always start out the same way. This real sad organ music would come on and Tommie would always say the same set of words.

"This is the hour for quiet contemplation and reverential reflection over the joys brought to us in life by our dear departed loved ones who have gone on before. This is the Memorial Hour, brought to you as a service and through the courtesy of the Gladstone Memorial Undertaking Funeral

Parlor. Remember at Gladstone's, we give the same tender care after that you gave before."

Now that was a lie! I had a cousin that used to work down there at Gladstone's and would tell me some of the things that was done to them poor dead bodies down there, you wouldn't believe it.

Anyway, on Sunday mornings Tommie had another program that would come on that radio, this time a gospel music program. Lord, have mercy them people sure got their money's worth out of Tommie Too-Tough Tucker; they sure did. I don't know this to be a tee-total fact but I don't believe them people to have paid Tommie no salary for all the time he spent working down there. He had to go around, hustle up his own advertising, then had to pay them people some money to be on they air.

Years went by and they finally come to figure it out: "Say, Jesse, there's a bunch of money to be made in this here colored music business. A bunch of money!" When they figured that out they kicked poor Tommie off the radio, hired a bunch of young college boys. They didn't know what was going on.

By that time Tommie had done got too old to go anywhere. All he knew how to do was that old funny radio talk. That's all he knew how to do. Didn't nobody want to hire no old colored man.

He stayed there in Four Corners. He's down there now, if you was to go down there right now you could probably see him. He's the one with them pointy-toed bee-bop shoes on; them wide-legged bee-bop pants, cinched in real tight at the ankles; and that wide-collar bee-bop coat; bee-bop hat, sitting off to the side and dark sunshades. I swear, if you was to wake up Tommie in the midnight hour I bet he would have those shades on.

He'd be doing that little funny bee-bop walk . . . he looked real normal, for Tommie; and he talked real normal, for Tommie; then all of a sudden he would stop and grab his head like this here. (Impersonates Tommie) You couldn't tell whether he got a headache all of a sudden or whether he was trying to find out what had become of his earphones.

Last time I was home I seen Tommie. He was sitting up in
a booth down at Bug's Underground Café, had it all fixed
up with stuff he'd done found to make it look like it might
be a radio station. Tommie would sit up in there for hours,
talking to a tin can tied on a stick, and spinning records
couldn't nobody hear but him.

Tommie Too-Tough Tucker is my doggone name
I'm the Bee-Bop Poppa that's my claim to fame.
I talk so much jive it's a crying shame
You might have heard it from the others but it's not the
    same.
I'm a real bad sucker
Got to sing far my supper
You won't need no other upper
Don't look another further
In your pocket there's a bucka
For you sweet corn shucker
Your buckaroo bucker.
I'm the man with a plan know all over this lan'
As Tommie Too-Tough Tucker, check it out now.
I'm Tommie Too-Tough Tucker, go on and shout now
I'm Tommie Too-Tough Tucker, yeah
I'm Tommie Too-Tough Tucker, yeah
I'm Tommie Too-Tough Tucker, hey!
I'm Tommie Tucker.

I'm the man with the music blow away you ills.
If you been on medication throw away your damn pills.
I make all the young women want to pay my bills.
I make the old women want to rewrite their wills.
I got the music that's a winner.
I got your midnight dinner.
I make the summer seem like winter.
I make you twenty pounds thinner.
I don't sing tenor
But if a woman's got it in her
Be an all-night sinner.

I'm the butter bowl stuffer known to every huffing puffer
As Tommie Too-Tough Tucker, check it out now.

I'm Tommie Too-Tough Tucker, check it out now!
I'm Tommie Too-Tough Tucker, go on and shout now!
I'm Tommie Too-Tough Tucker, yeah.
I'm Tommie Too-Tough Tucker, yeah.
I'm Tommie Too-Tough Tucker, hey!
I'm Tommie Tucker.

I know how it feels to work from sun to sun.
I know what it takes to put the Blues on the run.
When you ain't got no money, hell, it just ain't no fun.
Work all the damn day and you still ain't done.
It just ain't proper.
Lord, we got to find a stopper.
It's a sad sharecropper
No corn in the locker
For the pooped Bee-Bopper.
But I got no time to suffer;
Struggle only makes me tougher.
I'm Tommie Too-Tough Tucker, check it out now

I'm Tommie Too-Tough Tucker, go on and shout now!
I'm Tommie Too-Tough Tucker, check it out now
I'm Tommie Too-Tough Tucker, yeah.
I'm Tommie Too-Tough Tucker, yeah.
I'm Tommie Too-Tough Tucker, hey!
I'm Tommie Tucker.

I am the one who made St. Helen to blow her top.
I let them know it was the thing to make Miami hop.
Say put your foot on the rock and stomp it 'til the rock hop.
Put your foot on the rock—
Put your foot on the rock and hop 'til the rock hop
Put your foot on the rock—
Put your foot on the rock I bet your foot don't stop
I'm Tommie Too-Tough Tucker
Tommie Too-Tough . . .

Scene 7

Telling What I Told You

JUNEBUG: Well, it's done wound down to time for me to go now. So I reckon I better back up and tell you what you been told. I'ma break it down to you in words of this here fashion. It ain't no way 'air for one of y'all to get freedom and justice for yourself unless you're working just as hard as you can to get freedom and justice for common ordinary working folks like me.

The people in trouble is the ones to make trouble and there's more people falling off in trouble every day. At the same time it's a bunch of people representing themselves to be leaders, doing more for themselves than they ever dreamed about doing for the people they supposed to be leading. It's up to us to learn how to tell the difference between a leader like that and the way a leader supposed to be. The leaders we can't set straight we have to set aside. Can't nobody ride your back unless you first bend over.

Well, that's the idea I get out these old stories I been telling y'all. I hope when you get to where you going you'll see where it's an idea like that in there for you too. Hope I get the chance to see you all again sometime. If and when I do, I hope it ain't one of those times you done threw a rock and tried to hide your hand. Even worse, I hope it ain't one of those times I'm trying to hide mine.

So long.

(The Actor exits to the song "Don't Start Me to Talking or I'll Tell Everything I Know." He returns momentarily for a curtain call during which he may briefly address the audience from the contents of his own heart.

Exit.)

THE END

You Can't Judge a Book by Looking at the Cover

Sayings from the Life and Writings of
Junebug Jabbo Jones, Volume II

Production and Performance History

You Can't Judge a Book by Looking at the Cover: Sayings from The Life and Writings of Junebug Jabbo Jones was written by John O'Neal and Nayo-Barbara Watkins, with Steve Kent; additional dialogue by Timothy Raphael.

The play was directed by Steve Kent, with John O'Neal playing the leading role, Junebug Jabbo Jones, in all the performances since its premiere in 1985. The original music and sound engineering was by Michael Keck. The lighting design was by Ken Bowen.

The play premiered at the Wisdom Bridge in Chicago, Illinois, in 1985. Portions of the play were presented earlier as works-in-progress by Seven Stages in Atlanta and Theatre Fountainhead in Toronto.

This play began touring in 1985 and continued until 2002. It has been presented by most of the same theaters and presenting venues that first brought *Don't Start Me to Talking or I'll Tell Everything I Know,* as the audiences in those cities were eager to have a second visit from Junebug.

—*TRH*

Prologue

A walking blues like Freddie King's "I'd Rather Be Blind" plays as pre-show music. The lighting should feel like a clearing in the swamp at four A.M.

The stage is set with two stepladders, each positioned at a forty-five-degree angle at center stage. One ladder is eight-feet high, the other is six-feet high. A plank of wood rests on the second wrung between the two ladders.

Junebug enters through the house with a boom box blaring the same walking blues of Freddie King. He wears his usual outfit: old denim overalls, a blue work shirt, old high-top boots, a dull-colored sport coat, a red bandanna around his neck, a white handkerchief in his pocket, and a soft, well-worn wide-brimmed felt hat. His clothing is soft and worn, but very clean and tidy. He holds his beautifully carved walking stick. He carries a canvas bag containing a camp stool, a canteen, a tin cup, a bottle of rubbing alcohol and other objects that he considers important.

When he arrives on stage he unpacks his bag, placing the boom box on the plank, one camp stool downstage right, the other down left, and the rubbing alcohol on the floor by the upstage ladder. He opens his canteen and pours himself a drink. Then he sprinkles the circumference of the playing area with his libation, restores the boom box to his shoulder, retrieves his walking stick and raises a toast to the audience. He turns off the boom box.

Junebug sings "The Po Tatum Hambone Blues":

JUNEBUG:

Po Tatum, Po Tatum, where you been?
"Been to the city and I'm going again."
What you going to do when you get back?
"Take a little walk on the railroad track."

Po Tatum, Po Tatum, have you heard?
Junebug's here and he's spreading the word.
Telling everybody you was his best friend.
Telling everybody how you's done in.
Telling how you had to leave away from home.
Telling how you had to hit the road alone.

When Po Tatum was just a little bitty baby
His mam was known to be a real fine lady.
His daddy was a man with a special skill
Could make people laugh and he knowed how to build.

Had a nice little farm and a real fine house
As Po growed up he learned to run his mouth.
They was doing pretty well 'til things got funny,
They run out of work and they run out of money.

Need money for the farm, need money for the house.
Money for the cat, and for the cat to catch the mouse.
Need money for clothes, need money for school.
Even need money to feed the old mule.

You run to the city trying to get you some money.
You run to the city trying to find your honey.
When you run out of money come to the end of your rope.

You run out of money you run out of hope.
Po Tatum!

That's the "Po Tatum Hambone Blues."

It was because of Po Tatum that I finally come to understand that I was supposed to be a storyteller. I'ma tell y'all how that come about.

That's for Po. *(Pouring a libation)*

That's for y'all. *(Raising a toast)*

Act One

Scene 1

Goin' to Chicago

JUNEBUG: Po was the youngest one of Miz Adeline and Mr. Jake Tatum's three boys. There's Ralph, Skinhead and Po.

If you had seen him, you might have thought we called him Po 'cause he's so skinny. He's so skinny that he could get lost behind a telephone pole. But that ain't why we called him Po. We called him Po 'cause when he was seven years old, Miz Adeline, caught him eating a whole half a bushel of raw I'sh potatoes by himself. Miz Adeline, that's his mama, said, "Why you eat all them raw potatoes, son?"

He just grinned and said, "'Cause I was hungry!"

Why he didn't gain no weight I don't know, as much as he would eat. That boy could eat some potatoes! That's why we called him Po Tatum.

'Fore Po Tatum left home going to Chicago, he was one of the nicest fellows around. He'd go out of his way to try

43

and help people. He'd always speak to people and everything.

I remember one time, Mr. Raggs got drunk and fell in old man Quinland's cesspool. Miz Maybelle, Mr. Raggs' old lady, always beat him up real bad when he got drunk.

Mr. Raggs didn't always used to be like that, no! At one time he had one of the nicest little farms in Pike County. But then the City of McComb thought they could get a plant in there to make bullets for the war if they had Mr. Raggs' property. They told him he had to leave off his land and they took it over. Oh, they gave him a little bit of money for it, but they took away his pride. After that he was always getting drunk.

They never did get that ammunition plant in there neither.

Well, this particular time Mr. Raggs was trying to sneak in the back door, so to stay out of Miz Maybelle's way, and he misremembered and walked on them rotten boards over that cesspool and they give out from under him and he fell, *kerplush*, in all that stinky water! He made the biggest racket! Well, Po Tatum was the only one would help Mr. Raggs get out of that cesspool. Miz Maybelle wouldn't even beat him up 'til he went down to the Bogue Chitto River and got himself washed off.

Well, that's the kind of fellow Po was before he went off to Chicago. But he got to the city and his mind got turned around.

The Tatums come from this place out 'round the New Mt. Zion Community we called The Bottom. Mr. Jake was the Head Deacon at the New Mt. Zion Church and was the best carpenter around at the time. He had learned the carpenter trade from his daddy. Mr. Freeman Tatum, which they say he had been the main one to do most of the building on the Pike County Courthouse and most of the rich white people's homes around there. Mr. Freeman had built two homes for Colonel Whitten.

The Tatums had scrimped and scrapped for years 'til they was able to build a real fine home down in The Bottom,

as good or better than any they ever built for the white folk,
in some ways. And they built it out of scraps of stuff they's
able to save off whatever job they's working for the white
people.

The Bottom was a special kind of place. It wasn't nothing
but an old swampy piece of land didn't nobody want, but
them that lived down there. But for years and years white
folk just wouldn't go down there for nothing. It was said that
in years past a bunch of runaway slaves and Red Indians had
laid ambush and killed a bunch of white people there. For a
long time after that the white folk wouldn't go down to The
Bottom for nothing—not even the High Sheriff.

The first white man to go down there in modern times
was old man Ebenezer Winston, and he got there by accident. Eb was a sneaky, low-lifted sort of fellow, looked like
an old mangy dog. All slumped over with his tail sucked
up between his legs, he'd come sidling up to you and you
couldn't tell 'til he got right up on you, whether he's intent
to lick you or bite you.

It was during the Depression—one day old Eb had been
out looking for work and he fell asleep on his wagon. His
mule, which it must have had something to do with the
Tatums somewhere down the line, 'cause he wandered off
up in The Bottom and stopped right in front of the Tatums'
house. Eb woke up when the wagon stopped rocking from
the walking of the mule. He figured out where he was and
hightailed it back to town. He brought the High Sheriff
out there to arrest Mr. Jake, "'Cause can't no uppity nigger
afford a house that good no matter how hard him to work!"

But couldn't nobody 'round there figure out where Mr.
Jake or his daddy had ever done anybody wrong. They'd
nearly always finish whatever job they's working on on time,
and often was able to save people's money on the project
too. Since they couldn't find nobody to bring charges, they
had to let him go. But after that, Mr. Jake wasn't able to get
much carpenter work from the white folk. So, the way it
turned out, he had to work harder to try to make something
out that little swampy piece of land he had to call a farm.

It takes a heap of work and a heap of money to make do on a farm. Aw, you can pretty much stay in something to eat, but you pay hell trying to get ahead without no money.

The Tatums did some of everything trying to get ahead. They raised chickens, geese, hogs, some goats and a few cows, they had what was known to be the best bull thereabouts. People used to bring they cows from as far as Crystal Springs to stud off that bull. And you know a good bull is half your herd.

Miz Adeline kept a good-sized vegetable garden. They did they best trying to get ahead, but soon's they's able to get one step forward, something would come along and blow them two steps back.

Still and all Miz Adeline and Mr. Jake did as well or better than most. Things would probably have worked out all right 'cept for the fact that Mr. Jake got to bragging about how Phillip Anthony "Po" Tatum was going to be the first of they kin to go to college. Po wasn't even out of grade school yet but his daddy already seen him as the one who was going to put they family on a new footstand. "It's something about the boy. He look like a lawyer to me. Besides, he ain't never going to be fit for no real work, he too skinny!"

Po later told me that it many a night Mr. Jake would get that dictionary book down and say, "All right, son, read me something. If you going to be a lawyer, you got to know all kinds of things." He'd make Po read three or four pages out of that dictionary book.

By the time Po was twelve years old, he'd worked his way up to the letter "M" in that dictionary. His mind got stuck on the word "Meteorology." He wanted to know all about the weather. He told his daddy he needed a weather vane on top of the barn so's he could keep up with which way the wind was blowing. Mr. Jake didn't have enough money to buy one so he figured out how to make a weather vane out of scraps of stuff he had around the barnyard.

One Sunday afternoon after church, Mr. Jake set out to hitch that new weather vane to the hip of that tin-roofed barn when this freakish little summer storm blowed up. A bolt of lightning, just as red as blood, hit and knocked him plumb off that roof. He had to've been dead before he hit the ground. The body almost landed on young Po.

Miz Adeline wasn't 'nair bit of good after that. Seem like she just lost all interest in living. Miz Adeline was half Indian—long black hair down to here. *(He shows a spot far down his back)* It's a funny thing about them Indians—they get done living, they just ups and dies. She lingered on a good while, but she wasn't 'nair bit of good.

Like I said, Po was a nice young man, but with his daddy dead and his maw acting funny, Po got kind of lost. Guess he thought it was his fault what had happened.

Miz Caldonia Spencer, which everybody called her "Aunt Callie," had the farm next door to the Tatums. Being a retired schoolteacher she could see that neither Ralph, Skinhead nor Po's oldest sister, Miz Jeanine, was going to be able to do much with the young Po. Being an old friend of the family, she could see that there was little or no hope that Miz Adeline would ever get straight, so it didn't surprise nobody when she made it her business to try to keep Po from going sour.

Because of her arthritis she had to have help working the land so she would hire different people to help her do certain things—'course she wouldn't pay them nothing more than good will but everybody considered her to be hiring right on.

At the time. Aunt Callie had three young calves which she hired Po to take care of. He got into it too. Took to wearing a cowboy hat and everything. I wasn't but a child at the time but I remember wondering how Po thought he could be a cowboy with neither six-shooter nor horse to ride.

Her idea was to make a school for Po out of them calves. She would teach him the different parts of the calf, that would be his biology lesson. She would have him to figure up how much corn or hay it would take to feed them and so forth, so that would be his mathematics. For his English lesson she would have him make up little songs and things since he was so good with words. He had one song that went:

I'm an old cowhand from Bogue Chitto land.
My legs ain't bowed but my cheeks are tan.
I'm a cowboy who knows all about a cow.
I raise 'em real good 'cause I sure know how.
Get out of my way 'cause I'ma coming now,
Yippe-tie-yo-tie-yea!

Things were going on real good 'til one day Po come home from school to find all three of Aunt Callie's calves sick. He said, "Aunt Callie, what's wrong with my cows?"

"I don't know, son. Run over to Mr. Joe Whittie's and tell him to come down here to look at them.

He run all the way to Mr. Whittie's and told him to come look at his cows. Mr. Whittie come and he looked. He said, "Urn-hum, yeah. Urn-hum, yeah. Urn-hum, yeah. You got the red-tick fever, son. That's the red-tick fever. Aunt Callie you got the red-tick fever, that's what it is, urn-hum, the red-tick fever. You got to go in town and tell Doc Shultz that I said you got three calves with the red-tick fever out here. He'll give you a subscription and you take that to the drug store so you can get the medicine it takes to Rx the red-tick fever. Um-hum!"

Po ran to Doc Shultz' office and Doc Shultz told him, "If Joe Whittie said you got the red-tick fever out there, you got the red-tick fever all right. Joe Whittie knows something 'bout cows . . . and horses . . . and pigs and stuff like that. Here, you take this prescription to the drug store. It's going to cost you about seventy-five dollars for the treatment to cure all three cows." Before either Po or Aunt Callie could come up with the seventy-five dollars, all three of them cows died.

Po took and dug holes for them cows and buried them all by himself. It wasn't too long after that Po quit school and got a job at the Rainbow Sign Casino. He swore he wasn't never going to be without money again.

Now up to this time I reckon I'd have followed Po to the Gates of Hell. But when he start to get right wild, I begun to wonder. He took to fancy dressing and hanging out on weekends up in McComb.

He did have the gift of gab! That boy coulda talked St. Peter into letting the Devil pass through the Pearly Gates. He would make up little rhymes and sayings quick as you could turn around. And don't talk about no Dozens!

The Dozens is a game we play, which the idea is to take advantage of people. The way you supposed to take advantage of people is by making them mad and upset. The way you make them mad and upset is by talking bad about they mama. We call that game the Dozens.

Now if you like me, you wonder why they to call a game like that the "Dozens." What's a dozen got to do with your mama? So I did some research on the subject. The best idea I been able to get on the subject come from Miz Louise Anderson, a storyteller I know from Jacksonville, North Carolina.

Miz Anderson traced the story back to slavery days. 'Course you understand, didn't nobody want to be no slave, but if you had to be a slave, you didn't want to be no cheap slave. Say they sell one person for five hundred or a thousand dollars. It come your turn to hit the block won't nobody bid more than fifty or sixty dollars for you. That makes you feel bad.

Well, it was some slaves they couldn't sell for doodley-squat. You say, "Hey, boy, take this hoe go down there to chop that cotton." By the time you get down there to check on him he be sitting up on the fence row, waiting. You say, "Hey, boy, I told you to chop that cotton!" He say, "I can't." The hoe's broke. You say, "All right then, boy, you go up to the barn and pitch that hay." So you take the hoe to get fixed but by the time you get to the barn, the barn's on fire! You tell him, "Boy, go down to the crick and send some water up here so we can put the fire out!" By the time you get that fire out, that slave's done run off.

Well, a slave like that you'd have to sell by the dozen and didn't nobody want to be in the dozen. If you get put in the dozen, that would mean your mama didn't raise you right, so that's a bad reflection on your mama. That's the best idea I've heard on how the game got its name.

So, while everybody else be struggling to remember one or two bad names to call your mother, Po be running off a string of bad names. And he'd put it in rhyme!

Say your mother's name might be "Mary." Po would say:

Late last night, snuck in to see Miz Mary
Mighta tried to kiss her but her face was too hairy.
Your mama's got a face like a kitchen sink
She's got to sneak up on a glass just to get herself a drink.

I hadn't never heard of Po being beat at playing the Dozens or playing cards but one time. This fellow named Skipper Rowe come up from New Orleans. They called him "Tipper" 'cause he always walked around on his tiptoes like he's trying to sneak up on somebody. He always wore these little soft shoes that looked kinda like slippers. Said he had bad feet. He would always carry an umbrella rain or shine. Called everybody "Little" something. "Hey, where you at, Little Bro? What's happening, Little Mama?"

One time during "Spring Break," which always came during cotton-chopping season, a bunch of us fellows had gathered up in the back room of Bugs' Underground Café to play Tunk. Po was acting a fool that day. He was just sounding on folks and putting them in the Dozens. But Tipper was hanging right in there with him just as quiet as could be. Finally, it come down to just the two of them. Po, running his mouth, and Tipper, just running them cards.

Before he knowed what had happened, Po was down to his last money. Po pulled the Queen of Spades and slapped it on the table. "Doggonit, I told your mama not to send me no more other ugly pictures!"

Tipper pulled a card. Just as cool as could be, he said, "Hey, wait a minute, baby. You can say anything you want to about my mother or any one of her kin people. But if you just look like you going to say one bad word about your sweet mama, son, it's going to make me mad!" He laid down three aces and three deuces—ain't no way to beat that in Tunk. "You country hip, Little Poppa, but your game is

lame. Where I come from, we use chumps like you for bat-
ting practice."

"Now, Mr. Tatum, I'ma take your little chump change, go
up front and buy everybody a nice cool RC Cola." After that,
Po ain't had no more to do with Tipper and the Dozens.
Tipper be in a game of cards or somethin', Po go shoot
some pool.

'Fore long, Po got his mind made up that he's going to
the city. Every time you seen him he be saying:

Going to Chicago, baby
Heading for the city.
Going to Chicago, baby
Heading for the city.

Chica-Chica-Chica-Chica-Chica-Chicago
Chica-Chica-Chica-Chica-Chica-Chicago
Chica-Chica-Chica-Chica-Chica-Chicago
I'm gonna get the Northbound train.

I musta been about thirteen or fourteen at the time. It was
before I'd made up my mind to leave home myself. One
day I asked him, "Why you got to go way to Chicago to get
some money, they got plenty work right over here in New
Orleans?"

"And they got the same old mean-ass white people they
got here. Dan Skinner's got a first cousin down there's big-
timer in the Waterfront Union. Dan's down there two or
three times a year himself. He comes out to the Rainbow
Sign Casino just bragging about the "mellow yellow Creole
gals" he finds down there. Colonel Whitten's got a brother,
four nephews and a son down there. They own the newspaper, a radio station and a bunch of other stuff. No, siree,
Bob! It sounds too much like home to me. Besides, that's
where old-jive-time Tipper Rowe comes from. What kind of
rep you think I'm going to make with him around to get on
my case?"

I'm going to the city
Where the women's really pretty
And they tell me that the money falls like rain.
I'm tired of picking cotton
Mississippi's gotten rotten,
Gonna pack my bag and jump the quickest train.

Going to Chicago, baby
Heading for the city.
Going to Chicago, baby
Heading for the city.

Chica-Chica-Chica-Chica-Chica-Chicago
Chica-Chica-Chica-Chica-Chica-Chicago
Chica-Chica-Chica-Chica-Chica-Chicago
I'm gonna get the Northbound train.

Po kept on like that every time you seen him, but after two
or three months he just up and disappeared! It was a bunch
of rumors as to why Po left town so quick like that.

It was a well-known fact in a small circle that him and
Becky Sawyers was making time. She was a waitress out there
at the Rainbow Casino where Po was bussing dishes. Becky
Sawyers was good-looking in a way but she on the thin side.
She's so thin she could dodge raindrops in a good-sized
storm and not get wet. In that way her and Po made a good
pair. She always wore these two long braids. Them braids was
bigger than her legs. She was thin. But she was also white.

Some of y'all might be surprised that it was so much race-
mixing going on during the deep down Jim Crow days. But
I'm here to tell you that there was plenty of it. See, old-timey
segregation had more to do with sitting down together. If
you was standing up working or laying down working it was
all right.

The Sawyers was what we used to call poor white trash.
They wasn't nothing but sharecroppers just like the rest
of us, but that's what we used to call them. When she was
thirteen, Becky'd had a child for Dan Skinner, Colonel

Whitten's Overseer and Deputy Sheriff. Dan never made no
move to marry her 'cause she had the reputation of being a
bad girl—due to the child she'd had for him. 'Course Dan
wasn't in no shape to get married no way, financial or otherwise. "Aw, I'll keep her for fooling around, but you want a
wife, buddy, you got to get you a good girl."

So, when Po come along with his heavy line of rap, she
must have figured, "If he's got the nerve to try me, then
I sure got the nerve to try him." Plus, she knowed, if they
ever got caught, she could always claim he's raping her.

Rumor had it that one night Dan Skinner had caught ol'
Po with Becky in the smokehouse out back of the casino, shot
him dead and throwed his body in the Bogue Chitto River.
For years after Po disappeared, every time a body washed up
in the Bogue Chitto River, people would wonder, "Is that Po?"

A more likely story went that Po had found out where
Antonio Dominuis "Stonewall" Whitten was keeping his
money hid. Stonewall Whitten was Colonel Whitten's younger
brother. Colonel Whitten and their older brother, Beauregard
Caesar Whitten, owned the bank in McComb and half the
rest of everything around there. Stonewall didn't have a
dime's worth of confidence in his brothers or their bank.

Stonewall claimed that when their daddy died, his brothers had cheated him out of his share of the family inher-
itance. Two or three times a year he would bring a legal
action to try to get his money back. Every time he come
down there his case would be thrown out of court. Every
time they thrown him out of court, he would haul off and
start preaching on the courthouse steps.

"Brethern and Sisteren of the Righteous Cause of the
Confederation: Beware of the sins of sloth, greed and glut-
tony! Yeah, even also products of my father's seed, issue of
my sainted mother's loin, have made league with the Devil in
Hell in rapacious lust for your land and property. Through
the devilish device of this bank, aided and abetted by the
officers of this court, the police, jury, the sheriff, the mayor,
and the city council they are bleeding you dry, dry, dry! I say
we must rise up against this heathenistic oligarchy! Before

the South can rise again, we must purge ourselves of these fiendish devils sporting the cloth and style of gentlemen!"

He made it plain and clear that he was calling for a rebellion amongst the white folks. The colored people knew they'd need a passport to get within a block of the courthouse when Stonewall was down there preaching.

Stonewall would rather have died than put two pennies in that bank. Since it was the only bank around it was said that Stonewall had a way of stashing money in glass jars, strongboxes, anything, in places all over his plantation. Po had been heard to say that he knowed where Stonewall was keeping that money hid and that whenever Po needed some, he'd just sneak out there in the dead of night and take whatever he wanted.

You might can tell. Stonewall was somewhat peculiar. Where most folks would have used dogs for the purpose. Stonewall kept a pack of wild pigs to protect his property. Now that ain't necessarily as dumb as it first might seem. A hog is stronger, meaner and smarter than your average dog.

This particular story went that one night while Po was down there rooting for some of Stonewall's money, the biggest, baddest boar in the pack caught with Po 'fore he had the time to get out the hole with the money. Before Po was able to cut him bad enough to bleed it to death, that pig put a gash on the left side of Po's face from his ear to his lip.

Stonewall loved that wild hog more than he loved money. He's the first one I ever heard of to quit eating pork. He'd made his wife leave home 'cause she didn't want that thing sleeping in the bed with them when it was a baby.

After killing Stonewall's favorite wild boar and getting cut like that, Po knew it was time for him to grab his hat.

Po was feeling so low-down that the belly of a rattlesnake would have looked like a bridge. He went that night and hopped an IC freight train going to Chicago.

The old freight train's a rocking,
My aching head's a popping
Need me something just to ease the pain.

54

Had to leave my home and family
'Cause this crazy cracker jammed me,
I'm going and I won't be back again.

Going to Chicago, baby, heading for the city.
Going to Chicago, baby, heading for the city.
Chica-Chica-Chica-Chica-Chica-Chicago
Chica-Chica-Chica-Chica-Chica-Chicago
Chica-Chica-Chica-Chica-Chica-Chicago
I done gone and caught the Northbound train.

Scene 2

Home for the Funeral

JUNEBUG: It was five years more 'fore Po was seen again in Pike County. His mama, Miz Adeline, had pined and pined 'til she couldn't pine no more. After Mr. Jake was killed like he was she didn't have much use for the world. Year by year, as their land would go a piece at a time, she just went more and more into herself. Whilst all her other children was gathered around her dying bed she kept calling for her baby one more time.

The problem of it was the family didn't know where in the world Po was. They used to get a money order from him once every month for three or four hundred dollars. But they hadn't heard a thing for over a year now. They's sitting there trying to figure out what to do and Skinhead said, "By God," let's go up to Mr. Jimmy Knowles store and call Junebug. Him and Po's tighter than the twine on Aunt Callie's corset. If anybody'd know were to find him Junebug would."

At the time, I was running this shoe-shine stand at the Pontchartrain Hotel in New Orleans. They's kind of some-timey about me getting phone calls there. But when long distance called for me even the switchboard operator got excited.

"Pontchartrain Hotel, may I help you, please? . . . Long distance? . . . for Mr. J. J. Jones, one moment please . . . I'm sorry, Operator, we don't have a Mr. Jones registered at this time . . . What's that? . . . Junebug? Oh! You mean June-bug! Operator that's a Nee-ga-row! . . . Well! Excuse me please. What's this world coming to! Charles! Charles! Tell the shoe-shine boy that he has a long-distance telephone call!"

"Long distance? For Junebug? Boy-oh-boy! Boy-oh-boy! Boy-oh-boy! Long distance, for Junebug. Boy! Boy! You've got a long-distance telephone call in here. Florine says you'll have to call 'em back on the pay phone if it takes more than three minutes. She can't have you tying up her lines."

"If it takes a week, a week'll do, turkey. And from now on it's Mr. Boy to you. You just mad 'cause you ain't never had no long-distance telephone call . . . Hello. This is Mr. Jones."

"HEY, LI'L DAVID, THIS IS SKINHEAD."

Right away I knowed who it was. Didn't but one person call me by my given name like that beside my mama. "You keep on like that you going to break the telephone, Skinhead. What's going on?"

"WE TRYING TO FIND PO. MAMA'S LOW-DOWN SICK AND SHE BEEN CALLING FOR HIM."

"Miz Adeline's sick?"

"LOW-DOWN SICK. TELL YOU THE TRUTH, I DON'T THINK SHE GOIN' TO MAKE IT THIS TIME. WE AIN'T HEARD A WORD FROM PO IN OVER A YEAR."

"I ain't heard nothing from Po in the last little while myself, but I feel and believe that I can find him."

"ALL RIGHT, YOU GET TO HIM, THEN. TELL HIM HIS MAMA'S ON HER DYING BED AND SHE CALLING FOR HIM."

"All right, I'll do that, Skinhead. Tell all your brothers and people 'Hello.'"

"ALL RIGHT, LI'L DAVID. SO LONG, NOW."

It hurt me some bad to hear that. By me being so close to Po and all, Miz Adeline was next to my mama in my mind. But finding Po was going to take more'n a notion.

The trouble was, Po didn't exactly live in no particular where. If he got in tight with some woman he'd stay with her for a while but mostly he'd live in his car. Every now and then, being as Po was none too swift in the writing department, he'd have this one particular lady friend of his to write me a letter. Whenever I wanted to get in touch with Po I had to write to this lady, which her name was Consuela LeBeaux. She's from Haiti. That's just south of Miami off in the Atlantic Ocean.

It took me a while but I's able to get her number from information. The operator put the call through for me.

"Miz Consuela, I'm trying to reach Po— Well, I'll say, Phillip Anthony Tatum. I need to talk to him quick, fast, and in a hurry."

"You must be the one he calls Junebug."

I was knocked out. Not only did she know who I was, she sounded like the original honey-dripper!

"Philippe said you might call some day. Is there anything wrong?"

"Yes, ma'am, it is. I need to let Po know that Miz Adeline, his mama, is on her dying bed and she's calling for him."

It got real quiet on the other end of the line. I thought we'd been cut off.

"Hello. Hello, Miz Consuela . . ."

"Yes. I'm here. I will get the message to him right away."

I couldn't tell what it was, but I knowed something was wrong by the way she said that. But when she said that one of them would call me back the next day, I went on back to work feeling like I had done something worthwhile. Early that next morning the porter came back to my shoe-shine stand.

"Say, boy. You're getting to be a regular businessman around here. You got another one of them long-distance telephone calls."

"Aw, hush up, man! . . . Hello."

"SHE GONE, LI'L DAVID. YOU FIND HIM?"

"Yes, I found him—leastwise I found somebody said they could get a message to him. I'll call 'em back right away. When's the funeral?"

"SATURDAY."

"All right, I'll see you, Skinhead."

"I'LL SEE YOU, LI'L DAVID."

I called Miz Consuela right away. She was mighty upset 'bout Po's dear mama but she was more upset 'cause she couldn't promise that Po was going to be able to make the funeral that coming Saturday. I didn't say nothing but I did wonder what it was that Po was so tied up in that he couldn't make it to his own mother's funeral. I later found out that Po had been in jail at the time and Miz Consuela didn't have no idea whether Po would be able to come up with some scheme to get out of jail in time to be to the funeral.

Me, I got to Four Corners late that Friday afternoon. Next morning at the funeral, they had the front four rows at the church on either side roped off for the family. Reverend Wright preached a powerful sermon. I reckon he was glad to have a funeral to preach that he didn't have to spend most of his time lying about the poor departed. Miz Adeline was one of the best and nicest people you ever going to meet.

Reverend Wright was done preaching and was about to open the casket so we could view the remains when it came a great racket outside of a car sliding to a halt. The door to the church popped open and there stood this lady, on high-heeled shoes, which was more strap than shoe, she sorta pranced like a highbred filly, without touching the ground too hard. My eye followed her blue stockings up them long shapely legs 'til I almost embarrassed myself. Scared I was about to see something that I wasn't supposed to look at, my other eye jumped up to the woman's face which was covered by a little blue veil pinned to a little blue pancake hat tilted over her left eye. She licked her shiny red lips and dabbed her eye with this little blue handkerchief. She turned to hold the door open for Po Tatum!

He had on a white, double-breasted seersucker suit, with a black silk shirt and a white polka-dot necktie and this wide-brimmed white straw hat with a black-and-white polka-dot band. As he stepped in the church house, Po dabbed his forehead with his polka-dot handkerchief and, sure enough, there was a long scar running down his ear to his lip on this side of his face that made him look like he's smiling all the time.

He walked up the coffin, raised up the veil on the coffin, bent down and kissed his mama. Then, slow like in slow motion, he slumped down on the floor and cried like a baby.

Up to that point it had not been such a sad funeral. But it's a sad thing to see a grown man cry. Everybody in the church busted out in tears. Skinhead, who ain't never been heard to whisper a day in his life, said, "Well I'll be a ring-tailed monkey."

It took Reverend Wright and Willie Gladstone a good while to get the service back under control. They finally got the casket loaded out onto the hearse. That being done, Po come back to the center of attention. All his brothers and sisters was hugging him and holding him trying to find out all that he'd done, and how he was and such.

Me, I turned my attention to the Blue Lady. Still feeling obliged not to look below the pearl-looking necklace she wore, I said, "How do, ma'am? I'm Junebug. You must be Miz Consuela."

"The name my mama give me was Flora Belle. My daddy's name was Washington. Do that sound like Consuela to you? Po, Daddy, Po! You ready to go?"

She walked as much as that tight-fitting dress would let her to where Po was standing and he loaded her into that brand-new 1951, powder blue Cadillac for the trip to the burying ground.

After a funeral, everybody meets at the house of the nearest of kin to talk and sip a little spirits to help out 'til the grief be kinda lifted. They had some food out there that day. Seemed like everyone ever owed Miz Adeline a favor tried to pay her back by bringing food that day. Everybody was talking about Po and how well he had to've been doing, what with them fancy clothes and that fancy car and that fine woman, he had to've been doing all right!

Aunt Callie leaned back in the rocking chair, scratched a match on the floor to light her pipe and said, "I have seen them come and I have seen them go. You can't judge a book by looking at the cover. I'm here to tell you!" Nobody said nothing back to Aunt Callie. Not so much because it's impolite to back-talk old people, but because Aunt Callie's been known to put people in their place with little or no ceremony.

Knowing Aunt Callie, that got me to thinking.

Po still looked sad when the family got back from the graveyard, but the young boys crowding all around him would not let him have no peace. Out on the porch, all the young unmarried women fell in around Miz Flora Belle, which Po called her Flukey.

"Aunt Callie noticed how all of us youn'uns followed behind Po and Flukey with our minds. She rared back and blowed a big puff of smoke from her pipe and said, "Well, Phillip, it seems like you've gone off to the city and struck it rich, huh, son?"

"I wouldn't say that, Aunt Callie, I'm doing all right, but I ain't found no cows to tend in the city."

"What have you found to tend in the city that will afford you a Cadillac car and that fancy, fast-talking woman? Are you married to her? Or did you bring her here to make mock of your mother's funeral?"

"No'm, Aunt Callie, you know I wouldn't do nothing like that!"

"Then tell me just exactly what you have been doing, son. You happy enough to tell all these young boys, tell me.

Just then Ralph came in from the bedroom and said, "I'm sorry, Aunt Callie, ma'am, but Po, we need to speak to you in the bedroom."

Po was glad to get out from that session with Aunt Callie. But what he didn't know was that he's going from the fat into the fire. I couldn't get in the room to see what they was saying, but with Skinhead in there I didn't have to.

"HOW COME YOU DIDN'T COME HOME WHEN WE GOT BURNED OUT? WHYN'T YOU LET SOMEBODY KNOW WHERE YOU'S AT? YOU KNOW'D YOUR MAMA WAS SICK AND YOU'S HER FAVORITE! HOW CO—"

"I'm sorry, Skinhead," said Ralph, "but Po you know Daddy always did expect more out of you than he did any of the rest of us. We sure could use some extra help around here. If we don't give Whitten five hundred dollars by the end of the month, we stand to lose the twenty-acre plot the family place used to stand on, the one with all the graves on it."

It must have been Po's oldest sister, Miz Jeanine, said, "How dare you bring that 'Floozy' woman to your own mother's funeral!"

"Her name ain't 'Floozy'! And if she's woman enough for me, she ought to be good enough for you."

The bedroom door popped open and everybody but Aunt Callie jumped to get at something like they hadn't been listening. Po, just as cool as a cucumber, walked over to where I was standing, "Junebug, my man, I've got some business in New Orleans. If you want a ride, you let the doorknob hit you where the good Lord split you. Flukey, baby, we got to rise and fly."

"You know me, Daddy, I'm wake up in the morning ready to roll."

"Well, Junebug, you flying or crying?"

Everybody turned to see what I was going to do. Aunt Callie broke the silence by tapping the ashes of her pipe on the edge of the Prince Albert tobacco tin she was using as a spit can. She said to one of the young Tatum women standing nearby, "Help me up, darling. I believe I'm going back down to the kitchen, get some of that good yellow corn bread and some of that pot liquor off them collard greens." As she caned her way back toward the kitchen on her good foot, she sang:

Oh, I done done
Oh, I done done
Oh, I done done
I done done what you told me to do.

"All right, Mr. Po, I'm ready to go."

All the fellows followed us out to that new blue '51 Cadillac. Four or five of them fought to hold the door for Flukey, mainly so they could see her prance up to the car, bend in the middle, rotate those blue-stocking knees into the plush upholstery of the new-smelling car.

I cleared a space in the backseat for myself, but before Po could park hisself behind the steering wheel, they said, "Hey, Mr. Po, tell us where you going to go."

"That's for me to know and for you to find out."

"Aw, come on, Po. Lay one of them heavy rhymes on us, man."

Po thought about it for a minute and said:

My mama just died,
My dad's a long time gone.
I'm out here on the highway all a doggone 'lone.
I'm digging like a dog for his very last bone
Living for the city
Trying to make a new home.
I'm talking Chica-Chica-Chica-Chica-Chica-Chicago
Chica-Chica-Chica-Chica-Chica-Chicago
Chica-Chica-Chica-Chica-Chica-Chicago
I'm out here on the road all alone.
So long, y'all.
So long, home.

Po slammed the door of that Cadillac, dropped it in gear and gunned it so it cut a dusty gash in Ralph's front yard.

We's halfway to Franklinton 'fore I figured out what was going on. Miz Flukey had the map in her lap trying to tell him which way to go. I said, "Excuse me, ma'am, but Po, you know Highway 51's the best, most direct route to New Orleans."

"We know that, darling. But we figure as long as were out here in the country, we ought to take in the sights. Oh, Po, Daddy, look! There's a whole herd of bulls!"

"Ain't no such thing as a 'herd of bulls,' Flukey! Them's cows! To be so smart about the city, you sure are dumb about the country! You just lay back and let the groove do the moving, Junebug. See in these new Cadillac cars, you pay for your ride and get your rocking free."

I thought for a minute about why we's taking them back roads down to New Orleans and decided it wasn't none of my business and I was going to leave it alone.

That Cadillac rocked so steady that it wasn't long before I had dozed off to sleep. When I woke up Po was saying, "Wake up, Junebug, we in New Orleans!"

At the time, I's living in this little three-room shotgun house down the street from the Dew Drop Inn in New Orleans. Flukey didn't like it 'nair bit. She went with Po that first night to play cards with Tipper Rowe and I ain't seen hide nor hair of her since.

Four days later, Po came driving up to the hotel, where I's working, in a different car—a maroon-colored Lincoln Continental, fully loaded.

"Come on, Junebug, get you glad rags on. I'm gonna take you to Dookey Chase's restaurant for a high-class dinner."

The next day I came home from work and all of Po's stuff was gone. It was a hundred-dollar bill on the kitchen table with some printing in one corner. Said, "Keep this for good luck, Po."

It was a good while after that 'fore I caught up with Po again. But I later come to find that two days before Whitten was to foreclose the mortgage on the Tatum Family place which used to have that lovely house on it, Ralph and them got a money order from Chicago for five thousand dollars with a telegram from Po saying, "This is for my share of the funeral. I hope things work out fine."

Act Two

———

Scene 1

Letters from Jail

CHICKEN IN THE CAR AND THE CAR CAN'T GO
THAT'S HOW YOU SPELL CHI-CA-GO.

JUNEBUG: I be going around a lot telling stories and since I'm from the country, which most of us are in one way or the other, I tell a lot of country stories. Sometimes ci-ditty people try to hide from the light that shines through the tales I tell by just playing it off—they say, "Oh, that's jut another old country boy talking." But I'm here to tell you I might look like a farmer but I ain't no fool!

You don't know what that word "ci-ditty" means do you?

Back home Miz May Ellen Gladstone, now that's Willie Gladstone's mama—she's a Jeter by birth, her people come from down in The Bottom too—they had the place on the other side of Aunt Callie's place from the Tatums'. She's the one that built up the funeral home that Willie runs now. Miz

May Ellen is an A-number-1 good person. When the Freedom Riders first come to McComb they stayed at her house. When the sheriff set up road blocks to keep the director of this national Civil Rights Organization from coming to speak at the New Mt. Zion Church, Miz May Ellen sent a hearse to meet him at the airport in New Orleans, put him in a coffin, drove him through the road block straight to Reverend Wright's church. That's the kind of person Miz May Ellen was!

Right after Samella, Willie's little sister was born, their daddy Mr. Granville Gladstone had had a stroke. Miz May Ellen must have been too busy taking care of Mr. Granville, running the funeral home, and helping out with The Movement to take good care of those children. Willie's mean as a one-eyed cat, and Samella was all right before she got so "ci-ditty."

The summer before we started high school, Samella went to Chicago. She came back with all these fancy clothes 'n' everything. She even took to sticking her nose up in the air and talking funny. I asked her why she be dressing strange and acting funny. She say, "You are just too country, sweetheart, that's how we do it in ci-ditty—I mean THE CITY!" 'Fore long it got to be a saying when anybody got their hips up on their shoulders—got things turned bassackwards and upside-down—that there was "ci-ditty."

I don't know why Miz May Ellen couldn't see to do no better with her own kids 'cause she sure could see through everybody else.

When I came back from the Korean War, The Freedom Movement was in full swing in some places. My mind was made up and my heart was set. I went home and jumped right into it. Miz May Ellen was the only one of the so-called big-time colored people would have something to do with me and the Movement.

She once took me to a meeting of the Better Business League of Greater Pike County in the private dining room of the VF&W Rest and Lodge. I was trying to get them to come to a meeting to find out about the Supreme Court school desegregation issue.

Reverend Elmore Dooley, who ran Dooley's "One-Stop" Grocery Store and Grill—the reason they called it "One-Stop" is if you stopped there one time you wasn't likely to stop there no more—he was the first one to his feet.

"Mr. President, Madam Secretary and Members in Good Standing of the Better Business League of Greater Pike County. As a life-long resident of this community, as a responsible businessman, and a minister of the gospel, I feel it's my bounden duty to say before I go, y'all ought to leave this freedom mess alone! It ain't nothing but trouble and I ain't having nothing to do with it and if you was smart, you'd leave these shiftless Negroes alone too. These crazy white folks would just as soon's to kill any one of y'all as they would to shoot a wild dog."

There wasn't no way he could finish his march to the door without trying to get 'round Miz May Ellen. It wasn't no way she was going to let him get away clean.

"Reverend Elmore! I guess you ought to know a shiftless Negro when you see one. I don't know who or what you think you are. How much grocery do you sell to white folks? How many white folks thump your collection trays on Sunday morning? Hell! We're all just one step from the cotton patch anyway!

That was the spring of 1957. We never could get us a school case in Pike County, but that fall they did get nine children to start the white high school in Little Rock, Arkansas. After seeing the kind of stuff they had in the paper about Korea, I knew you couldn't trust what was in the newspaper so I figure I'd go over there to see for myself what was going on.

It was October before I got this letter forwarded from home:

July 20, 1957
Consuela LeBeaux
4818 Drexel Blvd.
Chicago, 111.

Dear Mr. Jones,
   Phillip wants to get in touch with you. Please let me
know where you are so I can put you on his mail list.
Write me at the above address or call me at CAlumet
2-4210.

Sincerely yours,
Consuela LeBeaux

It was two things seemed strange to me about this letter.
Number 1: this letter looked like it might have something to
do with business and I knew the only business Po's likely to
be in at the time was monkey business. Number 2: I couldn't
figure out why I'd have to get on a "mail list" to communi-
cate with my friend.
   I was staying at Mother Mason's Guest House on Elm
Street. Of course, I could have stayed at the Hilton but
I didn't want everyone to know my business.
   When my mail caught up with me it'd already been a
good while since Miz Consuela's letter had been sent. So
I decided to call on the phone and see what was going on.
   It turned out that Po had got himself put back in jail.
Miz Consuela, the honey-dripper, was just trying to help
out by finding me since I was the only one besides her he
wanted to write to. If you wasn't on their list, the jailhouse
wouldn't let you communicate with him. They had him at
the State Penitentiary in Joliet, Illinois. He was doing time
for attempted manslaughter and about four other things.
   It seems Po had won twelve hundred dollars in a poker
game from this white fellow who had tried to duck out on
him. Po had to run the man down to get his money. But
the game was in an all-white neighborhood. When they seen
this colored man with a scar on his face and an eight-inch

switchblade chasing this white man, somebody called the police. Even so, Po probably could have gotten away if he had just taken the money and gone on about his business, but no—he had to hang around giving the man a lecture about how honesty was the best policy and how it would put a bad light on his people if he didn't pay his debts in a timely way. So because of that he landed in Joliet with a twenty-four-year sentence.

Now I don't want y'all to misunderstand what I'm about to say because I don't believe that it's right what's happening in the jails of this country. You got to understand that something's wrong when over eighty percent of the people in the jails of this country is either black, Spanish, Indian, or some other denomination of poor people, when all took together, we don't make up forty percent of the population. It just ain't right when a man who steals a twenty-dollar ham for his family might get three years in jail, while a man who steals twenty million dollars will get a warning and a little fine. And if they just have to give him some time, they send him to a camp with horseback riding, golf, tennis courts and private rooms in little bungalows they can stay in with their wives and girlfriends or whatever.

No, I ain't in favor of jails and the way they are run, but I do think it was good for Po to get that little time when he did. The way he had been going, he might as well a tried to run through Hell in a pair of gasoline drawers. If they hadn't put him in jail when they did, they'd a had to put him in a pine box.

Po always did like to taste a little bit. But when he got to the city, somebody turned him on to dope. By the time he got busted he had begun to mess around with heroin—snorting it and every now and then he pump a little bit. But when they put him in jail he got to reading and studying and practicing on his writing and all kinds of stuff.

You can see the difference in Po by the letters he would write:

June 16, 1957

Dear Brother Junebug,

How are you? Fine I hope. Here I sit behind these four walls of bars. Sad and lonely and all alone I write from this empty cell and dream about the times we was fishing on the Bogue Chitto River, and wish that I had the wings of a dove and over these prison walls would I fly, but since I am not no angel and will be here for a while I wish that you would send me news of the world outside and books that I can read. *Please* don't tell my brothers and people where I am.

Your sad friend,
Phillip A. Tatum

December 18, 1958

Dear Junebug,

I figured, "What the hell?" So I signed up to go to college. Bet you didn't know you could do that in jail? The worse they can do if I fail is kick me out of here. Don't I wish! Well, I had to do something to pass the time. So why not try college?

I figured I'd start off easy so I took this English composition course. It was not as easy as I thought but I came out okay.

I only made a "C," but that isn't too bad for a fellow dropped out of the ninth grade, is it?

I met this guy in the library named Robert Watson. You might as well say he volunteered to go to jail because he's in here for what he called a "sitting demonstration" at a private club in Springfield. He's a pre-law student. He went and made a sitting demonstration to test the law that says black folks can't go to places like that. He won't even take bail while his case is still in court.

It sounds dumb to me. I'm getting out of here as quick as I can. What's going on out there? Have people gone crazy?

Your incarcerated friend,
Po

March 28, 1959

Dear Junebug,

I am into chess now. Are you hip to chess? There's this old dude in here that everybody thinks is crazy. Won't tell nobody his name or nothing. He has been here for thirty-seven years and nobody knows his name. They call him "Old Dude."

The only thing Old Dude will do is play chess. He won't do that with just any and everybody either. But he did offer to teach me what he know about the game. Through that we got to talking.

It turns out that the Old Dude had first been set up for five years for something they called "criminal syndicalism." I looked it up in the library here and near as I can understand, it's something like crime syndicate. The Old Dude had joined up with this syndicate they call a union. They were trying to get at the Pullman Porter plant outside of Chicago. Thirteen of them got busted.

After a month or two at Joliet the warden sicced one of his lap dogs on the Old Dude to make him rat on his partners. They got in a fight. The Old Dude hit the other guy with the handle of a wrench out the machine shop and called a guard. It took them so long to get that guy to the infirmary that he bled to death.

A month after that happened, they cut the other twelve guys loose but they convicted the Old Dude on a new charge of Murder 1.

I'm glad you got me to let my family know what's happening. Ralph and Skinhead both came all the way up here twice to visit me. I told Consuela, "I feel more like a man now that I ain't got nothing to hide." She smiled and said, "You look more like a man to me too." I can't wait to get out of here!

Send me something about these people in Montgomery, Alabama. What do they think they are trying to do? I don't have too much to do with preachers ever since Deacon Johnny Green pulled the covers off Reverend Doctor A. B. C. Golightly. But this King fellow from Montgomery seems to be different. Maybe he's the one who can lead us out the wilderness of North America.

Keep the books coming. After I get through with them, I put them in the prison library, so you helping at least a few more besides me . . . maybe.

Your studious friend,
P. A. Tatum

November 3, 1963

Dear Junebug,

I have to tell somebody! I'm still gloating about the fact that I did better in this course in "Modern Social Theory" than Babatunde did. Babatunde is just a thesis short of his master's degree, and the professor said my final paper was "insightful, innovative, very interesting, and that it deserves serious consideration." He gave Babatunde an "A" too but he wrote all over the brother's paper about how this point needed "further development" and so forth. I feel like I'm doing all right.

I wrote a critical review of the theoretical differences between W. C. B. DuBois and the White/Wilkins regime of the NAACP. It's really an interesting case study that reveals some of the basic problems that lie at the heart of the Afro-American struggle for freedom, justice and equality in America. If you're interested, let me know. I'll send you a copy of the paper.

Thanks for your help hooking me up with that NAA lawyer for the Old Dude. After a year and a half of correspondence, I got a letter last week from the lawyer saying that he's willing to try for clemency for the Old Dude, considering the circumstances and some recent rulings on similar cases.

The only problem is, we buried the Old Dude last month.

Yours with undying hope for freedom,
P. Anthony Tatum

P.S. I'm up for parole next week. Wish me luck.

Scene 2

The Danger Zone Is Everywhere

JUNEBUG: When I's in New Orleans, Mr. Ray Charles used to come to the Dew Drop Inn. He'd come out to the bandstand after the band got everybody all warmed up and say, "I want y'all to meet the Raelettes. The Raelettes are international stars. In case you didn't know what that word "international" means, it means "all over everywhere." The Raelettes are international stars. Help me sing the song girls. ". . . The whole world is in an un uproar, / and the danger zone is everywhere . . ."

The whole world was in an uproar and the danger zone was everywhere. That's what I's trying to tell Po when I went to visit him the last time 'fore he got out of jail, but he never heard a word I said. "No, Junebug, I'm a college graduate now. I'll get a good job when I get out of here and work my way through law school. I'm not fit for no real work anyway."

"How you think you going to get into somebody's law school, Po? You got a felony conviction record."

"Oh, Junebug, you don't understand. They have good lawyers meeting before the bar every day with records worse than mine!"

I wondered what kind of bar he was thinking about.

They put Po in a halfway house on the Westside of Chicago 'til he could find a regular job. It was in a real crowded part of town. That part of town wasn't much different than the jail Po had come out of, except the jail was cleaner. Everybody had they little roosts to go to. It reminded me of how chickens used to be stacked in crates on a flatbed truck on the way to market. You go to your roost, you fasten three or four locks and a chain and there you be—them four walls is what you got to call home.

I was working with the Mississippi Freedom Democrats at the time. I had jumped at the chance when they needed somebody to do some organizing work in Chicago in 1964. Miz Consuela took to inviting us to her house over on Drexel Boulevard for Sunday dinner. The first time I went I made the mistake of asking Po how he was coming on his job hunt.

"I can't stand these jive-time liberals, man! Things will be going on just fine 'til they find out I'm an ex-con, then the stuff gets funny. 'Mr. Tatum you're over-qualified.' 'Mr. Tatum you're under-qualified.' 'Mr. Tatum you're dis-qualified!' Give me a straight-up, stomp-down redneck any day!"

"You must learn not to be consumed by your own anger, Phillip."

"If I am 'consumed' by anything, it is my 'legitimate dis-content' as your Dr. King might say. I could go out of here this afternoon, after nine years out of circulation, and get a stake for gambling, or for selling drugs, for that matter, and have five hundred or a thousand dollars of my own to spend by tomorrow night. Now, with a college degree, I can't even find a straight job that will pay a hundred and fifty dollars a week! Don't worry I'm not going back into the life, but you have to understand that there's something wrong with the system that offers a man that kind of choice!"

He'd grab the Sunday paper and sit in the big easy chair by the window. He'd read a while, then he would stare out the window watching the children play while junkies went in and out of the empty brown brick building across Drexel Boulevard. Po would cuss the newspaper. Miz Consuela would ask him, "If you find the newspaper so disturbing, why do you continue to read it?"

"Information is an essential requirement of modern life. Brother Malcolm is right! 'He who manipulates the media manipulates the minds of the masses.' I have to keep up with what the Devil is saying so I know what not to think!"

He'd turn back to the newspaper in such a way that we knew not to say no more to him.

Finally, the brother got a job. They hired him to be a counselor at the halfway house. When I pulled out of Chicago on the IC Railroad, I felt like my friend Po was doing all right for himself. Me, I was tired of being where you couldn't see the sun go down for all the concrete and steel.

My work took me to a heap of different places. It was a lot of stuff for us Freedom Riders to do in the '60s. The next time I hit Chicago, he'd dug up Miz Consuela's whole backyard. Had some collard greens, I'sh potatoes, tomatoes, squashes, bell peppers, okra and some funny little plants he said was Miz Consuela's teas.

"Po, this garden looks near 'bout a good as back home."

"Yeah, Junebug, we've got to learn to get back to the land. As long as a people have a piece of land they've got something worthwhile. Junebug, my man, this is only the beginning. There's land all around here. A vacant lot there, one there. And there's people all around who can't hardly afford to eat. Now there's a likely combination: hungry people and vacant land! All I have to do is put all this land to productive use and I can feed the world!"

Sometime Po and me be talking and he'd jump track on me. I thought we was talking about a little backyard garden and he's the new messiah out to feed the whole world.

Still it made my heart feel good. He was almost like the old Po. Had a look in his eye I hadn't seen since before Mr. Jake died. He even started making up rhymes again.

I got a garden in the city.
My okra's really pretty, had no greens that taste so good
Since I was home.
Had to put aside my shopping
Grocery bill it got me rocking
Had to leave that doggone grocery store alone.

Living off my garden, baby
Garden in the city
Living off my garden, baby
Garden in the city.

Diga-Diga-Diga-Diga-Diga-Chicago
Diga-Diga-Diga-Diga-Diga-Chicago
Diga-Diga-Diga-Diga-Diga-Chicago
Trying to find a way to make a new home!

Po was running up and down different streets all over the South Side looking at vacant lots. He was still working at the halfway house but he had also organized something he called "Development of International Gardens in Chicago."

"DIG in Chicago, you dig it?"

"What do you mean by that 'International' Part?"

"All over everywhere! We got the potential to feed half the hungry people in the world right here in Chicago!"

That was the first time I met Little Johnny Tadlow. He was a fine-looking fellow with a black leather jacket, a little crimp-brim hat and a gold tooth right here. *(He smiles and points to a tooth)* Kept a big smile on his face so you could see it.

"Brother Junebug, we figure there's an average of three lots in every block where some house has been torn down, burned down or just about to fall down, you dig? So if we just take this six-block area from Drexel to Woodlawn and

from 43rd to 45th, that's approximately four acres. Now if
we convert that to productive land, it'll feed at least ten percent of the people in this neighborhood. When we get this
neighborhood organized, we're going to move on to the
next one and the next one and so on and so forth. Besides
affordable, fresh food for the people, this program will provide jobs for cats like us coming out of the joint, you dig?
Now that's what you call reversing the cycle, Brother. Dig it!

"And that's serious, real, productive work! Not some jive-
time make-work, dead-end gig for some dude downtown
that don't care no more about us than Colonel Whitten
cared for his brother's pet pig."

Well, it worked! By spring of '66, "DIG in Chicago" had
planted up a bunch of vacant lots on the South Side and a few
out west. People come in droves from all over to buy those
vegetables.

Those were the days! After they'd finish up the day's
work they'd meet up somewhere, talk things over and have a
nip. They was a fine bunch. Whenever I could, I'd be with
them.

There was this one fellow they called "Deadeye"—had
one eye—he lost the other one in Korea. He had the look
of a bloodhound.

Deadeye'd say, "Before I got to working in the garden
project, things had got so hard, man, that I didn't have
but a dollar forty-seven cents for lunch. I went to this little greasy spoon joint and this fine young sister come over.
I said, 'Hey, baby. What can I get good for a dollar forty-
seven cents?' She say, 'I ain't your baby, mister. The only
thing you can get in here for a dollar forty-seven cents is
hurt feelings. You need more than that to get a wish sandwich?' I said, 'A wish sandwich, what's that?' 'When you
get two pieces of bread and a paper napkin and *wish* you
had some meat.' Man, that woman offent my man-tality!
I got up and walked out of there so fast I tried to take the
door off the hinges. Went down to the corner store and
bought me half a pound of 'loney dog and saltine crackers!
And that's what I had to eat off of for three days!"

77

Then there was this other old cat in the group called "Hound." He looked kinda like a basset hound. He said, "Oh, Brother Deadeye, you're lucky you could afford that much. I was so broke when I became involved in the DIG in Chicago Project that I had to borrow eye-water to cry with!"

Those guys would carry on. When they weren't laughing and joking, they would be rapping on the problems of the world. When people get a sense of purpose in their lives, it seems like the whole world opens up to them.

Then, it come a day, that next fall, when it seem like the problems of the world blew in on them just as swift and mean as a cold wind off Lake Michigan.

The job fell to Po to try to explain to them what was happening. "Well, fellows, here's the situation. Fat Mack, the South Side numbers man, brought us a message from the mob. Said we have to start giving them half of what we make at our stores if we want to stay in business."

TADLOW: Forget that, man! My granddaddy left Mississippi to get shed of sharecropping!

PO: That ain't all, Tadlow. As if that wasn't enough, the man downtown has issued building permits for four out of six of our sites on the South Side. They've got low-income housing slated for these sites. Because of the money involved you can be sure that there's somebody big behind it. They plan to bring the bulldozers in tomorrow.

HOUND: They won't hold off long enough for us to get the harvest in?

TADLOW: They'll hold off as long as we make them hold off, Brother Hound! What we need is action! You dig?—action! When y'all get done flapping you lips, meet me and my boys at the battlefront.

DEADEYE: Cool it, Youngblood! Ain't no battlefront yet. We just got to make a plan for what we can all do together! And don't you forget, you still on parole.

TADLOW: And don't you forget that you got a good bunch of men depending on you for work and people counting on you for food, and all the guys counting on our organization for jobs. I ain't scared of the man or the mob. Besides,

it's the principle of the thing. Ain't that what you been trying to rap to us about, Po? Naw, man, meet me down at the
battlefront.

PO: Let him go. He'll be back when he cools out.

The rest of them stayed there to make a plan. It was a good
one too. They made leaflets, they got on the telephones,
they knocked on doors, all night long they contacted people to get them to know what was going on so they would
come out and stand with them. The next morning, before
sunup, the whole block was full of people. They sang and
bragged about how they wasn't "goin' to let nobody turn us
around," and "going to stay on the battlefield," "like a tree
planted by the river," and lots more of those beautiful old
songs. They had their arms locked, and rocked back and
forth. They was so many of them the trucks with the bulldozers on them couldn't even get in the neighborhood.

They were feeling real good as the early morning light
got bright enough to see into the garden somebody scream.
"What's that out there?" Po hollered, "Don't y'all go trample
down the product!" He fought his way through the crowd to
the middle of the field and there was Little Johnny Tadlow.
It didn't look like all that blood could have come from the
one small round bullet hole in the middle of his forehead.

Po didn't even try to plant a garden the spring of '67. He
just went to sitting in the window at Miz Consuela's house,
staring out. Reminded me of how Miz Adeline was after Mr.
Jake passed.

Miz Consuela would light candles in the window and sit
with him a while. She'd brew up these herb teas and get him
to drink a little. Said it was his medicine. I wished I could
have said something to make him laugh. A rhyme, a story.
Every time I'd go somewhere and come back Po look like he
was worse off than the time before.

Sometimes Po be there. Sometimes Po be gone. Nobody
know were to find him. He lost the job at the halfway house.
He come home hungry and tired. He sleep. He sit, looking
out the window. Sometimes Po'd pop up and say something
like he's talking to some people we couldn't see.

"A college degree offers little relief from the bondage of blackness in white America. A piece of paper is no passport from the prison of poverty! Brother Malcolm was right. If they won't let you win with the ballot, then you must lay claim to victory with the bullet . . . Somebody ought to do something about those buildings across the street."

When Po got to talking like that, I seen a kind of cold wildness in his eyes. Reminded me of old Stonewall Whitten back home preaching on the courthouse steps. I didn't have no recollection of Po being like that. His eyes used to sparkle and smile, even when he's talking bad about your mama.

Every summer was worse than the one before. Cities burning: Harlem, Watts, Newark, Detroit. Every time somebody got killed it seemed like a little piece of Po would die too. He'd sit there looking at reports on TV, rocking back and forth, making something that sounded like an Indian chant: "Burn, baby, burn. Burn, baby, burn. Burn . . ."

It rocked on and rocked on into 1968. That was the worse one of all. They killed Dr. King in Memphis, and the whole country went up in flames. They got young Bobby Kennedy in California. They brought the Democrats' Convention to Chicago and the whole world was watching.

I was watching the convention on television when up popped Po Tatum on the local news!

"Why are you trying to take over all these South Side Chicago buildings?"

"There's thousands of people with no place to stay and right now these empty buildings are nothing but shooting galleries for a bunch of junkies."

"But what you're doing is illegal, isn't it?"

"What is happening here now is immoral and destructive to the life of this community. We're trying to liberate these buildings."

"Mr. Tatum, isn't it true that you're blocking the rightful owners from acquiring permits for rehabilitation?"

"These buildings have been vacant for years. Why do you think these damn landlords just started this stuff when we started this action?"

YOU CAN'T JUDGE A BOOK BY LOOKING AT THE COVER

"Who is this 'we' you refer to? Isn't it true that you represent no real constituency?"

"That's not true. I represent the people."

"Isn't that rather vague, sir? And isn't it true, Mr. Tatum that you were recently released from Joliet State Prison on charges of attempted manslaughter, jail breaking, illegal gambling and a variety of other charges?"

"What the hell has that got to do with anything?"

"There you have it, Ladies and Gentlemen. We taped this interview earlier today with Mr. Phillip A. Tatum at the site of a building on Drexel Boulevard that he's trying to 'liberate.' We have just learned that Mr. Tatum has occupied the building, he is believed to be armed and is considered extremely dangerous. We will update the story as the situation develops.

"Meanwhile, at the Democratic Convention—"

I hit the street flying.
It was a hell of a storm blowing in off the lake.
"Taxi! Taxi!"

Chica-Chica-Chica-Chica-Chica-Chica-Chica-Chic—
El'll take too long.

"Taxi!"

"Drexel and 47th. Quick!"

"Loop's blocked off."

Gotta go way out the way.
Tanks in the streets of Chicago.
"Faster, man, faster!"

Rolling South through a sea of blues
Rolling South through a sea of blues
Rolling South through a sea of blues
In the Windy City.

Who knows which way the wind blows?
Who knows which way the wind blows?
Who knows which way the wind blows?
In the Windy City.

"Faster, man, faster!
Right on 37th! Move it!"

Clap of thunder split the sky!
Cop cars scre-e-e-eaming around the corner!

"Flashing lights ahead."
"Uh-oh! Something's wrong."
"Cops got the street blocked at 40th and Drexel."
"Let me out here.
Keep the change."

Strange.
Police.
Blockades.
A sea of blues!

Police squat down behind they cars.
Guns pulled!

People milling around like it's a show going on.
"It's a crazy nigger holed up in that building."
"Yeah, they going to kill a coon today."
"Let me through."
"What's he trying to do?"
"I don't know."
"Let me through!"

I couldn't tell what come first—whether it was the gunshots, the thunder or some other kind of explosion.

The newspapers said it was Po that fired the first shot and that old building, which wasn't none too strong in the first place, just come tumbling down. With all that thunder and lightning it wasn't too many willing to swear as to what really did go on out there that day. 'Cept for one old man who swore, "I seen the face of a man in the clouds when a bolt of lightning just as red as blood hit and danced all around that building just when the police opened fire."

It taken them three days to clear away the rubble of that building and find the two bodies that was left up in there. One of them looked like it might be Po except for one thing. Miz Consuela swore Po left home that morning with a clean red shirt on. The body they found had on a green shirt.

Me and Miz Consuela, we taken what we thought to be Po's remains, put them in the best coffin we could afford and took 'em down home. We buried it in a grave out there in The Bottom between Po's ma and pa.

Epilogue

You Can't Judge a Book by Looking at the Cover

JUNEBUG:

I'ma tell you a story 'bout my old friend Po.

Things he had to do, places he had to go.

Homeboy going out to get some money,

If it hadn't been so sad it might have been funny.

Told all about the way that he was misunderstood,

His family and his friends thought that he was just a hood.

Told how the man misunderstood himself.

He went to get some knowledge, left the book up on the
   shelf.

He got the cover off the book, but didn't get what it had
   in it.

What should have took a week, he tried to get it in a
   minute.

You can't judge a book by looking at the cover.
You can read my letter but I bet you can't read my mind.
If you want to get down, down, down, you got to spend
   some time.
I want to talk with you,
I want to talk with you,
I wanna, wanna, wanna, wanna rap with you.
Hey!

When you grown up in the country, things are hard,
   times are tough.
Growing your own food but it never seems enough.
You too smart for the country, you got to get away.
Got to move to the city, got to be a better way.
So you move to the city, put the country stuff behind.
But when you hit the city, it starts to messin' with your
   mind.
You struggle and you scramble just to do the best you can.
Think you working for a living? Hell, you working for The
   Man.
People stacked like chickens on the way to meet the
   slaughter.
Flopping all around the ground like fishes out of water.
Blind man on the corner, holding up a sign
It says, "No more water, y'all. The fire next time!"

You can't judge a book by looking at the cover.
You can read my letter but I bet you can't read my mind.
If you want to get down, down, down, you got to spend
   some time.
I want to talk with you,
I want to talk with you,
I wanna, wanna, wanna, wanna rap with you.
Hey!

THE END

Ain't No Use in Going Home, Jodie's Got Your Gal and Gone

Sayings from the Life and Writings of
Junebug Jabbo Jones, Volume III

PRODUCTION AND PERFORMANCE HISTORY

Ain't No Use in Going Home, Jodie's Got Your Gal and Gone: Sayings from the Life and Writings of Junebug Jabbo Jones was written by John O'Neal, Q. R. Hand and Nayo-Barbara Watkins, with additional text by Michael Keck and Steve Kent. The music was published by Rhythmatizm, ASCAP.

The play was directed by Steve Kent and John O'Neal, who played Junebug Jabbo Jones, with Michael Keck in the role of Jodie. The original music was composed and arranged by Michael Keck. The lyrics were written by Q. R. Hand, Michael Keck, John O'Neal and Nayo-Barbara Watkins. Theresa Holden was the Executive Producer.

The world premiere of the play was jointly produced by Junebug Productions and the Oakland Ensemble Theatre and premiered at the Oakland Ensemble Theatre, Oakland, CA, in 1989. Portions of the play were created and originally produced as a work-in-progress at the Department of Theatre Arts at Cornell University's Center for Performing Arts, Ithaca, NY.

The play began touring in 1989, and it has been presented by many of the same theaters and presenting venues across North America as *Don't Start Me to Talking or I'll Tell Everything I Know* and *You Can't Judge a Book by Looking at the Cover.*

Among other cities, *Ain't No Use in Going Home* was presented in California in Oakland, Riverside, Santa Barbara, Stanford, Santa Ana; and in Washington, DC; Atlanta, GA; New Orleans, LA; Dayton, OH; St. Paul, MN; Winton-Salem, NC; Las Vegas, NM; Ithaca, NY; Columbia, SC; and Knoxville, TN.

—*TRH*

Setting and Characters

There are two actors in this play. One actor portrays Junebug Jabbo Jones, the other actor plays Jodie, who is also a musician. A keyboard player, singer and actor must be cast in the role of Jodie. Both Junebug and Jodie play many different characters during the play. As in all Junebug plays, Junebug wears his same outfit: old denim overalls, a blue work shirt, old high-top boots, a dull-colored sport coat, a red bandanna around his neck, a white handkerchief in his pocket, and a soft, well-worn wide-brimmed felt hat. His clothing is soft and worn, but very clean and tidy. He holds his beautifully carved walking stick. Jodie wears dark clothing, which can indicate his role as a musician or, with a few props, his Military Service.

The playing area is defined by a series of rectangular boxes of various sizes. They are built so that each side is a function of nine inches or eighteen inches (that is, 9" x 18" or 36" x 36", etc.). There needs to be at least seven boxes with at least two matched pairs in the mix. The boxes may move within each scene to compose the environment/setting for the rising scene. Other boxes are arranged to facilitate the action of the Prologue and the Invocation.

The boxes are painted olive drab. There are at least two wool Army blankets that can be used to complete each of the images. There are three camp stools, one backpack, Junebug's walking stick, his boom box, and arms and munitions.

A 9' x 9' platform sits upstage right at a forty-five-degree angle to center stage. On this platform, the musician/actor and his elaborate electronic keyboard live. The large platform may be used to reveal or conceal the sound equipment as the action of the play requires.

Hard white light helps to define the military metaphor of the play—hard, inorganic, artificial, reductive analysis, exaggerated sense of mission and clarity upon which the military depends to provide the government it presumably serves with appearance of order and power that all governments depend upon for the support of the people whose interests they serve or presume to serve.

Spartan, olive drab, black and brown, the metallic stuff, illuminated in the main by bright, cold, white light, which contrasts sharply with any colors as they are highlighted by the action of the play.

Sound: omni-directional, high-definition. The show presumes a highly competent sound designer could be employed for the design and implementation of the show.

Prologue

Libation

Pre-show music ends. The pre-show music can include songs, such as "Jodie's Got Your Gal and Gone" and military songs, such as "We're in the Army now," etc.

Junebug and Jodie are on stage. Junebug has his ever-present red bandanna. Jodie sports a blue bandanna.

JODIE *(Pouring libation at center stage)*: This is for the sisters who have fought the good fight and have gone on before, who are with us in the spirit but cannot join us in the flesh.

JUNEBUG *(Joining Jodie at center stage, pouring libation)*: This is for the brothers who have fought the good fight and have gone on beyond, who are with us in the spirit but can no longer be with us in the flesh.

(They create a Sacred Circle around the playing area, meet again at center, raise toasts to all present and to each other.
Jodie and Junebug begin a military march.)

JODIE: Ashe!
JUNEBUG: Ashe!
JUNEBUG: Atten—hut!

JUNEBUG:	JODIE:
Your left!	
	Your left.
Your left!	
	Your left.
Your left right left!	Your left right left!
Your left!	
	Your left.
Your left!	
Your left.	
Your left right left!	Your left right left!
We're in the Army now.	We're in the Army now.
We're not behind the plow.	We're not behind the plow.
Wc're in the ditch	We're in the ditch
Where you'll never get rich.	Where you'll never get rich.
We're in the Army now!	We're in the Army now!
Your left!	
	Your left.
Your left!!	
	Your left.
Your left right left.	Your left right left.
Your left!	
	Your left.
Your left!	
	Your left.
Your left right left!	Your left right left!
Over hills! Over dales!	Over hills! Over dales!
We will hit the dusty trail,	We will hit the dusty trail,
As the caissons go rolling	As the caissons go rolling
along!	along!

JUNEBUG: Company forward . . . Face!

(They turn.)

Stockade shuffle . . . March!

(They comply for eight counts and halt!)

Company! . . . Halt!
     Company! Dismissed!
     To begin with we do NOT like war. War is a sin and an abomination!

JODIE: What is war anyway? The United States hasn't claimed a "hot war" since 1945. But still there's Korea, Vietnam, Iran-Contra, Iraq, and untold numbers of actions, "undefined" actions from Guyanna, Iraq, Afghanistan to, Zair, *Etcetera! Etcetera! Etcetera!* Since 1945 over how many U.S. soldiers have died on foreign soil? Call 'em "wars," or—

JUNEBUG: . . . or police "actions"—

JODIE: . . . or "sustained low-intensity conflicts."

JUNEBUG AND JODIE: All the blood that's shed is red and all of them that died *is* dead.

JUNEBUG: Now, just because we say we don't like war it does not follow that we don't like soldiers. Soldiers are just ordinary people like anyone else. Some of my best friends are soldiers, I was somewhat of a solider myself once—

JODIE: But they've taken and turned the whole thing upside-down. See peace is not the absence of war, war is the absence of peace!

JUNEBUG: Peace is the positive thing that we should strive for.

JODIE: War is the evidence of our failure to reach that goal.

JUNEBUG: My name is Junebug Jabbo Jones. I AM A STORY-TELLER. This here is my buddy, Jodie— *(Jodie motions a correction)* Well, his name is Joseph Montgomery, but I call him "Jodie Grinder." Jodie here is a Musicali-compo-techni-sician. That's a word I had to make up to explain to myself what the brother's into. What Jodie's into will make you remember stuff you never heard before!

JODIE: The way I think of myself is as a man who tells stories with music!

JUNEBUG: Yeah, you right! I must confess that at first I was surprised to hear such an idea come from one of the first "Musicali-compo-techni-scians" in the world, but my man, "Jodie Grinder" has his eyes on the prize. He came hunting for me.

I was telling stories in Los Angeles and I seen him! He was sitting way off in the back watching like a one-eyed cat peeking in a seafood store. As soon as I got done telling stories, he marched right up looking all militant and otherwise with this thing that looked like a toy piano and plugged it into my box. He started right out as if he were taking up where we left off a few minutes ago—

JODIE: It never starts the same way. This time I'm on stage playing the whole world through my keyboard. It was about six months after the poet Bob Kaufman died. I started having this weird dream.

JUNEBUG: My box starts to making sounds like I never heard before. As I really don't understand what's going down I try to be cool and go along with the program.

(*Jodie plays the dream. Junebug performs parts of the dream following Jodie's lead. A high-powered portable lamp may be used by the performers to heighten effects as needed.*)

JODIE: At first everything is real hip, man! I'm in the music and the music is in me and the people in the place are grooving. We're all together and I'm soaring like some brilliant, impossible bird who can climb the high winds like an eagle, then, in the twinkle of a grace note, hover like a hummingbird sipping nectar from the most beautiful of blossoms.

The first sign that something's wrong is the sound of this far-off train. It sounds big and it roars like thunder. I can see this one big strobe light on the front rocking and rolling back and forth like a drunk sailor.

As it lights up the crowd I recognize some people. My mama and daddy are dancing. My daddy's dancing! It's like he's trying to keep up with my sister, Aida, who's moving like a demon possessed. I'm playing as hard as I can but the only thing I can hear is the train.

I can see it now, big and shiny, and crusted with blood, the hellish engine roars right by me. Some of the train-crew members wear red, others wear white or blue. The train screeches to a stop in front of the bandstand, but I can still see the people as they start to dance all over each other trying to get in. My sister, Aida, leading the pack. Daddy dances right in front of me. He doesn't recognize me but as he passes by I can see that his suit is made of thousands and thousands of tiny feathers. I get sick from the smell of dead geese.

In one car of the train I see these guys I know playing basketball. They're playing so hard they are tearing up the train, breaking windows, drinking wine, laughing loud and cussing.

Toy soldiers lined up around the sides of the room begin to move like they're real. They carry their bayonets danger-ously low as the crowd begins to jam up the entrances to the train.

There's a commotion around this tree growing in the back of the hall. Some people are gathering around the tree to hear something. It's not loud but I can hear a voice com-ing out of the tree. I listen real hard but can't tell whether it's you or Uncle Touss telling stories and singing some old-time bluesy gospel about trains rolling through the grave-yard. The toy soldiers are trying to stop the singing and tell-ing but they can't. The tree keeps growing. The toy soldiers have these laserbeam guns. Every time one of them shoots at the tree, the beam bounces back at the speed of light to vaporize the gun, and the soldiers turn into little chil-dren lost and confused and frightened. They cry and search among those in the crowd for their parents.

The sound of an Ornette Coleman riff off of a wigged-out version of "We Are Soldiers in the Army" comes from somewhere behind me. On that side of the train some peo-ple dressed in overalls are smashing windows and breaking doors, pulling people off the train. One of the women who helps them looks like Linda, but she doesn't recognize me. I try to speak but my mouth won't move. All I can do is play. The harder I play the louder the train gets.

More soldiers come firing at the people who are trying to help the others off the train. The train revs up and the sky turns black and low. A blinding flash of sound splits open the sky. The floor begins to shake and crack apart in places. The train spirals down toward a yawning chasm that opens up below. Fires belch out as from some hellish furnace.

The train is gone. I can make no sound. There are no people left to see, only their shadows are still there in the concrete and on the walls.

"Al. Al. Where's Al?" Just then Al rolls out of the shadows bouncing a basketball. He looks after the train and sadly shakes his head. He turns and rolls back toward the place where the people are still singing and telling stories.

I'm playing as hard as I can but still no sound, no sound.

I wake up, and cannot go back to sleep.

JUNEBUG: To begin with I did not know this dude from Adam.

JODIE: I knew him right away.

JUNEBUG: I hadn't seen him for nearly thirty years and dreams are not my thing—

JODIE: I hadn't seen him either, but you didn't change that much.

JUNEBUG: I guess not. By then I was already a grown man and you were just a child. So I outright asked, "You sure do look familiar, but help me to call your name."

JODIE *(Singing)*:

> Ain't no use in going home,
> Jodie's got your gal and gone.
>
> Ain't no use in going back,
> Jodie's got your Cadillac.

JUNEBUG: I couldn't believe it was him. His brother, Al, had been one of my best buddies when I first got to the war in '52. We talked 'til daylight came and went again.

JODIE: It had gotten to the place where I couldn't sleep for dreaming. I needed someone to help me find the meaning of my dream.

JUNEBUG: We've come to the point in this dream-chasing where it's clear to us that the story of this dream is the story of the main part of Jodie's life. I believe that if he don't tell his story he just might explode. Jodie's story speaks directly to me because I'm part of it, but I also believe that his story might be some use to you all too.

Some of the Indian people have a saying that goes, "If we don't know our stories, how can we tell who we are?"

So if you're willing, we intend to share with you the unfinished story of one black man's—

JODIE: African-American's!

JUNEBUG: What's that?

JODIE: African-American. I'm an "African-American!"

JUNEBUG: One young "African-American's" effort to come to grips with war and his duties as a citizen of the U.S. of A.

JODIE: Now there're lots of different people in the stories we got to tell and only two of us to tell it.

JUNEBUG: So y'all got to be kinda swift on your seats to keep up with us. If you can't keep up with all the changes, don't worry; you'll understand it better by and by.

Act One

Scene 1

JUNEBUG: To figure out Jodie's dream and why it bothered him so much, we decided to start in 1941, five years before Jodie was born.

JODIE: My daddy actively supported the effort to win the right for African-American men to fight in the United States Armed Forces.

JUNEBUG: I'm more than certain that Jodie's daddy, Jacob Montgomery, must have felt a sense of personal victory when President Roosevelt shrewdly appointed the first black general in U.S. Army history.

JODIE: But like most folk, Daddy didn't know the story of what was going on behind the scenes down at Camp Stewart in south Georgia.

(Dissolve to:)

OFFICER OF THE DAY: General Benjamin O. Davis! Regiment, stand at ease!

GENERAL DAVIS: I just want to tell you three things. One: I may be your color but I'm not your kind. Two: if you are complaining about discrimination and segregation in the United States Armed Forces, forget it. Three: the problem you have mentioned in your correspondence about what happens to your ladies who come down here has nothing to do with the United States Army. That's your private business. The Army didn't tell you to get married. Humpht!

OFFICER OF THE DAY: Humpht! Regiment . . . dismissed!

(Dissolve to:)

JUNEBUG: Jodie's mama, Elmyra, had different ideas than Jake did about a lot of things.

(Quick cut to:)

ELMYRA: VOLUNTEER??!

JAKE: Elmyra, you gotta be ready for change. A man's got to do what a man's go to do.

ELMYRA: Jacob, you don't have to go. You've got a wife and two children. You're thirty-one years old. You're exempt from the draft. You've got a job, Jacob, what'll happen to us?

JAKE: Elmyra, in this life, you gotta be ready for change. Change means Opportunity! We, as a people, got a chance to prove what we could have been doing all along.

ELMYRA: Why you got to prove what's already known to be so?

JAKE: At Tuskegee, there's a Negro squadron, officers, pilots, hell, a Negro general! I may be too old to fly around in the sky myself but, Elmyra, I'm a qualified aircraft mechanic! And Elmyra, you know good and goddamn well we always have to do more with less!

   They need men like me to keep those planes in real good shape and ready. We got an opportunity to prove our qualifications for citizenship!!

ELMYRA: Opportunity to fight? What's that? Jacob, you're a man already. You've got a good job that's gonna get better—

JAKE: Woman, can't you see, working here wouldn't be the same as being a part of a once-in-a-lifetime? I want you all to be proud of me. Imagine Al and Aida when they see me in my uniform?

ELMYRA: You're only interested in how you look. I don't see that you have anything over there to fight for. How're we going to make ends meet when you're gone?

JAKE: Jacob Montgomery ain't married to no woman who ain't capable of her own independence. Now, ain't that right, honey? Ain't it?

ELMYRA: It's got nothing at all to do with "independence," Jacob. It has more to do with good sense!

(*Jake marches off to war.*)

Scene 2

JODIE: Daddy quit his job and paid his own fare to travel to Alabama before he had any guarantee that he would be accepted into the Service. His mind was made up. Like thousands of others, he was so anxious to join up and fight he didn't care who he'd have to kill or why. Daddy made it to and from World War II in one piece. Five years later, when I was only four years old, he figured it was my brother Al's turn.

(*Quick cut to:*)

JAKE: Al, ain't no way I could be doing as well as I am right now if I hadn't been in the Army first. I get preferential treatment over others. See, we're gaining ground, Al, you can't even imagine the change from the time I was your age 'til now . . . 'Specially with all the new industry around here in Oakland with government contracts on 'em: the shipyards—Kaiser, U.S. Steel. If you just have to go to college, you get that GI Bill. Right now you're just another young Negro without no qualifications. But when you come back from the Army, people look at you different.

AL: I'm qualified to play music! You said yourself that I already play as well as you do.

JAKE: A guitar ain't no qualifications! You see what it got me.

AL: I got applications in. Something might come through. Besides, I can work at Miz Esther's down on 7th Street and start college at night in September.

JAKE: You got to *make* something happen, boy! . . . or you'll be out there on 7th Street with the rest of 'em, waiting.

AL: Working not waiting.

JAKE: Boy, you got an opportunity to fight for the UN command under General Douglas MacArthur. Now the U.S. Army is an integrated fighting force . . . not like when I went in. *The White Man's* gotta take notice.

AL: He didn't notice me on the basketball court or in the band. I wanna teach music, Dad, all I need is—

JAKE: The opportunity you make for yourself by serving in the Armed Forces! That's what you need! Remember how I looked in my uniform? *(Al sneaks out)* It's like Touss used to say, "You'll go down if you don't stand up for your self" or something like that.

Just think when you get back from Korea . . . Al! Al! Don't you walk off while I'm talking to you!

(Jake exits.
Jodie sings "Brother to Brother":)

JODIE:

Now that you're gone away
The sunlit days don't seem as warm as they used to be.
When you're not here with me,
What once was clear, now seems all lost in mystery.

Brother, are you safe and well?
There's so much to tell, I need someone just to talk to.
Brother, won't you come home soon?
No one else can cheer me, no one else can chase away the gloom.

Brother, why'd you go away?
Brother, what's a hero?
Leaving home makes no sense to me.

Daddy said you had to go away.
Tell me what you're fighting for,
Brother, help me understand your war.
Brother, help me understand your war.

Stay safe, my brother,
Hurry home, my brother,
There is someone here, my brother,
Someone who needs you, and loves you.

(Spoken) Brother, what's a hero?
And why'd you have to go away to be one?

Scene 3

JUNEBUG: I first met his brother, Al, when I was a medic in Korea.

(Sounds of combat. A nearby explosion. Junebug hits the dirt. He starts crawling, clutching his leg. Voices and sound of many people running. Someone calls for: "Medic!" Flares. Junebug crawls toward the sound of an injured man.)

They broke through! Broke through! Bug out!

(There is general confusion. Harum-scarum.)

Oh, my God!

(As he tries to scramble to safety, Al begins to scream in pain for help from a medic.)

I'm coming, soldier. Hold on man, I'm coming.

AL: THE PAIN IS KILLING ME. IT'S KILLING ME, MAN!

JUNEBUG: Here I am, man. I'm here.

AL: My leg! My leg is killing me.

JUNEBUG: I'm going to give you something for the pain. But first I got to stop the bleeding! If I don't stop the bleeding you going to die, man! Shut up! Hold still, brother!

AL: My leg! What'd you do with my damn leg, man? Where the hell is my LEG, MAN. WHERE THE HELLL IS MY LEG?

JUNEBUG: YOU GOT TO BE QUIET, BROTHER. YOU CALLING FIRE OVER HERE!

AL: WHERE THE FUCK IS MY LEG, MAN? WHERE'S MY LEG?

JUNEBUG: HERE I'M GOING TO KNOCK YOU OUT MAN WITH THIS MORPHINE, BROTHER. WHAT'S YOUR NAME, BROTHER?

AL: MY LEG

JUNEBUG: TRANSPORT!

AL: FUCK THAT! MY LEG! WHERE'S MY LEG? WHERE'S MY OTHER . . .

JUNEBUG: I GOT YOUR LEG, BROTHER . . . TRANSPORT! DOUBLE AMP! HEAVY BLEEDER!

AL: MY LEG . . .

JUNEBUG: I GOT YOUR LEG . . . HERE—

AL: MY . . .

JUNEBUG: I GOT BOTH OF THEM. I GOT BOTH YOUR LEGS! WE MIGHT BE ABLE TO PUT THEM BACK ON! BUT YOU GOT TO COOL DOWN, BROTHER! THEY COME OVER HERE AND KILL BOTH OF US!

AL: BOTH MY LEGS, YOU GOT THEM BOTH? . . .

JUNEBUG: TRANSPORT! TRANSPORT! DOUBLE AMP! URGENT! URGENT! URGENT!

(Junebug drags Al to relative safety. The sounds of the battle subside into a momentary fade to black. Lights come up on Al sleeping. Junebug enters with a light.)

Need to roll you over, buddy, and give you this little stick in the butt. Make you feel better, all right?

AL: Aw, man! Here you come again, man, can't you get it through your goddamn head? I don't want to be woke up.

JUNEBUG: Just a little sting. *(He sticks him)* Okay, now it's all over. Didn't hurt a bit, right.

AL: Hey, June, listen. Just listen to me for a minute . . . Make a mistake. Take me out, man, a little morphine too much. That's all. Nobody would know. Please, man, just make one little mistake . . . for me.

JUNEBUG: What the hell is this, man? What kind of medic you think I am?

AL: Man, you know how it is back stateside. Everything moving, everybody on the go, gotta keep up. How'm I gonna deal with that? Aw, man, I just can't make it . . . no way, no way. There's nothing left for me to live for, man.

JUNEBUG: What would your people think? Your mama, your daddy?

AL: My daddy? Naw, man, not him. He wants a son he can be proud of. A whole man. What can I do now? Push matches in little boxes? That's not man's work. Now I'll just be dependent on welfare.

JUNEBUG: You still got your music, man. You been playing for years.

AL: Yeah, ever since I's a little boy . . .

JUNEBUG: Little old boy with a music jones, huh?

AL: Yeah. Just a little fellow but I understood. My main man was Charlie Christian. He was the first one to hook guitars up to amps. Charlie Christian did that. He was from over by KC.

JUNEBUG: Could he play?

AL: He could beat Bird wailing! He was to the guitar what Charlie Parker was to the alto sax. He was what you might call my idol.

JUNEBUG: So did Christian teach you?

AL: Naw, he was just passing through on his way to the coast. He gave me some words to encourage me and all. After he died they had a memorial for him. They were going to jam for my man, Christian. I was only twelve years old, but I told 'em I had to play. First they said no, but this old cat said I could use his ax. It wasn't a dry eye in the place when

I got through. But that was a long time ago. Before my daddy come back his war, before we left St. Louis, before Korea . . .

JUNEBUG: Your old man can't run your life now. So go on, play your music, dude.

AL: Naw. Just something that happened to me when I was a little boy.

JUNEBUG: But, Al, this ain't no little boy talking tonight. You're a grown man and you still got the music jones. It's in you, dude. I see the fire in your eyes. It's now. The music is now. I can see it. I ain't going to quit before you can see it, too. Don't you never let me hear you talking about nothing to live for. Never.

(Dissolve to:)

After the ceasefire in Korea, I was assigned to a special medical facility in Thailand. I took to spending as much leave time as I could in a little village about a hundred kilometers from Bangkok. I really loved it there. The people were kind and beautiful, the food was rich and spicy, the land reminded me of home. Before I left they started to call me "Doctor Brown Bug" 'cause they didn't know what a "Junebug" was.

About the same time that the word came that the Americans had started sending "military advisors" into Vietnam because the French had been beaten at Dien Bien Phu, I found out about the lynching of Emmett Till in Money, Mississippi. The people in my village couldn't understand why I was so upset about that one child being killed back home, when every month children all over that section were dying by the hundreds.

After we fought all over the world in the name of freedom, then to have a fourteen-year-old boy to be lynched in the "land of the free and the home of the brave" was just too much. That's when I knew it was time for me to go home. I was fighting on the wrong side in the wrong war.

The next week I got a letter from his brother, Al, saying that he was getting married but that he wasn't going to do it 'til I could be there to stand as his best man.

JODIE: That's when we first met. It was 1956. I was ten years old.

JUNEBUG: Still wet behind the ears—

JODIE: Wet all over!

JUNEBUG: You sure didn't think so at the time—

JODIE: Ignorance seldom recognizes itself.

JUNEBUG: No. You were real smart. It was just some things you didn't know, no way you could have known.

JODIE: But that's what ignorance is, isn't it?

JUNEBUG: When I got to the wedding in Oakland, it was like having to start a whole new life.

JODIE: I remember the way you would look at the Bay and the ships. I didn't know whether you were thinking about jumping or what . . .

(The following song, "Oakland Bay Blues," helps make a transition in time and place. At the end of the song, Junebug and Jodie are looking out on to the San Francisco Bay somewhere near the old dock. Junebug is surprised by the child's innocent invasion of his solitude. Junebug sings "Oakland Bay Blues (Gently Sail Away)":)

JUNEBUG:

      Sunrise over the mountaintops
      Sun sets in the Bay
      Moon tide ride me safely home
      Starlight guides the way.

      Oakland, Alameda, redwood, pines
      Graceful Southern sway
      Whispers of my father's home
      Gently sail away.

      Returning to my motherland
      My restless heart at ease.
      Still certain of the discontent
      That starves my dream of peace.

      Leaving peace and joy and love behind
      On strange and foreign shore.

Other wars and battles done,
Turned homeward facing more.

(Jodie enters quietly. He startles Junebug.)

Hyaah! *(Struggling to regain his composure)* Boy! Don't you ever creep up behind a combat vet like that! Never! Do you hear me?!

JODIE: Huh?

JUNEBUG: Do you hear me?

JODIE: Yeah. I hear you . . .

JUNEBUG: If you'd been two inches taller you'd a been seriously hurt if not dead.

JODIE: But you was Al's nurse in the Army. You the one supposed to be helping people well instead of hurting them.

JUNEBUG: Even a medic or a nurse learns to defend himself, Jodie.

JODIE: Joseph. My name is Joseph Montgomery, not no "Jodie."

JUNEBUG: I know, but they way Al used to talk about you, I had this picture of a nearly grown man in my mind. I was kind of surprised to find a fellow your age when I got here last week. Al and me, we just started to call you "Jodie" after the fellow the soldiers used to sing about when they would be marching:

Ain't no use in going home
Jodie's got your gal and gone . . .

I really didn't mean no harm. "Jodie's" the brother who stayed at home—

JODIE: My name is "Joseph." I would have gone to the war to help Al if I could.

JUNEBUG: Yeah, you right! *(Changing the subject)* Why'd you follow me out here?

JODIE: I ain't been following you. I got better things to do with my time . . .

JUNEBUG: What are you doing out here then?

JODIE: I came out here to meet Marty. This is our special hide-out. Ever since Al's wedding we ain't had time to talk things over and work stuff out. Marty say he's gonna meet me . . .

JUNEBUG: Oh, I didn't know this was your secret hideout. I'll leave.

JODIE: It's all right. I guess you can stay.

(Pause.)

JUNEBUG: That had to be the biggest batch of monkey suits I've ever seen together at one time.

JODIE: Monkey suits?

JUNEBUG: Tuxedos. You really looked good in yours but I don't think I ever felt any more uncomfortable in a Korean foxhole.

JODIE: Daddy was dead set to make it the biggest, fanciest wedding in West Oakland since Slim Jenkins got married.

JUNEBUG: Think we could groove, huh?

JODIE: What you say?

JUNEBUG: Naw, I got to keep on going. I'm making a slow trip of it but I'm on my way back home. There's work for me to do there. *(Pause)* Who's Uncle Touss? I don't remember meeting him.

JODIE: Naw, he didn't make it this time. It wasn't his kind of thing. Uncle Touss used to come over here, too, when he wasn't sailing in boats like that one there. He would go all over the world, would come out here to do his organizing.

JUNEBUG: "Organizing"?

JODIE: Yeah, he organizes things . . . unions and things like that. He said he did his best organizing out here in the quiet. This was one of his secret places, too . . . See that bridge over there?

JUNEBUG: Un-huh.

JODIE: There's a tunnel under there that will take you all the way back over by city hall. Want a see it?

JUNEBUG: Naw, Jod—Joseph, I've already seen more tunnels than I meant to see in this life.

JODIE: "What you see is what you get." That's what Uncle Touss used to say.

JUNEBUG: Sounds like your Uncle Touss had something on his mind. Yeah.

JODIE: Uncle Touss say people supposed to take care of each other. He say it's some places in the world where people do a better job of doing that than they do here, like in Africa and places like that. They named him after Toussaint— Toussaint Lowerdoor, or something like that. You know who that is?

JUNEBUG: Is he that general who led Haiti's war for freedom from the French?

JODIE: Yeah! That's right! You pretty smart!

JUNEBUG: Thanks. You pretty smart yourself, Joseph.

JODIE: All I know is what Uncle Touss and Al taught me. I sure ain't been learning nothing in school here lately. Uncle Touss taught me how to listen to things and Al taught me how to play music.

JUNEBUG: I'd say if you know how to listen you could learn just about anything.

JODIE: Yeah, un-huh. Whenever I would get ready to say something without thinking, Uncle Touss would say, "Sh-h-h-h-h! Listen! If you want to know something, you got to be quiet and listen. It's all kinds of stuff to learn if you just listen. We got to listen to the sound and we have to listen to the time between and around sounds. That's why they took our drums from us, thought they could make us forget how to listen. It was the sounds from the drums of the slaves in Haiti that defeated the French army. When L'Ouverture failed to listen to sounds of his people, he lost the revolution."

JUNEBUG: He sounds like somebody I would love to meet.

JODIE: No telling about Uncle Touss. He's the type to sneak in when you don't expect him. He ain't been coming around much here lately. Mama say that that organizing is real dangerous. Uncle Touss got hit in the head too often, he lucky to be alive. Daddy fuss at Uncle Touss all the time but Mama say it's important to take care of those who keep giving and giving, so Mama, she'll help to take care of him. Daddy say Uncle Touss don't make sense about certain things. You know what I think? I think Uncle Touss gets in fights with bad guys all over the world and they gang up on him. Then he gets away. He's smart like that. Uncle Touss say, "That's all right, you can kill a man but you can't kill an idea," and he goes right back to fight some more.

Come on, Junebug, let's walk over by 7th Street. I want to show you some places where the sounds really light up the sky. Slim Jenkins' Place and Esther's Starlight Lounge.

JUNEBUG: "Sh-h-h! Listen!" What do you know about stuff like that. You too young to be hanging out on 7th Street, aren't you?

JODIE: Humpt! I know everybody over there. Al started bring me down for my music lessons. One time when Muddy Waters was playing at Esther's, Al listened for a while and seemed like something just got in him. He said real soft, with tears running down his cheeks, "You do the music, Joseph. You do the music." He left me there all by myself. Miz Esther and Muddy Waters took me home that night. Ever since then I been going out by myself anytime I want to. But Al, he's doing all right I guess, but he ain't touched the guitar or give me one more music lesson since that night. That same week he got that fancy car, took the job that Daddy'd been after him to take and the next thing I know him and Alice was talking about getting married.

JUNEBUG: You going to miss him, huh?

JODIE: Nah. It ain't no big thing.

JUNEBUG: I had a big brother once. His name was Walter Lee. 'Course I got seventeen brothers and sisters still living—

JODIE: Seventeen!

JUNEBUG: Yep! Well, four of them's half-brothers: Matthew, Mark, Luke and John. My daddy made sure that all his children had Bible names. My mother's eldest is Mary, then came Adam, and Walter Lee—I don't know nobody beside my mama that would claim that name to be found in the Bible; she said it was her daddy's name and that it was in their family Bible, and that was good enough for her. After Walter, came Isaac, the twins Ruth and Rebecca, me—David by name—Miriam, Phillipa, Sheba, Micah, Jacob, Joshua, Peter and Little Esther.

Yep! Coming from a big family like that, you have to pick out one who's going to be your own special brother or sister, less you get lost in the shuffle. Walter Lee was mine. He could do anything too. He was the best scholar—black or white—to finish school that year but here was no scholarship waiting for him. That's why he joined the Marine Corps. He had already finished a complete tour of duty. Two weeks before his discharge, they found him dead underneath a rolled-over jeep outside of Camp Lejeune in North Carolina.

I didn't go to the funeral. I couldn't stand the idea of Walter Lee being dead. I didn't want him to be dead. I always thought they should have had an investigation. That's one reason I wanted so bad to get in the Marine Corps when I went to Service.

Now I know Al is not dead and I don't wish him no bad luck or nothing like that, but he sure would have made a hell of a blues man.

JODIE: Hey, Junebug . . . ?

JUNEBUG: Yeah?

JODIE: It'd be all right if you call me Jodie . . . Junebug, what's that song about "Jodie"?

JUNEBUG:

> Ain't no use in going home
> Jodie's got your gal and gone . . .

Scene 4

JODIE: After my brother, Al, got married, it seemed like Daddy would be lonely. He started trying to get me to do more things with him instead of me spending so much time with Mama. It seemed like he missed some important part of his life.

JUNEBUG: Like being able to go out hunting in the country and feeling the joy of tramping through the fields you know your grandpa tramped in too?

JODIE: Yeah, that's it!

JUNEBUG: It's hard to get that feeling of belonging to a place if you feel forced or don't feel fairly put there. Jodie's daddy, Jacob Montgomery, was like a rolling stone who didn't want to be one.

JODIE: My brother, Al, was born in Tennessee. My sister, Aida, was born in St. Louis, and I popped out in Oakland.

JUNEBUG: The man had no place to be somebody.

JODIE: My twelfth birthday present from my daddy was a gun, a shotgun, .410-automatic. My sister, Aida, was jealous of that gun. I had my own gun—and couldn't shoot it! Aida could light a match at thirty yards with the rifle that Daddy had given to my brother, Al, on his twelfth birthday.

JUNEBUG: There's something about black folk and guns and being "down home." For one thing, when you grow up poor out in the country, life and death don't seem so far apart. You see things dying and being birthed all the time. In the city you can easily forget that. Country folk see a gun as just another tool you got to learn how to use.

JODIE: When I made thirteen, Daddy started taking me goose hunting with him.

JAKE: Don't move now! You'll scare them away. Look at Old Blue there, see how alert and still she is. But watch when I bring down one of them geese. She'll be dead on him like white on rice! Now don't tell me you can't be as smart as a dog.

JODIE: Daddy always went hunting with a rifle, 'stead of a shotgun.

JAKE: I want the bird to have a fighting chance! All I need is one clear shot—dead through the heart and you don't have to worry about breaking your teeth on shotgun pellets scattered all through the flesh! Just be still and wait for your one clear shot.

JODIE: While we'd wait he'd talk.

JAKE: You got to learn how to handle a gun to gain the proper respect that's due you from the other man. Half the time "we" don't get no respect 'cause "we" don't deserve none.

Like Uncle Touss always says: "You don't own what you can't defend!" Remember that, boy, you remember that! If

114

you can't *protect your family* you be better off dead! Better off dead than to try to live without the respect due a *man*.

The white man's scared of a nigger with a gun. But a gun ain't no good if you don't know how to use it. When you get big enough to go to the Army you'll be that much ahead of everybody else.

Look a yonder! There they come. Be quiet now. Don't move! *(He shoots)* Go get 'im, Blue! Go! Go! That a gal! Go! Go!

JODIE: You shot it, Daddy! You killed it!

JAKE: That's the whole idea, boy. That's why we call it hunting! Hell, I've let your mama make too much of a sissy out of you. I'd done better bringing Aida out here. She would enjoy some good hunting.

JODIE: I'm ready to go! I want to go home!

JAKE: We ain't through hunting yet! You ain't fired the first shot of your gun today!

JODIE: I don't want to shoot it no more. I don't like dead geese. I like them better in the sky.

Act Two

———

Scene 1

Junebug and Jodie sing "What Did They Do with What They Took from You, Man?"

JUNEBUG AND JODIE *(Starting the chorus)*:
>What did they do with what they took from you, man?
>*What did they do with mine?*
>No use complaining what they took from you,
>They been stealing from us all a long time!
>
>I listen to the radio the other day,
>They was a talking 'bout the Japanese,
>Who were very upset 'bout what they planned to do,
>To reparate the Iran-ese.
>They got they battleships afloating in the Persian Gulf,
>Looking for some tension to ease.
>The Yankee ship is loaded with technology,
>And the difference they could not see

Between an airliner and a fighter jet,
The one they call the F-14.
Two hundred and ninety Iranian people,
They leave out there dead in the sea.
Uncle Sam, he won't say that he sorry,
He just tell them he pay them a fee,
For every Iranian loved one,
That "accidentally" fall down in the sea.

During the time of the Second World War,
They round up all the Japanese,
They put these American people in camps,
And brought them down to their knees.
They were so afraid of what the Nisei would do,
These American-Japanese,
The only way to get outta the camps,
Was to go and fight overseas.
Some of them go and they fight with distinction,
But when they return to their homes,
Many mothers an' fathers had died in the camps,
And the farms they had were gone.
Forty years now have come and go,
Before the Japanese are promised compensation,
Still they haven't been paid for the bad situation,
And the Iran-ese are set to go.
Japanese say, "Wait! You still got a date.
I got a tattoo on my arm.
Before you give them a penny, in fact don't give them any
'Til you pay for my family's farm!"

What did they do with what they took from you, man?
What did they do with mine?
No use complaining what they took from you,
They been stealing from us all a long time!

The black people hear the argument,
And they begin to see the light.

They think about the past and what about the future,
Pretty soon they get a fright.
They tell all the others it really wasn't right,
What they lost won't compare,
They say, "How can you get yours before we get ours,
We've paid more than our share."
Families disrupted, where is the justice?
Millions gone to the slave-ship sea,
With faith intact, they broke their backs,
Three hundred years of labor for free.
The only thing we asked when we finished the task,
Was for forty acres and a mule.
We asked and waited and asked again,
They look at us like we a fool.
It's been a long time since 1865,
And changes are slow to come,
So if they compensate everybody else,
Lord knows they better save us some!

What did they do with what they took from you, man?
What did they do with mine?
No use complaining what they took from you,
They been stealing from us all a long time!

Ancient red man chief stands looking in grief
At all the damage done to Mother Earth.
A lot of blood's been shed, through the years,
No shame can equal its worth.
Can't measure the sorrow of the Buffalo people
Who dwelled from shore to shore.
When the pilgrims began, it was the red man's land
Before they were forced to go.
Those that are left, a land-lost few,
Forced onto reservations
The Trail of Tears, battles lost and won,
Endless treaty manipulations.
They've been fighting in the courts,
Using the system,

119

Organizing a plan.
Standing with their brothers and sisters
They're winning back their land

What did they do with what they took from you, man?
What did they do with mine?
No use complaining what they took from you,
They been stealing from us all a long time!

It goes on and on with the women of the world
Screaming, "Give us the ERA!"
Equal jobs and pay all the benefits,
Lord help ya if you tell them you're gay.
'Cause they try their best to take what's left.
Hold on to your self-pride.
Greed is the villain and whoever is a willing
Can join in the militant line.
So don't be upset if we seem to forget,
And left out your personal beef.
We're all sisters and brothers if we're doing unto other
We all share the grief.
The battle's not easy, the path's rough and greasy,
It's gonna take a little more time.
It might take some effort,
But you and me together, can get to work 'til we find
What they did with what they took from you, man?
Let's find out what they did with mine.
No use complaining what they took from us,
Let's get it all back this time!

(Dissolve to "We Are Soldiers [In the Army]." Traditional.
Chorus:)

We are soldiers in the Army,
We have to fight although we have to die
We have to hold up the bloodstained banner
We have to hold it up until we die.

JODIE: '64 was the same year my daddy was ready for me to go to war and my mother was ready for me to go to college. That summer I met this young woman named Linda Villere from south Louisiana. Linda told me of this brother at Southern University in Baton Rouge named Alvin Batiste, musician-musicologist, master teacher that would help you give birth to what was in you if you were paying attention, and worked real hard to develop your talents.

There was no way I was going to the Vietnam War, so that fall I was off to Baton Rouge to study under this modern master. Batiste was great but otherwise school was a disappointment. A love for music is one of the things I took South to college, to The Movement, and to Linda.

> My father was a soldier. Oh yes!
> He had his hand on the freedom plow. Oh yes!
> One day he got old and couldn't fight anymore,
> He said, "I'll stand here and fight anyhow!"

> My mother was a soldier. Oh yes!
> She had her hand on the freedom plow. Oh yes!
> One day she got old and couldn't fight anymore,
> She said, "I'll stand here and fight anyhow!"

> My brother was a soldier. Oh yes!
> He had his hand on the freedom plow. Oh yes!
> One day he got old and couldn't fight anymore,
> He said, "I'll stand here and fight anyhow!"

> My sister was a soldier. Oh yes!
> She had her hand on the freedom plow. Oh yes!
> One day she got old and couldn't fight anymore,
> She said, "I'll stand here and fight anyhow!"

> We are soldiers in the Army,
> We have to fight although we have to die
> We have to hold up the bloodstained banner
> We have to hold it up until we die.

(Jodie enters a mass meeting in a church in Plaquemines Parish in 1967. He carries on a conversation with Linda. As the scene progresses, a suggestion of rural church folks singing a Freedom Movement rendition of "We Are Soldiers [In the Army]" slowly becomes louder.)

PREACHER:

    . . . From 1865 to 1965 is one hundred years.

    One hundred years and still counting.

    One hundred years is long enough to wait

    To obtain our rights, as citizens of these United States of
        America,

    To vote in the elections of this country,

    In this state,

    In the parish.

    The actions we take here today are connected to actions for

    Change all over this land.

    All over the Good Lord's earth,

    Wherever the privileges of some

    Take priority over the fundamental rights of others,

    That must end!

    Any system that puts the privileges of the few

    Before the rights of the many must change!

    And we must change it!

    It's time for a change!

    God knows, it's time for a change!

    If there's just one of us who's locked out of the polls

    Or written off of the voter's registration rolls

    Then *all* of us are locked out.

    Same thing about freedom.

    No one is free

    Until all are free . . .

    It's time for a change!

(The sound of the crowd swells underneath in a response that has been building throughout the sermon, with the spontaneous singing of multiple songs and responses, as has the singing of "We Are Soldiers." The volume reaches its peak as the verse "We are not

afraid . . ." from "We Shall Overcome" is heard and takes domi-
nance over the other sounds. The song is sung to its conclusion
underneath the following scene.)

Scene 2

JODIE: Working in The Movement was no picnic, but with Linda
. . . It was righteous, June.

JUNEBUG: You and her are soul mates, huh?

JODIE: And haven't seen each other in over twenty years, don't
have to. May never see each other again. Linda helped me
understand that men have no monopoly on the warrior spirit.

I was so excited about Linda when I came home from
school that summer, I couldn't wait to tell Mama about her.

(To Elmyra) Mama, Linda's so soft and sweet in person,
but when she starts to rapping at one of our meetings, she
makes Malcolm X sound like an Uncle Tom. They can't
call her an outside agitator because her whole family lives
right there in Plaquemines Parish. Even Boss Leander Perez
won't mess with Linda's family.

Mama Dolly, her grandmother, delivers half the babies
born there, black and white. She's eighty-seven years old
and will go anywhere day or night to deliver a baby, but
she keeps a well-oiled .38 in her baby bag and an automatic
shotgun hitched inside the door of her pickup truck. That's
where the warrior spirit in Linda's whole family comes from.

ELMYRA: Son, maybe it would be better for you could go to
school closer to home.

JODIE: Oh, Mama! I'm safer down there in the middle of the
night than you are here sitting on the front porch in
Oakland in broad open daylight. I already feel like a trai-
tor for coming home because, we had big plans for a voters'
registration campaign this summer.

ELMYRA: We made an agreement with your father that you
would earn at least a third of what it costs for you to stay in
school—

JODIE: I could have earned more playing piano around Baton Rouge and New Orleans.

ELMYRA: You know how your father feels about the music business, Joseph. You didn't have a "real" job—

JODIE: Mama, it would have worked out all right. I've got my union card, and there're at least four bands who would hire me.

ELMYRA: Well, I'm just as happy to have you home for the summer working for your father's friend, Mr. Lambert, in his restaurant. Maybe he'll let you play there some evenings.

JODIE: I know what the real problem is: Daddy's scared I'll go to jail and mess up his plans for me to get into some officer's training program. Well, I got news for him. I am not going to be an officer, in fact I am not even going to join the Service at all.

ELMYRA: Are you saying that as a private citizen you have the right to put the concerns of your own conscience above the law and that you're willing to go to jail for that and never be able to get a federal job or do lots of other types of work? Is that what you're saying?

JODIE: I haven't said anything about all that. That's not the issue.

ELMYRA: Those are the kinds of issues that you have to deal with if you're serious about this "Movement" business and refusing to go to the Military Service.

JODIE: What do you think I ought to do, Mama?

ELMYRA: War is never good but it is sometimes necessary. But what I think is less important than what you think, Son. I hope you think about it clearly, for we will all have to live with the consequences of the decisions that you make.

Scene 3

JODIE: The more I tried to get my mother to tell me what to do the more ways she found to make me think for myself. The more I tried to think for myself, the more my daddy tried to tell me what to do. During the summer of '65 it wasn't easy to be black and nineteen years old. In February, Malcolm X

was assassinated and the U.S. continued to escalate its involvement in the Vietnam war. That summer I spent more time on the streets of Oakland than I did in my father's house.

(Late August 1967 or thereabouts. It's 4:30 on a Friday afternoon. Jodie enters his parents' house. Al is drunk.)

Hey, Al! What's happening?

AL: Hey, man, where in the world have you been? Mama called me at work this morning and told me to come over here to wait in case you showed up. She went to the police station to see if they had anything on you.

125

JODIE: Police station?

AL: They have started picking up those Black Panthers around here lately.

JODIE: I got nothing to do with the Black Panther Party.

AL: You expect the cops to know or care about that?

JODIE: Something really important came up. I guess I forgot the rules around here since I've been out on my own.

AL: Hey, that's lame, man. It's no more than common courtesy to let your folks know what's happening. For two nights in a row, they said, they had no idea where you were.

JODIE: I know, Al, I know but it's really been intense.

AL: Intense, huh? I can dig it. All it would have taken is a phone call. You could have told them anything, you wouldn't have had to blow your cover, a friend from college, hell you could have told them you were at my house. I know how it is with you young college bucks. Sometimes things just come up, don't they? When things get "intense" you just have to get "intense" with it.

JODIE: No, Al, no. It's nothing like that. There's this guy at the gig on Wednesday night, a poet named Bob Kaufman. You know him?

AL: A poet? Hell no.

JODIE: He's a real important poet, right out there along with Ferlinghetti, Ginsberg, Baraka, and dudes like that. He's from New Orleans; been a labor organizer, like Uncle Touss, way back in the fifties he was doing his own freedom rides. Talk about the Beat Generation, they beat him black-and-blue. He reads poetry like a sanctified sax man. If I could just learn to play music the way he plays words.

AL: "Play words"? I'll be damned. Play words.

JODIE: I can't wait 'til Linda finds out about this, man! Bob Kaufman! We hung out all night then we went to this demonstration at the Federal Building.

(Jake and Elmyra reenter.)

JAKE: Where the hell have you been for the last two days—

JODIE: Daddy, I—

JAKE: No. Wait. Don't answer that, let me tell you. You been hanging out with dope fiends and pinkos burning draft cards. *(To Al)* You see? You see? This is the kind of stuff they teach 'em in college.

JODIE: It's got nothing to do with what I learned in college.

JAKE: It sure as hell ain't got nothing to do with anything you learned around here, so where did you learn to be a draft dodger, boy? On the streets of Oakland or hanging out with your pinko, dope-fiend, so-called "musician" friends?

JODIE: Daddy, you don't know what the hell you're talking about! I—

JAKE: Don't you raise your voice to cuss at me, boy. I brought you into this world and I sure as hell can take you out.

I ain't never been so outdone in all my life. That sorry-assed, C. J. Beamer, came all the way from the other side of the shipyard to meddle with me.

"Hey, Mr. Montgomery," he says. Says, "You got a boy that went off to one of them fancy-pants colored colleges, ain't you? I seen him on TV this morning, just as big as life *burning his draft card* with a bunch of other un-American, Commie sympathizers."

I was just that far from kicking all three of his teeth down his throat! He waited 'til the Vice Commander of the whole base was standing right there!

JODIE: You could have probably punched him out too, what the hell!

AL: Watch you manners, Jodie. He don't mean no disrespect, Daddy. *(To Jodie)* Be cool, man!

JODIE: I give him all the respect he deserves and then some.

AL: He works at a *military* installation, Jodie.

JODIE: I wouldn't care if he worked at the Pentagon.

AL: He went through eight investigations over the last fourteen years to get the security clearance required for this job.

JODIE: A competent chief mechanic can get a job anywhere. Our demonstration was intended to stir the conscience of the people in this community to oppose an illegal, immoral war of imperialist aggression—

JAKE: Goddamn, if he ain't learned the lingo too! Next you
    going to be telling me about the "downtrodden masses" and
    "the rising power of the working class." Funny how you work
    your butt off to get these young turkeys where they don't
    have to work and all of a sudden work gets to be glorious.

JODIE: I'm not talking about "the glory of work." I got one of the
    dirtiest, dullest jobs there is. Washing dishes at—

JAKE: You *had* a job! Cal Lambert called me about *that* last night.
    It was bad enough when I thought you were hanging out
    with some trifling floozy, but this!

    Beamer had a whole bunch of people over there for the
    midday news, including Vice Admiral Morton. I wouldn't
    have believed it if I hadn't seen it myself. There you were,
    just as big as day, leading the singing. He was the star of
    the show! Beamer and his buddies had a field day at my
    expense. They been after my ass ever since I got this damn
    promotion.

JODIE: I've seen Old Blue scare away as many as six white men by
    herself. As bad as you're supposed to be, don't tell me you
    can't run off white folks as good as a dog.

JAKE: Boy, I'll rope your ass like okra . . .

JODIE: If I was going to fight I wouldn't go all the way to Vietnam
    to do it. No Viet Cong ever called me "Nigger"—

JAKE: Take me for a clown!

JODIE: I ain't taking no more than you giving me.

JAKE: Well, take this, Mr. Political Genius. I'm through paying
    for you to go to that sorry-ass school. In fact, if you don't
    get down to the draft board first thing tomorrow morning
    to get a new draft card, I'm going to write you out of this
    family.

JODIE: You can't do that!

JAKE: Try me! I'll do it so fast it'll make your head swim.

    If you had any sense at all you'd be running to get *in* the
    Service, not away from it. If it's a fight you looking for, let
    them teach you how to fight.

JODIE: I took a stand on principle. I won't back out now.

JAKE: From now on you going to support your own principles
    with your own pocketbook and the sweat of your own brow.

I ain't got to have no son who's a duty-shirking draft dodger.
'Til he joins the Army . . . Tell him: until he joins the Army—

ELMYRA: NO! Jacob, NO! Please, Jacob! Please, please. Please!

JACOB: Tell him! Tell him! His name will not be spoken again
in this house. You tell him to be gone before the sun sets
tomorrow night!

ELMYRA: His name will not be spoken—

JACOB: His name. His name!

ELMYRA: Your name. Your name will not be spoken . . .

JACOB: . . . in this house . . .

ELMYRA: . . . in this house . . .

JACOB: . . . in this house . . . AGAIN!

ELMYRA: . . . in this house . . . again.
I'm done with it!!

(*Jodie's parents exit.*)

JODIE: Fine! *(To Al)* You tell him I'll be gone before the CLOCK
TICKS TEN MORE TIMES. *(After Jake)* I don't need you or
anything you've got in this house.

AL: Shut up, Jodie! You ain't supposed to talk to your daddy like
that!

JODIE: He ain't supposed to treat his family like that either . . .
don't worry about me, I'm history!!!

Scene 4

JODIE: And I didn't speak to him for twenty-four years, eleven
months, and two days, four hours and thirty minutes.

JUNEBUG: Hard time, huh?

JODIE: The worst part was being cut off, was being cut off from
my mama. 'Far as my daddy's concerned, it's not that
I think that he doesn't love me but I was never able to communicate with him. I don't know how my mother stood it
all these years.

JUNEBUG: Your old man stands by his word. I'll say that for him.

JODIE: Stubborn as a jackass.

JUNEBUG: I guess it runs in the family—

JODIE: Hey, which side are you on anyway?

JUNEBUG: You want a friend, or you want somebody to lie to you? It seemed to me that you were just as stubborn as he is as far as that woman Linda is concerned.

(Strains of "A Song for Linda" are heard.)

JODIE: That woman's special. An African queen if there ever was one. Her mouth's so full, lips so soft . . . Sometimes I'd be lookin' at her when she was sleepin' and get to her mouth and I would start quivering and couldn't stop. I'd put my arm around her and squeeze myself to sleep. When I'd tell her about it in the morning she'd smile from a deep place in her and say something about how silly men are.

JUNEBUG: Women feel that way lots a times, that's how they can be strong and sweet at the same time, but most men think there's something wrong when that happens until they learn different from a woman. I sure wish I'd a got that kind of education when I was young enough to use it.

JODIE: One time she said, "If you ain't tough enough, even the sweetness won't survive; but if you ain't sweet enough, all the toughness in the world don't mean a thing."

JUNEBUG: Teach! Teach!

("Ain't Gonna Let Nobody Turn Me Around" begins as Jodie, Linda and Junebug participate with others in demonstrations. Time passes. Jodie and Linda are in a conversation:)

JODIE *(On the phone with Linda)*: Linda, I can't go back home and school isn't doing enough for me anyhow. So maybe it's different for you . . .

Sure, I'm serious about The Movement but I have to work for freedom my way. I'll guarantee you one thing: there wouldn't be a Movement without music. I certainly don't have to stay in school to become a better musician. You've heard that sound in church, you don't learn everything in school, and technique? I'll get that by practicing and working with good musicians.

Ah . . . Linda there's something I've been meaning to talk to you about. You know how hard it's been for me financially, since my old man cut me off? Last night I was sitting in with this band. They just lost their piano player and they're getting ready to go out on a *European* tour. They will pay me six hundred dollars a week plus expenses.

Now I'll only be gone ten weeks and when I get back I'll be able to pay most of what I owe the school and still be able to work in The Movement.

No, it's not just about money, Linda, you know me better than that. These guys will help me learn to play better and I'm ready to fly, baby, I got to try out these wings.

Aw, Linda don't run that jive-bougsie line on me. My mama's a housemaid who teaches music on the side and my daddy, my ex-daddy, is a mechanic. Everybody can't be like you. You're the only one working full-time in The Movement who's a full-time law student, at the same time. And law, everybody knows that ain't about nothing but money and power, so don't be screaming on me about no bougsie trip.

I'm sorry, Linda, I really didn't mean that, but it hurts when it feels like you don't trust me. Most of the other Movement heavies come on the same way and frankly I don't trust half of them either. When I get that funny vibe I just get pissed off. You're the only one I'm close enough to talk to about it.

You know I trust you. I trust you with my life, but, Linda, I dream of freedom too. My dreams come to me as music. I have to set the sounds free in the world so you and everyone else can hear them too.

Yeah, I guess my mind is made up. But it's not like freedom's going to get here before I get back. I swear, Linda, I was born to love you and to make music. We'll have time to work all this stuff out. We'll have time when I get back. But right now, Linda, I've got to go.

("Ain't Gonna Let Nobody Turn Me Around" fades up. Junebug joins Linda and they rejoin the demonstration that's been going on. Jodie sings "Voices in the Rain." Then he begins "A Song for Linda":)

I'm like a bird with wide wide wings
I want to take off and fly
Riding the wind I'll find freedom
On golden wings through the sky
I need to soar way above the clouds
And play to all the world
Always coming back to you
To share my love.

I live my life like there's no tomorrow
My dreams wild and free
Can't escape mysterious visions calling after me
If we go our separate ways
My love for you won't fade away
There's a chance our dreams won't survive
If we stay.

I wish we could fly together
And never have to land
Sharing our wings, traveling dreams
You're the best friend I ever had.
There is nothing missing between us
I know you understand
I'll be there if you ever need me
I'll always be your man.

(Quick cut to:)

Scene 5

Music runs continually underneath the following scene. It's post–Sun Ra, Ornette Coleman, Rahsaan Roland Kirk, Kidd Jordan, etc. The sound is asymmetric, atonal, arrhythmic, improvisational music that captures the sonic chaos of the era.

JUNEBUG: For ten years Jodie worked regular with some of the biggest names in the music business but to duck the Selective Service System he'd have a different name for every job and would always be paid in cash. He kept hearing and playing a music that nobody else did. Finally, when he thought he was safe from the Draft Board, with money saved from the anonymous years, he organized his own band and took it on the road under yet another name.

JODIE *(Entering Syl's Place)*: Syl! Hey Syl! Syl! Syl! Hey Syl, I thought you were in here. You owe me, man! I got three cats waiting for a week's pay and the hotel's waiting for me to settle up with them too. You were supposed to pay me last night, that was our deal. The time came and you were nowhere in sight.

SYL *(Played by Junebug)*: Judging from the box office, it wasn't much of nobody else here. Neither.

JODIE: We played anyway. We didn't stop 'til afer three o'clock. Where were you?

SYL: It's my old lady, man. Last night was Marty's birthday. Ever since he came up missing in 'Nam, she celebrates his birthday like she really expects him to show up. I spent all day here at the club yesterday so I spent last night with my old lady.

JODIE: I'm sorry about the fact that Carrie is all bent out of shape because your boy got . . . hit in 'Nam, but that's beside the point. That's not the issue—

SYL: "Beside the point," huh? Easy enough for you to say. That's my flesh and blood, Little Joe, my flesh and blood.

JODIE: You know that's not what I meant, Syl. Marty was my best friend. He was in my first band, hell, I spent more time at your house than I did at home, but we got some business outstanding.

SYL: My old lady's half crazy. Ever since they told her that the boy's missing, she ain't been right. I had to quit touring she was so bad.

JODIE: You haven't given up all that much, Syl. There're lots of dudes who would kill to get booked into your club.

SYL: Yeah? Too bad my boy had to get ki—come up missing in order for me to get into it.

JODIE: That was eight years ago, Syl, you know you'd have heard from him if he was still living. If you don't get some help yourself, you'll soon be crazy too. But dig it, if you'll lay my bread on me I'll clear out.

SYL: Hey, you done got to be real big time, huh, Little Joe. All you care about is money. Just like your daddy.

JODIE: What's the issue, Syl? I got six dudes waiting and a bunch of bills to pay, man. Where's the bread, man? We played two sets a night for three nights.

SYL: And every time you played people got up and left! Those few that stayed quit drinking. Uh-unhh, naw, I've already lost money on you, Little Joe.

JODIE: I'm sorry, man, but a contract is a contract.

SYL: Naw, you got that wrong, Little Joe, a contract is a piece of paper. Who you gonna complain to?

JODIE: We agreed on a flat fee plus a percentage of the gate. I'll waive the percentage but I have to have the fee!

SYL: How come you changed you name, Little Joe?

JODIE: That's showbiz man, but that still has nothing to do with my money.

SYL: I was wondering. A dude from the FBI was here this morning, said he was looking for "Joseph Montgomery," also known as "Monty Josephs," "Jomo Jamil," and several other interesting—

JODIE: The FBI was here?

SYL: That's what he said. 'Course I don't know for sure no more than I know why you changed your name. He had pictures and everything. You think that looks like you? *(Shows him a photo)*

JODIE: What'd you tell him? Where's he at?

SYL: I don't know where he went, but cops is cops. I told him that Little Joe and his band left last night and I didn't know where they went.

I'll tell you what, Little Joe, what say I split the loss with you? Here's a hundred and fifty dollars, I'm willing to call it even.

JODIE: A hundred and fifty dollars? Man, I got a signed contract for four thousand dollars guaranteed, plus a percentage of the gate!

SYL: Okay. Here's four hundred dollars. Take it or leave it! You win some. You lose some. It's like my son. I wonder how much money he'd be making if he hadn't been killed in that war.

JODIE: This is killing *me*, Syl!

SYL: What makes you think *you* got the right to live, boy? It's just like war out here, Little Joe. You just the same as a dead man to me, Little Joe, just the same as dead.

JODIE: You killing me, man, you killing me.

SYL: I will tell you one thing: don' nobody want to hear that sad-ass stuff you be playing. They don't care what you think, they want something they can dance to, something with a tune and a beat to it. You keep up that stuff you soon be dead too.

JODIE: For two years more I kept at it but I kept putting out more than I was taking in. It doesn't take a genius to figure out that you can't stay in business long at that rate.

I ended up in Chicago with no money. I had told so many different lies about who I was to so many people I couldn't tell *any*body *any*thing. I had nowhere to run, nowhere to hide. The only thing that kept me halfway straight was the one keyboard I was able to hold on to. To keep from going totally insane I played basketball.

(The sound of a basketball bouncing on concrete, hitting a metal backboard and rim. They're going through shooting and dribbling and rebounding motions.)

JUNEBUG: That had to be some serious sandlot ball!

JODIE: I met this guy named "Big G." I was playing for my life but this guy would play harder than I did. He was six-foot-two, was built, and could fly, hang, and glide like he had wings.

They called him "Big G" because if this dude was after you, that was the only part of "JESUS" you'd ever get out before he finished you off. He had the biggest gentle brown eyes you ever did see. When they got narrow and he slowed down his speaking pattern—red light! That was a sign of clear and present danger.

After everyone else was gone, we'd go one-on-one 'til I'd be dog tired. I knew that there'd be no chance of sleep for me if I wasn't already too tired to dream when I lay down.

When it got too cold to play outside, G would take a piece of plastic, a stick, some wire, or a piece of dental floss and in a few seconds we'd be in any gym we wanted.

BIG G *(Played by Junebug)*: Leave the lights out. You got to be able to find your target in the dark.

JODIE: Hey man that does it for me. It wouldn't take much for me to crash right here.

BIG G: You can't do that, bro, that would blow the whole program.

JODIE: I know that, Big G, give me some credit. I may not be a second-story man like you, but—

BIG G: I ain't no thief! I ain't never stole nothing in my life.

JODIE: Then how'd you learn to pick locks like you do?

BIG G: Uncle Sam. I was a trained killer for Uncle Sam.

JODIE: That's what an army is for, G. You were just one among thousands.

BIG G: I was counterintelligence, with an Army cover. I never did get on the field with the enemy. My job was to eliminate "security risks," GIs, and some civilians thought to be selling information to the other side. Long as I was killing for them, I had a "walk on water pass," but now nobody knows my name. No Service record, no benefits, nothing! It's like I just don't exist.

JODIE: Oh. One night while we were sitting in the dark talking, two of the meanest cops on the South Side walked in on us. *(Light in the face)* We were just playing ball, man.

BIG G: "We were just playing ball, man"! *(Runs off)*

JODIE: Oh-oh, G's about to lose it!

(Fighting noise from offstage.)

BIG G *(Reenters)*: Make yourself scarce, blood. You'll never see me again.

JODIE: Before I could blink my eyes, Big G was gone.

JUNEBUG: I can imagine how many hundreds or thousands of young brothers came back from Vietnam, just like G. A good number of them bound to be living on the streets.

JODIE: The years after that had to be the roughest of my life, June, but I still had my music and my one keyboard to practice with.

(We hear the sounds of the riots and demonstrations, marches against the war, and other sounds of protest. These sounds yield to the sounds of isolation and self-centeredness that characterized the '70s.)

JUNEBUG: Riots, rebellions and urban unrest on both sides of the Atlantic. Malcolm X, Medgar Evers, John Kennedy, Martin Luther King, Robert Kennedy, assassination got to be just another way of doing business. A whole bunch of people were forced underground: Rap Brown, Angela Davis, the Weather Underground, Joanne Chesimard, Stokely Carmichael for a while.

JODIE: After that night with Big G in Chicago, I felt like a fugitive from the law, like an invisible man. I was paranoid! I thought everybody I met was out to get me. I finally found my way back to L.A. For a time I lived like a rat in bombed-out barrios and basements in Watts. I'd only come out to play ball. You could say that I had the same problem as some of those guys who came back from Vietnam. Those guys were like family to me.

(An outdoor basketball court at dusk, blacktop between a tenement and a brownstone. There's the sound of Otis Redding's "Satisfaction" and the sound of a ball bouncing, hitting a metal backboard.

Junebug and Jodie both play "Jodie": one from the past, the younger Jodie remembering his life; and the present-day Jodie. It is a surreal, dream-like scene, with Jodie "seeing himself" in both the past and the present.

Jodie is shooting baskets and talking apparently to himself. He looks around from time to time.)

JODIE *(As his younger self)*: I know that was my keyboard . . . I should have gone all upside his head anyway.

(He weaves and wobbles, but he's going through the motions. His head thuds on the backboard and he falls hard. It's unclear if he konks out before he hits the ground. He's hurt and like a boxer "on the daze" when he does finally rise.)

Help. Santi . . . Lester . . . Zeke! Hey, Coobah! Where you guys at?

JUNEBUG *(As Jodie in present time)*: The question is, what do you do with anguish?

JODIE *(As his younger self)*: Rickie, that you?

JUNEBUG *(As Jodie in present time)*: That's me there. Santi, Lester, Zeke and Rickie played ball there too.

JODIE *(As his younger self)*: Gimmie a hand!

JUNEBUG *(As Jodie in present time)*: Rickie said, "Hey, brother. You doing too much wine and reefer all the time. 'Specially since your keyboard got ripped off."

JODIE *(As his younger self)*: Rickie, you crazy. Gimmie a hand, Coobah, man.

JUNEBUG *(As Jodie in present time)*: Coobah isn't there either. They didn't know about the heroin-snorting a little more all the time. A little skin-popping, but not the main line. Because of that night, never did.

(Junebug—now as the younger, fallen Jodie—gets back to his feet, looks up slowly, recognizing night, and begins to walk, weave, wobble toward the basket. He loses his balance when he bends to pick up the ball and falls again under the basket and rolls on his back as the sound of Marvin Gaye's "What's Going On" fills the night.

Jodie—himself now the fallen Jodie—rolls over toward the pole and grabs it, pulling himself up. He leans against the pole, remembering the time Santi knocked him on his ass and what had happened earlier this evening.)

JODIE *(As his younger self)*: Lots of war talk on this court. Santi, a lanky, green-eyed Puerto Rican dude was real quiet and off to himself since he got back from 'Nam. Once I made the mistake of suggesting he wasn't playing aggressive enough. Damn, what'd I do that for?

JUNEBUG *(Still fallen, younger Jodie, looking at the sky)*: Damn, Santi, you didn't have to do THAT!

(The rest of the scene is played by Jodie, in his present self, remembering the past. Junebug continues to be the fallen, younger Jodie, lying in the background).

JODIE: People came back shell-shocked and didn't know it. Coobah had his own private language. If I hadn't been so crazy myself he'd have sounded damn near psychotic.

(The sound of night-club merengue music, then the beat becomes more diffused and varied, like a Haitian or Dominican merengue, then a louder and driving mixed Haitian and African drums. Starting above and continued throughout the following speech, Jodie listens to the sounds of the city. Then he spots a bottle of wine that he had left against the side of one of the buildings and had forgotten. He staggers toward it. The bottle slips from his hand and he juggles it, catching it before it hits the ground. He smiles, mumbles to himself. The mumbling becomes louder as the sounds of the active monster city diminish except for an occasional siren. The drums stop for a while. Jodie unscrews the top and does an enormous chug-a-lug. Then he holds the bottle to the light, again smiling with satisfaction that he hadn't finished it earlier. He relaxes. His head falls and rolls from side to side. He's now drooling and mumbling/moaning. The drumming begins again, low and slow.)

I don't remember anybody who was for the war. Santi said he was proud to of having been a rifle man when he was there but wouldn't go now. Look at me being a fool. A weaker body might have OD'ed, but it wasn't my time.

Lester could shoot over much taller dudes. He enlisted to fight in Korea at fifteen to get out of Georgia poverty and racism. Maybe he's scared of the devil, but that's the only being he might back off of. He said, "Damn Uncle Sam and his Vietnam." He'd tell anybody the war was wrong and it was righteous not to go.

(He sits down against the side of the building, legs spread out and flat against the ground. He holds the bottle up looking through it toward the street lamp, and smiles when he discovers how much is left in the bottle of Five Star Half and Half [port and sherry].)

But Lester re-upped and went back to 'Nam 'cause he couldn't find a decent job. He loved to get high and go out on his own. He said he couldn't find anything like the tension of combat, the sheer physical beauty of a firefight at night. When I heard that, I had these visions of Lester going out, getting high and going out to the field to fire on anybody and anything. I don't know what happened to him, he wasn't no patriot, that's for sure.

(The drums begin to get louder and moderately more fast. Jodie awakens almost as if from a dream or a nod or both, and slowly manages to push himself up, by exerting his unsteady legs, rubbing his back roughly up against the wall.)

I was trying to get the war out of my head any way I could, get back into my own life making music. But I was getting more angry all the time. War all around me and I couldn't tell if I was coming or going.

Who was crazier, Lester or me, I don't know. I was looking for oblivion and it wasn't far away.

JUNEBUG *(As the fallen Jodie, offering wine)*: Hey, fellahs, let's finish this off.

JODIE: Like the absurd, the war itself, "It don't mean a thing." The one thing I had left, my keyboard, was gone like everything else.

(Lights come up on an eerie unreal light, luminescent, lighter than real day and darker, like the moment before the deep dark of a sudden electrical summer storm. Jodie changes time/place with

Junebug. Jodie [as Jodie in the past] pours a little of the wine onto the ground, as if for the boys upstate. Jodie and Junebug deliver the following speeches on top of each other at counterpoint, exploiting every coincidence of meaning.)

For those who didn't make it.
Hey, Coobah, have a taste and pass it to Rickie
And then Les
And Santi— Aw shit, Rickie, man!
I know you don't.
Just wet your tongue out of respect.
And Larry

(He swigs at each name.)

And Johnnie
And Carlos . . .

(He starts drinking faster and faster.)

And Rickie
And Tony
And Featherstone . . .

(Reeling and frenzied, he flings the bottle into the night.)

Don't forget him
And Al. Oh, my God!
All my brothers all.
My sisters. Oh, Aida, help me.
All all all all, oh Linda . . .

(He falls down. The lights go on and off. He's still for a moment. The drums stop.)

Uncle Touss. Touss.
I'm history
Aren't we.

(Darkness. Then, from a small emerging patch of light comes the raspy voice of Uncle Touss:)

JUNEBUG *(As Uncle Touss)*: This way he explained it to me don't make complete sense 'til this day, no matter how many times I hear it. Like that dream, too much happening in too little space and you can't tell if it's a long time or short time but it's BIG. It's BIG and Jodie don't lie. He might embellish like any musician or poet or prophet, but Jodie don't lie. BIG MEANING.

He said it felt like all the forces in the world, human and otherwise, were twisting his body and mind something fierce. There ceased to be a Jodie, only hundreds of movies of vistas happening all at once, each momentarily distinct and all mixed up at the same time. Ringing, changing frequencies split his mind into fragments and then a sudden stillness.

All the members of his family, most he'd never met, some he'd never even heard of, in a tightening, silent circle getting smaller and smaller. He finds himself, as Big Jake, bending over to kiss a prodigal, alien Jodie. At the moment of touch everything dissolved into the smell of Louisiana marshland and the sound of a bottle-neck guitar. The same blues chord over and over floating like a detached lily on a bayou that Elmyra picks up and holds for Aida and Linda to enjoy the fragrance of nothingness.

(Jodie becomes Uncle Touss.)

JODIE *(As Uncle Touss)*: Sh-h-h-h! Listen! Look for the brother you found, Joseph Montgomery, look for the brother you found.

(Junebug, as Jodie, collapses into the hellish glow of the dream. Jodie, now a specter of his brother Al, approaches in a wheelchair. Train light flashing, he searches for Jodie.)

JODIE *(As Al)*: Hey, man, hey! You okay or what? You need help? HEY, MAN! ARE YOU OKAY? It's me, your brother, Al. I need you, man.

(Al falls to the floor as he tries to help his brother up. Junebug, as Jodie, is inert, maybe dead. Jodie, as Al, struggles until he is reduced to tears trying to get his brother to safety.)

Wake up, man! You can't do this to me! Get up, Jodie! Let me help you. Come on. Oh, hell! I got to get you out of here man. Don't worry I won't leave you out here like this. We'll be all right, just you wait and see. You hang in there, Bro, we'll make it through this, I'm going to get you through this. Help! We'll be all right. Medic. I'm not going to let you down, Jodie. I'll be there for you, man. MEDIC! MEDIC! I can't feel my legs, man! My legs are gone, man!

(The dream subsides.)

JUNEBUG : Hey, Jodie, are you all right? It's Junebug! It's all right, man. Let it go through you. You'll be all right! Hold steady. I'm with you. We're here for you.

JODIE: It's all right? Is everything all right?

JUNEBUG: Yeah, it's all right, Jodie. Let it pass through. Just let it pass.

JODIE: I was dying, June. Al was trying to save me, but couldn't. I was a casualty of war, June. I'm a casualty of war and I never even went to boot camp. Al was trying to take me home. This dream's been chasing me too long, Junebug. I got to go home.

JUNEBUG: I reckon it is time. Time to reclaim your name and birthright, Joseph Montgomery.

JODIE: I've been riding the wrong train, June. I need to get home.

JUNEBUG: You've got to ride that *other* train, Jodie.

JODIE: What train?

JUNEBUG: In the dream. It's in the dream.

JODIE: No, June. It's in the music.

JUNEBUG: What are you tal—

JODIE: Sh-h-h! Listen!

(Pause.)

JUNEBUG: I don't hear anything.

JODIE: Sh-h-h-h! You're not listening.

JUNEBUG: I'm listening as hard as I can and I don't hear a dog-gone thing!

JODIE: Then listen to this.

(He goes to the keyboard and begins to sing "The Only War That's Fair to Fight":)

> The only war that's fair to fight is the war to end oppression
> The only war that's fair to fight is the war to win your freedom
> The only war that's fair to fight is the war you fight to win your human rights
> The only war that's fair to fight is the war to end oppression.

JUNEBUG: Brother, what's a hero?

JODIE: And why do you have to go away to be one?
Ain't no use in going home.

JUNEBUG: Jodie's got your gal and gone!

(Stockade shuffle.)

JODIE: Mr. Jones.

JUNEBUG: Mr. Montgomery.

THE END

'Til the Midnight Hour

Sayings from the Life and Writings of
Junebug Jabbo Jones, Volume IV

Production and Performance History

'Til the Midnight Hour: Sayings from the Life and Writings of Junebug Jabbo Jones was written by John O'Neal, directed by Steve Kent, with lighting design by Mike Palmer. John O'Neal played the solo leading role of Junebug Jabbo Jones.

'Til the Midnight Hour was born of the relationship between the Carver Cultural Center of San Antonio, Texas, and Junebug Productions, which started in the early eighties. John O'Neal met Jo Long during a trip to San Antonio and discovered the Carver Center. Jo Long then presented all of the Junebug Jabbo Jones plays at the Carver and subsequently Jo and the Carver Center co-commissioned, along with Junebug Productions, the development of *'Til the Midnight Hour,* which is set in San Antonio. Theresa Holden was the Executive Producer. The play premiered at the Carver Center in February 2000.

The play has been performed in New Orleans and San Antonio.

—TRH

AUTHOR'S NOTE

Several of the elements in some of these stories were first published in *Southern Exposure Magazine* as part of a column I wrote
for that progressive Southern journal. Elements of the character Junebug Jabbo Jones initially appeared in *Data News Weekly*,
a long-standing news and entertainment journal that first featured Junebug Jabbo Jones in 1976.

SET

A 9' x 9' platform is placed on stage. There are six stackable boxes, constructed on multiples of 9". Some boxes are square, others rectangular. There are also two 9' boards on stage, and one sturdy table. Throughout the play, these boxes are used to indicate the space of the action: a living room, street scenes, etc. They are used to indicate alters, chairs, counters, etc.

Prologue

An Invocation

A pre-show soundscape of music that represents the themes in the play is heard: blues, rhythm and blues, etc.

Junebug enters the playing area. He wears his usual outfit: old denim overalls, a blue work shirt, old high-top boots, a dull-colored sport coat, a red bandanna around his neck, a white handkerchief in his pocket, and a soft, well-worn wide-brimmed felt hat. His clothing is soft and worn, but very clean and tidy. He holds his beautifully carved walking stick. His boom box plays "Amazing Grace" in long-meter congregational style while he makes a libation. The lighting emphasizes the sacred qualities of the space. His walking stick, a red-black-and-white serape, votive candles, and other items are placed on stage in a casual yet intentional way that only becomes apparent when the items are integrated into images called for by the action in the story.

While Junebug marks a sacred space with water, he speaks:

JUNEBUG: Here's to the water:

> The briny waters of the sea and of tears;
> The sweet, clean water of rain, deep artesian wells and
> mountain streams;
> The fierce, muddy water of floods.

Here's to the water.
Here's to the earth:

> The swirling speck of stardust that marks our spot in the
> universe;
> The rich, warm earth that yields up life, and all that it
> requires;
> The deep, damp earth that marks the places where we
> make our graves.

Here's to the earth.
Here's to the fire:

> The life-bringing fire of the sun and the hearth,
> The terrible fire of Maafa, holocaust and of battle
> The cleansing fire that purges before planting, the bond-
> ing fire of the forge.

Here's to the fire.
Here's to the air:

> The air that sustains our breath and sustains the bird in
> flight.
> The powerful air that makes the hurricanes and tornados
> The air that embraces all and rejects none.

Here's to the air.
Here's to each of you:

> Let us be grateful to all of the ancestors who have come
> and gone before.

Let us be grateful to all our relatives in the universe whose efforts have brought us together now in the opportunity that this moment offers us to increase the joy and decrease the suffering in the world.

Here's to each of you.

(Junebug completes the libation ritual. "Amazing Grace" continues to play.)

Act One

Scene 1

Amazing Grace

JUNEBUG: I grew up thinking that this was a black hymn because that was my experience as I grew up in the black church. But I got a different story looking at *Bill Moyers Journal* on TV. The same Bill Moyers who used to work as press secretary to Lyndon Johnson. LBJ, the first president from Texas.

You can imagine my surprise when I found out that the song was written by a *white* slave ship captain!

After some years in the slave ship business, this English fellow by the name of John Isaac Newton, began to worry about the condition of his soul. On one particular trip across the Middle Passage in 1837, they ran into a terrible storm at sea. Old Captain John lost several of his kidnapped Africans and some of his crew. As "a God-fearing man," so to speak, he fell to his knees and started praying. He promised the good Lord (and several other responsible white men), that if He'd just let him get through this trip, he would put slaving behind him.

Well, he made it back to Britain that time and I don't know why he didn't keep his promise to the Lord, but the next year he made his last trip to Africa for slaves. I can only guess what happened this time to make his soul so sick that he really gave up the trade in human flesh and freedom. He wrote the words to the hymn on board the ship and set them to the tune of this old British folk song. When he got back to his home port he took up preaching against slavery, singing his song, telling his story and never went to sea on a slave ship again.

Now everybody thinks the song belongs to them. I'll bet most of y'all know it. If you do, sing along with me!

(Junebug begins "Amazing Grace." He "lines the song out" for the audience who wish to sing, conducting the tune with his hands, indicating high and low.)

Amazing Grace, how sweet the sound
That saved a wretch like me.
I once was lost but now I'm found,
Was blind but now I see.

T'was Grace that taught my heart to fear
And Grace my fear relieved.
How precious did that Grace appear
The hour I first believed.

Through many dangers, toils and snares
I have already come.
'Tis Grace that brought me safe thus far
And Grace will lead me home.

It's a good song. No doubt about it! In point of fact, Captain John Newton had a lot to make up for, after his career as a slaver. But one good thing about it is that *no matter how bad off you are, as long as you're still drawing breath, it's never too late to beg pardon for your mistakes.*

Scene 2

Preacher in the Cornfield

JUNEBUG: My name is Junebug Jabbo Jones. I'm a storyteller. I was called to be a storyteller. I say "storyteller" 'stead of liar 'cause it's a heap of difference 'tween a storyteller and a liar. A liar's somebody trying to cover things over, mainly for his own private benefit. But a storyteller, that's somebody trying to *un*cover things so *everybody* can get something good out of it. I'm a storyteller . . . a storyteller. It's a heap of good meaning to be found in stories if you got the mind to hear.

My granddaddy was a jack-leg Baptist preacher and he used to tell me things. One time he told me, "Son, it takes three things to make a good preacher. First: you got to *tell the people what you're going to tell them!* Second: you got to *tell the people.* Three: you got to back up and *tell them what you told them.*"

The meaning and the message to be found in the stories I'ma tell y'all . . . is why I believe it's never too late to embrace our responsibility for your errors and shortcomings . . . for things we have done and failed to do, and that goes for everybody: preachers and politicians, children playing on the playground, and those who are getting ready to take our places among the ancestors . . . We can't take back things said and done while we have shared time and space among the living. We just have to accept responsibility for our actions and move on—*on* as best we can.

People sometimes ask me, "Junebug, you act like a man full of the spirit, doing these rituals and always trying to get people to change things . . . How come you so hard on preachers and politicians?"

The way I figure it, there's a good number of politicians and preachers too who pay more attention to showbiz and how to get over on people than they do to our public interests and spiritual needs. Some of them are always getting into trouble, but they don't get messed over by themselves. A leader can't lead if don't nobody follow. You got the call and you got the response. And it's not that I have anything against entertainment, I'm in the business myself, but we have to keep our priorities straight. Good preachers and good storytellers have somewhat the same job: to comfort the afflicted and to afflict the comfortable!

(He unfolds a serape, craeting a pulpit.)

The year I finished high school, my granddaddy (we called him "Pop-Paw"), Pop-Paw was running a revival at out church. He was deep down in his song and Miz Jeanine Tatum was deep down in it with him. She filled up the church with her response to his call.

POP-PAW: We need to round up all the wife beaters and give them a taste of their own medicine. As it says in the Book, "An eye for an eye and a tooth for a tooth!"

MIZ JEANINE: Listen to the man! Mercy! Tell the truth! Preach the word, Preacher!

POP-PAW: I'm talking to the gamblers, ramblers and back-biters! Great God Almighty's going to cut you down!

MIZ JEANINE: Say that! Say that!

POP-PAW: I don't believe all of y'all heard what I said!

MIZ JEANINE: You better watch out now!

POP-PAW: I'm talking about the damage done by these gossiping back-biters who feel they just have to be in on everybody else's business, spreading rumors and tales all about the community.

MIZ JEANINE: Humpht! All right now, Preacher. You done quit preaching and gone to meddling now. We don't allow no signifying in this church.

(Jeanine definitively goes back to her seat and sits in the "Amen Corner." Junebug removes the serape, disassembling the pulpit.)

JUNEBUG: After that Miz Jeanine made sure there wasn't a church in four counties that would hire Pop-Paw to be a pastor. Still and all it's where I got my idea about what religious people are supposed to be like. Because of him I expect religious people to be the best they can be. But a good many of the people in the ministry are only playing like they want to do better, so it gives the serious ones a bad name.

Some people say that a preacher won't steal
But I caught one in my cornfield.
One had a bushel and one had a peck,
One had a roasting ear around his neck.

"You can't judge a book by looking at the cover." I have known some scoundrels and scalawags in my day . . . some of them preachers. And like Pop-Paw, I don't mind talking about them.

Back in '73 I was doing research with a group called "Klan Watch." The Klan was very active in southern Ohio at the time. I got this job mopping floors at the state office building to pay the bills. *(Uses a stick as a mop)* I was working late one night when I noticed this heavyset dude sneaking into one of those fancy private suites up there on the fourteenth floor with a hefty, but good-looking, young woman. She looked to be in her twenty-threes.

The minute I laid eyes on him I knew I knew that man from somewhere! I guess my mop and bucket made me invisible to him. He was so busy grinning and flashing his gold-trimmed tooth at that good-looking woman that he never paid no mind to me or all the soapy water that I'd done put down on the floor. Well, the first thing you know, that man had slipped and fell! It seemed like the whole building shook when his bottom thumped that floor.

When that young gal stooped over to try to help him up, it struck me where I knew that man from. This here was the Reverend Dr. A. B. C. Golightly, BS, MS, PhD, DD, LID, and he had several more letters tagged on to his name. It was the self-same guy that Head Deacon Johnny Green ran out of my hometown of Four Corners, Mississippi, when I was twelve or thirteen years old.

From what I was to understand, the Reverend Dr. was doing very well for himself, in Cincinnati, big-timing it, running for the city council and everything. He was the first black man thought to have a fair to even chance of winning such a big job there.

'Course, back in Four Corners when I was a child, I could have told them it was something wrong—the man had to been lying! How come a fellow with so many figures behind his name would want to preach at a little church like that, in a little town like that, in Mississippi! But when I was coming up, you didn't back-talk no grown people and tell them they's wrong. When you'd get big enough to back-talk grown people, you's big enough to leave home too.

You ever notice how it is that people's child-rearing habits work out pretty much the same as the police those people have to deal with? See, when I was coming up, the High Sheriff was just bound to be the Grand Dragon of the Ku Klux Klan—it was part of his job! So our people had to be strict on us 'less they wanted to see us dancing through a bonfire or swinging on the end of a rope. *(He mops)*

What happened back then in Four Corners, was that those people hired that man, Reverend Dr. A. B. C. Golightly (BS, MS, and so forth), to be the pastor of the First Missionary Tabernacle of Calvary Free Will Church of the Hebrew Profits (Colored Division). As far as I know, ours was the only church of that denomination anywhere to be found. Bishop Johnson was the founder of our denomination and had been the pastor of our church for years and years, had never been sick a day in his life 'til he choked himself to death on a piece of fried chicken on the first day that we was to move into this brand-new church that he had worked so hard to build.

Lord, the way they mourned that man, you'd a thought Bishop Johnson was the Son of God Himself Almighty. It was so many people crowded up in and around that church— people came from four counties—it took them a hour and a half just to view the body.

(The set morphs into the church, still smelling of the flowers from the recent funeral.)

It couldn't have been no more than ten days after the funeral, when by *mere* coincidence, I'm sure, come Golightly showed up at the regular Monday Night Board Meeting in his 1952 Cadillac Coupe DeVille saying *(It's the Deacon Board Meeting at the church)* "Er-ah, I am a preacher! Er-ah, I am a member of the same denominational church! Er-ah, I was called to be a preacher by the late Reverend Dr. Bishop Johnson! Er-ah, I just finished up my schooling and I am ready to take up preaching on a full-time, regulation-type of basis!"

The people looked at him, looked out the window at that long black Cadillac car that Golightly had come in and said, "Well, Bishop Johnson . . . he passed away last week!"

The Reverend Dr. let out a scream and, big as he was, he jumped two feet off the floor and seemed like he floated to the floor landing on both knees just like James Brown (when he was young), and real tears commenced to rolling down his cheeks! "'Never alone! Never alone!' He promised never to leave me alone! He promised never to leave me alone! Before he introduced me to his congregation from his pulpit!"

Deacon Johnny Green, jumped up from his pew and sailed over the pew between him and the wailing Reverend Dr. and landed on the floor right in front of the new pulpit and nose-to-nose with the Reverend Dr. Deacon Green, wailing for the whole meeting to see and hear.

"'Never alone!' Bishop Johnson promised never to leave me before he introduced me, 'Never alone!'" The Reverend Dr. said. "And he told me the last time I saw him, that he wanted me promise him that I would preach my first sermon from his pulpit no sooner the day I finished my education in the ministry, which is the reason I drove straight down here, stopping only for gas and to relieve myself in the weeds on the side of these segregated Dixie highways."

And the Reverend Dr. said that in front of the Bishop Johnson he promised this to us before he died. And right then he could have gotten anything he wanted out of them people. That's how he got the job.

At first, everything seemed like it was going all right. Golightly wasn't no Bishop Johnson but the man could preach. You put him in a pasture, he could make the cows shout. Things seemed to be going fine 'til Head Deacon Johnny Green found out that Reverend had took to fooling around with Sister Mary Martha Rose Hill. That wouldn't have been so bad, except for the fact that the Dapper Deac thought he was the one who had Sister Rose Hill's nose open. So Deac didn't waste no time making sure that Reverend's wife got the news about Reverend and Sister Rose Hill.

Now Reverend's wife was a great, B-I-G woman: Reverend Mother Gilda Golightly—she was a preacher too. She had to weigh at least three hundred fifty pounds! She was over six feet four inches tall, had one eye, which kinda wandered around by itself, especially when she got excited.

(He makes a booth out of some planks.)

To pay the note on the new church, on Saturdays we would go down to the courthouse square to set up a booth to sell crispy fried catfish or chicken or chitterlings dinners with potato salad and green beans. They set up there right between the white Baptist church and the white courthouse.

Sister Rose Hill was known to be a shouting lady. She would shout if you's to holler, "Jackie Robinson was a baseball player," if you could get it in the right key. But Sister Rose Hill could sell them dinners. It was more than a few would come to town for no other reason than to buy from her. Joe Blankenship used to say, "I'd pay fifty cents for a slice of white bread if I could just stick the money in Sister Rose Hill's purty little hand!" And that was when you could buy a whole loaf of bread for twenty cents.

That very next Saturday, Sister Rose Hill was down at the courthouse selling, and here come Reverend Mother Gilda just a preaching and saving souls that day. She had started preaching around that chicken and chitterlings stand, and it wasn't long before Sister Rose Hill got happy and started shouting all over herself. Before she knew what she was doing, she knocked over that big kettle of chitterlings and slipped and fell all up in the stinky stuff.

Reverend was passing by in his Cadillac car at the time. *(He turns a trunk into a car, a hat into a wheel)* He seen Sister Rose Hill slip in the chitterlings. He stopped his car right in the middle of Main Street. He ran over and bent down to help Sister Rose Hill out of the chitterlings but he slipped and fell down plumb on top of her.

All the time Reverend Mother Gilda ain't stopped preaching and saving souls yet, 'cept it taken Reverend too long to get up off of Sister Rose Hill. Reverend Mother cut one eye over at Reverend and Sister Rose Hill down there wiggling in the chitterlings. Her wandering eye locked in on that big pot of grease they were frying the chicken in. She taken that big Bible she was preaching with and swung it so that it knocked over that big kettle of grease so that it spilled right on the seat of Reverend's hundred-fifty-dollar suit! Sister Rose Hill stopped shouting and both of them got out of their chicken-hot, chitterlings-funky clothes no sooner than you could say, "Jack Johnson!" It was a mess. *(Mops up the mess, then restores the mop and bucket to its original place)*

But that's not why they fired the man. While Deacon Green was sneaking in behind Reverend, trying to find out about his private business, he found out that several thousand dollars of church-building fund money was missing. On top of that, he seen where Reverend had snuck and had the deed to the church property transferred over into his own name. That's why they fired the man—the nigger was a thief!

Now the question comes up if I passed a report on Rev's background in Four Corners to the people in Cincinnati. No, I did not. There was three reasons for that. Number one: he was the first black man with a good chance to win a seat on the city council. Number two: here I was a stranger in a foreign land, and those people there didn't have no idea who I was or nothing but I wasn't the only manual worker in there that the big shots there didn't pay no mind to, unless it was someone with a camera around.

They would whisper to one of the little fellows always be snuffling up behind them, this little busybody would come over and say, "What's your name, brother?" The white ones would say, "Sir . . . What's your name, sir?"

"My name is MISTER Junebug Jabbo Jones."

They run back over to the Big Shot and act like they wasn't whispering back to him. He come and put his arm around you. "J. J., my man, how long have you been with us? Fellows, get a picture of Mr. Jones here. Mr. Jones is a man who knows the dignity of a well-mopped floor . . . J. J., my man, I too have mopped floors in my day. Never give up hope, my friend . . . Did you get that picture, fellows?" And before I could get a word in edgewise they'd be tramping all over my "well-mopped floor."

But the third reason that I didn't pass a report on Rev's background in Four Corners to those people in Cincinnati was the fellow Golightly was running against for that city council job. He was the lawyer for the Cincinnati chapter of the Ku Klux Klan. On top of that he was known to be in good company with the people from the Mafia in that territory. Now if you know anything about the Klan and the Mafia, you might be surprised to find out about that since the Klan is known to be just about as hard on Catholics and Jews as they are on black people.

That's all I got to say about that. It ain't that I'm scared. I just don't have no more to say.

(Singing:)

You don't tug on Superman's cape.
You don't spit into the wind.
You don't mess around with the Lone Ranger
And you don't mess around with Jim.

Scene 3

Of the Earth (As in Mud)
The Brass Balls of Handsome Bailey

JUNEBUG: There are some things that just have to be done. The Irish have to kiss the Blarney Stone, Muslims have to make it to Mecca, salmon have to go back to where they were born to hatch a brood before they die . . . and Handsome Bailey has to lie. Me, I believe I'd die if once or twice every three or four years I couldn't get back to the place in south Mississippi where I was born and raised, go to the old home place, stir up some mustard greens with some collards, a few turnip tops, wild dandelions and poke salad mixed in. Cook 'em down with lots of garlic and onions, some okra and a few pods of pepper and serve them with pan-fried, cornmeal spoon bread . . . for that I'd walk into a meeting of the Ku Klux Klan and slap the Grand Dragon all up in the face!

I call it "Mustard Mecca" because there's no better dirt anywhere in the world for raising mustard greens. It's like yellow onions from Vidalia, Georgia, it just don't get no better than this. I'd been back to Mustard Mecca just long enough to make my first pot of greens, and here come a chauffeur-driven Cadillac car long enough to put a pool in! Out steps His Honor, Congressman Handsome Bailey.

Why they called that child "Handsome" I don't know. His ears stick out at different angles like a first grader was trying to make a head out of clay and didn't know where the ears were meant to go.

Handsome was "a child of wishes." His mama, Miz Mildred, wished the boy didn't look like he'd been beat about the head with an "ugly stick." Still she acted like the sun rose and set on her "Handsome." His daddy wished he could be certain that the child wasn't his.

MR. ONE STOP: It don't look like nothing that so much as passed through the neighborhood where my family lived!

JUNEBUG: The rest of us wished Handsome just wouldn't talk so much.

As he stepped from his limousine, in his high-priced, patent-leather shoes, he slipped in a fresh cow pie. Knowing he'd track mess all over our house without a second thought, I put aside my greens, went out the screen door and stood so he couldn't get to the steps.

HANDSOME BAILEY: Hey, Brother Junebug, I'm so glad you're back in town, man. I've got the "Backlash Blues." They're trying to gerrymander my district so I can't get elected. We need to relight the flames of struggle, brother. They're trying to rip us off again.

(Looking around to be sure there're no white people within earshot.)

These crackers are trying to kick me out of office again, man.

JUNEBUG: That ain't news to me, Handsome, and it oughtn't be news to you. I don't know why you think I'd give a tinker's damn about keeping you in office, considering how you voted on health care, welfare, education, Affirmative Action, and everything else that you weren't in position to make BIG BUCKS on.

HANDSOME BAILEY: I didn't make the rules, Junebug. I'm just trying to keep us in the game, brother. You know I've always been down with the struggle . . . in my heart! *(On the sly)* I need you to hook me up with that brother from the Voters' Education Project, what's his name, Rap Brown?

JUNEBUG: I am not a violent man, but it was all I could do to keep from grabbing the shotgun that hung over the kitchen door. I wanted to insult the man, hurt him, embarrass him, as if I didn't know that was impossible! I wanted to tell him that the cow dung he was standing in smelled better than he did, but it didn't matter. His mouth was running like a bell clap. He was in the zone. I tuned him out and thought, "Handsome always has had brass balls! He was born in that condition."

If it hadn't been for Handsome and his daddy, we'd have had a lot of black people to vote a long time ago. In the time it took for him to walk from his car to the back porch, my mind raced over our history together.

(He lowers a plank onto the top of the sawhorse in order to make the counter of a store.)

Handsome's no-count daddy, Mr. "One Stop" Bailey, had a store at the New Caledonia Crossroads right near Four Corners. We called it "One Stop" 'cause if you stopped one time you wouldn't be likely to stop no more if you could help it. Mr. One Stop tried to act tough among black folk, but was known to be more than a little skittish around white people.

(Unable to get around Junebug, Handsome sits outside the store.)

What got me so upset with the Baileys had happened thirty-five years before, right after I'd come back from Korea. I'd joined the NAACP and the Pike County Voters' League. We'd organized "voter education" classes. In order to vote, people had to pass the so-called "literacy test." That meant they had to be able to read and interpret any one of the 187 sections of the Mississippi State Constitution well enough to satisfy a Registrar of Voters who couldn't read too well himself.

If that wasn't hard enough, they were still killing people for trying to vote in those days. But even so we were able to get a few people brave enough to come out. So to keep people from coming out to classes "One Stop" started the rumor that I was "shell-shocked," dangerous, violent and liable to pop off any minute like Mr. "Pud" Johnson still did from time to time.

Finally, I'd had enough. I went out to the store to have it out with him. He couldn't see me by the door when I got there. One Stop was holding court like a judge. Most everyone there depended on One Stop for credit, so had to be careful what they'd say.

ONE STOP: I know from shell-shocked. I seen many a one in my day. From World War I and World War II. Junebug's worse than Pud was when he first came home waving that German Luger and wearing that French hat, singing "How You Going to Keep Them Down on the Farm After They Seen Paree?" Junebug's got to be crazy! Why else would he be running around the county trying to stir up stuff with the white folk? Just when I got things cooled down after the Parker boy got himself kilt four years ago for trying to get people to vote.

JOE: Well, it come to Junebug natural, yes it did. His grandaddy never did take no stuff from white folk or anybody else. I know for a fact that ever since they got Willie Parker, the Klan has regular meetings on the back side of Whitten's plantation. Somebody needs to stand up to them.

BEN TUCKER: That's what Frozine Johnson's was doing when they got him last year.

ONE STOP: That boy had an accident on the way to the hospital in Jackson.

JOE: He didn't need no trip to the hospital when Whitten's man, Deputy Dan Skinner, and his gang picked him up. They beat him so bad . . . the undertaker, Willie Gladstone, told me that he had to wire that boy's jaw to his cheekbone to keep his mouth shut for the funeral.

BEN TUCKER: That would've been the only way to shut that nigger's mouth anyway. He wasn't scared of nothing!

ONE STOP: That boy wasn't brave, he's crazy! And you's a fool to think otherwise. Now here's Junebug! I tell you he ain't the only one headed for funeralization if he keeps on trying to get people to register to vote. He's crazy as a rabid dog and shell-shocked too. He's worse than his granddaddy.

JUNEBUG: I'll take that as a badge of honor any day! (One Stop jumped like I had shot at him.) Mr. Bailey, you should be ashamed of yourself! You claiming to be a "race man" too.

ONE STOP: It's a difference between a race man and a fool, Junebug. I been here a long time and intend to be here a good while longer.

JUNEBUG: If you scared of the white folk, just say so, but we've had as much as we're going to take. He's even got his fifteen-year-old son going all over the county lying on me. You ought to be on our side. You got your own business and

I sure don't see no white folk in here spending their money making you rich. It sure as hell ain't no white folk paying you rent for them little shack houses you got all around the county. Is somebody paying you to keep us from voting? If it wasn't for a pity, I'd take you out and whip your butt myself.

ONE STOP: See! What'd I tell y'all? He's just like Pud Johnson! People need what I got to offer, Junebug! And they don't need you. You so crazy you don't see the gun that's pointed at your butt, boy. You can go anywhere, do anything you want, but we got to live 'mongst these crazy crackers. Why don't you go on about your business and leave well enough alone?

JUNEBUG: It took some years before I found out what made One Stop act like he did. One Stop was up to his eyeballs in debt. What money he did get, Miz Mildred spent buying Handsome everything she thought he might want as quick as she could get her hands in One Stop's pocket.

See, One Stop did his banking with Colonel Whitten up in McComb. Like most of the other property owners around there, white as well as black, One Stop couldn't go outside to relieve himself without Whitten's say so. If Old Colonel said, "jump!" One Stop would have said, "How high?" If he'd heard Whitten say, "I don't see where niggras need no vote," that would've been all One Stop needed to know that I had to go.

With One Stop and Handsome working one side of the street and Whitten's gang working the other, I was between a rock and a hard place.

But Whitten, One Stop and the others like them had mis-read history. They couldn't keep us from getting our right to vote. But years later, when it got so it was safe for black folk to run for office, we let our guard down. Handsome Bailey, true to his raising, was the first one to jump to the front of the line. He claimed he had been a leader in the struggle for our rights. And that was the least of the lies he told.

(He uses his bandanna as an apron, moves to the porch. The Supremes sing "Stop! In the Name of Love.")

All this was running through my mind while Handsome Bailey was tracking the cow dung toward my back porch. I hadn't heard a word he'd said, but I knew I hadn't missed a thing.

HANDSOME BAILEY: . . . so that's why I need to get your buddy, Rap Brown, down here from the VEP. He'll scare the devil out of them.

JUNEBUG: Ed Brown.

HANDSOME BAILEY: What's that?

JUNEBUG: Ed Brown. His name is Ed Brown. Rap's his baby brother.

HANDSOME BAILEY: Whatever. I just want you to get him in here, quick!

JUNEBUG: (I said more to myself than to Handsome) Some things just have to be done!

I grabbed him by the scruff of the neck and the seat of his pants and tossed him in the dirt beside his Cadillac car and told the driver, "You better get him out of here before he really gets hurt."

It was the next day before I could enjoy my greens like I wanted to.

Time went by. One Stop died from a stroke while ringing up a sale in his store. Too cheap to buy a grave for his daddy, Handsome closed the store, buried One Stop in the driveway, and used the gas pump for a headstone, and put Miz Mildred in a rest home.

Colonel Whitten's over a hundred now. He's too mean to die. He wound up with the first statewide bank in Mississippi. Here lately I heard he financed Handsome in a string of convenience stores called "Handsome's Pantry, One Stop Stores."

The Voter Education Project is gone now. Toward the end, my friend Ed told me he called on Handsome to help with some fundraising for VEP. Handsome had told him:

HANDSOME BAILEY: What do I need to get more people on the rolls for? The ones already registered are the ones that voted me in.

ED: You burning the bridge that brought you over, man.

JUNEBUG: But that didn't stop Handsome. He stood for three terms in the State Legislature before they elected him to the U.S. Congress. I couldn't say that *all* politicians lie as much as Handsome does but he does seem right at home in that business.

Meanwhile, the average black person is worse off than we were in '56.

(He sings an old blues song:)

Nobody loves me but my mama, and she could be lying too.
I feel like a rabbit being chassed by a bunch of hounds,
I just don't know what to do.

Scene 4

Brer Bo and the He-Ro

JUNEBUG: What I been thinking about is how come Brer Rabbit was such a hero to the slaves and other black folk? That's what I've been thinking about. White folk just take him for a scamp and say that's how they are, but what makes black folk like him so? He almost never helps anybody but himself so what is it about him that we pull for him to get over?

Okay, he's smart enough to outwit people who are stronger than he is; he's tricky; he's got the gift of gab; you have to get up early in the morning to beat him. But it seems to me that taking advantage of a bad situation isn't the same as transforming or rising above it.

Here's another question: what would it take to turn Brer Rabbit into a respectable fellow?

(He stands the trunk on end to begin setting up a bar for the next scene.)

When I moved back to New Orleans in '69 to go to nursing school, I met this fellow named Bo Willie Boudreaux who reminds me of Brer Rabbit like some of these other scamps and scalawag we been talking about. He's a wiry little guy with a reddish tinge to his hair and skin. Couldn't a been no more than twenty years old when we met. The reason I say he reminded me of Brer Rabbit is he was smart, tricky, could work his way out of any little tight spot you get him in and didn't care about nothing or nobody but himself.

His family owned the main joint in the neighborhood, which was around the corner from my house. They called it "The Famous Bar on Barracks Street." They say the bar had been in the Boudreaux family for three generations. Bo played the saxophone over there from time to time but he seemed more at home in Orleans Parish Prison than he was here in the neighborhood that he'd grown up in.

(He moves the plank to the top of the trunk to make a bar.)

One Saturday afternoon I was working on the backyard of the camelback double-shotgun I was renting when Bo Willie stumbled around the corner with a used battery in his hands.

(As Bo Willie, he picks up a box and uses it for a car battery. He sings:)

BO WILLIE:
>Shake rattle and roll.
>You won't do nothin' to save your doggone soul.

Say, brother man, que paso-o? Whoee! This battery is heavy!

(He leans down to rest the old car battery.)

They call me "Bo Willie," and you're "Junebug," right?
JUNEBUG: That's right, Junebug Jabbo Jones.
BO WILLIE: The word is that you're a homosexual. Is that right too?

JUNEBUG: What?

BO WILLIE: The word in the neighborhood is that you go to a nursing school and that you a homosexual. I figure no better way to find out than to get it from the horse's mouth.

JUNEBUG: I hear you spend a lot of time in jail. Does that make you gay? Far as I'm concerned it ain't your business what I do if it don't include you. In point of fact I am using my GI Bill to go Flint-Goodridge Hospital School of Nursing.

BO WILLIE: Who ever heard of a male nurse? I bet you're the only man in that nursing school over there. Hmm, come to think of it, that could be a pretty hip get-over. I hadn't thought of that. That's hip, bro. That's hip!

JUNEBUG: It's a good way to use the experience I got as a medic in Korea, plus the fact that nurses can get work anywhere. They got plenty of scholarships for the program. As smart as you are, I know you could qualify. It's a good line of work.

BO WILLIE: No, no, no, no, no! I'm allergic to W-O-R-K, bro. I can't even say the word. Brothers and sisters been slaving in this country for three hundred and thirty-six years and what has it got them? More broke and more broke down. I'm with Smiley Lewis: "The harder you work the faster your money go." Naw, Junebug, it ain't no future in W-O-R-K, bro. I'm getting on the Rockefeller Plan: you do the slaving and bring the money to me! I'm an entrepreneur, me, yeah.

JUNEBUG: Oh, yeah? Like there's a lot of buying and selling going on in Orleans Parish Prison, huh?

BO WILLIE: You'd be surprised, bro. But OPP ain't no big thing. When rich people take a risk and lose, it costs them a little money. When I miss on a bet, it costs me a little time. It's just the cost of doing business. Say, Junebug, you interested in a good used battery with plenty of fire in it? Look a here . . .

(Bo Willie connects two poles to the car battery. A bright, hard spark flares up.)

See that! This battery's got plenty of life in it. It'd be a real good deal for you, Junebug.

JUNEBUG: No, thank you, Bo. The spark in my old struggle-buggy's shown no sign of weakness yet.

BO WILLIE: For you, Junebug, I'll knock five dollars off the price.

JUNEBUG: Thanks, but no thanks, Bo Willie.

BO WILLIE *(Exits, singing)*:

Shake, rattle and roll.

Shake rattle and roll.

You won't do nothin' to save our doggone soul.

JUNEBUG: Later that night my old car was just as dead as a door-nail. When I raised the hood to look and see what was wrong with it I was shocked. I had no battery at all! Bo Willie had been trying to sell me my own damn battery!

I guess you can see that Bo Willie was a lot like Brer Rabbit. It wouldn't take too much effort to find more than a few sermons in his story. He'd take advantage of a bad situation in a minute. And if the situation wasn't bad enough he'd do whatever was necessary to make it worse. I have in mind to tell y'all more about Bo Willie but it's likely to get a little complicated, so I think we better take a little break here.

Act Two

Scene 1

Of the Earth (As in Fertile Ground)
Bo Willie Strikes Again

Junebug returns to kill the intermission music. He restarts music on the boom box before he exits again. The house returns to preshow light settings.

JUNEBUG: Another thing Bo Willie had in common with Brer Rabbit was *impatience.* Bo Willie would rather turn to the back of the book for the answer than to learn how to solve the problem. Sometimes you have to crawl around in the mess before you can climb out of it. Lots of the great spiritual teachers talk about stuff like that. The ancient Egyptians had the scarab. That's what a Junebug is. The Buddhists have the Bodhi tree and so forth. *The difference between a pile of manure and a pile of "fertilizer" is what you do with it.*

When Bo Willie's daddy, Mr. Chink Boudreaux, got too sick to run The Famous Bar on Barracks Street, Bo Willie's sister, Bernice took over. Bernice is a serious, church-going Catholic convert, but it didn't stop her from being the life of the party.

BERNICE: When Daddy got sick everybody in the family helped out but Bo. He always claimed he was too busy with his music or some other get-rich-quick scheme. All he's really doing was hustling. He's always in jail! They got a bunk in the parish prison with his name on it. They ought to be charging him rent there.

JUNEBUG: Bo Willie was a real fancy dresser when he wasn't in jail and he loved pretty women. Every time you'd see Bo Willie he'd be with a different one. When one girlfriend opened an account at Rubenstein Brothers for him, he started hanging out seriously with this woman by the name of Velma Gautier. She was somewhat past her prime but was still a good-looking woman. Velma used to sing with the Raelettes. She'd lost her job with Ray Charles because she had to go to jail in East Texas. A man in a nightclub told her:

MAN IN NIGHTCLUB: Come on, baby. Everybody knows that to be a Raelette you had to "let Ray," so why don't you "let me"?

JUNEBUG: She shot him. It being East Texas she only had to spend about four years in the pen.

It was very much of a surprise to me when Bo Willie showed up in August of '74 with a very pretty little creole-looking woman named Carmelita. She had a little boy and twin girls. Bo started introducing them to everybody as his family. He moved them into a house down the street from me. The first chance I had to get him alone I asked him, "So Bo, that little boy must be three or four years old. Where you been keeping the family hid?"

BO WILLIE: Carmelita's been staying with her family in Texas. I didn't want them over here 'til I could get better situated. Bernice said she would help us out so I told her to come on.

JUNEBUG: Raising a family's a big responsibility. You going to be able to handle it?

BO WILLIE: "Handle it?" What you mean, Junebug? I'm Bo Willie Boudreaux, remember? I'm "The Man," man!

JUNEBUG: One night that fall, late in the evening, I was on my way to The Famous Bar on Barracks Street for a nightcap.

(The last phrase of Wilson Pickett's "Wait 'Til the Midnight Hour" plays as Junebug opens the door.)

Velma Gautier didn't even say "excuse me" as she busted out the door.

(She wheels around on one high heel as she clears the sill. She pulls her tight-fitting print skirt down with as much dignity as she can manage and shouts back into the dusky room:)

VELMA GAUTIER: Bo Willie, you ain't said nothing to me about no wife! I bought and paid for everything he's wearing down to his silk drawers, baby! I'd sooner see him dead than in your bed, baby! If you don't believe it, let him be here when I get back!

(She wheels around, almost knocking down Junebug.)

JUNEBUG: Hey, everybody.

(He gathers himself in order not to fall.)

Carmelita, was sitting with Bo Willie at a table near the juke-box. Her jaw was tight, tight, tight, and he was intense, too. You could feel the tension in the room. Everybody had been waiting for this to happen but . . . Bo Willie.

Bo Willie's sister, Bernice, usually the loudest one in the place, said quietly, "Hey Junebug." She dug down into the cash-box and came from behind the bar with a fistful of quarters.

She rolls her eyes at Bo as she rocks from one hip to the other in front of the jukebox punching buttons. "The Thrill Is Gone! . . ." B. B. King's guitar, "Lucille" underscores the point.

I felt for Carmelita. She was the only one in the place that didn't know that Velma had just got out of jail for manslaughter!

Fast talking DJ, Henry Turner, who called himself "The Soul Burner" on his radio program, chug-a-lugged the last half of a Miller horse and said:

DJ HENRY TURNER: I got to go see a dog about a bone. I'll plant y'all now and dig y'all later.

(Henry looks both ways before disappearing into that good night.)

JUNEBUG: It was quiet for a minute. The rest of us in the bar tried to keep conversation going but everything pointed back to Bo Willie and Carmelita at the table by the jukebox, leaning into each other, talking quietly so no one else could hear what they said. After a while I heard a big racket over by the jukebox! By the time I got turned around, Bo Willie had flung the small cocktail table aside with one hand and Carmelita was sliding down the wall next to the jukebox staring at Bo Willie with fierce and fearsome eyes. The little man looked down at his "wife."

BO WILLIE: Bitch! I told you to stay home with the chil'ren and back your butt out of my business!

CARMELITA: "Business"? What business? We don't even have a scrap of bread for the children and you're out here buying beer for this *punta.* You a sorry excuse for a man, William! A sorry, sorry excuse!

JUNEBUG: Bo glared at her for a moment like he was intending to reach down and separate her soul from her body with his two hands.

CARMELITA: You a sorry excuse. A sorry, very sorry excuse.

JUNEBUG: Bo crammed his glasses back on, turned and walked out, slamming the heavy wooden door behind him.

I went to help Carmelita up from her crouch beside the jukebox. She jerked back from me. "Don't you touch me, man! You don't know me! I can take care of myself." She rose. With puffy cheek and still tearless eyes, she collected her purse, up-righted the table and chairs, looked at each of us in the room, and without a word walked out of the bar. Velma busts through the door, her right hand jammed into a heavy pocket.

(A Marvin Gaye song builds to very loud.)

VELMA: All right, mother— HUH! They better've been gone! Give me a goddamn Heinekcn, Bernice.

JUNEBUG: Armed with no more than the spirit of righteousness, Bernice stepped from behind the bar.

BERNICE: You come in here gunning for my brother, with that filthy language dripping from your mouth, and you think I'm going to give you a beer. You better get out, and think twice before you come back again!

VELMA: You wrong, Bernice.

BERNICE: You'll find out how wrong I can be, if you don't back your butt out that door . . . and don't come back 'til you calm your ass down.

JUNEBUG: The next day Bo Willie came over to my house, wearing the same *Super Fly* outfit he'd had on the night before.

BO WILLIE: I'm sorry you had to see that yesterday. I blew my cool, okay? Bernice told me I had to apologize to you.

JUNEBUG: I'm not the one you plastered up the side of the wall, Bo Willie! You ought to apologize to your wife and beg for her forgiveness.

BO WILLIE: What I need to apologize to her for? She's the one who started all the mess! She didn't have no business coming in there last night.

JUNEBUG: So I guess I should have apologized to you for leaving that battery in my car so you could steal it, huh! . . . How could she be the one to start "the mess" when it was you and Velma messing around?

BO WILLIE: Because. She's the one that ought to apologize to me. By the time I got home this morning she'd took the kids and was gone! Man! Gone!! Man!!!

JUNEBUG: By the time you got home . . . this morning . . . ?

BO WILLIE: Yeah, Junebug, *this* morning! . . . She-e-e-e-i-it! I'm proud of what I've done, Junebug, proud! Yes, proud! Every one of these people in here—these men in here—look at me as a hero! Yes sir, a hero! A HERO! Damnit! They only wish that they could do just *once* what I do every day . . . sometimes three or four times a damn day! Hell, I'm proud of what I do! I'm a hero, Junebug! A goddamn hero and I'm proud of it! A hero!! I'm a Superhero! I intend to have my own Marvel Comic Book Brand.

JUNEBUG: About five years after that I was beginning to get storytelling work kind of regularly. I was walking down Lynch Street in Jackson, Mississippi. I heard this rocking gospel choir singing a super hip version of "Love Lifted Me!" As I approached the church, I saw a hand-painted banner that said:

A Powerful Revivalist from New Orleans!
THE REVEREND WILLIAM R. BOUDREAUX!!

"Naw!" I said to myself. I slipped into the back of the church. The place was crowded. I looked around for Carmelita, but she was nowhere to be found.

The local pastor did the introductions "We are so happy to bring before you a full gospel preacher. You may not have heard of him before, but after today you'll never forget him . . ." The preacher went on with his introduction for several minutes before he said, "I present to you the Right Reverend Doctor William R. Boudreaux!"

The "Reverend Doctor" came out from the pastor's study off to the left-hand side of the pulpit. He got down on one knee and bowed down like he was deep in prayer. He had on a beautiful black velvet robe, an open-front dashiki and what they call a "dog-eared cap" made of the same kente-cloth material. This guy playing the elaborate electronic keyboard outfit started singing the lead part in "Love Lifted Me." He segued into an up-tempo version of "Long as I Got King Jesus! I Don't Need Nobody Else!"

Two men and two women came out of the different sections of the choir. I noticed that they were each dressed in the kente-cloth outfits like the costume the preacher had on. The Right Reverend Doctor was still on his knees pray-ing. When Bo Willie felt that they had the choir and the con-gregation about as high as they could go, he let loose a blood-curdling, "Lon-n-ng as I got King Jesus!" Each of the succes-sive voices followed Bo Willie with their own version of the run until all six of them were gathered about the keyboards doing the holiness dance and singing their hearts out!

The Right Reverend Boudreaux hit a long run and came up from under the pulpit with his alto sax draped around his neck. He sounded like a full-fledged John Coltrane! I couldn't believe it. This guy couldn't have been nobody but Bo Willie!

When the excitement in the church reached a full cre-scendo, Bo Willie opened his sax into a parachute and brought the congregation in to a soft landing. "My subject this evening is 'God is Love! Love is God.'" He read from a long section of St. Paul's lesson on the nature of love. I'm no student of the Bible, but the boy walked all around and through the Book of Ecclesiastes. After preaching and sing-ing, he raised an altar call for all who were ready to accept the Lord Jesus as "their personal Lord and Savior" regard-less of their denominational preference . . .

BO WILLIE: This is a nondenominational service. Regardless of your preference, we can help you get to where you feel you need to be. We can hook you up with The Holiness Church! The Baptist Church! The Methodist Church! The Church of What's Happening Now! We've even got a Catholic and Presbyterian, back there in the corner! If you don't have a church home we'll do whatever is necessary to help you find one.

JUNEBUG: Then Bo got down to the real business of the eve-ning—the collection. Bo spent as much time raising the offering than he had preaching. It was a big offering too. First he asked for everyone who had checks to give.

Afterwards I waited for him outside the church. He and that pretty woman who had been directing the choir were about to get in this big, brand-new, black Cadillac. "Bo Willie? That is you, ain't it?"

BO WILLIE: Junebug! What in the—world are you doing here?

JUNEBUG: What are you doing here is the question. I was work—

BO WILLIE: Whoa, man! You know how I feel about that word. Where're you staying? Let me give you a ride?

JUNEBUG: I can't imagine you as a preacher, Bo Willie.

BO WILLIE: I'm a new man, Junebug, I've been "born again." If I had known how easy this racket is, I would have been all up in it a long time ago. It's easier than running a barroom and a lot less dangerous.

JUNEBUG: But do you believe what you're preaching about?

BO WILLIE: As long as *they* believe it, I stay in business. That's what's important. You can see how well I'm doing. I'm on my way to Virginia Beach. I want to join up with the Christian Hundred TV Club. I've heard that they want to crack the black market. Who better than me to lead the way? Hey, man! Why don't you come with me? I could use a highly skilled man like you on my ministerial team.

JUNEBUG: Naw, Bo Willie. You move too fast for me.

("Papa Was a Rolling Stone" rises on the sound system.)

He was already on the run from legal complications in New Orleans when I saw him in Jackson. Then he'd gotten caught up in what I call the "Golightly Gambit." The pretty woman who was lead singer in the choir had a jealous husband who thought that Bo was doing his lady on the side. Just like Deacon Johnny Green had dug up the dirt on Golightly, that man in Jackson found out that Bo Willie had mixed up money from the church with the money in his pocket. When all that stuff got uncovered, Bo Willie landed in Angola State Penitentiary from 1981 to 1991.

Scene 2

Elmo Fudge's Fingers

JUNEBUG: I didn't see Bo Willie again 'til about a week after the Million Man March in August of '95. The Carver Center in San Antonio, Texas, had hired me to tell stories. By that time I had gotten to the place where I was just as interested in *hearing* people tell their stories as I was in telling stories to them. After my show that night, I invited people who wanted to stay for a while to share stories. And there was Bo Willie! I was surprised to see him 'cause the word from home was that Bo's preaching scam had crashed on him and that he was in jail at Angola State Pen in Louisiana. I was looking forward to hearing from him.

The group stayed a good while but Bo Willie never said more than a polite word or two. He passed every time. That got my attention, knowing how much he loved to talk. Something about him was different and I really wanted to know what it was. When we got done, I asked Bo Willie to go with me to get something to eat at one of the restaurants in the old Mexican Market.

BO WILLIE: What would you say about a real, down-home Mexican joint in the neighborhood? Better food at half the price.

JUNEBUG: People need their stories in order to live. The harder it is for people to live a decent life the more they need their stories and the harder those stories are going to be. Prison stories are some of the hardest.

BO WILLIE: I hated it in the joint, man. You couldn't get clothes to fit. If you weren't large or extra large you're just shit out of luck.

The average man would sooner die and go to hell than to spend ten minutes cutting sugarcane or cotton on the prison plantation in Angola. I'll tell you what it's like down on The Farm, but I warn you, it's not a pretty picture.

I had it pretty easy, 'cause I was a pretty good horn player. They put me in the prison band the first week I was there.

181

I'd played with two of the other guys in the band. The fact that I had the privilege to go out from time to time made the other inmates think that I had some pull with the warden or something, so they gave me a little room. It's a good thing they did too. I don't know how I would have dealt with those big muscle-building thugs that started smiling and talking about "fresh meat on the yard" as soon as I walked in the gates.

One of the meanest dudes there was was this little chocolate brown, bald-headed, muscle-bound killer who looked like Elmer Fudd. (You remember the little bald-headed dude from the comic strips and cartoons?) His name was Elmo. That's why we called him "Elmo Fudge." "Even the screws called him "Elmo Fudge!" I couldn't tell you his real name right now!

Elmo Fudge was only about five-feet-five-inches tall, but he was built like a Sherman tank. I knew he was a killer before anyone ever told me. His eyes were cold, like a shark. I never saw him blink. He wouldn't eat like other people do, by chewing his food. No matter what it was—government-surplus horse meat or stringy green beans from a tin can— he'd just suck it down.

One day, after he'd already finished his half-cooked rice and watered-down red beans, before anyone else had finished complaining about how dry the cornbread was or how much sugar and saltpeter was in the Kool-Aid, he banged his plate on the table, belched, and said, "Gimme your beans." I looked around to see who he was talking to. "Gimme your goddamn beans, bitch." Three dudes slid their plates over to the evil little man. I'd have given him mine too, if I'd thought he wanted them, but he never looked at me.

Most of the fights happened on the way to or from meals. That's when it was easiest for people to get together and hardest for the guards to stop them. To tell the truth, the guards didn't give much of a damn as long as the prisoners only beat up on each other.

There was this big fight between Elmo Fudge and this guy they called "Big Mack." Big Mack was a nice guy. He stood about six-feet-eight and weighed three hundred and fifty pounds. The day before, Elmo had reached to get a piece of pickled pork fat off Big Mack's plate and, without even looking to see who it was, Big Mack had backhanded Elmo Fudge, knocking him clear across the dining room floor.

For anyone else, it would have been an honor that they just *survived* a lick even from the back of Big Mack's hand, but for Elmo Fudge, it might as well have been the kiss of death. See, in the joint, a man is no better than his reputation, and Elmo Fudge had the reputation of being a killer. If he ever backed down from a backhand slap, even from Big Mack, he was dead meat, so everybody knew Elmo had no choice.

Fudge had made a knife by filing down a spoon handle and wrapping the end with newspaper and shoelaces. He laid for Big Mack the next day at the corner where the wooden walk turned to go from the mess hall to the recreation area at the back of the main yard. When Elmo Fudge jumped him, Big Mack pulled a cane-cutting knife that looked like a machete he'd hidden down his pant leg. Seeing Mack head for him swinging that machete, Elmo yanked a length of a one-by-four from the wooden sidewalk to block with.

Big Mack had the size, the strength and the better weapon, but Elmo was a natural born killer. He had Big Mack's back up against the wall.

You could see the fear in Big Mack's eyes. He made a desperate swing of his weapon. Elmo ducked and moved to block the blow with his one-by-four. I can still hear the soft sound as the machete sliced through the flesh and bone of the bottom two fingers of Fudge's left hand. The blood spurted out as his fingers flopped a bit before they fell off. And Fudge kept right on fighting. Big Mack's mouth dropped open. He was surprised by the force that kept Fudge fighting.

That little pause was all that Elmo needed. He was into Big Mack's midsection with that homemade knife: once, twice—on the third time the flimsy blade bent on a bone in Big Mack's side. Before Fudge could kill him with the one-by-four, the guards broke it up.

The next day, on the way to lunch, there was another fight at the same spot. The guards broke that up pretty fast. It was two dudes that worked in the kitchen. They were fighting over which one of them would get Elmo Fudge's fingers.

They wanted to use the meat to season their beans.

Life went on.

That next week, we wrote a real wild jazz tune for the band. It was really out, man—outside the scales, outside the harmonies, outside the rhythm. I mean OUT! You should have heard it. It was wild. We called it "Elmo Fudge's Fingers."

It wasn't long after that we were taken to play for a reception at the governor's mansion. We used the tune to close the last set. It was heavy, man. When we got through, half the crowd just sat there. Not talking.

In that silence I came to know that if I kept on down the road I was traveling I was going to end up as the meat in somebody else's beans.

I didn't mean to ruin your appetite, bro . . . Come on, Junebug. You like stories. There's one you just got to hear.

JUNEBUG: I followed him out Commerce to Olive Street and down a few blocks. It wasn't the same old Bo Willie. I thought about the time Brer Rabbit almost landed in the Brer Fox's cooking pot.

Scene 3

Of the Fire: Silence Is Golden . . .

JUNEBUG: The silence between us didn't bother me. When I was a kid my daddy used to tell me all the time, "If you ain't got nothing to say, for God's sake don't say it! . . . Silence Is Golden! Be Rich!"

Still, I have to say that it somewhat depends on what brings on the silence.

We came to this nice house. That appeared to be dark. Willie headed down the driveway toward the back porch. "Ain't it kind of late to be going up in somebody's backyard?"

BO WILLIE: It's all right. She's always up this time of night.

"Tia Eloisa, I got that storyteller I told you about with me. I told him you'd tell him a story."

JUNEBUG: She was a little woman with Mayan features. Straight hair pulled back in a bun. She reminded me of Carmelita. She offered me a firm handshake.

TIA ELOISA: Oh, how nice of you to come.

JUNEBUG: The soft light from the kitchen spilled into my lap as I settled in a wicker chair across from her. She said to Bo Willie:

TIA ELOISA: Please get Sergeant Bright's picture off the mantelpiece.

JUNEBUG: I listened to the night sounds until he came back with the picture.

Mr. C. J. Bright. He was a large, dark-skinned man with a bald head and a full, deep, well-satisfied smile. Listening to her was like watching a movie.

TIA ELOISA: I believe Sergeant Bright loved me almost as much as he loved life itself. I knew him as well as you can possibly know another person. We both grew up in the same neighborhood on the South Side of Chicago. From the very first time we met we knew that we were meant for each other. We would have been married thirty-six years on this coming June 24th. I don't believe he ever lied to me. There were a few times when I wished he had . . . lied . . . believe you me. He had a silver tongue. You just couldn't stay mad with him. At first my father didn't approve of our relationship. I don't think it was because Mr. Bright was Negro but because Papa thought we were too young to wed.

We graduated together from DuSable High School on that Saturday. We got married the next Tuesday. The next Monday I followed him here to San Antonio where he had

Basic Training at Lackland Air Force Base. Michael, our oldest, was born that December, on Christmas Eve.

Although I had grown up with my parents in Chicago, San Antonio is my family home and I was happy to be back here. Sergeant Bright was surprised by the Mexican culture here but he was more surprised by the white people. We'd never gotten to know any white people in Chicago. If you didn't do housework or yard work you didn't have to deal with them. He was most surprised by the Southern whites—"crackers" he used to call them. Later he came to prefer the term "gringo." The most surprising thing about the gringos to him was how . . . nice they could sometimes be, after you got used to their accents.

We liked it here in San Antonio . . . after we retired from the military and got this pretty little house we just didn't have occasion to see many of the gringos anymore. Our world was black and brown . . . and Bright. What brightened our world the most was our grandchildren. Timmy and the girls were so sweet and intelligent.

The only thing that I did not like was the way Timmy became enamored of the gangster culture. He was a really nice, really smart child and he loved us dearly. I didn't mind that he stopped combing his hair so much, but he started wearing these trousers that would fit down below his buttocks. If he were standing still he'd have to pull his pants up every few minutes to keep them from falling. I said to him, "Sweetheart, don't you worry about having your pants fall off?" He'd grin and say, "That's the style, Grandma. It's supposed to look like a gangster. That's the way my daddy does it."

JUNEBUG: I felt Bo Willie wince when she said that.

TIA ELOISA: I spoke to our daughter about it and she agreed with me. But Mr. Bright said that we shouldn't try to make him do anything about it. "Boys will be boys," he said. "He's only thirteen, he'll grow out of it in due time."

(Pause.)

Mr. Bright was here when the cops broke down the door with their guns drawn. They had knocked him down when he asked them what they were doing. He was watching when our little thirteen-year-old grandchild came out of his room to find out what all the noise was about. He was watching as the three of them told little Timmy to "take the position."

He was screaming, "What are you doing in my house with those guns?"

He was knocked back to the floor as one of them said, "Make that old nigger shut up!"

"What's going on?" Timmy wanted to know.

"Get your hands up, boy! You're under arrest; suspicion of drug-trading! I said keep your hands up, boy!"

"Do what he says, Timmy. Do you all have a warrant?"

"I told you to shut up, nigger!"

"Leave my grandpa alone!"

"You keep your hands up!"

My husband was watching as Timmy reached down to pull up his baggy pants to keep them from falling. He was watching as that young white policeman squeezed off the one round that tore a hole in Timmy's chest big enough to stick your fist in. He was holding little Timmy in his arms when the life went out of him, without enough air in him to get the question, "Why?" from his eyes to his lips.

Mr. Bright hardly spoke at all for the next three years. While the case drug from one court to the next, all he did was watch. Something snapped inside Mr. Bright when that policeman who killed Timmy walked out of that courtroom free and clear. I heard it just as plain as a bat against a ball. That morning I knew something was wrong.

"Good-bye, baby," he said.

"Where you going?" I said.

"I'm going to see if I can find some justice," he said.

I didn't even know he owned a gun. He killed the judge and seven other people before they shot him down. Two of them worked for the court and the others were policemen. All of them were white. He didn't even try to defend himself. The silence had built up in him 'til the dam just had to break.

He was a good man. I love him still.

JUNEBUG: We sat together for a long time, listening to the silence, the crickets, and looking at the bright, shining stars in the south Texas night.

(Donald Harrison's modern-jazz sax rendition of "Amazing Grace" plays in the background.)

Scene 4

To the Air I'll Fly Away

JUNEBUG: Way after a while Willie said, "You need anything, Miz Eloisa?"

TIA ELOISA: No, I'm fine, Willie. The twins went to a party. I suppose I'll sit here 'til they get in safely.

BO WILLIE: All right then. I'll see you tomorrow.

TIA ELOISA: That might not be such a good idea. Carmelita will have the day off.

BO WILLIE: Oh, yeah, I forgot. Guess I'll see you next week then. Come on, Junebug. We got one more stop to make.

JUNEBUG: We didn't talk as we walked.

We turned by the cemetery on Olive Street.

BO WILLIE: The boy that the cop killed that day, Junebug, was my son Timmy. The old man who killed the cops and the judge that day was Carmelita's daddy.

I was in jail when it happened. Carmelita called Bernice to tell her about Timmy being killed. I didn't find out about what happened to her daddy 'til I got out of jail myself two years ago.

JUNEBUG: The full moon shone bright. I was surprised at how nice it was in the neat little park.

He stopped walking near a large stone marker that read: "To the unknown dead."

BO WILLIE: The first people known as Buffalo Soldiers are buried here. Mr. Bright's granddaddy was a Buffalo Soldier. Mr. Bright is buried here. That one there is Timmy.

JUNEBUG: The gravestones were the same except for the writing on them. One said, "Master Sergeant C. J. Bright: A man of honor who fought for freedom and died for the lack of justice." The other said: "Timothy Bright Boudreaux, a brilliant promise snuffed out too soon, like a candle in the wind."

BO WILLIE: When I did get out of jail and found out what had happened, I moved over here to San Antonio. I wasn't much of a father to my son, but I still have twin daughters who're two years younger than he was. I've been helping Carmelita and her mother with them. The girls are talking about going over to New Orleans to go to college next year. I'm working as a body and fender man in a Buick dealership and going to night school myself. I'm taking up nursing.

Carmelita still don't want to see me no more than she has to. I don't blame her.

(Bo Willie lights two blue votive candles and places them on the headstones.)

JUNEBUG: We stood there in silence for a good while. I reached out to shake his hand farewell. He brushed my hand aside and took me in his arms. He held me tight for a long moment.

BO WILLIE: If you get back to New Orleans before I do, go by The Famous Bar on Barracks Street and tell Bernice that I'm doing all right.

JUNEBUG: That's a promise, Bo Willie.

As I turned to leave, Willie said:

BO WILLIE: Oh yeah, I almost forgot.

JUNEBUG: He handed me a brand-new hundred-dollar bill. "What's this for," I asked.

BO WILLIE: It's what I figure I owe you for that battery. As it turned out it wasn't much good after all. It wouldn't hold a charge but I owe you for the inconvenience.

189

JUNEBUG: As I went back through the star-bright moonlit night
I sang:

> One bright morning when this life is over
> I'll fly away. To my home on yon' celestial shore. I'll fly
> away.
> I'll fly away. Oh glory I'll fly away.
> When I die hallelujah, by and by I'll fly away.

(Wilson Pickett's "Wait 'Til the Midnight Hour" plays. Anyone who feels like it should be encouraged to dance.)

THE END

Trying to Find My Way Back Home

Sayings from the Life and Writings of
Junebug Jabbo Jones, Volume V

Production and Performance History

Trying to Find My Way Back Home was written by John O'Neal, with additional text by William O'Neal. The play has seen two versions and there have been productions of both, first in 2005 and again in 2011. The first version of the play had music and composition by Loyd Daly and was directed by John O'Neal. This same version of the play was subsequently directed by Gilbert McCauley, with lighting design by Penny Remsen and featured William O'Neal in the lead role. The first version had one lead character, Duppi, who becomes the next Junebug Jabbo Jones (William O'Neal), and one musician on stage (Loyd Daly). Theresa Holden was the Executive Producer.

The first version premiered at Ashé Cultural Arts Center, New Orleans, LA, in June 2005; and at New WORLD Theater, Amherst, MA, in April 2006. The play, and first production of *Trying to Find My Way Back Home,* was created with support from four co-commissioners: Junebug Productions of New Orleans, LA; The New WORLD Theatre of Amherst, MA; Reston Community Center of Reston, VA; and the National Performance Network of New Orleans, LA. The first version of the play was also presented at the International Festival of Arts & Ideas in New Haven, CT, in June 2006.

The second version of the play featured two actors on stage, one playing the young Duppi/Junebug Jabbo Jones and one his friend, a musician, who also played many different characters in the play. This version was written by John O'Neal, with much of the same music and composition from the first version, by Loyd Daly, with additional music by Kwame Ross. This production was directed by John O'Neal and featured Gamal Chasten as Duppi, and Kwame Ross as his musician friend Sundiata. This production premiered at Ashé Cultural Arts Center, New Orleans, LA, in August 2011.

The second version of this play is the one included in this anthology.

—TRH

A Note on Style

The style of this piece relies on our recognition and celebration of the importance of the sacredness of *all* living things—from the smallest things known to the greatest, of continuity between things known and unknown, of things common and uncommon, of things mythic and grand, of things ordinary and plain. The rituals gain their value from their ordinariness and frequent repetition. Myth gains its power from its ability to render small, ordinary things that are often overlooked in large and easy-to-perceive terms; to render things that are opaque in sharp, clear and manageable terms; to present things that are often seen as dense and difficult as simple and clear. We seek to explore core principles like the unity of opposites.

Setting and Characters

There are two actors in this play. One plays the young Duppi, who is to become the next generation of a Junebug Jabbo Jones. He is a young, powerful singer on his way to seeking fame. The other actor plays Duppi's friend, a musician, Sundiata. Both of these actors play their "main" character and many other characters to tell the stories in the play.

The set is a bare stage, with a platform upstage for the musical instruments used throughout the play. There are a few boxes and chairs that are used to create the various scenes in the play.

Scene 1

Pre-Show

A pre-show concert of recorded music that highlights the way love lights the way for the living. The concert ends with the best rendition of Percy Sledge's "A Lover's Prayer," followed by a recorded version of "Duppi's Rap" in the voice of Duppi with rhythmic and vocal support from Sundiata.

DUPPI *(Recorded):*

> We got a story for you, a love story.
> It's about the wonder of a woman and the glory of a man
> Though they were out of joint with time they had to take
> a stand.
> They had the power of a vision, they met the challenge
> of the time.
> When it came the time to struggle they were the first to
> fall in line.

They had the ocean-deep commitment where Medgar
    got his flow.
They had the deep burning fire within where Myrlie got
    her glow.
They had the rat-a-tat-tat-tat power that helped Malcolm
    rock and roll.
They had that clear, still water deepness that rested Betty's
    soul.
They had the soaring wings of faith that raised Martin
    mountain high.
They had the stainless-steel commitment that raised
    Coretta to the sky.
They had all that and then some. He was strong and she
    was winsome.
Still you never heard their names.

Just their families and a few loving friends are all that call
    their names.
You never saw their names in lights, they never ever had
    no fame.
Just a few knew what they were into, but they still had
    plenty game.
He was a man among the many, who stood out among
    the few.
She didn't seem to be that different from me or from you.

We want to celebrate that woman, we want to celebrate
    that man.
We want to celebrate you, we want to celebrate me.
We want to celebrate the way we got to be the way we are
And the way we're going to be
When we learn the way to see.

We have it in us
We have it in us
We have it in
We have it in
We have it

We have it.
Believe it when I tell you.
We have the power!

(Offstage Duppi fades the recorded music. Sundiata becomes a visible presence on stage as he completes the construction of a Haitian version of the Sankofa emblem, made from white corn meal, on the center of the stage floor. Upon Sundiata's completion of the emblem, all light fades to almost total blackness. Offstage, from the black, Duppi reads a quotation from I Corinthians 13:10–23. Light slowly rises on Sundiata, who dances to the text.

Offstage live voice:)

Though I may speak with the tongues of men and of
    angels
and have not love,
I am just a sounding brass or a tinkling cymbal.
And though I have the gift of prophecy and understand
    all mysteries,
and all knowledge;
and though I have all faith, so that I could remove moun-
    tains,
and have not love,
I am nothing.
And though I bestow all my goods to feed the poor
and though I give my body to be burned,
and have not love,
it profits me nothing.

Love is long suffering and is kind.
Love envies not.
Love does not flaunt itself.
Love is not proud
and does not behave in unseemly ways,
does not seek her own,
is not easily provoked,
and thinks no evil.
Love does not rejoice in iniquity but rejoices in the truth.

Love bears all things,
believes all things,
hopes all things,
and endures all things.

Love never fails.
But where there are prophecies they shall fail.
Where there are tongues they shall cease.
Where there is knowledge, it shall vanish away.
Now we know in part and we prophesy in part.
But when that which is perfect is come,
That which is in part shall be done away.

When I was a child, I spoke as a child,
I understood as a child,
I thought as a child.
But when I became a man
I put away put away childish things.
Now we see as through a glass dimly but then face to face.
Now I know in part but then shall I know even as also
    I am known.

So now abides faith, hope and love of these the greatest
    is love.

Scene 2

Invocation

*After Sundiata's dance, Duppi enters singing "Indian Red," the Mardi
Gras Indian hymn for the dead. When he arrives on stage he makes a
libation, blessing the performance space by honoring the six directions.*

*Haitian and Mardi Gras Indian images are projected on the rear-
wall scrim. "Indian Red" continues and Duppi and Sundiata sing
along. As the song progresses it grows in intensity. We see more and more
Mardi Gras Indian images.*

The actors wear tunics that are reminiscent of Harry Belafonte during his brightest, sexiest days. Beautiful bright colors that flow and move around their bodies like water. Duppi's base color is red with white and black accents. Sundiata's base color is blue with yellow accents. Duppi's totem is a walking stick that images a snake. Sundiata's totem is the djembe.

They sing "Indian Red":

DUPPI AND SUNDIATA:
> Mighty coux de fie yo!
> Indian Red! Indian Red!
>
> Here come the Indians, Indians
> Indians of the nation, the whole wide creation
> They won't bow down, not on the ground
> Oh, I love to hear them call my Indian name.
>
> Here comes my spy boy, spy boy . . .
>
> Here comes my flag boy . . .
>
> Make way for the Indians! Indians!
> Indians of the nation, the whole wide creation
> They won't bow down, not on the ground
> Oh, I love to hear them call my Indian name.
>
> Here come the elders of the nation
> The whole wide creation
> They won't bow down, to the dirty ground
> Oh, how I love to hear them call my Indian name.

(Duppi pours a libation after each toast:)

DUPPI: This is for all of those who have gone before. *(Pours a libation)*

We honor all of those upon whose land we stand, those who sanctified this land with their blood for so many centuries before we came to stand here. *(Libation)*

This is for Big Chief Toottie Montana and all the Mardi Gras Indians who devote themselves to bringing Beauty and Joy to their peers and to the world. *(Libation)*

That's for all the brothers and sisters who have ever been incarcerated and those who lived to celebrate the victory of life over death and who live now to celebrate that victory. *(Libation)*

That's for all the Junebugs in the world who live to tell the stories of our people's struggles. *(Libation)*

This is for all of those who have died that we might live. *(Libation)*

(Singing:)

Oh, my Indian Red.
My Indian Red.
How I love to hear them call my Indian name.

Scene 3

Who Are We That Sing, Dance and Tell Stories to You?

DUPPI: My name is Toussaint Antonio Duplessis. My Friends call me "Duppi the Liberator"!

We work in the ancient storytelling tradition of the mythic Junebug Jabbo Jones, without whom none of us would be here. Thank you for joining us in this place.

Junebug says it takes three things to make a good storytelling. One: You gotta tell the people what you're *going* to tell them. Two: You *tell* the people. Three: You tell them what you *told* them.

SUNDIATA: Yeah, you right! We're going to sing a little, dance a little and rap a little to tell how we came to believe that even when profound revolutionary change is firmly rooted in a clear understanding of history, *it will fail if the effort is not also rooted in Love For All Living Things*! Love is the key. It's what binds all living things together!

That's what we are going to tell you.

DUPPI: This here is my cousin, Sundiata Adelabu Ajaya! My spiritual guide, my teacher in the drum and dance. Sundiata's going to help me tell these stories today/tonight. Sundiata!

(Sundiata takes a brief drum solo. Duppi takes over the bass drum. Sundiata tags the rhythmic break with a flourish.)

SUNDIATA: Thank you! Brother Duppi. Thank you!

My mother says I started dancing and drumming when I was in her belly and I've been doing it ever since.

(Duppi carries on with the musical subtext for Sundiata's story:)

Everything in the world! Everything that ever existed, everything that ever will exist, everything has its own distinctive beat. When you lose that beat you lose your lease on life.

(Duppi takes over the bassline on the big drum, allowing Sundiata more freedom for his solos. Sundiata's rhythmic mastery claims the power of the African root, which ultimately claims parentage of all people of the planet. Sundiata focuses on the way New Orleans culture is like the link between ALL people of the African Diaspora, which ultimately includes all human beings in the world. He closes the rhythmic essay with a flourish. On the bass drum Duppi picks up the second line beat hidden in the pattern that Sundiata has been playing.)

It all depends on rhythm. I live to celebrate the rhythm of the universe as that rhythm reveals itself to me.

I was born in Haiti but moved to New York City when I was eleven. My mother is Haitian, my father is Barbadian. Both families were sailors and fishermen until the big companies and the pollution in the ocean destroyed the fish! Now we do whatever we can to eke out a living. My family goes back six generations on *both* sides in the Islands, man!

It's just a question of where you got off the boat. What happened before that, nobody knows but the *"bones! Black bones in the sea! Black bones!"* *

The reflection of the ocean in the sky, smell of shrimp and oysters; crawfish and crab shells; and the rhythm of the city is what called me to New Orleans.

I was touring with a great dance company from New York, the Urban Bush Women. The tour had closed in Dallas so I was headed back home to New York. I had a flight change in New Orleans but we missed our connection because of "mechanical problems." We had to circle the New Orleans airport for nearly two hours! They said we couldn't land 'cause the landing gear was jammed. Fire trucks, ambulances, all kinds of emergency stuff out to meet us! Happily, we got down okay. But then the airline tried to change their story! They told us we'd be stranded for at least two days 'cause of a blizzard on the East Coast. Since it was "weather-related" the airline would be responsible for no expenses! I wasn't too hyped about flying in the first place so I pitched a serious fit! They tried to make *us* pay for *their* mistake!

I got busy organizing all of the passengers who weren't intent to stop in New Orleans in the first place. I found forty-three people! Before I was done they had given us four days at the Fairmont Hotel and first-class tickets to wherever our tickets said we were going.

I took this as a sign. I was *supposed* to stay in New Orleans! . . . which I did. Basically, I've been living there ever since!

This young man right here was one of the first people I met in New Orleans. The way it happened was kind of funny.

My first night in the Crescent City, I didn't sleep no more than two hours. I was so excited about just being in New Orleans. Sunday morning I had breakfast in the hotel, took "Jenny D'Jembe," my big bass drum, and went looking for the source of *the rhythm of the city.*

I walked down Rampart Street and came to "Louis Armstrong Park"! Right away I saw what I was looking

---

*From the poem "Names, Places, Us" by Kalamu ya Salaam.

for! New Orleans is an African city! The buildings have European designs but they were built, maintained and rooted in African culture! That's it! The whole city was saying, "Welcome home, Home Boy! Welcome home!"

I came to Catlett's bronze tribute to the great musician, here in his own park in his own hometown! I was awestruck!

I sat down on the grassy knoll in front of Satchmo. I must have dreamed the conversation between us. I was more than a little cheeky when I asked him, "All due respect, Baba, but why the hell you keep that handkerchief in your hand, that big snaggle-toothed grin, and how come you always laughing and rolling your eyes so much. Why you got to act like you a dumb 'Rastus' in a damn minstrel show?! How come you have to embarrass colored people so?"

I saw myself the same size as the statue. Had my finger all up in his face.

"Were you raised to talk to your elders like that, son? . . . One more thing . . . *(Slipping his hand into his back pocket)* . . . if you don't get that finger out my face quick fast and in a hurry, you're going to draw back no more than a nub!"

The Dirty Dozen sounded like they were right on top of me! They were playing an upbeat version of "Blue Monk." It was still a new sound to my ear! I woke up to see them marching from Congo Square over to where Baba Louis and I were talking. The parade marshall, a cat named Darriel, stopped them and the crowd that was marching with them between where I was sitting on the grass and Catlett's giant. I got up and moved to a spot on the little footbridge nearby so I could see and hear the whole band better. They played the most sad, sweet version of "Do You Know What It Means to Miss New Orleans?" I'd ever heard.

Satchmo had quit smiling and took a solo on the last chorus. He was looking dead at me as he played. I tried to avoid his stony gaze as he stepped back up on his pedestal as the sad song ended. Darriel counted off a snappy street beat (on his whistle) and led the way down St. Claude Avenue to the heart of Treme. Somebody started singing, "I Got a Big

Fat Woman Just as Sweet as She Can Be! . . ."—and a new song was born right on the spot! You couldn't tell the Saints from the Sinners on that Sunday afternoon.

SNARE DRUMMER: Can you play that djembe, or are you just toting it for show?

SUNDIATA: It's all right for me to play?

SNARE DRUMMER: Yeah, man! Especially if you can tighten up that brother with the beer bottle and the case knife!! I don't know if he's drunk or if he just can't feel the beat. He's throwing everybody off.

SUNDIATA: I put on my djembe, got right up next to the cat with the beer bottle and fell into the groove between him and this sister who played the tambourine to a fare-thee-well! I couldn't tell if she was in the band or not, but if she wasn't, she should have been!

I played so loud there was nowhere for him to go but to the beat. Every time he started to drift away from the beat I smacked him back into line!

St. Augustine Church was only two blocks away. As we came close the priest came soaring out of the church like a black angel! Four or five guys who looked like they could have held their own with any one of the lead dancers of the Alvin Ailey Dance Theatre made themselves a chorus to the tall dark-skinned man with a premature white afro! The moment I saw him I knew he lived in the light of the Cleansing Fire! The padre was all up in it!

I wondered how any *Catholic* church could tolerate all that Africanity!

I heard this swinging beat I'd never heard before. It was twelve-year-old Duppi beating on a five-gallon bucket! Him and the priest got off so deep in it!

When the rest of the band got tired, Duppi and me carried on. That woman with the tambourine, this kid with the sheetrock mud-tub *and* me! Before we got through, all the people in earshot were dancing in the street! All the young girls and some of the older ones circled around Duppi and took turns each one trying to outdo each other. And I'll tell you that second-line dancing is some sexy, yeah!

At first I wasn't sure Duppi was intentional about what he was doing, but he knew what he was doing all right! He could turn it off and on like he had a faucet!

Duppi spied this attractive middle-aged, brown-skinned woman sauntering down the street from Back O' Town on Governor Nicholls, hollered out, "Mama Marese! Calinda! Ville d'Lis, Calinda!" He started to play out the rhythm. His Mama Marese started doing a dance that I'd only seen my mother do before. She'd told me that only people from their village do that dance.

"Mama Marese" must have grown up in the same little Haitian village that my mama came from! She'd told me if I ever got to New Orleans, to look for her friend "Marese from Ville d'Lis." But she couldn't tell me what last name she would be going by because, like so many people in Haiti at the time, she was one of those who opposed the regime of Haitian President Francois "Papa Doc" Duvalier.

DUPPI: Mama Marese looked at him so very carefully and said, "You play that calinda so very well. Where did you learn that style?"

SUNDIATA: I was also born in Ville d'Lis.

MAMA MARESE: Are you . . . the middle child of Denise Lebeaud.

SUNDIATA: Yes. My mother sent me to find news of you.

Before my first day in New Orleans was over, I'd found my mother's friend!

(Duppi's drumbeat marks the end of Sundiata's introduction.)

DUPPI: I didn't know it at the time, but that was one great leap forward in my search for my birth family. When I heard Sundiata tell the story about his family running back for six generations!, it comforted me but it stung me too.

Most of the kids I grew up with in New Orleans could count back four or five generations, but I felt like I was alone. All I had was Mama Marese and her friends: Big Duck, Mr. Montana and his family, and that was a lot—a hell of a lot! But everybody else had a lot of aunties, uncles, cousins for days! Grandparents! Nannans! Parrans! But where did my bloodlines run to? Who were *my* ancestors?

That very afternoon Mama Marese claimed Sundiata as my "Ville d'Lis Cousin." She told him for as long as he was in New Orleans her home was his home! Sundiata has been my Big Brother Cousin ever since.

SUNDIATA: Now you have six generations of Haitian kin people spread across the USA, the Caribbean and everywhere else too.

Before the second-line ended that day Padre had hired me to give African drumming and dancing classes at the church. Duppi was in the ninth grade that year. We worked together all through his school years.

DUPPI: Like Mr. Montana, Father LeDoux and Mama Marese, Sundiata and I became a team! If anybody in Treme had a problem they couldn't handle on their own, that's where they took it, to the kitchen table around the corner from St. Aug at Mama Marese's house! It's the old African way. Their motto was: "Strength through unity!" We claimed their motto as our own, "Strength through unity!"

SUNDIATA: Mama Marese was an emergency room nurse at Charity Hospital. She'd been there since the '50s when she first came over from Haiti. She was real good at it too. If anybody in Treme got sick and didn't have insurance, they didn't call a doctor! They called Mama Marese! There were many nights people would call or come knocking to ask Mama Marese to help them. She always did.

DUPPI: On top of that, she was good friends with Father LeDoux and Mr. Montana who, in addition to being the Big Chief of the Yellow Pochantas, was a master plasterer and was highly respected by his union brothers. With my new cousin teaching me about dancing and drumming, taking me on gigs with him whenever I could make it, I was making pretty good money. We were well known in Treme!

SUNDIATA: One day, late in the summer, Jerome said he was coming by to talk to Mama Marese and me about Duppi. Frankly, I was a little worried. He had just made sixteen and had started hanging pretty tough with some people that neither of us knew. Some of those dudes were pretty fast, so yeah, I was worried.

DUPPI: Straight As, point guard on the basketball team, captain of the drum line during the football season, I don't know what they could a been talking about! *(Seeing Jerome approach, he welcomes him in)* Hey, "Big Duck" what's up?

JEROME: You the boss, Duppi, you the boss!

DUPPI: Not around here. Mama Marese is the boss here!

MARESE *(Entering)*: And don't you forget it! Hey, Jerome. Sorry I'm running a little late.

JEROME: I got some good news!

MARESE: Good news? GOOD! GOOD! GOOD! I couldn't take no more bad news today! Duppi, make Baba Jerome some tea and bring me some café olé, please.

JEROME: What bad news you dealing with, sister? What can we do to help?

MARESE: All the helping's been done, now, bless her soul. *(Making the sign of the cross)* You all remember the cute little Logan girl from around on Villere Street? Celestine, I think? Yeah. Father LeDoux brought her over to Charity. Someone messed up an abortion! She was already in shock by the time Father LeDoux and her mother got her over to the hospital. She'd already lost too much blood. We did all we could do to save her, but she was just too far gone.

DUPPI *(Returning with coffee and tea)*: You mean Celestine?

MARESE: Yes, Celestine.

DUPPI: Dead?!

(Duppi exits abruptly. Pause.)

SUNDIATA: She's his best friend, girl. He didn't know there was anything wrong with her.

MARESE: I should have been more sensitive. You have good news, Jerome?

JEROME: Yeah, good news. But look, I can come back later if you want to—

MARESE: I could use some good news now, Jerome. I need it. He's tough. I'll attend to him later. Please, continue, *s'il vous plaît.*

JEROME: Y'all know that we've been doing everything we can over at Tambourine and Fan to raise scholarships for our kids for the last few years. This year Duppi's application came out head and shoulders above everyone else. He's got a four-year, all-expenses-paid scholarship any school he wants in the state of Louisiana.

SUNDIATA: You serious, Jerome?

JEROME: Serious as a heart attack! Here's the paperwork, see here! "Toussaint Antonio Duplessis ". . . full scholarship for academic excellence and community leadership . . ." It's all in the package here! Let me be the first to congratulate him on the good work he's done! All he has to do is to maintain his grade point average and he's "in like Flynn"!

DUPPI: Jerome came to my room to holler before he left that night. He gave me the papers on the scholarship and tried to cheer me up, but he didn't understand what I was dealing with. He thought that Celestine was my "girlfriend" and that she was having my baby. But, no, that wasn't it! It wasn't that we didn't want to but . . . I was deep in love with her. Neither one of us thought it would be the right thing to do. What we had was deep, deep, deep! From the time I was thirteen years old!

Celestine had been at St. Aug that day I first met Sundiata. I had admired her from a distance for a long time. She lived around the corner from us on Ursulines. I always thought she was pretty, and eventually came to know that she was deep too. She was one of the dancers in front of the church that day. In fact, it seemed like she could see straight through me into my spirit. Like she could see what I was going to do before I did it. I could see what she was going to do before she did it.

On that day when we first met over by St. Aug Church . . . Everybody crowded up around me, clapping me on the back and stuff, and she came toward me and the crowd opened up like magic. I thought she was just sweating real hard, but, no, she was crying. Tears were just rolling down her face, but, no, she was smiling. We had never even said a word to each other before, but she walked up close to me and kissed me—with her mouth open she hugged me real tight and put her tongue in my mouth. Then she turned around and went back to her house. I was sweating hard too. I wiped my face with my T-shirt. Both my cheeks were wet and salty. Then I realized that I was crying too.

That night I had my first wet dream. I was so embarrassed. Nobody in the room but me. Still I was so embarrassed. I didn't know what was happening to me. I didn't know what was happening to my body. I woke up in the middle of the night and turned my lamp on. My pj's were soaking wet. I got some fresh pj's from my drawer and put them on. I heard Mama Marese in the kitchen. I smelled the sassafras she always drank when she had trouble sleeping.

MARESE: You couldn't sleep either, huh?

DUPPI: Nah. Thought I'd have some of that tea you're having . . . Mama Marese . . .

MARESE: *Oui.*

DUPPI: Mama Marese. How can you tell when you're in love?

MARESE: In love?

DUPPI: Yes, ma'am.

MARESE: You think you're in love?

DUPPI: Yeah. I think so.

MARESE: Have you—

DUPPI: Oh no, ma'am! No, ma'am!! I want to . . . we want to . . .

MARESE: Celestine is a very nice young lady. But do you think you're ready for a family?

DUPPI: I been thinking about it . . . and I got a lot of big plans. But I haven't got that part figured out yet.

MARESE: I think you better "get that part figured out" lest you find yourself with a big surprise. In the meantime I would advise you to keep your conversations in the parlor. Don't try to work things out in the bedroom. When passion rises words often fail . . . I must get a little sleep before rude sunlight comes to rouse us. I'll surely have a busy day at the hospital tomorrow. *Bon soir, mon fils.*

DUPPI: *Bon soir, Mama.*

MARESE: *Toussaint* . . .

DUPPI: *Oui, Mama.*

MARESE: *Mon cher* . . . sometimes judgment fades in the heat of passion. Take these condoms . . . Just in case . . . You do know how to use condoms, yes?

DUPPI: Ah . . .

MARESE: Here, *mon fils*, take this pamphlet. If you have questions, we can talk again. *Oui?*

DUPPI: *Mais oui, Mama!*

MARESE: Oh. Take this pamphlet for Celestine.

DUPPI: Mama!

MARESE: Well, she might need the information in it also. What lovers need and want more than anything else is love—true love, real soul-satisfying love! Love! The kind of love that you know will be there when all else fails. *Bon soir, mon cher.*

DUPPI: *Bon soir, Mama.*

That conversation between me and Mama Marese happened two years before Celestine died! When I thought both of us were still virgins when she died!

I knew that I was.

Scene 4

The Death of Mama Marese

DUPPI: Thanks to Baba Jerome I finished the MBA at SUNO before I was twenty-one years old. I'd gotten into hip-hop and made up my mind to be the first big world-beat hip-hop sensation from America—singing, rapping and raising hell. Called myself "Duppi the Liberator!" I got my own publishing company for my songs: "DuppiWrites!" My own record label: "DuppiWorks!" My own clothing line: "DuppiWear!" I had it all mapped out and the plan was working! I was a conglomerate 'bout to bust out.

By September 2001 I was featured on a Russell Simmons All-Star Show on a tour across the north-central states. On the ninth of September we were working at this big theater in Chicago. Soon as I stepped on stage I saw this real fine sister! I couldn't take my eyes off of her the whole time I was on stage.

I didn't want to go to the after-show party 'cause she didn't look or feel like that type of woman to me, but the minute I walked into the ballroom they had set up for the party I saw her at the punch bowl. I made a beeline for her. "Hey, lady. I'm 'Duppi the Liberator!' Aside from 'Angel,' what people call you?"

ROSE *(Before she turns)*: I know who you are.

DUPPI: Then you have an edge on me . . . I couldn't see nobody but you the whole time I was on stage. Your boss 'fro waving like a flag every time you bobbed one way or the other. I felt like I was doing the whole show just for you!

ROSE: I know. Thanks. I could feel it . . . I'm Rose. Rose Marie DuBois.

DUPPI: "Rose. Rose Marie DuBois." A beautiful name for a beautiful lady.

ROSE: This is really interesting. Could it be that your stories know more about people than you do? . . . Aside from being just a little corny, it's truly unnecessary. But you do remind me of this storyteller from Pike County, Mississippi. He goes by the name "Junebug Jabbo Jones." You know him?

DUPPI *(To the audience)*: Now that hurt my feelings, some bad, yeah! *(To Rose)* Here I am trying to get with you and you *ranking* me by saying I remind you of some old dude from Mississippi—who I've never heard of—telling *children's* stories!

ROSE: You're a storyteller too and your stories are definitely not for children. Grown people need their stories too! . . . Some of us call it "history." . . . An Ojibwe woman once told me, "If we don't know our stories, how can we say who we are?"

Look. You don't have to *scheme* to get with me. You're the only reason I came to this party. My mind's already made up. I'm telling you, you must see this show! That's why I'm asking you to go out on a date with me . . . if you've got the time.

DUPPI: The woman of my dreams was asking me out on a date! It made my head swim! What else could I do?

Scene 5

Duppi Meets Mr. Jones and Po Tatum

DUPPI: On the tenth of September, I went with her to see this "Junebug Jabbo Jones" tell stories. That night changed my life! He told stories that touched me so deep deep deep! Listening to this dude tell stories was like listening to a good blues singer! I laughed, I cried, I got mad enough to punch somebody . . . But most of all I wanted to talk to this "Junebug" man about how much of his story was true.

SUNDIATA: Mr. David Walker, aka Junebug Jabbo Jones, said Po grew up in Pike County, Mississippi, in a section they called The Bottom. Said the story was intended to honor his mentor, a man named Phillip Anthony "Po" Tatum. He called the show, "You Can't Judge a Book by Looking at the Cover: Sayings from the Life and Writings of Junebug Jabbo Jones, Volume II."

His stories helped me understand why they call it "Down Home"! He started with "The Po Tatum Hambone Blues" and ended with the title piece of the show.

Not only did he tell a bunch of stories, he did some old-school rap with nothing but some heavy rhythms that he played on his thighs and other parts of his body.

(Duppi and Sundiata perform "The Po Tatum Hambone Blues" as a duet:)

DUPPI AND SUNDIATA *(Singing)*:
"Po Tatum, Po Tatum, where you been?"
"Been to the city and I'm going again."
"What you going to do when you get back?"
"Take a little walk 'cross the railroad track."

HAMBONE!

"Po Tatum, Po Tatum, have you heard?
Junebug's here and he's spreading the word.

He's telling everybody you's his best friend.
Telling everybody how you's done in.
Telling how you had to leave away from home.
Telling how you had to hit the road alone."

PO TATUM!

When Po Tatum was just a little bitty baby
His mama was known to be a very fine lady!
His daddy was a man with a special skill,
Could make people laugh and he knowed how to build.
Had a real nice farm and a real fine house,
As Po grew up he learned to run his mouth.

They were doing pretty well 'til things got funny,
When they run out of work and they run out of money.
Need money for the farm, need money for the house;
Need money for the cat, and for the cat to catch the mouse;
Need money for clothes, need money for school;
Even need money to feed the old mule.

So you run to the city, try to get your people some money.
You run to the city, trying to find your honey.
When you run out of money, you come to the end of
    your rope.
You run out of money, you run out of hope, no hope, no
    hope, no hope!

That's the Po Tatum Hambone Blues!

DUPPI: By the time Junebug finished his story and summed up
the lessons he'd learned from Po Tatum, I felt like I really
knew Po Tatum well!

*(Together, they launch into "You Can't Judge a Book by Looking at
the Cover":)*

DUPPI AND SUNDIATA *(Singing, alternating lines)*:
    You can't judge a book by looking at the cover
    You can read my letter but I bet you can't read my mind.

If you want to get down, down, down, you got to spend
   some time!
I want to walk with you.
I want to talk with you.
I wannna, wannna, wannna, wannna rap with you.
Hey!

SUNDIATA:

When you grow up in the country, things are hard, times
   are tough.
Growing your own food but it never seems enough.
You too smart for the country, you got to get away.
Got to move to the city, got to be a better way.
So you move to the city, put the country stuff behind.
But when you hit the city, it starts to messin' with your
   mind.

DUPPI AND SUNDIATA *(Alternating lines)*:

You struggle and you scramble, try to do the best you can.
Think you working for a living? Hell, you working for
   The Man!
People stacked like chickens on the way to meet the
   slaughter.
Flopping all around the ground like fishes out of water.
Blind man on the corner, holding up a sign

(Singing this last line together:)

It says, "No more water, y'all. The fire next time!"

DUPPI: In between this beginning and this ending, he told a
story about black people growing up and living through
Mississippi from the 1930s to the 1960s and how *his* mentor,
Po Tatum, a guy only four years older than he was, inspired
him to become a "Junebug Jabbo Jones Storyteller" fighting
for justice.
   The show was peppered with songs like the ones Po
Tatum sang at different times of his life. There was only one

man on stage, but it felt like I was living through history in living color.

Before he left Pike County, Po fell in love with the idea of himself as a high-rolling, no-limit poker player. When he got there he found out there's a big difference between "no-limit" poker in Cook County, Chicago, and Pike County, Mississippi. On the other hand, the difference in racial justice in northern Illinois and southern Mississippi wouldn't amount to a hill of beans. From all I can figure out, Po had to spend about five years in the Illinois state pen for chasing down this white man for trying to sneak off with about five thousand dollars worth of Po's money!

As you can see, this was some pretty heavy stuff, but the way Junebug told it, it was really funny. These letters he wrote to Junebug while he was in jail give a picture of his progress. Look at this. *(Showing a letter:)*

December 18, 1958

Dear Junebug,

I figured, What the hell? So I signed up to go to college. Bet you didn't know you could do that in jail? The worse they can do if I fail is kick me out of here. Don't I wish! Well, I had to do something to pass the time. So why not try college?

I figured I'd start off easy, so I took this English composition course. It was not as easy as I thought but I came out okay.

I only made a C, but that isn't too bad for a fellow dropped out of the ninth grade, is it?

I met this guy in the library named Robert Watson. You might as well say he volunteered to go to jail because he's in here for what he called a "sitting demonstration" at a private club in Springfield. He's a pre-law student. He went and made a sitting demonstration to test the law that says black folks can't go to places like that. He won't even take bail while his case is still in court.

It sounds dumb to me. I'm getting out of here as quick as I can. What's going on out there? Have people gone crazy?

Your incarcerated friend,
Po

Now compare that to this. This is the first letter that Mr. Walker got from Po. It looks a lot like chicken scratch, doesn't it? It's dated June 1957. The one I just read, dated December 1958, looks like a college student. Clearly Po was a man of great "potential," but like Richard Pryor, he had the habit of doing things the hard way.

Po came out of jail in 1957 a changed man. But the world he came out into was changing too. Little Rock, Arkansas; Montgomery, Alabama . . . In 1960 the sit-ins spread across the South like wild fire. 1961: the Freedom Rides. 1962: major campaigns in Albany, Georgia and Cairo, Illinois. And el-Hajj Malik Shabazz assassinated under cloudy circumstances. Harlem burns. 1963: Bomb-ingham, Alabama. Medgar Evers and John Kennedy, assassinated. 1964: Bobby Kennedy, Martin Luther King. More American cities burn, the whole nation goes up in flames: Memphis, Watts in Los Angeles, Kansas City, Chicago, Detroit, Baltimore, New York, Miami, Atlanta, Washington, DC.

No longer were black people rushing North, East and West to escape from racial disaster of the South, because racial disaster was everywhere. Many came to prefer the disaster they knew to the one they did not know. Some summed up the situation by declaring that:

Chicago is just North Mississippi!
There's no running away!
Chicago is just North Mississippi!
Do you hear what I say?

Miz Consuela was his saving grace. She was his anchor in a raging sea from the time he first met her when he got to

Chicago, during the whole time he was in jail, and after he got out. Like Mama Marese, Miz Consuela was from Haiti. It wasn't long after his parole that Po moved in with her on the 4800 block of Drexel Boulevard.

Whenever he ran into things he hadn't heard of before, he talk with her about it. She'd help him to figure it out. She was working as a full-charge bookkeeper for the Supreme Life Insurance Company when they met in Chicago, and was studying to become a certified public accountant. Consuela convinced him that poker was not a reliable way for him to send money home to his family, because the odds in poker were always heavily in favor of the one in the game with the biggest bankroll.

First, he worked as an employment counselor with other ex-cons. Soon he had organized an urban gardening project to reclaim abandoned lots in the city, and that soon developed into food co-ops that he called Development of International Gardens in Chicago ("DIG in Chicago!" You dig it?)

At first the DIG in Chicago project was going great. They had three gardens and a big co-op farmers' market on the South Side and they got ten big gardens and a good-sized market on the West Side. But, by Summer of 1966, the stuff hit the fan. Po didn't know that the wholesale food business in Chicago was controlled by the mob at the time. They made Po and his gang one of those famous "offers you can't refuse":

MESSENGER: So dig up, buddy. The Family told me to make you an offer you can't refuse, you dig? Ain't nothing I can do but bring a message, take a message, and give you's boys my opinion if you's boys is interested, ya see? But it ain't my deal, y'see? I am nothing but a messenger. Ya dig?

Good! So here's the deal it ain't nothing I can do but tell you what it is, you dig? Okay, here it is: the Family will give you one hundred percent of the expenses of the business, in advance, to be repaid at the end of the season at a flat ten-percent-compounded-daily, to do all the bookkeeping and banking in return for sixty-five percent of the profits.

Failure to comply with the terms of this agreement and the "borrower"—that's you: the "borrower"—forfeits all right to gain. All arguments will be submitted to the Family for final resolution. Okay?

PO TATUM: Hell, no! You tell your Boss that slavery is what we fought the Civil War about!

MESSENGER: I'm stoned down with you man, brother, brother man! Dig it! Remember that I'm just a messenger, you dig? Mother—no! I mean—no—Jesus, Mary and Joseph! Oh my God! I'm getting too old for this work! *(He takes a pill)*

PO TATUM: We left sharecropping when we left Mississippi. You tell your Boss to take this so-called "loan" and shove it up where the sun don't shine!

SUNDIATA: The next morning they found Po's best organizer in the middle of their biggest garden . . . dead. Had a single .22-caliber bullet hole in the back of his head.

The day after that, the City of Chicago took over all the lots they had gardens on and arrested all the parolees working on the project for "consorting with known criminals."

DUPPI: That killed the DIG project, but Po tried to stay strong for his boys. And Miz Consuela tried to stay strong for Po.

A lot of the guys in the DIG movement didn't have decent places to stay.

SUNDIATA: Po organized those who didn't have parole to worry about, and started squatting in empty, run-down buildings, fixing them up and stuff. Well, that movement caught on too. By March of '68 it looked like things were going pretty good again, but once more the ceiling crashed in on them. Once more, the city moved in on them. Long-standing court cases were decided in favor of the city and the DIG squatters were kicked out of their homes.

After that, for weeks at a time, Po would not leave Miz Consuela's house on Drexel Boulevard. Miz Consuela and Junebug both really got worried about him.

DUPPI: Junebug had come to Chicago that summer because of his work for the Mississippi Freedom Democratic Party. They were organizing to get the MFDP recognized as the fairest representative of the Democratic Party in Mississippi. Their strategy was to expose the immorality of the Democratic National Convention. They lost control over the plans for (and gave over to) the young white *kids* who thought they knew more about what to do than the MFDP did. Junebug and them let it go. They knew that they were in over their heads. The white kids had no idea what they were up against. They saw the cops, the Illinois National Guard, the FBI, and all the others, but I guess they didn't believe that they would use all those weapons on them, especially with the media from around the whole world there. Their slogan was: "The Whole World Is Watching!" *The whole world is watching!*

SUNDIATA: And they were right about that much. The whole world was watching as the troops waded into the crowd with tear gas, billy clubs, horses, tanks, planes, helicopters, water canons, bullets, and everything else you can imagine. It was awful!

Since then I've gone back to look at television footage of what happened while those poor little white kids from all over the world were smoking dope, wearing flowers, singing and dancing like it was some kind of party going on.

DUPPI: Mr. Walker said he was looking at it on TV when, on the local news, up popped Po Tatum!

NEWSMAN: Why are you trying to take over all these South Side Chicago buildings?

PO TATUM: There's thousands of people with no place to stay, and right now these empty buildings are nothing but shooting galleries for a bunch of junkies.

NEWSMAN: But what you're doing is illegal, isn't it?

PO TATUM: What is happening here now is immoral and destructive to the life of this community. We're trying to liberate these buildings.

NEWSMAN: Mr. Tatum, isn't it true that you're blocking the rightful owners from acquiring permits for rehabilitation?

PO TATUM: These buildings have been vacant for years. Why do you think these damn landlords just started this stuff when we started this action?

NEWSMAN: Who is this "we" you refer to, sir? Isn't it true that you represent no real constituency?

PO TATUM: That's not true. I represent the people.

NEWSMAN: Isn't that rather vague, sir? And isn't it true, Mr. Tatum, that you were recently released from Joliet State Prison on charges of attempted manslaughter, jailbreaking, illegal gambling, and a variety of other charges?

PO TATUM: What the hell has that got to do with anything?

NEWSMAN: There you have it, ladies and gentlemen. We taped this interview earlier today with Mr. Phillip A. Tatum at the site of a building on Drexel Boulevard that he's trying to "liberate." We have just learned that Mr. Tatum has occupied the building, he is believed to be armed, and is considered extremely dangerous. We will update the story as the situation develops . . . Meanwhile, at the Democratic Convention . . .

(Duppi tells the story of what Junebug did when he heard about Po Tatum. He also plays Junebug in the story.)

DUPPI: Junebug hit the street flying! Chica-Chica-Chica-Chica-Chica-Chica-Chica-Chica-Boom-Boom! It was a hell of a storm blowing in off the lake:

    (As Junebug) "It'll take too long! Taxi!"

    "Taxi!"

    "Drexel and 47th. Quick! Man. Quick!"

    (Himself) Clap of thunder split the sky! Cop cars scre-e-e-eaming around the corner!

    (As Junebug) "Flashing lights ahead."

    "Uh-oh! Something's wrong!"

    (Himself) Strange . . . Police . . . Blockades . . . A sea of Blues! Police squat down behind they cars. Guns pulled! People milling around like it's a show going on.

SUNDIATA *(As bystander voices)*: "It's a crazy nigger holed up in that building."

    "Yeah, they going to kill a coon today."

DUPPI *(As Junebug)*: "Let me through."

SUNDIATA *(As bystander voices)*: "What's he trying to do?"

    "I don't know."

DUPPI *(As Junebug)*: "Let me through!!!"

(Back to telling the story of what happened) The newspapers said it was Po that fired the first shot. That old building, which wasn't too strong in the first place, just come tumbling down when the police opened fire. It took them three days to clear away the rubble of that building and find the two bodies that was left in there. One of them looked like it might be Po except for one thing. Miz Consuela swore Po left home that morning with a clean red shirt on. The body they found had on a green shirt.

Miz Consuela and Mr. Walker took what was thought to be Po's remains, put them in the best coffin they could afford and took it to Mississippi. They buried it in a grave in The Bottom beside Po's ma and pa.

You could have heard a pin drop when Mr. Walker laid the red shawl that represented Phillip Anthony "Po" Tatum in the trunk that represented his coffin.

I turned my head so Rose Marie wouldn't see the tears rolling down my cheeks. I don't know about the others who were doing it, but I was crying for the death of a man that I just knew had to have been my father!

There were just one or two small problems:

According to Mama Marese I was born in Port au Prince, Haiti in 1974. According to Junebug, his man had died in August of 1968 in Chicago.

A few moments passed in silence. Somebody down front jumped up and started clapping. Junebug came out and invited anybody who wanted to stay around and talk.

ROSE: How'd you like the children's stories?

SUNDIATA: It's all right. Naw. Naw, don't let me lie—it was good! Damn good! But they aren't children's stories.

ROSE: I didn't say they were children's stories. You said that.

SUNDIATA: Rose, I got to meet this man. Do you think that his stories are true?

ROSE: No reason to doubt him as far as I can see. He got the historical information right anyway.

SUNDIATA: We made our way to the stage. When he spotted me he looked like he'd seen a ghost or something.

JUNEBUG: Boy, if you ain't the spitting image of Po Tatum!

SUNDIATA: Po Tatum? Me?

Nobody had ever told me that I looked like anybody before. He wanted to talk to me as much as I wanted to talk to him. We—Junebug, Rose Marie and I—went to eat together and the three of us hung out that whole night talking. We were still sitting in the diner in Hyde Park when the news came on the TV of the two planes crashing into the Twin Towers.

We had both been scheduled to fly out the next day but clearly nobody would be flying *anywhere* that whole week after 9-1-1-0-1. So Rose Marie and I spent the time with Junebug talking about what had happened in New York, what was going on in the Middle East, and whether Po Tatum could have been my daddy.

I really didn't want to leave Chicago. Let me correct myself—I didn't want to leave Rose Marie and Mr. Walker. They were both certain that Phillip Anthony Tatum was my daddy, but the known facts didn't add up.

What happened to Po in that confrontation with the cops in Chicago in 1968? Did Po survive the shootout with the Chicago police? What happened then? Who was buried in that coffin?

My life would never be the same.

The last time we saw Mr. Walker that week, he gave me this box.

MR. WALKER: This right here is all the stuff I've been able to keep from my old buddy, Po. I had the idea in my mind to make a book or something of it. But now, since meeting you, I think it'd be more fitting for you to have it to do whatever you think best. There're thirteen letters from Po Tatum and one from Miz Consuela, which seems like it ought be there too. This is the wrapping paper it came in. I guess they put this old newspaper on to help keep the Cuban cigars that came in it fresh. 'Course the cigars are long gone. But if you want these things you're welcome to them.

(He hands him a wooden cigar box, carefully wrapped in brown paper. He opens it. Two layers of a Haitian newspaper are inside,

used as an inner layer to protect the hand-rolled Cuban cigars that
came in it. On its lid is a rendition of the Sankofa emblem, which
Tous wears around his neck.)

I got the box in October of '76 from Teddy Marchand, a
merchant marine that I knew. He said a skinny Haitian guy
named Phillippe, who knew that he was from New Orleans,
gave him fifty dollars to deliver it. That was a hell of a lot of
money in Haiti in those days.

SUNDIATA: Po Tatum, he was a like a good ballplayer who doesn't
know the difference between being *in sync* with the team
and *being* the team. I could see myself heading in that direction. Still, the more I learn about him, the more I like him.
He was really committed to the fight for justice. And the
main woman in Po Tatum's life was Consuela Lebeaux,

DUPPI: As I packed to leave, I told Rose Marie, "I'm going to Pike
County. I have to know if I'm connected to these people."

ROSE: Did you intend to leave this newspaper?

DUPPI: Naw, but it looks like it was just stuffing. I don't think it
matters much.

ROSE: It could be important. Do you mind if I hold on to it? It
will be like holding on to a piece of you.

DUPPI: You've already got the most important part of me, Rose
Marie. You've got my heart.

She smiled. We kissed. I walked out the door to the taxi
that was waiting.

When I got to New Orleans I didn't even go home, I went
directly to McComb. I got a room at the Holiday Inn. Late
as it was, I took a drive around town to get the feel of the
place. As I drove around that night, something about the
place felt familiar to me.

(Duppi sings "Chicago Is Just North Mississippi":)

Black folk up North, trying to build a bigger kitty,
People young and old moving to the nitty-gritty.
One day you here, the next day it's a pity,
Country culture in the city, got to keep it all with me.

Everybody that you run into is acting all siditty,
Children hustling and bustling in the city-pimping diddy.
Every nationality assimilates to the way
The lust for money substitutes for honey
While the city falls in decay, I say:

(Duppi and Sundiata sing the chorus together:)

DUPPI AND SUNDIATA:
Chicago is just North Mississippi,
We keep running away.

DUPPI: When I got back to the Holiday Inn, I needed to talk to
Rose Marie. She sounded a little sleepy when she answered
the phone. "I hope it's not too late to be calling."
ROSE: I was hoping you would call. In fact, I was waiting on you.
DUPPI: In that exact moment whatever barriers I might have had
left around my heart started their final fall. Although there
were eight hundred miles between us, I felt the warmth of
her embrace take the chill out of the sheets on the hotel
bed. It was like she was there with me. The smell of vanilla
filled the room. A living vision of her filled the space about
me no matter where I placed my eyes. I missed her, but
I was not lonely. The words I found to tell her how she made
me feel were simply too thin, too pale to carry the message
across the telephone line to where she was. So for the next
hour we talked about what had happened: "Even though
I grew up right next door in Louisiana, I guess I don't have
a very realistic picture of Mississippi in my mind."
ROSE: That happens to a lot of people when they get to Mississippi. Let me know what happens when you meet the
Tatum family tomorrow.
DUPPI: You better believe I will!
The phone line filled up with silence. I felt awkward.
Here I was a poet, a rapper, "the next big sensation," and
all the words that I could think of seemed only to cheapen
what I knew we both were feeling. I wanted to say, "I love

you." I wanted to hear her say that she loved me. The phone filled up with silence. Finally I said, "I guess I better crash. It'll be a big day tomorrow and you got to go to work."

ROSE: Toussaint . . .

DUPPI: Yeah?

ROSE: I'll dream of you.

DUPPI: Thank you so much, Rose.

ROSE: *Good night, chéri.*

DUPPI: Good night.

When I got to Magnolia the next morning I drove around town for a while just looking at houses. Some sections looked a lot like some of the older houses in Treme where I grew up. I stopped to ask this old man sitting on a soda pop case in front of a convenience store how to get out to the Tatum place.

MR. WEDDERBURN: Which Tatum you want? Jimmy Tatum owns this place right here, his wife LeeEsther runs it *now*. Jimmy's cousin, M.L. owns the feed and grain company up in McComb. He worked there for years for old Colonel J. C. Whitten and his brother. Neither one of the Whittens had any children, so when they died, M.L. went to court and got hold of it. Jimmy's nephew, Malik, is the principal of the elementary school and—

DUPPI: It sounds like half the people in town are Tatums.

MR. WEDDERBURN: Might near it.

DUPPI: What about Skinhead?

MR. WEDDERBURN: Oh, Skinhead? He's the best carpenter around these parts since his daddy died. Old Man Jake Tatum got hit by a bolt of lightning when I was a young boy. He was up on a tin-roofed barn trying to hook up a lightning rod for Skinhead's brother when he was a child. They called him "Po." I didn't know him either, but I seen him once, when he came home for his mama's funeral. He must a been about your age now when he did that. From what I recollect, you look a lot like him . . . My name is Junior Wedderburn. Pleased to meet you.

DUPPI: I'm Toussaint. Toussaint Antonio Duplessis.

MR. WEDDERBURN: You kin to the Tatums?

DUPPI: I really don't know for true. If I go down to The Bottoms, you think I'll find Mr. Skinhead out there?

MR. WEDDERBURN: He'll be there all right. You reckon you know how to get there.

DUPPI: Junebug said I should go south on County Road 1712 toward Four Corners. When I get to the New Mount Zion Church, circle the graveyard there to get the New Caledonia Road, heading out toward Seven Waters. Stay on that for about twelve miles. Pass the hairpin turn at Dead Man's Bend, keep on past the Devil Crossroads to the Twin Oaks—

MR. WEDDERBURN: So you know Junebug?

DUPPI: Yes, sir. I met him last week in Chicago.

MR. WEDDERBURN: A good man, that Junebug. He told you right except for one thing. Last year one of the Twin Oaks died, so if you get to the little white house beside a big red barn where Aunt Callie used to live, you done gone too far—

DUPPI: I figured that I'd better get while the getting was good. Mr. Wedderburn had plenty to say and was just getting warmed up.

"I believe I can make it, Mr. Wedderburn. Thank you, very much."

I followed that trail for several twisty miles through a swamp so thick that at times I couldn't tell where the road was. In his story the week before, Mr. Walker had told about how this place had been the headquarters for Indians and runaway slaves who fought against white people back in the day. I could easily see how nobody could have gotten ambushed up in there.

Finally, I came to an opening. There was this big, three-story house that looked like a mansion! I couldn't believe what I was seeing! I stopped the car and just sat there. When I opened the door to get out, a group of about six dogs with motley markings of black, white, brown and tan seemed to come from nowhere. They had me surrounded at about twenty to thirty feet. The hair stood up on their backs and I could hear them growling low to make it clear that I shouldn't move. The big, gray, muzzled one barked a little, like he was calling somebody.

A big man, who looked like a brown-skinned Mr. Clean, came out of the barn with some hickory splits on his shoulder. He nodded and the dogs moved off.

SKINHEAD: I was beginning to think you didn't make it pass the sinkholes out there. Grab another one or two of those logs. Just drop them down over here. Yeah, Po could have spit you out all right.

DUPPI: A side of pork, some beef ribs, about ten chickens, and some other stuff was laid out on a huge construction of brick and mortar that looked like a little house with its own little patio with benches and tabletops built in. Skinhead saw me notice the shotgun and a military style automatic rifle leaning on one corner of the structure.

SKINHEAD: The Catahoula hounds are pretty good, but we got all kinds of varmints around here. You can't be too careful.

I'm Jacob Freeman Tatum, II. Around here people call me Skinhead. I reckon you'd be Toussaint Antonio Duplessis?

DUPPI: How'd you know?

SKINHEAD: Everybody knows everybody out here in the country. Our survival depends on it. Plus Little David told me you was coming.

DUPPI: I'm not used to being known like that. Living in the city in a one-room flat, you're just one among many, just another rat.

SKINHEAD: You just like my baby brother all right. He'd make rhymes like that all the times!

DUPPI: You did it too.

SKINHEAD: I did? I guess I do. You looked like you was kinda surprised to see our house.

DUPPI: Shocked would be more like it.

Skinhead: Most people are, the first time they see it. Colonel Whitten hired Dan Skinner to bring a gang of white sheets down here and burn everything to the ground on the first of November in 1951. We was lucky enough to get everybody out without nobody being hurt. I been working to bring it back like Daddy wanted it ever since. The "other man" can't stand for nobody to get ahead.

DUPPI: He showed me around the whole place. It's a really beautiful Victorian with eight bedrooms, a double parlor, dining room, and a big kitchen with a screened-in porch on the ground floor. A two-car garage connected with the kitchen. He had rebuilt the barn too and put the handmade weather vane that his father had made for Po on top of it. "I heard Mr. Walker tell this story in Chicago last week. He said your daddy used to make Po sit at the kitchen table and read the Webster's dictionary—"

SKINHEAD: Thorndike-Barnhart. I never will forget that, Thorndike-Barnhart dictionary book! That's why Daddy had to build that weather vane, 'cause money was hard to come by during the Depression and he couldn't afford to buy one.

DUPPI: Junebug said a bolt of blood red lightning came out of nowhere to hit Mr. Jake and kill him.

SKINHEAD: Junebug got that right. He's dead before he hit the ground. The body almost landed on young Po. Po wasn't but twelve years old at the time, but he thought it was his fault what happened.

(Skinhead stops to hear a dog bark. The dog barks again—one, then three times. After a couple of seconds the dog barks the same pattern again.)

Here come Ralph and his wife and grandchild. We might as well set up the ice box. They'll have the cold drinks with them.

DUPPI: How'd you know that?

SKINHEAD: Ol' Blue. He said they's one car with three people in it. Ralph and his family are the ones most likely to come in a group of three. I'd be surprised if it's anybody else—they always come early.

DUPPI: After that I watched to see if Skinhead was telling the truth or just "funning" me. Every time I noticed, Ol' Blue was right about the number of people coming. Soon they had a whole yard full of Tatums. They ran from infants to great-grandparents and most all of them looked like me. More important, I *felt* like I fit in. I was the center of attention. Everybody was talking about how much I looked like Po, and was telling stories about him.

The older ones talked about how nice Po was as a youngster, how everybody liked him, and how his daddy had decided he would be "the one to put their family on a new foot stand," how he turned "sour" when Mr. Jake got killed and Miz Adeline "lost herself." For all the stories that Mr. Walker had told and all the songs that he had come up with, there were dozens of other stories told that day. The younger ones had made up their own songs about the stories that they had heard told time and time again.

Some of them had taken what seemed like different chapters of Po's life and picked up the verses of the songs that Junebug had sung and made it like it was all one song.

(He sings:)

Going to Chicago, baby,
Heading for the city.
Going to Chicago, baby,
Heading for the city.

Chica-Chica-Chica-Chica-Chica-Chicago
Chica-Chica-Chica-Chica-Chica-Chicago
Chica-Chica-Chica-Chica-Chica-Chicago
I'm gonna get the Northbound train.

I'm going to the city
Where the women's really pretty,
And they tell me that the money falls like rain.
I'm tired of picking cotton,
Mississippi's gotten rotten,
Gonna pack my bag and jump the quickest train.

Going to Chicago, baby,
Heading for the city.
Going to Chicago, baby,
Heading for the city.

Chica-Chica-Chica-Chica-Chica-Chicago
Chica-Chica-Chica-Chica-Chica-Chicago
Chica-Chica-Chica-Chica-Chica-Chicago
I'm gonna get the Northbound train.

The old freight train's a rocking,
My aching head's a popping,
Need me something just to ease the pain.
Had to leave my home and family,
'Cause this crazy cracker jammed me,
I'm going and I won't be back again.

Going to Chicago, baby, heading for the city.
Going to Chicago, baby, heading for the city.
Chica-Chica-Chica-Chica-Chica-Chicago
Chica-Chica-Chica-Chica-Chica-Chicago
Chica-Chica-Chica-Chica-Chica-Chicago
I done gone and caught the Northbound train.

My mama just died,
My dad's a long time gone.
I'm out here on the highway all a doggone lone.
I'm digging like a dog for his very last bone
Living for the city
Trying to make a new home.

I'm talking Chica-Chica-Chica-Chica-Chica-Chicago
Chica-Chica-Chica-Chica-Chica-Chicago
Chica-Chica-Chica-Chica-Chica-Chicago
I'm out here on the road all alone.
So long, y'all. So long, home.

SKINHEAD: Hey, Skeeter! Run around to the front yard and tell
your grandpa I said to come on, the soup's on.
DUPPI: Ralph and most of the other elders in the family were
sitting in the rocking chairs on the front porch of the big
house. Ralph stood up and said, "Thank you, baby. You go
tell your grandpa we'll be there in a minute." As he sang
others joined in. I followed at a distance.

RALPH *(Singing)*:

> Will the circle be unbroken
> By and by, Lord, by and by?
> There's a better home awaiting
> In the sky, Lord, in the sky.
>
> I was sitting by my window
> On a dark and rainy day
> When I saw the hearse wheels rolling,
> Come to take my mother away.
>
> Undertaker, undertaker,
> Undertaker please drive slow
> 'Cause the one that you are driving,
> Lord, I hate to see her go.

Let us pray. We bow our heads and humble our hearts and stretch forth our hands to the spirit that brings life and takes it away to and from everything and everybody. We are grateful to be here and to have this opportunity to give thanks to all who have come before and who have gifted us with the example of your lives. We're asking y'all to be with us and stand by us now and in the future as you have been with us and stood by us in the hours of our greatest need.

You been fathers to the fatherless. You been mothers to the motherless. You been our battle ax in the time of battle, our shelter in the wintry storm. You have been our all in all.

We're asking y'all to pay particular attention to this young man who comes as a new relative whether by the direct tics of blood and kinship or by the bonds of our common humanity and the love of justice for all our relatives scattered near and far throughout the universe known and unknown. Aid him in his journey. Throw your strong arms of protection about him as he goes on his way. Arm him and us with the knowledge that his struggle is our struggle, as the struggle for justice is one.

Consecrate the food we're about to receive that you all have provided us with the means to acquire. We pray for all

those who have worked so hard to prepare it for us. We pray
for the souls of those plants and animals who had to die for
us to have this celebration today. May we further consecrate
what we eat (their sacrifice) by using the energy that it pro-
duces in us to increase the joy and to decrease the suffering
in the world.

And finally, we beg for your active presence among us
today and for more of the love that runs from heart to heart
and from breast to breast.

If anyone else wants to add anything, now is the time . . .
Hearing none, let us all say amen.

Brother Toussaint, Skinhead is famous for his barbecue,
so it goes fast. If you want any, you better try to beat me
down the hill.

DUPPI: The festivities continued late into the night. By the time
everyone had left most of the cleaning had been done. But
while I helped Skinhead's twin grandchildren clean up,
Skinhead dozed in a rocking chair. Ol' Blue, with one ear
standing straight up like a soldier, looked like he was resting
at Skinhead's feet. I sat quietly across from them.

SKINHEAD: You boys help Mr. Duplessy pour that tub of ice left
over from the beer and soda pop on the coals in the barbecue pit. Then y'all go on upstairs and go to bed. I don't want
to hear no racket up there either!

DUPPI: I watched the glowing embers on the barbecue pit cool
down. The wet embers crackled, sputtered and made steam.
The night birds sang their evening songs. Frogs croaked.
The crickets sang. In the far distance, more dogs barked.
Ol' Blue stirred ever so slightly.

SKINHEAD: Everybody loved you, boy.

DUPPI: I love them too.

SKINHEAD: You fit in good . . . for a city boy.

DUPPI: Yeah. It feels good. Real good . . . for a city boy, you know.

SKINHEAD: Ol' Blue likes you too.

DUPPI: Yeah.

SKINHEAD: I think that mess at the graveyard is kind of strange
though. I don't go up there any more. Ralph up there talking to dead people! They ain't paying him no mind.

DUPPI: You aren't nervous living so close to all these dead people?
SKINHEAD: I don't care nothing about no dead people. It's the
living that can hurt you.

(Pause.)

DUPPI: Skinhead . . .
SKINHEAD: Yeah?
DUPPI: I . . .
SKINHEAD: Yeah?
DUPPI: I don't think that it's Po buried up there in that grave
with his name on it.
SKINHEAD: You don't?
DUPPI: No, I don't. The fellow in that grave just didn't say any-
thing to me . . . I couldn't feel anything . . . you know what
I mean?
SKINHEAD: 'Course he didn't say nothing to you, he's dead!
Humph! You just like Ralph, going around here thinking
you can talk to dead people! Jesus Lord, help!
DUPPI: Thought you didn't talk to dead people. *(Pause)* Jesus
died over two thousand and five years ago, didn't he?
SKINHEAD: You hear that, Blue? Don't start no mess, boy, it won't
be no mess.

(Pause.)

Anyway, you ain't the first one to wonder about who it was
in that coffin. In the shoot-out Po had with the cops up in
Chicago, they messed up the body so bad they had to have
a closed coffin funeral. Miz Lebeaux was in a big hurry to
get him in the ground. Then she made haste to get out of
here the same day. Junebug said she had to get back to Haiti
where she come from.
No sir, you wouldn't be the first to wonder.
DUPPI: I called Rose and tried to tell her what it was like to find
the Tatum family. We talked 'til 3:30 in the morning.
ROSE: You going home tomorrow?

DUPPI: Yeah. I got to get ready to go to work next week. Why?

ROSE: What time you plan to get there?

DUPPI: I don't know. Why?

ROSE: It's been over a week since I've seen you. If I get there on the 3:25 P.M. will you be able to pick me up?

DUPPI: *That's beautiful, chéri!* I'll be there even if I have to fly!

ROSE: Let me do the flying. You just get there when you can. I don't mind waiting . . . for you.

DUPPI: That night I slept like a baby and had the sweetest dreams . . . The next morning at breakfast:

SKINHEAD: That lady, Miz Consuela, who brought Po home for burial, her and Junebug stayed with me. I was living in Four Corners at the time. This place wasn't fit to live in until '75. I told Junebug she left some expensive-looking jewelry here. He told me, "Just keep it. If it's important, she'll probably call for it." She ain't never called. It's too nice to throw away. I dug it out this morning. You might figure out what to do with it.

DUPPI: That's the same Sankofa symbol of the box of letters that Mr. Walker gave me. It symbolizes the importance of how we must sometimes look back in order to go forward.

SKINHEAD: Sounds like some more of that African mumbo-jumbo to me.

DUPPI: The next morning, as I made my way down I-10 back to New Orleans, I was certain that I had found major clues about my own history and a new family, whether by ties of blood and kinship, or by the bonds of our common humanity and the love of justice for all our relatives scattered near and far throughout the universe known and unknown.

As I chugged on down the highway, my mind settled on the song Mr. Walker closed his show with:

You can't judge a book by looking at the cover.
You can read my letter but I bet you can't read my mind.
If you want to get down, down, down, you got to spend
   some time.
I want to walk with you,

I want to talk with you,
I wanna, wanna, wanna, wanna rap with you.
Hey!

I didn't want to leave the Tatum mansion hidden in the swamp, but I was so excited about Rose Marie's first trip to the city that I loved. We ate dinner at Dookey Chase's Restaurant. Then I took her to my favorite place on the Mississippi River. The yellow moon was big and fat. It shimmered off the river.

I dropped a five-dollar bill in the case of this guitar player who was playing just for us on the levee.

She wrapped her shawl around her shoulders as we settled on the metal bench by the River Song sculpture. Its silver petals waved gracefully in the evening breeze. "I hope it not too chilly for you."

ROSE: We've already had our first frost in Chicago. It's just a little breezy that's all.

DUPPI: I ordered the breeze so you would have to sit close to me.

(Pause.)

ROSE: If you'd really wanted to be close to me, we would have been home by now. Not that I don't want to know about the city that has done so much to bring you to where you are . . . as Chicago has helped to shape me.

DUPPI: His family really loves him. He was really committed to "the revolution" too.

ROSE: When he found The Movement, he got a foundation to stand on.

DUPPI: Yeah, It's like when you find a purpose in life, the whole world just opens up to you. But there're plenty of new mysteries too: What happened to Po in that confrontation with the police in Chicago in 1968? If it wasn't Po, who was buried in that coffin? Why was Miz Consuela so anxious to leave after the funeral? Who was Mama Marese to me? Did she send her that letter? Was that letter about me?

ROSE: What about your mama? You can't have a daddy without a mama . . .

DUPPI: Mama Marese?

ROSE: No. I'm talking about your *birth* mama. You're so busy trying to find your daddy and his revolutionary struggle, you're forgetting about your mama? If, in fact, Phillip Anthony Tatum is your daddy, he couldn't have turned his life around to become the man he seems to have become without your mama.

DUPPI: What up? What you trying to say, Rose?

ROSE: Revolution or relationships, in the final analysis, it's all about love.

(Rose sings:)

When you give yourself over to a thing
That is greater than yourself,
You find yourself a song to sing
That leaves nothing on the shelf.
Then you find yourself on a shining path,
You find a peace more powerful than knowing.
It settles deep down in your soul,
You find a light within you glowing.
Even in the darkest night,
You know you've found your goal.
Still there's something more you hunger for,
You know you need to be made whole.

It's not just how long you fight,
It's not even that you win,
It's not about the hype,
It's not about the shape you're in.
It's not "You're wrong!" "I'm right!"
It's not being thick or thin,
It's not money in the bank,
It's not who you have to thank.
The final analysis is
It's all about love.

DUPPI: Now you can see the picture that was taking shape in my mind. Mississippi, New Orleans, Chicago, Haiti, David Walker aka Junebug Jabbo Jones, Phillip Anthony "Po" Tatum, Miz Consuela and me—Toussaint Antonio.

ROSE: You remember the Haitian newspaper Mr. Walker wrapped the letters in? You were going to throw it away, said it was just wrapping?

DUPPI: Yeah. Mr. Walker said he got the box in the fall of 1976 from a merchant marine he knew here in New Orleans. It was filled with a bunch of Cuban cigars. The sailor said that a skinny black American in Port-au-Prince named "Phillippe," who was also from New Orleans gave him fifty dollars to deliver it.

ROSE: Well, I had a French-speaking friend of mine to look at it. One section of the paper included some birth notices. One of them was about the birth of a Toussaint Antonio to Mrs. C. Lebeaux and her husband Phillipe Tatum on August 22, 1975.

DUPPI: Why didn't you tell me?!

ROSE: You've hardly let me catch my breath since I first got off the plane. Besides, I was waiting to show to you when we got home.

DUPPI: That would explain a lot, wouldn't it?

(Rose's friend: a recorded voice in French.)

1 Novembre, 1977
Port-au-Prince, Haiti

My dear, dear friend,

It is impossible for you to know how much I appreciate what you are doing. There is no place in our beloved homeland that may be considered safe for those who value freedom. The merest peasant on the smallest rocky plot of land on the tallest mountain in the most forlorn and desolate part of our lovely island who even breathes the name of freedom in his dreams—that peasant is not safe from the vengeance of les infant Duvalier l'terrible—I refuse to grant him the honorific appellation, "Doctor." He uses the Tonton Macoute to satisfy his macabre personal vendettas. No one who opposes the wicked excesses of the regime is safe. He trades the health, wealth and welfare of the Haitian people for the mere pittance that is represented by the anachronistic pretense to the standards of European royalty. All this decadent extravagance is bought and paid for by the government of the United States of America. Your government has recently increased its support for the pitiful petty tyrant.

Shame. Shame. Shame.

Please forgive that I use these precious moments to vent my spleen, not for your information, but so that I can feel better for having said it.

You probably will not hear from us again unless we win. "In revolution, one wins or dies."

If it must be so. My dearest one and I are ready to give our lives in this struggle for human dignity and the welfare of our dear Haiti and her forlorn, yet still heroic, people. But we are unwilling to foreclose our connection to the future by condemning our gift from the ancestors. That is why we are both willing to pass the gift of our love on to you, and are honored that you are willing to become the parent and protector of the child that we were blessed to bear.

Be wary of the Tonton Macoute, for they have a long reach and are supported by the government of the United States.

Thank you profoundly for the generosity of your spirit. We know how you have longed for a child of your own.

Best wishes for success in the journey upon which you have embarked.

Pray for Haiti and for your friends who struggle here.

C. L.

"It's All about Love . . ."

(Duppi sings:)

When you give yourself over to a thing
That is greater than yourself,
You find yourself a song to sing
That leaves nothing on the shelf.
Then you find yourself on a shining path,
You find a peace more powerful than knowing,
It settles deep down in your soul,
You find a light within you glowing.
Even in the darkest night,
You know you've found your goal.
Still there's something more, for you hunger for,
You know you need to be made whole.

It's not just how long you fight,
It's not even that you win,
It's not about the hype,
It's not about the shape you're in.
It's not, "You're wrong!" "I'm right!"
It's not being thick or thin,
It's not money in the bank,
It's not who all you have to thank.
The final analysis is "It's all about love."

You think about where you've come from,
All those who've gone before,
And where it is you're going.
You think about the many wrongs
That they have fought and borne.
There are times we know
When selfish greed prevails,
When all that's just and fair
Is martyred, locked up in jails.

You know the painful time will come
When the price is charged in blood.
You know that there'll be times you'd rather run

241

Than to face the fearsome flood.
There will be times when the selfish and the greedy
Use bald-faced lies and bold deceptions
To get the hungry and the needy
To take up arms and to provide elaborate conceptions
To justify their deceit.

It's necessary, but not sufficient, to believe you're right,
To raise the force to fight and maybe even win.
It's necessary, but not sufficient, to study military might
To master history, politics, science; the ways of enemies
     and friends.
It's good, but still not good enough, to learn math and
     chemistry, literature and art,
Architecture, economics, agriculture, engineering, physics,
The healing arts and such and such.
All these things and more contribute to the part:
That we need to build a just society. Then build it again
     and again.
But none of this means a thing
If whatever we do is not grounded in true love for our-
     selves and others.
No matter what else we've learned, their respect must be
     earned
Over and over and over and over again.
'Cause in the final analysis, "It's all about love."

*(Duppi and Sundiata reprise "You Can't Judge a Book by Looking
at the Cover":)*

DUPPI AND SUNDIATA *(Sing)*:
     I told you a story 'bout my old man Po.
     Things he had to do, places he had to go.
     Homeboy going out to try to get some money.
     If it hadn't been so sad, it might have been so very funny.
     Told all about the way that he was misunderstood,
     His family and his friends thought that he was just a hood.
     Told how the man misunderstood himself.

He went to get some knowledge, left the book up on the
  shelf.
He got the cover off the book, but didn't get what it had
  in it.
What should have took a week, he tried to get it in a
  minute.

You can't judge a book by looking at the cover.
You can read my letter but I bet you can't read my mind.
If you want to get down, down, down, you got to spend
  some time.
I want to walk with you,
I want to talk with you,
I wanna, wanna, wanna, wanna rap with you.
Hey!

When you grow up in the country, things are hard, times
  are tough.
Growing your own food but it never seems enough.
You think you too smart for the country. You got to get
  away.
Got to move to the city, got to be a better way.
So you move to the city, put the country stuff behind.
But when you hit the city, it starts to messing with your
  mind.
You struggle and you scramble, just to do the best you can.
Think you working for a living? Hell, you working for
  The Man!
People stacked like chickens on the way to meet the
  slaughter.
Flopping all around the ground like fishes out of water.
Blind man on the corner, holding up a sign
It says, "No more water, y'all. The fire next time!"

You're running through the world, trying to make yourself a life,
You be digging on your people, you see their struggle
  and their strife.

JOHN O'NEAL

You think you're slicing through your problems like a
  hot butter-cutting knife,
But all of the time you know that something's missing
  from your life.
You try to find the hope, you try with all your might!
You get enough to work with, you think your game is
  really tight.

Then the roots you thought were dead and gone, come
  back blasting through,
You've got a life that's all brand-new.
I hope my story brings some hope to you.
Do you hear what I've said?

THE END

244

SECTION 2

Like Poison Ivy

Indigo Variations

———————

Production and Performance History

Like Poison Ivy: Indigo Variations premiered in New Orleans, LA, in August 2003. The play was written by John O'Neal, directed by Steve Kent, who also served as dramaturg and designer. The composer and musical director was Michael Keck. The lights were by Jeff Zielinski for the premiere and by Matt McClane for the touring production; set and props were by Douglas Redd and the costumes were by Theresa Holden. The cast included Linda Parris-Bailey (Antoinette), William O'Neal (Shack), Lloyd Martin (Fess) and Troi Bechet (Celestine). Theresa Holden was the Executive Producer. Other members of Junebug Productions who contributed to *Like Poison Ivy* include Adella Gautier, Michael Holden, Donald Lewis, Leia Lewis, Karen Kaia Livers, Lloyd Martin, Stacey Morton, John Pult, Kenneth Raphael, Frozine Thomas, M. K. Wegmann, Therese Wegman and Angela Winfrey. The music was published by Rythematizism.

The play was co-commissioned by the following organizations who supported the development of the play and its production: The Contemporary Arts Center, New Orleans, Louisiana; The Carpetbag Theatre, Knoxville, Tennessee; and the South Dallas Cultural Center, Dallas, Texas.

Like Poison Ivy grew out of Junebug Productions' 1998 Environmental Justice Festival Project held in New Orleans. It is based on stories collected from people in the Agriculture Street Landfill Community, the Gulf Coast Tenants Association, The Ladies of Treme and "Cancer Alley," the eighty-mile toxic corridor along the Mississippi between New Orleans and Baton Rouge and others in The Environmental Justice Movement who have fought and continue to fight for clean, healthy places to live, work and play. The play celebrates the memory of those who have succumbed to the ravages of environmental racism and celebrates the efforts of all the others who continue the fight for justice.

This play is dedicated to the memory of Kenneth C. Raphael, who died in April 1999. Kenneth was a member of Junebug Productions and he helped to collect the stories upon which some of the characters and the situations in this play are based.

The play has been performed in New Orleans, LA; Knoxville, TN; and Dallas, TX.

—TRH

SETTING AND CHARACTERS

Four actors play the main characters. They are all friends and live in the same neighborhood:

CELESTINE: A beautiful spiritualist, healer and fine singer.
ANTOINETTE: the wise older woman of the neighborhood, called "The Storyteller of Treme."
SHACK: A younger man who is a poet and a union organizer.
FESS: Dr. Norman Jackson, from Nova Scotia, a professor of American history and a preacher. He is called "Fess."

These four characters tell the story of a family affected by environmental racism. The family of Michael Claude Treem, called "Big Mike." During the play, Fess plays "Big Mike." Celestine plays his wife, Maudine. Shack plays their son, Junior. They also play other characters as needed.

Particular attention should be paid to color. Each primary character is associated to the color appropriate to the West African deity to which that character is associated. Since the Senegambian peoples and traditions have been dominant in New Orleans history and culture, we give priority to those traditions. I think of Antoinette as a devotee of Yemanja, or her equivalent, whose colors are blue and green. Shack is associated with Shango, whose colors are red, black and white, etc.

I also wish to honor the traditions of the American Indian nations native to this land. There should be visual imagery that connotes this aspect of our heritage and the libation may be done to honor the six directions.

The setting is primarily a bare stage. A few boxes, benches and chairs are used to create the scenes. At the opening of the play there is an "altar" created from these boxes, draped with a cloth. There is a chalice on the "altar."

Scene 1

Invocation

The pre-show entrance music ends with Willie Mabon's "I'm Just Like Poison Ivy."

Senegambian percussion. The four primary characters move from the house onto the stage. Sister Celestine takes an appropriate chalice from the altar and creates "the vessel of the spirits." Upon the completion of the circle she pours a libation. The vessel is passed on to each person in turn. An African percussion overture continues beneath the ritual.

CELESTINE: This is for all of those living and dead whose lives and efforts make our presence here now possible. We honor all who have gone before because we know that we couldn't have come here by ourselves and that we can't go on from here in the best way without giving honor to their presence in our lives. Blessed are the memories of those who have gone before.

ALL: Ase! Blessed are the memories of those who have gone before.

FESS: Ase! This is for the sixty-six million who started on the Middle Passage and left their bones in the bottom of the sea. *(Pouring another libation)* For the memories of the sixty-six million.

ALL: Ase! For the memories of the sixty-six million.

ANTOINETTE: Ase! We pour a special libation for those among the sixty-six million who chose to go to their watery graves because they believed that it was "better to die for a noble cause, than to live and die a slave." Blessed are the memories of those who have struggled!

ALL: Ase! Blessed are the memories of those who have struggled.

SHACK: Ase! This is for the untold, unnamed millions who suffered through two hundred and forty-four years of chattel slavery, one hundred years of legal segregation, thirty-three years of illegal discrimination, and who, throughout it all, have struggled for justice and kept the flame of hope alive.

ALL: Ase! Blessed are the memories of those who have kept the flame of home alive.

ANTOINETTE: Ase! This is for the mighty Mississippi that cradles our city in her arm like a mother holds her baby to her breast; a river that bears the poison waste of half a nation to the sea. Blessed is the river.

ALL: Ase! Blessed is the river.

FESS: Ase! This is for all of those whose lives are cut short and whose quality of life is reduced because we breathe poison air, drink dirty water, eat food without nutrition, work in dangerous places, and play in pools of pollution. And for all among that number who fight for clean, healthy places to live, work, and play. Blessed are those who struggle.

ALL: Ase! Blessed are those who struggle.

(Percussionist puts a period at the end.)

Scene 2

Introductions

ANTOINETTE: It always hurts me to see y'all spill perfectly good gin on the ground like that.

CELESTINE: It takes real spirits to get real spirits.

ANTOINETTE: You telling me! Gimme that! I need to freshen up my glass.

CELESTINE *(To the audience)*: Better to spill it on the ground than to let it knock us down.

ANTOINETTE: My name is Antoinette Smith. They call me "the Storyteller of Treme," And you know black folks got a whole lot of stories to tell. Good ones too! This here is Narcisse Trudeau—

SHACK: Better known as "Shack Daddy."

ANTOINETTE: "Shack Daddy." Uh-huh! *Narcisse* is a poet and a union organizer.

SHACK: Yeah, you right!

ANTOINETTE: This is Celestine Bernadette Casenave. Sister Celestine is a spiritualist and healer and a fine singer.

CELESTINE: Merci beaucoups, Miz Antoinette. Shack and I were in the first class to go to school in "Miz Antoinette's Backyard." We played "fly the coop," "red light," "double-dutch," singing "Eicho, eicho."

(Celestine and Shack play the games and sing the songs.)

CELESTINE AND SHACK *(Singing)*: "Eicho, eicho, eicho an de! . . ."

ANTOINETTE: Children! . . . Children!

CELESTINE AND SHACK *(Playfully)*: Yes, ma'am.

ANTOINETTE *(Regaining control)*: And y'all are two of my favorite children, baby. Now this here's Reverend Dr. Norman Jackson, from Nova Scotia of all places. He's a professor of American history and a popular pulpit guest at several churches in New Orleans. He's writing a book about Treme. Now anything you want to get straight about the last hundred years or so in Treme, you check with me, okay baby?

FESS: I'll be sure to do that. Now . . . Treme is the oldest black community—

SHACK: She's just jiving, man. She's old, but not that old.

ANTOINETTE: Hush up, Narcisse! You know what I mean. I didn't have to be there to know what happened. I've been collecting stories about Treme for years.

FESS: Excuse me!

SHACK: I didn't know they had black people way up in Nova Scotia.

FESS: Excuse me. Please!

CELESTINE: Shack! Chill a minute and let the man say what he has to say!

FESS: My ancestors settled in Nova Scotia in 1769 after fleeing from their masters in Virginia. They wanted to fight with the British, because the British promised the slaves freedom if they would help them win the war against the rebellious American colonies to the South and the French from the West.

    Our people weren't motivated by the imperial designs of the British. We weren't motivated by a particular hatred for the French. We were motivated by a love for freedom.

ANTOINETTE: Say that! Say that!

FESS: We were motivated then by the desire to be free from slavery; we were motivated then by the profound desire to see justice roll down in torrents and floods.

CELESTINE: You better watch it now!

FESS: Just as we are motivated now by the quest for freedom from environmental racism and for justice. We haven't yet won the war but we've won enough battles to know that we can win. If we just keep on fighting.

ANTOINETTE: That's right, baby!

FESS: Listen to me now my friends! When our vital interests are under attack we must fight effectively, we must examine our stories in their appropriate historical context. We must recognize the patterns and trends. We must see how our personal stories fit together to make up our families. Sharing our family stories gives us a sense of our community and our various communities sharing their stories can give us a sense of our common cause and help us build a movement.

CELESTINE: Hello!

ANTOINETTE: Teach!

SHACK: Shh-i-i-t!

FESS: We are all tempered in the cauldron of History! We carry our history in us like so many vestigial organs or seeds that are subject to pop out at any given moment. Be not misled by fabrications and trickery! Be not confused by the deceptive accounts of our people's past. What is generally considered as history is written by those who prevail in the fight. Understand this now! The victor tells his story not my story, not your story.

ANTOINETTE: HIS-S-S-STORY!

FESS: I subscribe to the sentiment expressed by Martin Luther King, Jr., when he said, "There is in the universe a great and unyielding arc that bends inevitably toward justice."

SHACK: This brother can rap!

FESS: The day will come when our efforts will be crowned by victory: ". . . the battle is neither to the swift or to the strong, but to he that endureth to the end."

ANTOINETTE: Amen?

FESS, CELESTINE, SHACK: Amen

ANTOINETTE *(To audience)*: It's okay, y'all can say "Amen" anytime you feel like it. Amen? Amen!

Scene 3

The Indigo Thing

ANTOINETTE *(Twirling and showing off her beautiful indigo-colored ensemble)*: How do I look? I found the best sale yesterday at Tar-jhay.

SHACK: Hey, you know you looking good Miz Antoinette.

CELESTINE: Yeah, sale, wholesale or retail, it's still blue. You always buying something *blue*. *Blue* is all you wear. You need help diversifying your closet. Her bathroom is blue. Her bedroom is blue. Everything in your house is *blue*. Why don't you put some of that stuff on eBay so somebody can give you a pile of money?

SHACK: So she can go out and buy more *blue* stuff.

ANTOINETTE: INDIGO! INDIGO! This is *indigo*. It inspires me, soothes me. It's deep, it's rich, it's luxurious, it's royal! It's historical!

CELESTINE: And it's your favorite color, we got it. But it still looks like *blue* to me.

FESS: It is historical! But getting the indigo color out of the plants was quite difficult.

CELESTINE: Disgusting.

SHACK: Yeah, you right!

FESS: When they got to Louisiana, the Africans found a variety of the plant used to make indigo in West Africa. The process required large quantities of urine; euphemistically referred to as "chamber lye."

CELESTINE: African women old and young had to work the toxic cesspool with their bare feet and hands for hours at a time to draw out the pigment.

SHACK: Phew! I can smell it now.

CELESTINE: The sickness and disease. Rashes and sores. Feet and hands that must have stayed blue for a whole season.

SHACK: Makes you wonder why the slaves didn't get sick from the stuff when they made it for themselves!

ANTOINETTE: But if they did it was their choice.

FESS: There's a difference between making a little for yourself and making a lot to ship all around the world.

SHACK: For money!

FESS: Indeed! The object of American slavery was to build the wealth of the slave masters at the expense of the slaves. The thing that's often overlooked is that the slave masters didn't just appropriate their labor, they also appropriated the knowledge.

ANTOINETTE: The Africans, caught in a terrible situation, used knowledge they brought with them from home to make something beautiful from otherwise useless bushes. The slave masters find out about it and take it to make the circumstances of the slaves even worse.

FESS: One could call it "the indigo syndrome."

CELESTINE: I can hear the echoes of the slaves' songs of comfort and hope. My ancestors. Your ancestors. Toiling. Toiling and singing. Long days. A relentless sun. Soaked by the rain and their own blood from the driver's lash! Cane. Cotton. Indigo.

(She begins a mournful chant/blues with slow, rhythmic, rural work-related movement.)

SHACK *(Sings)*:

You say you feeling low down, you 'bout to flow down
You know you got to find a way so not to go down.
Each day that goes by, you want to find out why
You got to live this life of a slave, you wish you could die.
I'm talking moody, moody blue, way past blue, I'm talking indigo!

So you survived the Middle Passage, but don't know just where you are
Can't even find a star to guide you home, you know it's way too far.
For two hundred and fifty years you fight, try to make a better way to be
Looking to make it so that you and all your children will be able to be free.
You gotta do something while you're waiting, trying to make it a better day
But everything you think to do, Old Master takes away.

Out into the swamp you go to rest and find some indigo, Old Master didn't know
How to get the beautiful blue color out from the roots and make the fabric glow.
To him the bush is just some trash, but then they find your stash.
Then he turn it all 'round into a way to make it into cash.
But you don't let the setback stop you from living to fight another day

You telling the stories to the kids so they can remember
   what you say.

Although you feeling low down, you 'bout to flow down
You know you got to find a way so not to go down.
Each day that goes by, you want to find out why
You got to live this life of a slave, you wish you could die.
I'm talking moody, moody blue, way past blue, I'm talking
   indigo!

You're going down in an ocean full of trouble,
You're in the bottom of a barrel filled with shit,
Don't know how to keep on living,
Think you might as well go on and quit.
But you think about those who've gone before
All bound in chains on old Goree's shore,
Heading for the Middle Passage,
Stacked up and tied down like so much rice or wheat.
That's what they paid for you and me,
So you figure that you'll have to go on, you think you'll
   flow on,
We got to figure out a way we got to go on.

ALL:

Plantation by the river, sweet magnolia all around
See all the happy darkies scratching all around the ground.
Listen to them singing sweet sad songs from far away.
They sing about times long since gone and of a brand-
   new day:

When we were free and unrestricted and when we will be
   once again
When the profits from our efforts return to our own
   hands.

So you figure that you'll go on, you better find a way to
   flow on
We got to figure out a way we got to go on.

So when you dig the dancing darkies, see old Sambo
    prance and strut,
When you hear the black folk laughing hard enough to
    bust a gut,
When you hear a mother screaming for a child laid dead
    and cold,
Curled up upon the concrete not even twelve years old.

Because some untempered man-child or some other
    mother's foal
Felt the call to punch two tickets off to Heaven or maybe
    off to Hell
Had no better reason than that, "I heard this brother
    heard that brother tell . . ."
"Damn, man! You ain't got no understanding at all!"

So you figure that you'll go on, you better find a way to
    flow on,
We got to figure out a way we got to go on.
Although you feeling low down, you 'bout to flow down,
You know you got to find a way so not to go down.

Each day that goes by, you want to find out why
You got to live this life of a slave, you wish you could die.
I'm talking moody, moody blue, way past blue, I'm talk-
    ing indigo!

Scene 4

Big Mike and Maudine

FESS: Indigo was big on River Road. The same place they call
    "Cancer Alley" now, mainly because of uncontrolled pollu-
    tion from the oil business.
ANTOINETTE: Recently I took Norman on a "toxic tour" out on
    River Road so he could see what it's like for himself. In some
    places where indigo used to grow you can see sugarcane ris-

ing from the banks of the Mississippi River around the big old plantation homes with their oak-lined lanes, which now stand like soldiers in front of the oil-processing plants.

FESS: Huge pipes and flaming smokestacks that pour potent poison into the air, land, water and, thence, into the bodies of all who are touched by them. The surrealistic beauty of the place hides the truth of what has happened and still goes on there.

ANTOINETTE: Like I told you: we're telling a story about environmental racism—

SHACK: Just a new name for the same old game.

ANTOINETTE: Our story is about Michael Claude Treem—

SHACK: Better known as Big Mike.

(The Company sings "Big Mike's Poison Ivy":)

He wasn't trying to be bad

CELESTINE:

He didn't mean to do wrong

FESS:

But when he got to be sad

ANTOINETTE:

He knew he had to be strong

He didn't try to be mean
He didn't mean to be cruel
But if you messed with Big Mike
It's all over for you.

ALL:

Well he sometimes liked to brag
And sometimes he'd act the fool
Just like poison ivy
He'll break out all over you.

You might have all the power,
You might be really smart;

But he'd fight when he's right
And he had a whole lot of heart.

Well, he sometimes liked to brag
And sometimes he'd act the fool
And just like poison ivy
He'll break out all over you.
Just like poison ivy
He'll break out all over
Break out all over
Break out all over you.

ANTOINETTE: Big Mike was always brash and forceful.
SHACK: But he met his match when he met Maudine Henry . . .

(Urban traffic. Truck brakes to idle. Horn sounds.)

BIG MIKE: Hey little school girl, I want to make you mine.
MAUDINE: I know you aren't talking to me. I deserve and I get
  more respect than that from children on the playground.
  I know that a strong, intelligent, proud black man like you
  would have more taste and intelligence than a child.
BIG MIKE: Whoa now! Knocked me down and put me in my
  place just as sweet as you please. Where'd you learn to talk
  like that?
MAUDINE: Who didn't teach you how to speak to a self-respecting
  black woman is the question.
BIG MIKE: I got to get some more of this. *(He gets out of the truck)*
ANTOINETTE: Big Mike stopped his tractor trailer right in the
  middle of the street and got out of the cab.
MAUDINE: Man, you can't leave that truck parked in the middle
  of the street like that!
BIG MIKE: My name is Michael Claude Treem, ma'am. I'm from
  Natchez, Mississippi. I want to beg your pardon for my flip
  lip, but I ain't never seen, much less met, a woman like you
  before in my life! I just got beside myself. If you'll just tell
  me how to get in touch with your people, ma'am, I'll be on
  my way.

MAUDINE: My people?

BIG MIKE: Yes, ma'am. I was raised to do things the right way. I intend to let your daddy know about my intentions, make a proper courtship and gain his permission for us to get married. 'Course, I'll have to let my people know up in Mississippi, but I know right now that you're the woman I want to marry.

MAUDINE: Marry me?! Man, you got to be crazy! Neither my daddy nor my mama tell me what to do. They raised all of us to be free and independent. So what permission you don't get here you won't get at all. You've got your nerve! You don't know me, mister, and I don't know you.

BIG MIKE: I knew I was right! From way across the street I could tell. You are full of fire and got a passion for freedom. I got the same fire burning in my heart, ma'am. But if it's just the same with you I still have a desire to talk this thing over with your people.

MAUDINE: Any man who qualifies to marry me has to have better sense than to leave an eighteen-wheeler in the middle of Claiborne Avenue and propose marriage to a perfect stranger. I hope you don't think I'm a fool. They got places to put people like you, and if you don't move that truck you're going to get there soon.

BIG MIKE: That don't worry me none, Miz Lady. The white folk know better than to mess with Big Mike Treem. So don't let it be a botherment to you.

Scene 5

It Ain't What You Do but the Way That You Do It!

The Treme home of the Henrys. Shack becomes Mr. Henry. Antoinette becomes Mrs. Henry.

MRS. HENRY: I don't see nothing funny at all about my daughter's love life being the subject of conversation among a

bunch of stevedores, hanging out on the Esplanade Wharf.
I didn't raise my daughter to be the subject of common talk
among common people.

MR. HENRY: There's nothing wrong with the good longshoremen
in my union. That's the most powerful bunch of Negroes in
the city and you know it! Besides, they meant to be looking
out for her.

MRS. HENRY: They were looking out all right!

MR. HENRY *(Talk-singing)*:
  I love it when you talk that way

MRS. HENRY *(Singing)*:
  What way you mean you heard me say?

MR. HENRY:
  When the blood comes up to flush your cheek
  Your eyes start to flash and my knees get weak.

MRS. HENRY:
  I'm talking about our daughter's life
  And some low-life clown wanting to make her his wife!

MR. HENRY:
  The blood's done made your cheeks, lips and nose
  Turn rosy red! I wonder where else the red blood flows

MRS. HENRY: Man, don't you be no crazy fool! It's twelve o'clock
in the afternoon.

MR. HENRY: So what has twelve o'clock straight up got to do with
it?

MRS. HENRY: Oh Henry! You know what I mean.

MR. HENRY: Why? What'd I say?

(Big Mike arrives and starts to listen.)

MRS. HENRY: I'm talking about Maudine.

MR. HENRY: I am too. What did I do?

MRS. HENRY:
    It's not what you say, but the way that you say it.

MR. HENRY: What'd I do?

MRS. HENRY:
    It's not what you do but the way that you do it!

MR. AND MRS. HENRY:
    It's not what you say but the way that you say it.
    That's what gets results.

MR. HENRY: You know I'm down with you, baby.
SHACK *(Knocking at the door)*: This is the Henry residence, ain't it?
MR. HENRY: Man, you better find a better place to park that trac-
    tor trailer or I won't waste no time calling the cops!

(Shack quickly goes to move the truck.)

MR. AND MRS. HENRY:
    It ain't what you say but the way that you say it.
    It ain't what you do but the way that you do it.
    It ain't what you say but the way that you say it.
    That's what gets results.

(Quick cut. Ten minutes later.)

MR. HENRY: So how did you find us, Mr. Treem? You from Mis-
    sissippi, you didn't have no name, no picture or nothing?
BIG MIKE: Oh, it wasn't hard, Mr. Henry, sir. From the minute
    I saw her, her picture was printed on my heart in living
    color. I got a better picture right here than Mr. Kodak will
    ever make.
MR. HENRY: It's a long way from a picture "on your heart" to our
    house here on Ursiline Street.
BIG MIKE: Begging to differ, sir, not when the picture is as clear
    as mine.

MRS. HENRY: Your words are full of flowers, sir, but you ain't yet said nothing about how you found us.

BIG MIKE: I should have knew that the queen of my heart would have a mama like you!

MRS. HENRY: The question was how did you find us?

BIG MIKE: Why, y'all are famous, ma'am. I believe if I'd a stopped the first person I saw on Canal Street and asked, "Who's the finest woman in New Orleans?" they'd have sent me here.

When I got to the Esplanade Wharf to unload my truck, I couldn't stop talking about the vision of a black angel that I'd seen on Canal Street. I said, "She wore that Freedom hair like a crown and carried herself like the Queen of Sheba." The longshoremen who handled my load said, "That ain't nobody but Elton Henry's daughter!" They showed me her picture in the *Black Dispatch* where Miz Maudine was the Queen of Carnival for the Royal Flush Social Aid and Pleasure Club for 1965. I been carrying this with me in the cab of my truck ever since.

MRS. HENRY *(To Mr. Henry)*: So much for Mr. Kodak and the picture in his heart.

BIG MIKE: Another driver said, "So you the fool that had traffic tied up at Canal and Claiborne. I thought it was a wreck down there!" I told them, "It wasn't no wreck and it wasn't no accident, boss. I just ran into my future right there and it stopped me in the middle of the street. Buddy, that's the woman I'm going to marry!" 'Course, they laughed at me. Said, "Mr. Henry's the head of the Longshoremen's Union, the most powerful Negro in town!" And they told me about your mama, Mrs. Bordelon, ma'am. They said she's one that runs a big catering business out of the Aristocrat Club, and said anybody want a job in the food business or play music in New Orleans got to come through you.

'Course, I don't need a job. I own the truck I'm driving, paid cash on the barrelhead for it two years ago and I'm the only heir to a nice-sized farm outside of Natchez, Mississippi. You'll come to know that I'm a man of my word and that I'm equal to my responsibility. All I need is your permission to court Miz Maudine and for y'all to know that it's my intent to marry her.

MRS. HENRY: He's got his nerve and a silver tongue. I'll give him that.

(Maudine enters.)

BIG MIKE: There she is! The queen of my heart.

MAUDINE: I've already told you, Mr. Big Mike Treem, that my people raised me to be free. What permission you don't get from me you won't get at all.

BIG MIKE: It ain't what you say but the way that you say it.

ALL FOUR *(Singing)*:
> It ain't what you say but the way that you say it!
> It ain't what you do but the way that you do it!
> It ain't what you do but the way that you do it!
> That's what gets results!

ANTOINETTE: Six months later they got married. It wasn't the fanciest wedding they ever had at St. Augustine Church, but I don't remember one before or since that had more people. Big Mike sold his big rig, went to work on the riverfront and moved into a place on Barracks Street in Treme.

CELESTINE: Everybody was so happy that the Queen of Treme had a new title: "Mrs. Queen Treem."

SHACK: The people in Treme liked Big Mike so much that the Royal Flush Social Aid and Pleasure Club made him "The King of Spades for Life" (as long as he stays married to the queen).

CELESTINE: For six years they tried but didn't make any children. But they had a wonderful life together. It looked like one of those happily-ever-after stories. Maudine was working and going to nursing school too.

ANTOINETTE: When they finally had a boy, Big Mike was really happy. He didn't know it but his family was descended from the white man, Claude Treme, who the neighborhood is named after.

SHACK: It's a good thing he didn't know it, considering how he felt about white people.

CELESTINE: See Big Mike was Creole and didn't know it.

ANTOINETTE: Maudine's people are Creole too. They know it well enough but most of them suffer the sin of darker skin.

ANTOINETTE: So the new baby was named Claude Michel Treem. They called him "Junior." Big Mike passed out two boxes of Cuban cigars. Everyone said it was the prettiest baby they had ever seen.

CELESTINE: Until the child was eight years old Maudine had him wearing a big afro like hers. People would stop them on the street and say things like, "Oh what a pretty little girl!" Junior got so it was automatic for him to say, "I'm a boy!"

FESS: He's still a very good-looking young man.

ANTOINETTE: Big Mike was as happy as he could be. Now he had a man-child to carry the family name into the future. Junior was Big Mike's pride and joy.

SHACK: He spent all his free time with his son. They did everything together: football, basketball, boxing. Soon as the child was nine years old, Big Mike would take him hunting and fishing, everything. And Junior was good at everything they did.

ANTOINETTE: They had the normal kind of problems. Hey, everybody has problems! That's how you know you're alive.

CELESTINE: Yeah. But basically everything was cool for them until the Treems moved out of Treme.

Scene 6

Moving Day in Treme

ANTOINETTE: Things changed for Michael and Maudine just when she was finally about to graduate from the nursing program at Dillard University.

MAUDINE: I struggled for seventeen long, hard years to get that precious piece of paper. I can't believe it, Michael. I had to

trade shifts to get time off for graduation. I won't be home
'til after work tomorrow. I hope you don't mind.

BIG MIKE: No. I'm taking the weekend off. Me and Junior got
some business to take care of.

MAUDINE: Just think, Michael. Soon I'll have no school bills to
pay and I won't have to be bowing and scraping in front of
the white folk at Charity Hospital to keep that little nickel-
and-dime job as a nurse's aide. I'll be a bona fide RN!

BIG MIKE: Hold up, Maudine. No wife of mine's got to be bowing and scraping in front of white folk or nobody else no
time. You working because you want to, not because you
have to. No wife of mine's got to work at all. I don't like it.
I never have. I never will.

MAUDINE: But, Michael, this is not about you. It's about me. I'll
be the first one in my family—either of our families—to
get a college degree. It's taken me seventeen years, but I'm
proud of what I've done, and I'll be prouder still when I can
start putting money into our future. Finally we'll be able to
get our own place.

BIG MIKE: Maudine, I'm going to say this one more time. You
doing this because you want to; not because you have to.
I don't need you in no school. I don't need you working on
no job. I need you at home taking care of Junior and making us a family. I don't stand second to no man. I'm equal to
my responsibilities . . . and then some.

MAUDINE: And I am equal to my responsibilities, Michael. Look,
I'm proud to be your wife. I'm proud of you, but I've worked
hard to realize my dream. I want you to be proud of me too,
but if you're not, it won't stop me from doing what I have
to do.

BIG MIKE: The whole neighborhood could fall apart and you
wouldn't know a damn thing about it.

MAUDINE: Anytime I need to know something about what's happening in the neighborhood I can go by Miz Antoinette's
backyard. She's got the skinny on everything.

BIG MIKE: Don't worry about us. Like I say, me and Junior got
business to take care of.

MAUDINE: What kind of business you got that's so important?

BIG MIKE: It ain't about you, Maudine. It's about me. It's a big deal. I been working on it for a long time. I got to tie the whole thing up tomorrow. Don't worry.

(Quick cut to "Cash on the Barrelhead." Big Mike sings:)

> I've bought my piece of the American dream
> And I'm making that dream come true.
> I don't care what anybody says
> I'm gonna do what I've got to do.

> They say bull corn walks and money talks
> When people try to push you around.
> Ain't taking no more stuff
> Getting ready for whatever comes down.

> But when you put cash on the barrelhead
> You got cash on the barrelhead
> They got to respect all the words you said
> When you lay that cash on the barrelhead.

MAUDINE: Michael Claude Treem, what in the world is going on in here? Are we being evicted? What have you been doing with the rent money?

BIG MIKE: All this time and you still don't know me. The white folks are buying up this whole ramshackle neighborhood from under us. It's only a matter of time before they come telling us we got to go. But not to worry, baby. I'm taking T-total care of every little doggone thing. The white folks want Treme, I say let them have it. It's a brand-new day, baby. We don't have to be dependent on white people no more. I done bought us a brand-new house. Happy graduation day, baby! You are the queen, I am the king, and these right here are the keys to the castle.

MAUDINE: You bought a house?

BIG MIKE: Brand-spanking-new! Cash on the barrelhead.

MAUDINE: Where'd you get that kind of money?

BIG MIKE: You ain't married to no fool, baby. You married to a working man, baby. A hardworking man. I keep telling you, Maudine, my intent and purpose is to take care of my responsibility. I been saving my money for years. On top of that, I sold the old family farm up in Natchez, and I paid cash on the barrelhead, saved me some big bucks. I don't believe in no credit. If you can't pay for it when you want it you can't afford it.

You think I don't know what I'm doing, but I'm dead on the case, baby. I don't have to go to no college to know what I'm doing. I'm tired of being pushed around. Every time somebody else decides they got a problem, they decide I'm it. I own—you hear me—outright own my own piece of land in the city, now. Can't nobody make me get up and do nothing until I'm good and ready to do it. We property owners now, baby.

MAUDINE: Michael, how could you do such a thing without me.

BIG MIKE: You think I don't know what I'm doing, but I'm dead on the case, baby. I don't have to go to no college to know what I'm doing.

MAUDINE: Where is this place? What's it look like? How will it work for us?

BIG MIKE: 2731 Agriculture Street, out in a new all-black development down the way from the Desire Projects in Old Gentilly. Here's a picture of it. It's got a big yard and everything.

MAUDINE: Desire? Old Gentilly? I don't know anybody out there. Me and all my people have always lived here in Treme.

BIG MIKE: Look, baby, I . . . we ain't going to be pushed around no more. We own, you hear me, outright own our own piece of land in the city now. Can't nobody make me get up and do nothing until I'm good and ready to do it.

MAUDINE: Here I can walk everywhere I need to go.

BIG MIKE: 'Til I teach you how to drive, you can take the Desire bus. It'll get you to town in no time. You'll get use to it, baby. I came from up around Natchez. I gave all that up to be down here with you.

MAUDINE: Now you're "The King of Spades" in Treme.

BIG MIKE: "Long as I'm married to the Queen." We got our own
place in the city now, baby. If I can move to a whole new
state for you, I know you can move across town for me.

MAUDINE: I don't know what to say.

BIG MIKE: Don't worry. It'll come to you.

(Maudine sings "Maudine's Blues:)

MAUDINE *(Sings)*:
How can I do this?
How can I carry on?
When everything that's dear to me
Turns out to be so wrong?

I don't know
I know I don't know
I just don't know
I don't know!!

All day I work and study to do the best that I can do.
I give you all my love,
But the point doesn't come through.
How can I do this? How can I carry on?

I need more room to try my wings
I need more space to fly.
You want to keep me in a cage
Where I could never try.
How can I do this?

I know you mean to do no harm,
But your love's the choking kind.
Your embrace is like a chain that's wrapped around my
neck.
I need a love that's more like the wind beneath my wings.
How can I do this?

Scene 7

The Sweet Life Turns Sour

ANTOINETTE: For all their pride and spirit, Big Mike and Maudine still suffered because there was one story that they had
trouble telling even to each other. Like my old Cherokee
grandmother used to say, "If we can't tell our stories, how
can we say who we are?" Finally, Maudine could no longer
stand the silence.

BIG MIKE: That don't make no sense, Maudine, it don't make
no sense to me at all. How's the boy going to be a . . . a . . .
like that when he don't know nothing about sex at all? He's
a good boy.

MAUDINE: He is a good boy, Michael. I simply think we must be
prepared for the possibility though.

BIG MIKE: I don't want to hear it. He can box, beat you in any
sport. Hell, you call the game, he can shoot better than
I can. No son of mine is going to be a . . . a—it's unnatural!
Sick! I love that boy. I don't want to hear it! Do you hear
me?

MAUDINE: Our son is as natural and as healthy as they come,
Michael. Yes, he is a good athlete, and we should be proud
of that. But ability to box or throw a football is not what
it takes to be a good person, a decent person. Our son is
smart; he's motivated and respectful. He's also a sensitive,
kind, well-rounded human being, who may very well turn
out to be a doctor. But we need to be ready if he turns out
to be . . . different.

BIG MIKE: I don't want to hear it!

MAUDINE: Well, you are going to hear it. And hear it every day
until it sinks in. I'm not going to stand by here and let you
treat my flesh and blood—your own flesh and blood—like
there's something wrong with him.

BIG MIKE: He's all right. Just you wait and see.

ANTOINETTE: The next year, in a desperate effort to make himself fit Big Mike's image of a man, Junior made himself a

father. Despite the fact that the boy was not married to the child's mother, Moniqua. Big Mike was ecstatic. He took it as proof of his belief that his son was "all right."

BIG MIKE: See there, Maudine, I told you that there's nothing wrong with my boy. See there! The baby looks just like me, don't he. *(To Junior)* Boy, you going about this thing the wrong way, you know that. So when you planning on getting married?

ANTOINETTE: When the baby was three months old, Junior finally had to confront his father . . . Man to man. He asked his mama to stay out of it.

JUNIOR: Daddy, we need to talk.

BIG MIKE: We way past due as far as I'm concerned. Maudine, get in here. This thing's been drifting on too long. When you going to do the right thing by that girl and go on and get married so you can be a proper parent to this baby?

JUNIOR: It's just between you and me, Daddy. Man to man . . . I've spoken to Mama already. You and me, we need to talk.

BIG MIKE: That's what we doing, ain't it? What you think I'm trying to do? That baby's a Treem. And we Treem men, we live up to our obligations. You know that. So it's time for you to stand up like a natural man and meet your proper obligations. I know things are different now from when I was coming up, so I been trying to be understanding, but as a man you have certain obligations. So when you plan to do the right thing? As a man, a Treem man.

JUNIOR: I'm trying to do the right thing, Daddy. I . . . we need to talk, Daddy—

BIG MIKE: I'm talking, but you just flapping your gums. You got a decent job. That gal is decent enough. She's not the one I would have chose for you, but she's clean, she's honest, she's polite.

JUNIOR: But I . . . She's . . .

BIG MIKE: You don't love her like I love your mama, is that it? Well, let me tell you, not many people love each other like me and your ma do. It's wonderful if you do love your wife, but you don't have to. Anyway, it's too late for that now. You just have to do the right thing. You done already made this baby now, so it's a whole 'nother deal, don't you know. You've got a baby now.

JUNIOR: Daddy, would you be quiet for just a moment, please? I'm trying to tell you . . .

BIG MIKE: Well tell me then, I'm listening. You a man. Represent yourself as a man. You going to do the right thing by this baby and his mama or what?

JUNIOR: That's your baby, Daddy.

BIG MIKE: What you talking about, boy? Maudine, your child's done gone crazy.

JUNIOR: That's your baby, Daddy. I made it for you.

BIG MIKE: Where you at, Maudine!

JUNIOR: Don't get me wrong, Daddy, I love the child, he's truly beautiful. And Moniqua's a really wonderful person. I think she really loves you and Mama. She worships the baby. I even think she loves me, but . . .

BIG MIKE: Maudine, you better get in here!

JUNIOR: And I've tried to do it, Daddy. Believe me I've tried—

BIG MIKE: Maudine! Where you at? Get in here! I don't want to hear this.

JUNIOR: I've tried to be the kind of man you wanted me to be, Daddy—

BIG MIKE: Maudine!! I don't want to hear this!

JUNIOR: You've got to hear me, Daddy. See me, Daddy.

BIG MIKE: Maudine!

JUNIOR: Listen to me, Daddy—

BIG MIKE: No.

(Big Mike punctuates the following with efforts at negation.)

JUNIOR: I am a homosexual, Daddy. I make love with men, Daddy. Daddy, I'm gay.

MAUDINE *(Speaking apart from the men)*: Michael. Son.

BIG MIKE: No. No. No.

JUNIOR: Don't look at me like that, Daddy.

BIG MIKE: No.

JUNIOR: I need you to see me, Daddy. I need you to love me, Daddy. *(He reaches for his father)*

BIG MIKE: No. Don't touch me!

MAUDINE: Michael!

JUNIOR: I need you, Daddy.

BIG MIKE: Don't touch me.

JUNIOR: I love you, Daddy. Love me.

BIG MIKE: Don't touch me. Get out!

MAUDINE: Michael! Don't!

BIG MIKE: Get out! Get out!!!

(Junior exits.)

MAUDINE: Michael, you can't do that!

BIG MIKE: It's done, Maudine.

MAUDINE: That's not all that's done here, Michael!

(Maudine begins singing "No Longer Safe in My Father's Home." Unable to find the words to express his pain, Big Mike moans along.)

> There's no way I'll let you make me drive my child away
> I don't care what you think he's done or how he got that
>   way
> I tried to help you prepare for the day
> You wouldn't listen to what I tried to say
> I truly love you but I can't stay
> When you don't have the kind of love that would let him
>   stay.
> There's no way that I could have lived life my way
> If I was no longer safe in my father's home.

JUNIOR *(Reenters; apart from his parents)*:
> I wander out on the streets alone
> No longer welcome in my father's home
> The hearth's gone cold, my base is gone
> No longer safe in my father's home.
> I could have kept on lying, could have feathered the nest
> I need a sound foundation if I'm going to do my best
> I weathered the storm; I'll weather the rest
> Though I'm no longer safe in my father's home.

ANTOINETTE:

> I love you so much but I don't know how to say so
> I want to hold you so much but I don't dare to.
> I want to pour out my heart but I don't think
> You'd care to hear what I'd have to say.
> I love you so much
> But I just don't know how to make you know just how
> I feel.

ALL:

> Like a flower needs the sun to grow
> My arms yearn to hold you so
> But I can't find the way to let you know
> I tremble when I hear your name
> I swing to and fro from joy to shame
> I love you so much but I just don't know how to.
> To make you know that it's safe in your father's home.

Scene 8

The Poison Legacy

ANTOINETTE: Maudine left that night. She moved back to Treme with her mama and them.

SHACK: That damn near killed Big Mike. But Maudine really worried about him and Junior too.

FESS: For a long time, Junior and Big Mike had nothing to do with each other. The pain between them was too deep. He wandered around quite a bit: West Coast, East Coast, Canada, taking odd jobs.

ANTOINETTE: He'd send me money for Moniqua and every now and then he'd come home to visit.

FESS: Not wishing to aggravate the situation anymore, Junior would avoid his father on these visits.

ANTOINETTE: Maudine, Moniqua and the baby moved into half of the double-shotgun camelback house that the Henrys had on Treme Street.

CELESTINE: Big Mike wasn't doing well at all that year. He must have lost forty, maybe fifty pounds. Most people thought he was sick.

SHACK: The blues will do that to you, man. Put a pain on your ass that make you wish you hadn't ever been born.

Scene 9

Ain't Too Proud to Beg

ANTOINETTE: They lived that way from October to March.

CELESTINE: Big Mike would come by three or four times a week when Maudine and Moniqua weren't home to visit with the baby.

ANTOINETTE: One night he came by when he knew Maudine would be at home.

MRS. HENRY *(Entering)*: I didn't think that child would ever go to sleep! I don't know how you and Moniqua keep up with him!

MAUDINE: Yes, ma'am. He's just like Junior was when he was that age.

MRS. HENRY: There's a reason why young people are the ones to have babies.

MAUDINE: Mama, the least you and Daddy could do is let me pay y'all the note on the house. I've been here for four months now.

MRS. HENRY: And you can stay here as long as you need to. Mr. Henry and I got this house for you in the first place. Besides, if Junior's going to that expensive school in Atlanta like you say, you're going to need all the money you've got.

MAUDINE: I think he's going to work it out so that he can get that full scholarship to the pre-med that they offered him over at Morehouse.

MRS. HENRY: Full scholarship or no, they won't be paying him enough to send money home for the baby. And that little server's job I helped Moniqua get over by Chez Helene will help out but she's in school too. You save your money, baby. Hmm, you know, if Junior's going to be in Atlanta, I'll call my friend at Paschal's place over there. They have nice traffic. If they don't have a place for him, they'd know where to send him to get a good position. Junior knows his way around the food business. I made sure of that. So now you say he's going to be a doctor.

MAUDINE: "My son, the doctor!"

MRS. HENRY: With you a nurse and him a doctor and Moniqua going to school to be a medical technologist, nobody in our family need to worry about getting sick.

BIG MIKE: Maudine! You in there?

MAUDINE: Michael. This is where I live. What you doing here?

BIG MIKE: I need to talk to you, Maudine. How you doing, Mrs. Henry?

MRS. HENRY: I was just leaving—

BIG MIKE: No need to leave on my account, ma'am. Fact of the business, ma'am, I could use a witness for what I'm about to say.

Maudine, I come here to ask you—no, beg you, to come home and bring the baby and Moniqua. "I ain't too proud to beg!"

I can't eat. I can't sleep. Life don't mean nothing to me without the baby and you. So I come here tonight crawling on my hands and knees to beg you to come home.

You know I love you. And that baby means life to me. Your mama knows. I be over here every day while you at work. That boy don't want for nothing, and won't, for as long as I'm able.

MAUDINE: Get up off your knees, Michael. It's not becoming to you.

Yes, I know you love me, and God knows I know you love that baby. But you've said nothing about our son. What about Junior?

MRS. HENRY: He's going to school over in Atlanta to be a doctor!

BIG MIKE: A doctor? Is that right?

MAUDINE: Looks like they're going to let him have that scholarship they offered him last year.

BIG MIKE: Well, he's your child so you know he's naturally going to be smart, but who's going to go to a doctor . . . like that?

MAUDINE: Most people are more concerned about how good their doctors are than how they live their private lives. Look, I'm not going to be sneaking around to spend time with our son.

BIG MIKE: I'm willing to try, Maudine. I'm willing to try. But I ain't going to lie to you or to him, Maudine. I wasn't raised with that stuff. I never expected no child of mine to go that way. But I'll say this: I do love him. And it might take me a while, and I'm willing to try, but truth be told, it's going to take a while.

ANTOINETTE: Of course Junior did well in school. It didn't take him long to find work as a waiter in a fancy restaurant in Atlanta. Soon he was making enough money to pay for his classes and send money to Moniqua for her school and the baby.

When he came to town to spend time with the baby, they worried more about how to avoid Big Mike than they did the baby. He looked healthy enough, but when the child was eighteen months old he still wasn't walking. The poor thing could only stay awake for two or three hours at a time. When they took him to the doctor, she said that some children are just slower than others.

FESS: They accepted the doctor's judgment until Junior went to a lecture about environmental justice and sustainable alternatives at Atlanta University. The professor, a Dr. Bullard, spoke of how bad things were in Louisiana's "Cancer Alley." Naturally that perked up Junior's ears. The upshot of it all was that Junior got a second major in environmental studies and became one of Dr. Bullard's star students, and became very active in the environmental justice movement.

CELESTINE: When the time came for baby Claude Henri Baker-Treem to start preschool, Junior almost came face to face with Big Mike for the first time in four years.

BIG MIKE: Maudine, who was that driving off with Moniqua as I pulled up?

MAUDINE: That was our son, Michael.

279

BIG MIKE: That's your son. I ain't ready for him to be coming 'round here yet. Don't encourage him . . . What was he doing here anyway?

MAUDINE: Henri starts preschool in the fall. Junior and Moniqua went over to meet the teachers at Moten School.

BIG MIKE: What you let him do that for? All that's under control. He act like we don't know how to raise a child.

MAUDINE: Henri is his child, Michael, and I am proud of him for providing for the child and taking responsibility. I think it's evidence that we raised him well.

BIG MIKE: I know I know how to raise a child.

MAUDINE: It's not our job to raise Henri, Michael. Thank goodness we don't have to. Moniqua's a good mother, Junior is doing as much as he can.

BIG MIKE: Not to my mind. And I'm done with the conversation.

(Pause.)

MAUDINE: Anyway they're worried about sending the child over there to go to school.

BIG MIKE: What kind of sense do that make, Maudine. Moten's a brand-new, state-of-the-art, multimillion-dollar school. You said yourself that Mrs. Simms is an A-number-one principal and that they got good teachers. What else could anybody want? Next thing you know he's going to be trying to make Moniqua and the baby move out of my house.

MAUDINE: They are closing Moten down next year. Junior says they are studying about the situation here in their classes at the university in Atlanta. They say Moten School and our neighborhood here are classic examples of environmental racism.

BIG MIKE: Do you mean to tell me that it's got so bad a nigger got to go to the university to find out that a cracker will kick your butt every chance he get? Maudine, please!

MAUDINE: You know from your own business with the truck, two or three times a year you have to go back to the same places to carry off the trash that comes up out of the ground around here.

BIG MIKE: You want to know what they don't like about Moten
School and our neighborhood out here? I'll tell you what they
don't like. It's black people being in charge of something.
Black people finally making some money off a something.
That's what they mean. It's a beautiful school and a beautiful neighborhood, and black people are in charge of everything from the school board on down. Hell, we even got our
own city councilman. If the neighborhood is good enough
for me, the school is good enough for my grandchild.

MAUDINE: Well, the child's parents don't think so. Moniqua's
found a place uptown. Junior was in town to help them
move this morning.

BIG MIKE: What?

MAUDINE: Moten is moving uptown by the old Holy Redeemer
campus. Moniqua's new place is near there so they'll still be
using Moten School.

BIG MIKE: See there! What'd I tell you! That little faggot has got
his nerve—

(Celestine slaps him.)

ANTOINETTE: Are you all right, Norman?

FESS: Uhm.

SHACK: She wasn't supposed to hit him that hard, was she?

ANTOINETTE: Hell no!

CELESTINE: I'm sorry, Fess. I didn't mean to hit you like that.
I guess I got carried away.

FESS: Your apology is accepted.

ANTOINETTE: You ought to have more control over yourself,
sister.

CELESTINE: The spirit moves in mysterious ways sometimes,
doesn't it?

SHACK *(To Fess)*: You just make sure that the spirit don't send you
over there to tag me like she tagged you.

FESS: Don't worry. I am not vulnerable to such mundane emo-
tional outbursts.

ANTOINETTE: I'm sure that Celestine didn't intend to get carried
away like that either.

SHACK: They say pride leads the ride to a fall, Fess.

CELESTINE: It sounds like the pot trying to out-black the kettle black, to me.

(Celestine sings:)

If you don't like the song I sing, still I've got the right to
    sing it

If you don't like the song I sing, still I've got the right to
    sing it.
If you don't like the story I tell, still I've got the right to
    tell it.
So I'll tell my story, yes and I'll sing my song
And though I never beg you for your love
Your love would help to make me be strong
Your love would help to make us both be strong.

There are many folk in history who suffered a tortured
    youth
Because they were homosexual and didn't see how they
    could tell the truth
To those who knew and loved them. They had to keep
    so many
Secrets just when the world was most confusing
They felt that there were not any
For them to love without the stain of sinning.

How many precious gifts have been damaged or destroyed
Because some adolescent youth had families who blindly
    toyed
With their emotions when their budding flowers
Had to find ways to bloom in darkness?
How much greater would have been their powers?
How much greater would have been their powers?

Scene 10

Power to the People

ANTOINETTE *(Intoxicated)*: When Maudine came back home it seemed like that got Big Mike up out of his blues. He went to Moniqua to tell her that it would make his life complete if she would bring his grandchild back home to Agriculture Street. But Moniqua politely told him that she couldn't come back to live there unless he could prove that it was a safe place for her to raise Little Henri.

CELESTINE: Then the superintendent closed Moten School. It was the first time in living memory that working-class black people could remember that their complaints were supported by the decision of a major public institution.

SHACK: I believe that's one of the main reasons they ran that brother out of town too.

FESS: Shortly after the school was closed, the federal government classified the whole area as a "Super-Fund Site." The EPA has a policy that makes the most toxic areas of the country eligible to draw on a Super-Fund, the idea being that the most toxic sites should be given top priority in the cleanup effort. The only problem is they've already got thousands of so-called Super-Fund Sites identified, and there's not enough money in the Fund to clean up more than a few hundred.

SHACK: It's like the government is saying, "Hey, y'all, guess what? The place you live is going to kill you, and we don't give a damn!"

FESS: The EPA appointed a black man to head the regional office of the EPA, Colonel Jacob Lamont Darrensbourg. Upon retiring from the U.S. Army Corps of Engineers, the colonel had taken a job as the Affirmative Action/Environmental Protection officer of the biggest energy company in the Gulf South. When EPA hired him away from big energy it was a very controversial appointment. Environmentalists argued that Darrensbourg was not qualified for the post for lack of interest in or commitment to protecting the environment.

SHACK: He wasn't no more than the "Spook Who Sat by the Door"!

ANTOINETTE: As it turned out, Colonel J. L. Darrensbourg is also from Natchez, Mississippi, where Michael Treem grew up. They went to the black school there and played on the same football team. Big Mike was sure that the whole thing was no more than a racist conspiracy to depress the value of his property, keep his grandchild from him, and to keep his high school friend from power.

CELESTINE: Up to that time, Big Mike hadn't paid much attention to ordinary politics.

SHACK: He didn't care nothing about no white people. He'd be the first one to step up if he saw a white person mistreating a black person, no matter where it was.

CELESTINE: But he hadn't paid attention to the more complicated issues like environmental racism. He was the type of fellow who needed to see it plain in black and white so to speak. He hadn't even registered to vote because he couldn't see where it would do any good.

ANTOINETTE: But he did believe that he could get the proof he needed for Moniqua from his old friend, Darrensbourg, and that his precious grandchild would be back in no time. Big Mike waited outside the colonel's office.

BIG MIKE: Hey, man. How you doing?

DARRENSBOURG: I beg your pardon, sir, that's Darrensbourg, Colonel Jacob L.

BIG MIKE: I know who the hell you are, Jake. I been knowing you. It's me. M. C.

DARRENSBOURG: Hey, that's got to be somebody from Natchez, Mississippi. What's happening, homeboy? Everybody else calls me Colonel Darrensbourg. You're looking good, my friend. What's happening? You getting plenty, big bro?

BIG MIKE *(Refusing to shake hands)*: No disrespect intended, Jake, but I was hauling some trash this morning. Gotta rash. Must a stirred up my allergy, probably some poison ivy, poison oak, or something I didn't notice. I was just going to the drugstore to get some calamine lotion and decided to pass by here to see if I could catch you. I been trying to get an appointment with you for two weeks, but your secretary always says you's busy or something.

DARRENSBOURG: Sorry to hear about your problem, brother.

BIG MIKE: I told her, "You tell him it's M. C. Treem, better known as 'Big Mike.' I know him well."

DARRENSBOURG: I'll speak to the girl.

BIG MIKE: Dig up, man, I ain't never needed nobody to do my talking for me. What I do need is some information on this environmental stuff. Some people have convinced my weak-minded daughter-in-law that it ain't safe for her to be raising my grandson in my house. So she moved out on me, man. I told her, "I got connect. I know the top man. I'm going to get this whole thing straightened out."

DARRENSBOURG: I bet she broke your heart, hey bro?

BIG MIKE: You know it, man. That little boy is the main reason I'm living for right now. Main reason . . .

DARRENSBOURG: Wait a minute. Treem, Treem, Big Mike Treem! I remember you! You used to have a big afro out to here—

BIG MIKE: I was the best blocking tight end and receiver ever to play for Carver High School while you was quarterback—

DARRENSBOURG: You organized the student walkout—

BIG MIKE: Yeah, you was our negotiator—

DARRENSBOURG: We had to have somebody on the inside. I'm still playing the inside game, brother. What you need, man?

BIG MIKE: I know these racist crackers is doing everything to try to cut you down, bro. They hate to see the black man do for self. Long as a brother come begging with his hand stuck out, they grin all up in your face. But stand up, represent yourself like a man, they don't want to see that. Your own people be the first ones trying to tear you down. Like fleas in a barrel.

DARRENSBOURG: "Like fleas in a barrel"?

BIG MIKE: Cash in a barrel . . . no, I mean . . . crabs on a barrelhead.

DARRENSBOURG: Aw, crabs on a barrel?

BIG MIKE: That's it. Yeah, that's it, brother. You know what I mean.

DARRENSBOURG: You got it, bro. Yeah, you right! Say, where is this place you're living in?

BIG MIKE: I'm the one that paid cash on the barrelhead for the house at 2731 Agriculture Street.

DARRENSBOURG: Oh. Agriculture Street. So what do you want me to do?

BIG MIKE: I thought I could come by your office and pick up something that I could use to show her that it's safe to live out here.

DARRENSBOURG: There's no reason in the world that lovely little neighborhood needs to be on the Super-Fund list. It's beautiful out there. I've driven all around out there. I intend to straighten everything out. We'll have you off that Super-Fund list in no time. No need for it at all. You tell her I said so. Okay?

BIG MIKE: Yeah, Jake, I'll be back over here tomorrow. You tell somebody to put something together for me.

DARRENSBOURG: You got my word on it. You can take that and put it in the bank, Big Mack.

BIG MIKE: Hey, Jake: "Power to the people!"

DARRENSBOURG: "Right on, brother!"

Scene 11

. . . And Then I Got Mad

ANTOINETTE: Moniqua and Little Henri hadn't been uptown a year before he was singing and dancing like everybody else. He was rapping like the Sugar Hill Gang.

CELESTINE: That night there was the main thing that got Big Mike to accept that there was something wrong in the place where they lived. He loved Little Henri more than he loved life itself.

ANTOINETTE: More and more often Big Mike would wait while Maudine went to meetings about the problems in the neighborhood. Finally he began to add up two and two.

(The players make the following speeches as if in a story circle. By the end, this circle transforms into a large meeting. The performers change characters as appropriate.)

CELESTINE: They tell us to "keep the kids off the bare spots in the soil."

FESS: The school is pressing down on a bunch of buried drums and forcing the stuff out of them.

CELESTINE: I moved here in 1972 and I've had a rash ever since.

ANTOINETTE *(Holding her grandson)*: My grandson has one large and one small kidney.

FESS: The testers came in white protection suits and oxygen masks.

ANTOINETTE: The animals are all sick. One dog died and another has no hair. One rabbit got sick and another had the good sense to run away.

SHACK: We didn't know how to fight. At least in Vietnam we had ammunition!

ANTOINETTE: Nothing grows in my backyard. It gets up to about this high, and up and die.

CELESTINE: I planted a vegetable garden. I worked in it all the time. I was so proud of it. One day my daughter came home and said, "This ground is toxic. Whatever you do, don't feed my baby anything out of your garden." I told her, "They wouldn't do anything like that. We're people." She said, "Don't forget . . . we're black!"

ANTOINETTE: My little girl had a condition with her lungs. It wasn't nothing to be done. They had her up at Charity Hospital. I sat with her day and night for a month. She just kept getting weaker and weaker. One day she perked up. Got stronger. Sat up in bed and said, "Turn on *The Guiding Light.* I want to see *The Guiding Light.*" She hardly ever looked at TV, but I turned it on for her. She said, "You go out and take a break. You been sitting there all night long." And she held her arms out for me to hug her. I went out for a while and when I came back she was dead.

SHACK: EPA, my ass! You know what it really stands for . . . Exploiting Poor People in America!

BIG MIKE: At first I tried to ignore it. Things kept getting worse. Then I got scared and that didn't help. Now I'm angry, damned mad in fact.

(Big Mike sings "And Then I Got Mad":)

At first I couldn't look at what was plain for all to see,
The stuff I thought was going down, I knew it couldn't be.
But when my eyes were opened and I had to take it in,
I didn't want to see it, "No way no way!" That couldn't
have been.
They were falling all around me; the truth came rush-
ing in,
I had to see we'd been misused, we'd been deceived,
we'd been sold out,
We had been taken in.
Fire in my belly began to burn, my blood began to boil,
Smoke came rolling out through my ears and nose,
And I began to choke and sputter.

And then I got mad, mad, mad!
Yes I'm mad, mad, mad!
Now I'm mad, mad, mad!
And I got to move!

ANTOINETTE: They figured the only thing that would help was
to organize. Some big, high-powered national organizations
came in. But not only were they loaded with high-powered
arguments that nobody could understand, they were strangers, and nobody could tell who decided when they were
doing their jobs correctly or who they were accountable too.
Still, Big Mike didn't feel like he had to get involved until
one day the Environmental Protection Agency sent some
teams down to inspect the neighborhood. They all came in
hazmat outfits that looked like space suits.

DARRENSBOURG: I think everything in the neighborhood would
be all right to live in if they just kept their houses reason-
ably clean.

BIG MIKE: Hold up, Jake. Just hold it right there. What the hell
you mean, "We got to keep our houses clean." If there ain't
nothing wrong with the dirt we standing on, why the hell you
all got those space suits on to come out here just to run a few
tests? How come you put us on the Super-Fund list? What
about our children? We supposed to keep them from play-

ing outside? What about the water pipes they run through that same dirt. Even if we do go out to buy some drinking water, we still have to take a bath and wash our clothes.

My grandchild had to move out of my house before he could learn . . . I mean basic things like walking and talking. He was three years old and still talking baby talk. Six months after he moved out of my house he was almost to normal. Now he's doing everything other kids his age can do. I lost the pride of my life from my house. I consider I'm lucky.

Y'all think it's okay to live out here—you give me your house and I'll give you mine. No, I'll take that back. I won't wish this condition on the Devil in Hell.

The worst thing I ever did was to pay cash on the barrel-head for my house. I wish I could close it up and walk away right now. We want the government to buy this property and close it down so nobody is exposed to these conditions. Give us the money we paid for our houses and let us be free.

We been waiting for the city government, state government, national government, anybody, somebody to say they'll buy us out like they did the people in Love Canal. What do we get? Some people in space suits to tell us that we'd be all right if we knew how to sweep and mop our damn floors. And you a black man, my homeboy!

Sisters and brothers, I believe we going to have to raise our plea to a higher power. These people don't have no good intentions as far as we concerned. At first I didn't believe it could be as bad as it is out here. My wife tried to tell me, my . . . boy tried to tell me, but I was in denial. Nobody would put people in bad conditions like this and keep them there on purpose. But it got to where it was too bad to ignore. Then I got scared. Scared for my grandchild. Scared for my children. Scared for my wife. But my fear froze me up, I couldn't do nothing but worry. This place is killing people. Think they'll do something about it? Hell, they still building more houses out here. Wonder why? Look around our neighborhood and you'll understand where our problems come from. Everybody living out here is black. That's the difference between us and Love Canal. It's racism.

That's why we can't find no justice. Well, now I'm mad. And I ain't going to rest 'til we get some justice out of this thing.

Things have gotten so complicated that niggers need a college degree to figure out that the white man will kick your butt every chance he gets. Some of us got the degrees. My wife's got a degree and she's not the only one. So we'll study. We'll figure it out. And we'll fight to get it right. We got to take our plea to a higher power. Environmental racism's got to go. No justice, no peace.

(Big Mike sings a reprise of "What You Don't Know Can't Hurt You!":)

The Big Shot said stop complaining,
Just relax and I'll do some explaining.
You got a roof over your head and three meals a day,
You got questions, I got answers;
Keep you blind, so you can't see.
Skillful political misdirection:
Money! Power! Greed!

What you don't know can't hurt you,
No need to worry, go on and have a nice day!
What you can't see, a poisonous evil
Slowly steals your life away.

Don't worry 'bout breathing smoggy air.
Don't think twice 'bout drinking from your tap.
There's no record of what's buried underneath your
    house:
Nasty slime, gunk, and other toxic crap.
You got more questions, I got more answers
Run you 'round bring you to your knees
I got the keys to the corporate kingdom
Money! Power! Greed!

What you don't know can't hurt you,
No need to worry, go on and have a nice day!

What you can't see, a poisonous evil
Slowly stealing your life away.

Help me, Doctor, something ain't right,
Losing weight, no appetite,
Aching joints, sleepless nights,
Don't feel like sex and that ain't right.
Limping, wheezing, coughing and sneezing,
Feet so cold ain't got no feeling.
Aching head, burning eyes.
Other than that, doing just fine.

What you don't know can't hurt you,
No need to worry, go on and have a nice day!
What you can't see, a poisonous evil
Slowly steal your life away.

Scene 12

To Speak of Home-Going

ANTOINETTE: It wasn't long before Big Mike became one of the main organizers for the Agriculture Street Group. Being that he was already retired and drawing a pension, when they needed somebody to represent the people of Agriculture Street they called on Big Mike because he spoke so well and was free to go.

FESS: Maudine was still working but she would be in on all the strategy sessions, and when they needed some information on one thing or another she'd get Michael Junior to work on the case. By this time the brilliant young man was working full-time on environmental racism for a national church. Maudine and her son became key members of the brain trust that guided Agriculture Street strategies.

CELESTINE: But two boils in the Treem-Henry family had swollen to the breaking point: one thing was that Mike's memory kept getting worse. Junior thought it was because of the toxicity in the neighborhood.

ANTOINETTE: The other thing was that despite the fact that they were really working together, Big Mike still refused to see Junior, and he was scared to death of his homosexuality. The situation was really dumb. It was holding up their work. Something had to be done.

(Jump cut.)

JUNIOR: I had to drive the truck home, Mama. I didn't believe it! I had to drive his truck home. He was sitting there in the middle of Gentilly Boulevard in rush hour, crying. I'd never seen him cry before, Mama. Here I am almost thirty years old and I've never seen my daddy cry. He had the traffic all tied up for blocks.

At first I was so pissed off I didn't recognize the truck. I saw it but traffic was so bad I couldn't pull over 'til I was a block away. I walked back to where he was still sitting . . . crying.

He looked at me but I don't think he knew who I was. He wouldn't come down out of the truck or even turn loose the wheel. At first he seemed kind of normal. I couldn't tell what was going on. He kept saying, "I'm trying to get home." I said, "So what's stopping you." He just kept saying, "I'm trying to get home." I said, "Well, go on then." He said, "I can't." I said, "Why not, Daddy." He cried, Mama. He cried and said, "I don't know where the hell it is!"

MAUDINE: Franklin and Gentilly? That's just down the street.

JUNIOR: You know that. I know that. And there was a time when Daddy knew that.

MAUDINE: He'll be okay when he wakes up.

JUNIOR: Will he, Mama? Will he? He had no idea who I was.

It's funny, Mama, I was coming home today to tell you that I'm not going to sneak around trying to duck Daddy anymore. He owes me an apology and I meant to get it. Besides, all this foolishness about his attitude about my being gay is interfering with our work.

Instead I find him out there crying in the street because he can't remember how to get home. But the worst thing, Mama, is that I don't believe he recognized me. Why, Mama? Why didn't you tell me it was like this?

MAUDINE: I . . . it wasn't "like this." Today is the first time anything like this has happened. I guess I could have seen it coming. I was hoping that things would get better.

JUNIOR: Have you taken him to a doctor? What do they say?

MAUDINE: Not much.

JUNIOR: You're a nurse now, Mama. Don't you know about this kind of stuff?

MAUDINE: They just don't know that much, baby.

JUNIOR: There must be a specialist somewhere who knows about this.

MAUDINE: Don't worry, baby. It's all right.

JUNIOR: No. It's not all right, Mama. I let him take the last ten years of my life in this family. No one should have to start off in life having to hide or apologize for being who or what they are. No more than people should have to live with all this poison. There must be healthy, loving, caring room for me among all the rest who accept the responsibility for it in our family and in our community. I was coming here today to ask you to help me in the fight to make it happen in our family. Now, I'm afraid I may have taken too long to get here.

(Junior sings "When You Love and Don't Know How To":)

I love you so much, but I don't know how to say so.
I want to hold you so much, but I don't dare to.
I want to pour out my heart, but don't think you care to
Hear what I'd have to say.
I love you so much, but I just don't know how to make you
Know just how I feel.

Like a flower needs the sun to grow,
My arms yearn to hold you so,

But I can't find the way to let you know
I tremble when I hear your name,
I swing to and fro from joy to shame.
I love you so much, but I just don't know how to . . .
To make you know just how I feel.

Scene 13

For Generations Yet to Come

ANTOINETTE: About a month after Big Mike got lost on Old
Gentilly Road, Junior and Maudine thought it might help
if they took Big Mike with them to a statewide meeting on
environmental racism. Maudine was elected to speak on
behalf of the Agriculture Street Landfill Association.

MAUDINE: The committee asked me to tell you some of the facts
about where we live. So here I am.

My name is Maudine Henry-Treem. My husband and my
son are . . . were the speakers in our family. But anyway . . .
I lived in Treme all my life 'til my husband spent our life savings on the house at 2731 Agriculture Street sixteen years
ago. The only problem is that we live on top of what used
to be the biggest dump in the city of New Orleans. In 1970,
they closed the dump. In 1974, they plowed it over, put
some fresh dirt on top of it, and started building some scattered, site housing projects, some low-rise housing units for
senior citizens, and the middle-income single-family units
where we live.

Everything looked just fine. It doesn't look bad now. We
had basic shopping facilities, convenient transportation,
and they had built a brand-new state-of-the-art school. In
fact, they're still building new homes out there and some
people are still buying.

BIG MIKE: I want to say something. I paid cash for my house.
That's the worst thing I ever did. The worst thing I ever did.

Ever. Ever. I worked hard all my life. Hard. I mean *hard*. My mama and my daddy they worked *hard*. Put their meat and their blood in this farm. They did that for me. Me. That's the money I put in my house. I ain't from here. Mississippi. My mama did. I sold my property in Mississippi—the worst thing I ever did. Mother's blood. Father's blood. What have I got to give my children? What I got for my grandkids, generations yet to come? Trade my mother's blood. What have I got to give my children? What I got for my grandkids? Generations yet to come? Trade my mother's blood for poison. These good times are killing me. The worst thing. I love my baby. I love my son. I love my boy. Love baby love son poison best thing love love.

MAUDINE: You need to stop, baby.

BIG MIKE: Huh?

MAUDINE: You need to stop now, baby.

BIG MIKE: I can hear the words but I can't tell what they mean.

MAUDINE: That's all right, baby. You did real good.

JUNIOR: That's my mother. And that's my daddy. My daddy has lost his mind, because of environmental racism. Environmental racism's robbed my daddy of his memory. My mother is the only one he can recognize now. Now he doesn't know who I am.

    When I was a little boy growing up in Treme, I was smaller than most of the other boys, and was not known to be a fighter at the time. One day my daddy sent me to the corner store to get some sugar for my mother. I came home with a bloody lip, crying. Daddy asked me, "What's wrong with you, boy?" I told him, tears rolling down my cheeks, "The big boys on the corner took my money." I wanted him to hug and comfort me and tell me everything was going to be all right. But no. He said, "You let them chase you home with your tail tucked up twixt your legs? You do anything wrong to them?"

    "No sir," I told him, "I was just going to the store like you told me."

    He looked me dead in the eye, and said, "When people mess with you for no good reason, you got to fight. You go back down there and do whatever you have to do to get me my money and bring your mama her sugar."

He stood out on the porch, watching, while I went back to that gang of mean boys, every single one of them bigger than I was. I was scared. I said, "I want my money back."

The leader of the gang said, "What's that?"

I said, "Please . . . May I have my money back, please." The gang leader started laughing at me. That made me real mad. I grabbed a St. Joe brick from the sidewalk and threw it at him as hard as I could. I missed him, but grabbed another. When they saw that I meant business, they said, "Here, take your old dirty money." I went on to the store and got the sugar for my daddy and never had another moment's trouble from those bullies.

When I got back home, Daddy told me, "Stand tall. You're a Treem man! We equal to our responsibilities."

That's how I remember my daddy. He's the one who taught me how to fight.

If we want to get rid of the poison in our air, our water, our land, we have to fight for it—no matter how big and bad the bullies we have to go up against. We have to fight these big corporations that have the government under their thumbs.

Some people try to tell us that there's no use fighting back: they're too big, too rich, too powerful. Well, if all that's true, we might as well lie down and let them have their way. All we can do is figure out what to do to get the best we can get out of it for ourselves. They're going to win anyway. There's nothing you can do but relax and enjoy it.

Well, tell that to Mrs. Davis, who lost her beautiful, little sixteen-year-old daughter. Tell that to the parents of these brain-damaged children. Tell that to the hundreds of cancer victims in Cancer Alley. Tell that to my daddy, my mother. Tell it to me.

We don't have to live like this. We don't want to live like this. We won't live like this.

If we want to get rid of the poison in our air, our water, our land, we have to fight a bunch of greedy, selfish bullies for it. We have to fight not just for ourselves, but for our

children and our grandchildren, and for the generations
yet to come.

(*Junior leads the group in a traditional song:*)

We are soldiers in the Army
We have to fight although we have to die
We've got to hold up the blood-stained banner
We have to hold it up until we die.

My father was a soldier, oh yes!
He had his hand on the justice plow.
One day he got old and couldn't fight anymore
He said, "I'll stand here, and fight anyhow!"

ANTOINETTE: That's what I'm talking about! If I didn't know better, I'd have thought that Junior snuck in here while I wasn't
looking. You got him, Shack.

SHACK: Yeah, you right! He might have been another Martin
Luther King or Malcolm X! It's too bad Junior couldn't get
his stuff together.

FESS: Just wait a minute. I've had about as much of this as
I can stand. What "stuff" are you talking about, Narcisse?
He seems to have "his stuff" very well "together" so far as
I can see. He got his education (on his own I might add),
he's taken the responsibility for parenting his child, he's a
leader in this community, and he is playing a role of growing importance in the region and the nation. And now he's
taken on a major leadership role in his family. And he's still
a young man. All in all, I'd say he's very much together.

SHACK: Aw, Fess, you know what I mean.

FESS: No. I don't know what you mean. You've been making
rude and insensitive remarks for the entire time we've been
working on this project.

CELESTINE: What's the matter, Shack? You jealous?

SHACK: Look, man, I'm sorry if what I said offended you, okay?
Everybody knows that Junior is real smart. I'm just saying
that the boy could have done a whole lot better for himself
if they'd raised him right. You dig? He's funny.

FESS: I don't believe this.

SHACK: Ain't nobody going to follow a fairy in a fight. It just ain't natural. You know that for yourself.

FESS: I don't believe this!

SHACK: The least he could do is not be rubbing it up in everybody's face. He looks normal enough.

FESS: Keep everybody in the closet, huh?

SHACK: "Don't ask, don't tell."

FESS: Do you hear what he's saying?

CELESTINE: I heard him.

ANTOINETTE: Uh-huh.

FESS: What does "funny" look like?

SHACK: Man, you got to be crazy!

CELESTINE: Crazy! He called the man crazy!

ANTOINETTE: Oh-oh! Celestine . . . ?

FESS: Answer my question, damn it. What the hell is "funny"?

SHACK: You getting on my nerves now, man.

CELESTINE: He said "funny"; what's so funny?

ANTOINETTE: Celestine!

FESS: No. Better yet, what's "normal"?

CELESTINE: Come on! "Normal." What is "normal"?

ANTOINETTE: I don't believe this. I must be drinking too much.

SHACK: You can't be serious.

FESS: Just as serious as the Angel of Death.

CELESTINE: "Swing down, sweet chariot!"

ANTOINETTE: Lord have mercy!

SHACK: Normal? You want to know what's normal?

CELESTINE: The brother wants to know.

FESS: I want to know what you think, if you think.

ANTOINETTE: Don't let him get up in Shack's face like that.

CELESTINE: "Think" about what you're trying to do to me.

SHACK: Man, don't get up in my face like that!

ANTOINETTE: All right now, that's enough!

FESS: Think. What's the matter? You having trouble thinking?

CELESTINE: Oh, I say think.

SHACK: Don't touch me.

ANTOINETTE: Think. Think.

FESS: Yes: think. Think "funny." Think "normal."

SHACK: I told you to get out my face, man.

CELESTINE: Come, Ogun. Ring the bell of truth in here.

FESS: What's the matter? You can't take the pressure?

ANTOINETTE: This wasn't supposed to be like this.

CELESTINE: Come, Shango! Give us courage to face the storm, the terrible storm that precedes and follows truth when she comes anew.

SHACK: Don't touch me!

ANTOINETTE: Y'all just stop it, right now!

FESS: Think. What is funny?

SHACK: What's the matter with you, man?

FESS: What is normal?

ANTOINETTE: Norman.

SHACK: Don't touch me.

CELESTINE: Come, Yemanja. Wash us with your healing love.

ANTOINETTE: What's the matter with you, Narcisse?

SHACK: Normal? You want to know what's normal?

CELESTINE: Come now, oh spirits of our ancestors.

FESS: Yes. I want to know what you think.

ANTOINETTE: Lord, help us all just get along.

SHACK: What's funny is men loving men and women loving women and making a mess. What's normal is men loving women and making babies. As far as I'm concerned, as far as most people is concerned, we'd all be better off if Junior and all other funny people would keep their business to themselves.

FESS: We can't.

SHACK: What?

FESS: When we are silent, you kill us.

SHACK: You mean—

FESS: I mean . . . Claude Michel and I are lovers.

SHACK: What?

ANTOINETTE: What?

CELESTINE: Say the words. Speak the truth.

FESS: When Michel and his mother return from this trip that they're on, he and I are moving into the house on Ursuline Street together. One reason for taking this trip with his mother is so that he can tell her about our plans.

SHACK: Ain't this some shit!

ANTOINETTE: This is a surprise.

CELESTINE: Junior will be surprised too when he comes back to find that you've come out in public like this.

ANTOINETTE: Why didn't you, I mean, come out before?

FESS: I am a Christian minister and I teach at a very conservative university, okay?

CELESTINE: How long y'all intended to sneak around? You think you're the only gay preacher in town? Fess, really?

FESS: I really love teaching. It's my calling. My life's work.

ANTOINETTE: Tell the truth and stay in church!

SHACK: If I had a kid, I wouldn't want him fooling with him at church or at school, I'll tell you that. I ain't going to be following no fairies in a fight.

ANTOINETTE: We've all been following Junior in this environmental justice fight. You going to quit on us just because Fess has come out?

CELESTINE: Shack ain't going nowhere, Miz Antoinette. If he makes one step toward the door, I'll break his leg. Look, Shack, you got to give up that reactionary foolishness—we're all in this together and we can't give up any of our soldiers, least of all the good ones. We need you, Fess. And, Shack, we need you too. I think that it's wonderful that you and Junior are getting your stuff together, Fess. I wish you the best for both of you.

FESS: Thank you, Miz Casenave, but—

CELESTINE: Sister Celestine.

FESS: Thank you . . . Sister Celestine.

Scene 14

In Closing

ANTOINETTE: I guess we let this thing get a little out of control.

CELESTINE: When you call the spirits in, there's no telling what they'll do when they get here.

ANTOINETTE: I'm going to get us back on the plan and wrap this thing up before another spirit breaks out up in here.

CELESTINE: The main thing is that we're all in this together. In order to determine what we must do to make it better, we must understand how Agriculture Street is tied in with the battles of people from all over Louisiana, all over this country, and all over the world. We have to listen to each other's stories.

ANTOINETTE: The Agriculture Street Landfill Community in New Orleans isn't isolated in this struggle. We identify with, and celebrate, the successful efforts of the Citizens Against Nuclear Trash. They call themselves CANT. They fought for nine long, hard years to keep a nuclear dumpsite out of their community. And they won!

SHACK: We celebrate the efforts of people in Taft, Louisiana, who fought against the Formosa plywood factory and won.

CELESTINE: The little town of Convent, Louisiana, which is eighty-percent black and already has more than twenty-six waste-producing factories in it, went to war with the governor of the state to keep Shintech Plastics out of their little community. A group of the heroic leaders—

SHACK: Like Big Mike!

ANTOINETTE: Yeah, but most of them were women!

CELESTINE: . . . from Convent went all the way to Tokyo, Japan, to tell the president of Shintech, "If your factory is all that good, keep it for yourself!" And the people of Convent won!

SHACK: All these fights are connected. We have to support each other. We can't win in south Louisiana without support from north Louisiana and New York and California and Hawaii and Puerto Rico and Snow Flake, Alabama—because these struggles are all tied together.

ANTOINETTE: Everyone, everywhere, deserves safe, healthy places to live, work and play. Everyone has a right to clean air to breathe, clean water to drink, clean soil to build their homes on, to plant their food in.

I hope you hear what I'm saying, Shack.

SHACK: We're doing this show everywhere we can because we want to make sure that Big Mike and others like him didn't die in vain.

CELESTINE: I'm sorry to say that we can't report a complete victory in the Agriculture Street Landfill yet. The longer they have to stay out there, we know the more sickness and disease we're going to see among them.

SHACK: Sometimes it's a victory just to keep on fighting for another day. At least we know what the problem is out there. There are hundreds, maybe even thousands, of communities that don't even know they got a problem.

ANTOINETTE: We say Big Mike is a hero because he came to understand that he was wrong about conditions in his community. He gave up his wrong idea and became a leader.

FESS: But Big Mike lost his memory and died before he could embrace the son who loved him, and loves him still, without a lie.

CELESTINE: I have a new idea for the closing. I know we didn't plan on it, but there's no telling what happens when the spirit comes down.

Most of us have some things that are holding us back from doing the best that we can do to move our struggle forward (like Big Mike couldn't give up his fear of homosexuality). I want us all to think about the things that are holding us back from doing our best and throw them away.

ANTOINETTE: I like that plan, Celestine, because ideas are pretty useless if they're not connected to actions. Maybe we can put things on the altar or light these candles to symbolize the things we have to release in order to be more effective in our lives. Like I might put this glass on the altar, because I intend to give up my dependence on alcohol.

CELESTINE: Miz Antoinette!

SHACK: What you say!

ANTOINETTE: That's just an example.

(The actors put objects of their own choosing on the altar and say a few words. Those who haven't an appropriate object light a candle. Celestine begins a ritual: she raises a toast to Big Mike. Fess lights a candle and commits to bringing the light of truth into the dark places in his life: to give up his grasp on silence. Shack gives up the

unexamined faith in tradition, just because it's tradition. He hugs
Fess and lights a candle.)

Big Mike was on a slow walk to the grave, like most people.
But unlike most of us, up until he lost his memory anyway,
Big Mike knew why and more or less when he was going to
die.

CELESTINE: We have a special way of dealing with death down
here in New Orleans.

SHACK: Death is no big thing, everybody does it. What you live
for and how you die is the thing. If you don't stand for something, you'll fall for anything.

ANTOINETTE: Big Mike died with dignity. Although they had
moved out to Agriculture Street, when he died, Michael still
belonged to the Royal Flush Social Aid and Pleasure Club
and, man, did they give him a beautiful home-going: they
had two bands at the wake and three for the funeral, and a
second line that lasted way up into the night, Cher!

SHACK: It was almost as bad as Sonny Dupree's funeral.
Remember that? When they got to The Famous Bar on
Barracks Street, they took Sonny out the coffin, set him up
at his favorite place on the bar, and when Professor Long
Hair's "Big Chief" came on the jukebox, they got him up
and danced all the way around the block before they put
him back in the coffin and finished the slow drag to the
burying ground.

ANTOINETTE: It was better than that, Narcisse. Big Mike's funeral
had all the spirit and dignity too. Norman, all the club members, had on black tailor-made suits trimmed in indigo with
indigo accessories, silk shirts, ties, handkerchiefs, and silk
socks. Each of them carried a black-and-indigo ostrich
feather fan. They wore black fedoras with a Jack of Spades
tucked in the band.

CELESTINE: Ase! This is for the memories of those particular per-
sons you remember to have struggled for justice. We invite
each of you to speak their names so that we may honor
them here, and, now, by remembering their contributions

to our ongoing struggle, to leave the world a better place than we found it. We invite you now to speak the names of those living and dead whose efforts have inspired you to such struggle.

(Allow time for people to fill the silence with the spoken names. A percussionist accents each name that is spoken. When it seems that no more names will be spoken, or when enough time has been allowed:)

Michael Claude Treem!
ALL: Ase!

(Celestine closes the ceremony by inviting the audience to light the candles on the altar of memories, as she pours the final libation.)

CELESTINE: Ase! We light these candles as symbols of those who live in our memories. Our circle can only be completed by giving honor to those who have gone before. None are truly dead until those who are living no longer remember them and no longer call their names.

May the memories of these honored ones fuel the passion for justice within us and provide light for our continuing struggle. Ase!
ALL: Ase!

(The percussionist puts a period at the end.
The Company sings "The Power Is in Your Hands," alternating lines in small groups:)

FIRST GROUP:
    Friends and family gathered, yes they came from miles around

SECOND GROUP:
    Tambourines ringing, umbrellas swinging, feet hardly touch the ground.

THIRD GROUP:
    There's a second line in New Orleans in the place we call Treme

FOURTH GROUP:

> Where the man they call the King of Spades has drifted
> on away.

ALL *(In unison)*:

> Sing glory! Glory! The power's in our hands.
> We can build a future, we can take a stand.
> We will tell the story of a man who stood up tall.
> He did what was right, he had the courage to fight!
> Justice! For one and all!

FIRST GROUP:

> We came to tell the story of how a hero lived and died.

SECOND GROUP:

> He didn't change the world around, Lord knows he
> really tried

THIRD GROUP:

> He set his sights on justice. He did the best that he could
> do

FOURTH GROUP:

> When the bell is rung and the job is done, his light will
> come shining through.

ALL *(In harmony)*:

> Sing glory! Glory! The power's in our hands!
> We can build a future, we can take a stand!
> We will tell the story of a man who taught! Taught us all!
> He showed us what's right, gave us the courage to fight!
> Justice! For one and all!

> Sing glory! Glory! The power's in our hands!
> We will build a brand-new future, together we stand!
> We can tell our story, how we stood up tall!
> Doing what's right, the courage to fight!
> Justice! For one and all!

Sing glory! Glory! We got the power in our hands!
Building our new future, together we stand!
Telling all our stories, and singing all our songs!
The power's in the hands of every woman, every man!
Justice for one! Justice for all! Justice! One and all!

THE END

The Collaborations

Junebug/Jack

Co-created by:

Junebug Productions
Roadside Theater

Co-written by:

John O'Neal
Ron Short
Donna Porterfield

PRODUCTION AND PERFORMANCE HISTORY

Junebug/Jack was written in 1989–1990 by John O'Neal, Ron Short and Donna Porterfield, and directed by Dudley Cocke and Steve Kent. Original music was composed by Michael Keck, John O'Neal and Ron Short. Set and lighting were designed by Ben Mays, and dramaturgs were Dudley Cocke, Steve Kent and Donna Porterfield. The play and production were a joint project of Junebug Productions of New Orleans and Roadside Theater of Whitesburg, Kentucky. Theresa Holden was the Executive Producer.

The original cast was Tommy Bledsoe, Angelyn DeBord, Michael Keck, Kim Neal Mays, John O'Neal and Ron Short. The first touring cast was Michael Keck, Kim Neal Mays, John O'Neal, Nancy Jeffrey Smith, Ron Short and Latteta Theresa. Joining subsequent casts were Adella Gautier, Shawn Jackson, Carl Le Blanc and Kenneth Raphael.

Junebug/Jack premiered in Atlanta, Georgia, on October 4, 1990, at the Alternate ROOTS performance festival, and continued touring for the following nine years to big cities and small towns alike, reaching 22,719 audience members in eighteen states, as well as in London, England. The play became the occasion for communities to convene conversations about race and class, which Junebug/Roadside artists supported with return visits. In a number of tours, ecumenical community choirs were formed, rehearsed the play's music over several months, and then were staged into the production.

—TRH

Setting and Characters

There are six actors: three are with Junebug Productions, an African-American theater company; three are from Roadside Theater, an Appalachian theater company.

Junebug Productions actors and singers:
JOHN O'NEAL
KENNETH RAPHAEL
ADELLA GAUTIER

Roadside Theater actors and singers:
RON SHORT
KIM NEAL
NANCY JEFFREY SMITH

The actors use their real names as they introduce themselves at the beginning of the play. Throughout the play each actor plays many characters in the stories they are telling.

The stage is bare, with just a few chairs on each side, which will be used throughout the play to create the environment of the various scenes. The lighting is very important in this play to help create the various settings.

The Company enters singing "Homeward Now Shall I Journey":

> Homeward now shall I journey
> Homeward upon the rainbow
> Homeward now shall I journey
> Homeward upon the rainbow
> To life unending and beyond it
> Yea homeward now shall I journey
> To joy unchanging and beyond it
> Yea, homeward now shall I journey.

(The Company repeats the song, then speaks to the audience:)

KENNETH: Hello! I'm Kenneth Raphael. This is John O'Neal and this is Adella Gautier. We're from the Junebug Theater Project, which is based in New Orleans, Louisiana.

KIM: This is Nancy Jeffrey Smith, that's Ron Short and I'm Kim Neal. We're a part of the Roadside Theater from the Appalachian Mountains, 'round Kentucky and Virginia.

ADELLA: So what you got here is two groups of hard-headed people. Over fifteen years ago, out of concern for what was happening in *both* of our communities, we decided that whenever we could, we'd get together, share stages and trade audiences. Junebug would play for Roadside audiences in the mountains of Appalachia, and Roadside would play for Junebug audiences in the Black Belt South. And we have had some fun. Some more fun than others. Out of these efforts to work together we created tonight's production of *Junebug/Jack.*

RON: What we soon found out was that the people in both our communities have a lot in common, especially music and storytelling. Junebug-slash-Jack—some people spend a lifetime studying those slashes. Junebug is a mythic African-American storyteller invented by young people from SNCC (the Student Nonviolent Coordinating Committee), during The Civil Rights Movement. He represents the collective wisdom of struggling black people. For mountain people, Jack represents the triumph of the human spirit, no matter how hard the times get.

NANCY: And tonight we've all come here together to share some of our songs and stories with you.

ADELLA: See everybody has a story, their own story. I bet you all got some pretty good stories, too. But it seems like it has come to the place where people think their stories aren't worth anything anymore.

KENNETH: Trouble is, seems like some people are always wanting to tell our story for us.

KIM: But, we got to tell it ourselves! Otherwise how we gonna know it's us.

JOHN: And if we don't listen to the stories of others, how we gonna know who they are?

NANCY: Our ancestors came over to this country on big boats with big sheets on 'em looking for freedom.

KENNETH: Our ancestors came over to this country in the belly of big boats.

NANCY: They got here and lots of them got kindly wild . . .

KENNETH: Off the boats in shackles and chains they filed . . .

NANCY: Some of 'em took to running after game . . .

KENNETH: Sold off and given a white man's name . . .

NANCY: Some of 'em died out . . .

KENNETH: Some of 'em just died . . .

NANCY: But some of them kept on climbing . . .

KENNETH: Kept on climbing . . .

NANCY: A little bit further on up into our mountains.

KENNETH: Further and further away from their "masters."

(The Company sings "I've Got a Home Somewhere":)

NANCY:

    I've got a home somewhere
    I'm leaving today
    I've got a home somewhere

NANCY AND KENNETH:
    I'm leaving today

ALL:

    I've got a home somewhere a heartbeat away

KENNETH:

    I want to taste freedom

NANCY AND KENNETH:

    I'm leaving today
    I want to taste freedom

ALL:

    I'm leaving today
    I've got a home somewhere a heartbeat away.

KIM: 'Course now when our people got here, there were people already here. Some say five million people, maybe
more. Already been here ten thousand years. They already
knowed about this land, and how to survive on it, and our
people learned from them.

KENNETH: I've got Native American blood on both sides of my family . . .

RON: Ain't a family in the mountains ain't got some Indian blood in them.

KIM: Wasn't long though, some of us started acting like they weren't people at all—started calling them names—heathens, savages. Next thing you knowed, we started calling each other names:

KENNETH: Rednecks . . .

NANCY: Coons . . .

JOHN: Hillbillies . . .

RON: Niggers . . .

(The Company freezes.)

KIM: Wonder why that happened?

RON *(Sings)*:

    Which side are you on?
    Which side are you on?
    Which side are you on?
    Some day
    This is a war we're
    Fighting
    The battles not yet done
    We gotta stick together
    Until this war is won.

KENNETH *(Sings)*:

    We shall overcome
    We shall overcome
    We shall overcome

    Deep in my heart
    I do believe
    We shall overcome
    Some day.

ADELLA: You know sometimes a story or song can start out one place and end up someplace else entirely different. *(Dixie starts to sing in the background; Ron plays "Dixie" on the fiddle)* Now take "We Shall Overcome." It began as a hymn in the black church and was changed to how we know it today during the 1930s Tobacco Workers Strike in North Carolina.

KIM: "Which Side Are You On?" comes out of a coal miners' strike in Harlan County, Kentucky. It was written by Florence Reece.

NANCY: Now that tune Ron's playing . . . you may not recognize it, but that's "Dixie."

ADELLA: And some of us have real strong attitudes about it, too.

KIM: "Dixie" started out as an Irish dance tune.

KENNETH: Then it got "borrowed" by African slaves who used it for their own dances.

NANCY: Then it got "borrowed" by a white musician for his minstrel show.

JOHN: Then the Confederate Army took it and used it for their own damnable purposes.

(Ron ends "Dixie," and Kenneth begins "Jubilo.")

ADELLA: Hear that? Change a few notes of "Dixie" and make a brand-new tune: "Jubilo." "Jubilo" is a song that celebrates the "Juneteenth": the time the slaves got the news about the Emancipation Proclamation.

JOHN: Black folks "borrowed" back the dance tune from all them other people and used it for their own celebration.

KENNETH: Speaking of songs with a complex history, here's one that everybody knows:

(Kenneth begins "John Henry":)

> John Henry was just a li'l baby boy,
> No bigger than the palm of your hand,
> He picked up a hammer and a li'l piece of steel,
> Said, "I'm gonna be a steel-drivin' man."

ALL:

> Lord, Lord.
> Said, "I'm gonna be a steel-drivin' man."

KENNETH:

> John Henry said to the captain,
> "A man ain't nothin' but a man,
> But before I let that steam drill drive me down,
> I'm gonna die with a hammer in my hand."

ALL:

> Lord, Lord.
> "Die with a hammer in my hand."

KENNETH:

> Now the man that invented that steam drill,
> Thought he was doing mighty fine,
> John Henry drove steel fourteen feet,
> The steam drill only made nine.

ALL:

> Lord, Lord.
> Steam drill only made nine.

KENNETH:

> John Henry hammered on the mountain,
> His hammer was ringing fire,
> He hammered so hard he broke his poor heart,
> He lay down his hammer and he died.

ALL:

> Lord, Lord.
> Lay down his hammer and he died.

KENNETH:

> Early Monday morning,
> When the blue bird begins to sing,
> Way up on the mountaintop,
> You can hear John Henry's hammering.

ALL:

> Lord, Lord.
> You can hear John Henry's hammering.
> You can hear John Henry's hammering.
> Lord, Lord.
> You can hear John Henry's hammering.

ADELLA: John Henry was a black man. 'Course some people say
that John Henry was not a real person at all.

KENNETH: They'll tell you he's just a story—a legend.

ADELLA: There's nothing wrong with telling stories and legends.

KENNETH: 'Course now it depends on who's telling the story and why.

ADELLA: Now here's a fella who hails from south Mississippi and goes by the title of:

KENNETH AND ADELLA: Junebug Jabbo Jones!

JUNEBUG: I am a storyteller. I say "storyteller" 'stead of liar 'cause there's a heap of difference between a storyteller and a liar. A liar, that's somebody want to cover things over—mainly for his own private benefit. But a *storyteller*, that's somebody who'll take and *un*-cover things, so that everybody can get something good out of it. I'm a storyteller, storyteller. Oh, it's a heap of good meanin' to be found in a story if you got the mind to hear . . . A mind to hear.

I am not the first one to carry the title of "Junebug Jabbo Jones." Neither the onliest to have that name. The very first Junebug started out life as a Negro slave. From the time that he was big enough to see straight, his maw took one look at him and said, "Lawd have mercy, this here's going to be one of them bad *boogers!*" Booger was so bad as a child he would not take funk from a skunk. Right away his maw seen it wasn't half a chance for him to make a full grown man 'fore the white folks to kill him.

So when he made seven years old, his mother got together with an auntie—who some people say could work root—they took him down to the river and pretended that he got drowned down there.

(Humming from the Company begins.)

They mourned, had a funeral and everything. Wore black clothes for three weeks! But in actual fact, they snuck around the backway, took him down to the Cypress Swamp, turned him over to Crazy Bill to raise. Now, Bill was so crazy, he decided to run off and live in the swamp by hisself rather than to live his life as a slave. That's how crazy Bill was. Bill belonged to what they used to call a "good master."

ADELLA: A good what?

JUNEBUG: A "good master"! Baptist preacher. He taught Bill how to read and everything. He had every intention to make a preacher out of Bill. Bill had to run off one night during a thunderstorm because that preacher had a fit of rage when Bill showed him where it say in the Bible: "It's a sin 'fore God for a man to own a slave or to be a slave. It's in the Book!"

That preacher got so mad at what Bill showed him in the Bible he went to grab hisself a gun. Bill took off running in that thunderstorm. That preacher got Bill lined up dead in his sight. About to pop down on him. Bill stopped, seed where that preacher had the drop on him. Stood stark still. Throwed his hands up in the sky, hollered out something loud in African. Well, don't you know, a bolt of lightning come down out of the cloud, hit the barrel of that gun, sealed it up plumb shut, knocked that preacher down on his butt and turned every hair on his body from jet black to silver white—right on the spot!

Bill came back over there, looked at that preacher all sniveling up in the mud and the rain, smiled kind of sad like to himself, and *walked* on down in that swamp. And stayed down there too.

From that night on, anytime you'd pass that white-haired preacher's house, you could see him sitting on the porch with four or five guns beside the one that got sealed shut by that bolt of lightning.

He swore, "I'll kill any man that goes down in my swamp to get Bill before I get ready to go for him." But he ain't never went down there. And he ain't never again stood astride a pulpit nor let his shadow fall across the face of an open Bible.

There's lots of people scared to go down in that swamp. Some said they was haints, but they ain't no haints. It was that first Junebug and Crazy Bill. That first Junebug stayed down there with Bill from the time he was seven years old 'til he became a full grown man. Many nights they sat up all night long, reading, studying. Since they didn't have to spend all their time working like all the other slaves had to do, they had plenty of time to think. They studied everything that went on around there. They saw everything inside of thirty or forty miles in every direction. They saw that in spite of the terrible conditions most of the colored people were living up under, in most sections it was more of them than there were white folk. If people could have just seen that, there's no telling what could have happened. (Ain't like it is up in here tonight.) Then again there was a whole bunch of white people that might as well to have been slaves for all they could get out of life. They seed that between the colored slaves and the poor white people, didn't hardly nothin' get done around there unless they were the ones to do it. They seen where people would make little stories and songs to make their days go faster and make their load seem lighter and they put secret meaning in their stories and songs. But everybody was so busy trying to keep their own heads from getting cracked, that they didn't take the time to stand back and look at the big picture that had everybody in it.

Right there, that first Junebug, and Old Crazy Bill, seen where there was a job that *needed* to be done. It's a job that need to be done. They knowed it was a bunch of people that would have killed them for teaching people how to read or spreading news that they did not want spread. They knowed that. "But they was a job needed to be done. And we got to be the ones do it. We got to do it!"

As soon as that first Junebug got big enough to leave out the swamp on his own, he commenced going from plantation to plantation, living by his wit. He'd listen to what people was saying, watch what they were doing, and then, so people could get a better idea what they could do to help change things, make things better, he would tell these over here what these over here been up to. That way the people that were struggling to make things better would feel support and encouragement. And those who weren't doing all they could, maybe should, would be uncovered, and be made to feel ashamed.

Whenever that first Junebug would find somebody who looked like they might make a pretty good storyteller, he'd help them figure out how they could run away. He'd take them down in the swamp, turn them over to Ol' Crazy Bill. Bill would teach them how to read, make their figures, everything they needed to know to be good storytellers. Before long there were a lot of them going around, watching, listening, and learning, and telling stories to whosoever wanted to hear. All of them doing it under the title of—

ALL: "Junebug Jabbo Jones"!

KENNETH: Wait, wait, now that's not his real name. It's just a title of a job that need to be did.

JOHN: Yeah, like "king."

ADELLA: Or "queen."

KENNETH: Yeah! And they all don't have to be black.

JOHN: And they definitely don't have to be men.

KIM: That's right, Junebug. There's lots of women up in the mountains like to tell stories. Good ones, too. There's one about where I come from. You see, there was this family lived way up on the side of the mountain and they lived like folks lived in that time.

NANCY: Which was grubbing out a living.

RON: And having young'uns to help grub out that living.

NANCY: Well, this family sure had a—

KIM, RON AND NANCY: *A lot* of young'uns.

RON: The first young'un they had they'd named Jack.

KIM: A purty good name.

NANCY: And after that they just named their young'uns whatever they could.

KIM: Well, they got a lot of the names out of the Bible, from Abel to Zebidiah.

RON: They went through the Sears Catalog. Named one Hardware!

KENNETH: That's a name to live up to!

NANCY: Then one morning they woke up and Mommy had another little baby with her.

RON: Well, for the life of her she couldn't think up a new name for this little young'un.

KIM: But they put their heads together and they decided to call him—

KIM, RON AND NANCY: Jack!

NANCY: Reckon by now they'd forgotten that was their first one's name.

KIM: And when they figgered out what they'd done it 'uz too late.

RON: So they started callin' the oldest boy—

NANCY: Big Jack!

RON: And they called the youngest boy—

KIM: Little Jack!

NANCY: Now Little Jack and Big Jack, they really took up with each other.

KIM: Little Jack follered Big Jack everwhere he went.

RON: But then Big Jack went off to work for this rich feller down the road.

NANCY: We'll just call him "King."

JOHN: "King Coal."

KIM: "King Cotton."

ALL: Always a "King"!

KIM: Little Jack wanted to go with Big Jack.

NANCY *(As Big Jack)*: No, you got to stay home!

KIM: Now there was plenty brothers and sisters for him to play with, but Little Jack missed Big Jack so much.

RON: Then, early one morning Little Jack seed Big Jack coming up the mountain.

KIM: Little Jack was just about to give him a big bear hug.

RON: But they was somethin' bad wrong. Big Jack looked awful. They helped Big Jack back up to the house and put him to bed. But when they took off his shirt they seed—

KIM: Three big strops of hide missing out of Big Jack's back!

RON: They doctored him best they could, but he kept on getting' worser. Finally they knowed that Big Jack was gonna have to have some medicine from the doctor if he was going to get well at all.

KIM: 'Course, now they didn't have no money to be goin' out buying medicine with, not to buy nothing with.

RON: Folks just didn't need money much.

KIM, RON AND NANCY: But doctors sure seemed to!

KIM: Well, one morning Little Jack come down to breakfast with his best little suit of clean clothes on and a little gunnysack with his working overhauls in it.

RON *(As Mommy)*: Just a minute. Just where do you think you're a goin'?

KIM *(As Little Jack)*: I'm heading off to work for the King so to get some money for Big Jack to have some medicine.

RON *(As Mommy)*: You're too little to be goin' off to work."

KIM *(As Little Jack)*: Well a man has to do what a man has to do, Mommy.

RON: And off he went.

NANCY: It didn't take Jack long to get down to that King's house. Went up and knocked on the door. King come out and Jack says:

KIM *(As Little Jack)*: Excuse me, King, but I was wondering, do you need any work done?

RON *(As King)*: Well, you're a mighty scrawny little rooster, but I reckon I can get my money's worth out of you. Pays a dollar a day. You interested?

KIM: Jack was right in for that.

RON *(As King)*: Oh, by the way, there's one more little deal . . . Anybody works for me goes by my rules. Whichever one of us makes the other one mad first gets to throw that one down, take three strips of hide out of his back. See now, if I make you mad, I get three strips of hide out of your back, and I don't have to pay you nothin'.

KIM *(As Little Jack)*: And if I make you mad, King, I get three strips of hide and my wages?

RON *(As King)*: Yeah. If you make me mad. I'll tell you what, Jack, I'll throw in a bushel of gold, 'cause you can't make me mad. I'm the King!

KIM *(As Little Jack)*: Well, King, we'll see about that.

NANCY: Jack had come a long way and was awful hungry, but he was awful proud too, and his mommy had raised him not to beg, so he says:

KIM *(As Little Jack)*: Reckon I better wash up before I eat supper.

RON *(As King)*: Eat! Boy you ain't done nothin' to deserve no supper!

KIM *(As Little Jack)*: But . . .

RON *(As King)*: Why, now, that don't make you mad does it?

KIM *(As Little Jack)*: No, I ain't mad. Just hungry.

RON *(As King)*: Oh, good. Now you see that corn crib out there?

KIM *(As Little Jack)*: That's a corn crib?

RON *(As King)*: No. That's your hotel for tonight!

KIM *(As Little Jack)*: Now just a minute, King. I come all the way from Mommy's house, you won't give me nothin' to eat, and now you expect me to sleep *there*?!! . . ."

RON *(As King)*: Um . . . Yeah. It doesn't make you mad, now, does it? You don't mind do ye?

KIM *(As Little Jack)*: Shucks no. I don't mind.

RON *(As King)*: Oh, good. Now get. You got a hard day's work ahead of you.

NANCY: Next morning Jack went up to the King's house bright and early, but the King met him outside.

KIM *(As Little Jack)*: Uhhh, King, something smells good! What's for breakfast? I could eat a hog.

RON *(As King)*: Breakfast? You just don't get it, do you, boy? You ain't done nothin' to earn no breakfast.

KIM *(As Little Jack)*: Look here, King, I'm getting awful hungry!

RON *(As King)*: Why, Jack, you ain't getting' mad are you?

KIM *(As Little Jack)*: No, I ain't mad! It's just low blood sugar.

NANCY: The King took Jack out to the barn. Showed him his fine flock of sheep and says:

RON *(As King)*: Jack, take my sheep up to the high meador. Don't you lose a one of 'em!

KIM: So Jack took them sheep way up in a high meadow. But he was so weak that he just layed down underneath a shade tree. Felt like his stomach was playing tag with his backbone. When this purty little lamb went skippin' by, saying:

NANCY *(As Lamb)*: Baa . . . Baa . . . Baa . . .

KIM: But Jack was so hungry, it sounded like that little sheep was saying:

NANCY *(As Lamb)*: LUNCH, LUNCH, LUNCH . . .

KIM: Jack banged him on the head, built him up a fire, and had him a fine lunch of roast mutton.

NANCY: That evening he took the rest of the sheep back to the King's house. There was the King counting the sheep . . .

RON *(As King)*: 996, 997, 998, 999 . . . Jack, where's my little prize lamb with the black ears?

> *(To an audience member)* Excuse me, have you seen my lamb?

KIM *(As Little Jack)*: Well, King, you hadn't given me nothin' to eat and I was mighty hungry, so I eat him.

RON *(As King)*: You eat my lamb? That was my little prize lamb I was raising for breeding.

KIM *(As Little Jack)*: Yeah, King, it was a good lamb all right, tasted mighty good.

RON *(As King)*: You good for nothin' . . .

KIM *(As Little Jack)*: Why, King, are you mad?

RON *(As King)*: No. I ain't mad.

NANCY: But that night the King fed Jack a real good supper.

KIM: And fed him a good breakfast the next morning, too.

NANCY: Took Jack out to the field where he had a fine horse hitched up to a plow.

RON *(As King)*: Can you plow? I want you to plow up this patch for me. I aim to put in some turnips.

KIM *(As Little Jack)*: Of course, I can plow. So, Jack giddy-upped that horse and set out plowing these long, straight furrows.

NANCY: The King watched him, got satisfied Jack knew what he was doing, went on back to the house.

KIM: About that time this old woman come down the road riding this old rickety horse.

NANCY *(As Horse and Woman)*: Rickety, rackety, humpity, bumpity.

KIM: You could hear its bones clanking together, it was that poor.

> *(As Little Jack)* Hey, good morning, Moms. That sure is a mighty fine horse you got there.

NANCY *(As Woman)*: Why, Jack you ortn't make fun of a ol' woman who's got the best she has!

KIM *(As Jack)*: Now, no, I think that is a fine horse. Why, I bet the King wishes he had one like that. I don't suppose you'd be willin' to swap horses with me?

NANCY *(As Woman)*: It's a deal. *(She gallops off)*

KIM: Jack hitched that old rickety horse to the harness and set in to plowing that field.

KIM AND NANCY: Just as crooked as a dog's hind leg.

NANCY: When the King come back:

RON *(As King)*: Hey, Jack, how you doin'? Wait a minute! Where's my horse?

KIM *(As Little Jack)*: Right here, King. That big ol' fat horse eat too much, so I swapped him for this'n. This'n won't eat much.

RON *(As King)*: You swapped my fine workhorse for this bag of bones?

KIM *(As Little Jack)*: King, you sound mad. You ain't mad are you?

RON *(As King)*: No, I ain't mad. Low blood sugar.

NANCY: But the King decided he wasn't gonna let Jack near no more of his animals. The next morning Jack was to pick apples.

RON *(As King)*: You do know how to pick apples, don't you?

KIM *(As Little Jack)*: Sure do.

RON *(As King)*: Well, get to it.

NANCY: The King sent Jack up to the orchard with some bushel baskets and a ladder.

KIM: But Jack snuck back down to the house and got a big double bit ax.

NANCY: And went to cutting down them big fine apple trees.

KIM *(As Jack)*: TIMBER!!!

NANCY: And then picked the apples off of the limbs, once they's down on the ground.

KIM: It's the modern way!

NANCY: When the King came out:

RON *(As King)*: Hey!! What in the devil are you doing?

KIM *(As Little Jack)*: Pickin' apples.

RON *(As King)*: Boy, you're gonna ruin me, you big dumb hillbilly. Don't you know nothin'?! You don't chop down the trees. This is how you pick apples.

NANCY: And he took the ladder and set it up against one of the trees, climbed up the ladder, and went to picking apples and putting them in his sack.

KIM *(As Jack)*: Well, that's one way of doin' it, all right, King. But what if somebody was to come up to you and do this . . .

NANCY: And he yanked that ladder out from under the King. The King just had time to latch his arm over a limb.

RON *(As King)*: Jack, you let me down. Put that ladder up here this minute!

KIM *(As Little Jack)*: Uh-uh. I don't like the way you been treating me, and I don't like the way you treated my brother. But I'll put the ladder back if you'll get your wife, the Queen, to make me a big deep-dish apple pie.

RON *(As King)*: Okay, okay, go tell her I said to fix you one.

KIM: So Jack went running down to the house, knocked on the door, and the Queen come out:

NANCY *(As Queen)*: Yeah, what do you want?

KIM *(As Little Jack)*: Queen, the King said for you to give me a great big . . . kiss.

NANCY *(As Queen)*: In your dreams, sonny boy.

KIM *(As Little Jack)*: Hey King, she says she won't do it!

NANCY *(As Queen):* Am I supposed to do what he says?

RON *(As King)*: Yes, yes, give him what he wants right now!

(Kiss.

The King gets out of the tree and moves to the house.)

Now you're gonna get it! I'm gonna bust your head wide open!

KIM *(As Little Jack)*: What's the matter, King. Are you mad?

RON *(As King)*: You're durn right I'm mad!

KIM: Jack throwed him down right then and there.

NANCY: Cut three big strips of hide off of the King's back.

KIM: Collected a bushel of gold and went on back home. He went in to where Big Jack was and seed he was bad off. Family was sure he wouldn't make it 'til morning. But Jack took them three strips of hide out of his pocket, washed 'em off real good, and laid them out on Big Jack's back. They fit real good.

NANCY: Next morning, Big Jack was up eating breakfast. It wasn't long 'til he was up and working around the place, feelin' fine.

KIM: And to this day:

NANCY: Big Jack,

KIM: Little Jack,

NANCY: All their children,

KIM: Grandchildren,

NANCY: And greats,

KIM AND NANCY: Are doing well!

KIM: And folks still say that that entire family has got:

KIM AND NANCY: Royal blood in their veins!

(Ron begins "Down on the Farm":)

RON:

       Cornmeal bread and cornmeal gravy
       They'll make you fat
       But they won't make you lazy.
       Talking 'bout the good ol' things down on the farm:
       Black-eyed peas and collard greens.
       They'll fill you up, but they'll
       Keep you clean.
       Talking 'bout the good ol' things down on the farm.

London, England, Paris, France,
Ain't none of them places stand a chance.
Talking 'bout good ol' things down on the farm.
Don't care 'bout Betty Crocker's Gold Medal.
Ain't nothin' no better than my mama's iron kettle.
Talkin' bout the good ol' things down on the farm.

ADELLA:

Rabbit stew and squirrel gravy:
Drive you wild, but it won't make you crazy.
Talkin' 'bout good ol' things down on the farm.
Fried squash!

RON: Fried 'maters!
JOHN: Fried corn!
ALL: Fried 'taters!

Talkin' 'bout good ol' things down on the farm!

NANCY:

Apple pie and strawberry jam:
Makes me sweet as I am.
Talkin' 'bout good ol' things down on the farm.
That ol' wild turkey and wild corn,
Make you glad that you was born.
Talkin' 'bout good ol' things down on the farm.

KENNETH: I live in the big city now, but I grew up in the country.
My grandfather had over eight hundred acres of good bottom land in south Mississippi. We still own a nice little farm
down the Dog Leg Branch off from the Twin Oak Trees on
the New Caledonia Road. New Calendonia Road? That's the
road that runs from Seven Waters over to Four Corners. Four
Corners! Now Four Corners ain't too far from Magnolia,
which is a big little town sits on old State Highway 27, about
nine miles south and a little bit west from McComb . . .
Mississippi . . . I don't believe they know where that's at. You

know where Jackson, Mississippi's at? Well, take that for New
Orleans. And this is Jackson. My home is right there. Right
there. Part of Pike County.

RON: Pike County? Pike County is in Kentucky.

KENNETH: Well, this Pike County has got to be different. You see,
there used to be plenty of people up in there; it was almost
enough black people for us to start our own little town, but,
now, my brother's the only one still got a working farm up
there.

(*Junebug reminds him to say more about Charlie Moffett.*)

Oh, Charlie Moffett still on county registry, but he's working two jobs in McComb to pay rent on the land he was born
on, in a house his daddy built with his own hands.

RON: It's the same way in Pike County, Kentucky. There was a
time when if you had the right to a piece of land and was
willing to work, you could make a living off that land. But
then it got to the place where you couldn't do a thing if
you didn't have money. When they brought money into the
mountains to help us out, the people started moving out . . .
take our land away.

JOHN: There was a time when black people gave blood, sweat
and tears to get forty acres and a mule. But now black-
owned land is being lost at the rate of about forty-two-thou-
sand acres a month. It's hard to see it, when land is being
lost, 'cause the land don't go nowhere.

NANCY: Now it's not that hard to see in the mountains, 'cause
they'll cart off a whole mountain in the back of one of them
dump trucks to make a strip mine. Still and all, when people
lose their land, they sort of drift off a few at a time, so you
don't really notice what's happening 'til they been gone for
a while.

I don't rightly know when things started to change. They
never did for me really. Saw all my young'uns marry off and
leave, but even 'fore then, it wasn't the same. I never liked
the idea of my children moving off, nor going to work in
the coal mines, but they wasn't nothing I could do about it.

Once they knowed about them things they didn't have, it was too late.

We worked hard and I can rightly say my young'uns never went cold or hungry for lack of something to wear or food to eat. We never had much, but we always had plenty. It's not what you've *got*, it's what you're *satisfied with*.

I know children are different from their parents, but they's things that they want that I don't even know about, nor care to. But I guess that's the whole thing. You know what you know. It's kinda like that little story about Adam and Eve. It wasn't the apple that got 'em into trouble, it was what they knowed after they eat it. And they ain't no turning back from that.

KIM: When we went to Dayton, I was so excited about living in a big city. I was gonna get new clothes and go to the movies. I was gonna play with kids that wouldn't be my cousins. But I never did fit in. I tried, but I was just too different. Mommy said it wasn't me different, it was them, but it didn't seem that way to me. I got to thinking there was something wrong with me. You know it seemed to me like going off to Dayton was like headin' for the Promised Land . . . But I ended up in the wilderness, believing in nothing or nobody.

(The Company sings "Cities of Gold" in G-sharp/A-flat:)

RON:

> Tell me where do you come from
> Tell me where will you go
> To the mountains around you
> Or the Cities of Gold?

ALL:

> Cities of Gold, Cities of Gold
> Oh so lonely and so cold
> You can lose your very soul
> Living in Cities of Gold.

RON:

> Now the people, they said to Pharoah
> You better let our children go
> 'Cause we're tired of livin' our lives
> So you can build your Cities of Gold.

ADELLA: Everybody in my family could sing. Our dog Red Rover, you could give him a harmony part and he'd hold it. No matter how tired Mama was when she got in from work, she's a house cleaner, she cleans houses for people; she'd be in the kitchen humming to the pots and pans. After dinner, my brother, my sister, my daddy would start harmonizing on some old church song and it'd be no telling how long before we went to bed—two-, three o'clock A.M.

But we were not the only ones could sing. We had ourselves a powerful singing preacher at our church. Sister Reverend Gary didn't just sing, she knew how to bring the music out in people. Our whole church would be rocking. Music tied our family together, united the members of the church and community. Music was everywhere: revivals, funerals, weddings, or big rally of some sort, marching with my daddy in The Movement. And we'd be there singing.

One Sunday morning, my cousin Sheila paid us a surprise visit at our church. Now before Sheila moved to Dayton, she was the best singer around. When she walked in, she looked like a picture straight out of *Ebony* magazine. She took her seat in the choir. A hush fell over the church. Reverend Sister Gary said, "Sheila sing us a song." Sheila stood up, cleared her throat, and cut loose. Child, three people asked to be accepted into membership before Sheila finished singing.

Sheila told me, "Girlfriend, the only reason you won't get what you want in the City is if you don't have the gumption to stoop down and pick it up!" The very next day I said, "Mama, I'm going to Dayton where Sheila live."

Mama said, "Dayton or no Dayton, you finish high school 'cause I ain't gonna to take care of your children in my old age!"

NANCY: Amen!

ADELLA: See how they all stick together! Well, I finished high school, mainly for her, but the ink wasn't dry on my diploma before I was on the bus heading for Dayton.

When I got to Dayton, Sheila looked like a different person at the Greyhound station. Her face was all pinchy and she was coughing all the time.

This white man said, "You got your claim check?" And I said, "Yassuh, right here." Sheila said, "Girl, you better leave all that country stuff at home. You don't have to be sniffing up to no white folk here in Dayton. Here, man, just give her her stuff!" Sheila got me a job in the plant where she was working. I worked side by side with this white woman: Kim. Me and Kim hit it off pretty good. Both our hands going nonstop to keep the assembly line moving. We hit production and then some. One day we found out we knew some of the same old church songs. We just started singing together, while we worked, during break, after lunch, just for the heck of it. 'Course she sang like white folks sing, and I sing like black folks, but we ended up laughing our heads off about how it sounded when we put that together. And we found out that neither one of us was scared to speak up for our rights. We didn't take no stuff off of nobody. That's how we became union leaders.

And we seen that of all the promotions that year, not one had been a woman, a black, or a Mexican. So we spoke up about it. Sheila coughed and said, "You better leave that crazy white girl alone. Ain't neither one of y'all got no sense." But before long a black man got promoted.

The mess really didn't start 'til we seed all the supervisors and the managers walking around wearing these white protective masks over their faces when they were on the floor. Well, we didn't have masks on the line. We were the ones working right in the pollution and we didn't rate to be protected. Me and Kim said, "Hey, what's up with that?"

We went to the boss and he listened. "Um-huh. Um-huh. You fired. And you fired, too, gal." Me and Kim, we lost our jobs. Sheila kept her job, and kept on working there. But Sheila never sang no more. Sheila died before she was thirty-two.

JUNEBUG: I was eighteen years old before I got set to leave home. A lot a fellers hung around back home 'til they was big enough.

NANCY: Or bad enough . . .

JUNEBUG: . . . to go in the Army. But the first one I ever remember to outright leave home with no intention to return, was my friend, Phillip Anthony "Po" Tatum.

KENNETH *(As Po)*:

I'm going to the City
Where the women's really pretty
And they tell me that the money fall like rain.
I'm tired of picking cotton!
Mississippi's gotten rotten
I'm gonna pack my bags and jump the quickest North-
bound train.

JUNEBUG: 'Fore long, everybody was singing Po's song.

CARL *(As Po)*:

I'm going to Chicago, baby
Heading for the City
I'm going to Chicago, baby . . .

ALL:

Heading for the City
Chica-Chica-Chica-Chica-Chica-Chicago
Chica-Chica-Chica-Chica-Chica-Chicago
Chica-Chica-Chica-Chica-Chica-Chicago
I'm going to catch a Northbound train.

ADELLA: "ZUDIO!"

(The Company sings "Zudio":)

ALL:

> Here come Zudio, Zudio, Zudio
> Here come Zudio all night long.
> Step back, Sally, Sally, Sally
> Step back, Sally, all night long.
>
> Walking down the alley, alley, alley
> Walking down the alley all night long.
> Looking down the alley, what did I see?
> A *big, fat* man from Tennessee.

JUNEBUG: There he is!

ALL:

> I betcha five dollars that you can't do this!
> To the front, to the back, to the side, side, side!
> You lean way back, then *ball the jack*!
> You lean *way* back, you get a *hump* on you back
> You lean *way* back, you get a *hump* on you back
> You lean *way* back, you get a *hump* on you back.
> You do the *camel walk*, you do the *camel walk*
> You do the *camel walk*!

JUNEBUG: By the time Po got to the city, there were lots of games like Zudio to be learned, but Po already had his mind set on other kinds of games—games where there was money to be made. He started playing with the boys from the big time, ended up in jail. Years later, I found Po in Chicago. One of the things he was trying to do to straighten himself out, get his life back together, was making a garden in the city and organizing others to do the same. By that time he had changed his tune:

KENNETH *(As Po)*:

> I got a garden in the city
> My okra's really pretty
> I ain't had no greens that tastes so good since I was home
> I had to put aside my shopping

That grocery bill left me rocking
I had to leave that doggone grocery store alone.

I'm living off my garden, baby
Garden in the city
I'm living off my garden, baby
Garden in the city.
Diga-Diga-Diga-Diga-Diga-Chicago
Diga-Diga-Diga-Diga-Diga-Chicago
Diga-Diga-Diga-Diga-Diga-Chicago
Trying to make myself a brand-new home.

JUNEBUG: Yeah, my man Po, seemed like the system just got the best of him. He went out in a blaze of glory, trying to change the whole thing all by himself.

(The music to "You Can't Judge a Book by Looking at the Cover" plays. Junebug and Po sing along.)

JUNEBUG AND PO:
You can't judge a book by looking at the cover
You can read my letter
But I bet you can't read my mind.
If you want to get down, down, down
You got to spend some time
I want to walk with you, I want to talk with you
I wanna, wanna, wanna, wanna rap with you.

PO:
When you grow up in a country
Things are hard
Times are tough

JUNEBUG:
You growing your own food but it never seems enough
You too smart for the country

PO:
You got to get away

JUNEBUG:
> You move to the city
> Got to be a better way!

PO:

> So you move to the city
> Put the country stuff behind

JUNEBUG:

> But when you hit the city
> It starts to messing with your mind
> You struggle and you scramble
> Try to do the best you can.

PO:

> You think you working for a living?
> Hell, you working for The Man!
> People stack like chickens on the way to meet the slaughter
> Flopping all around the ground like fishes out of water.

JUNEBUG AND PO:

> Blind man on the corner
> Holding up a sign
> "No More Water, Y'all, the Fire Next Time."

(Scene shift:)

RON: AT EASE!

KIM *(Skipping rope)*:
> GI Haircut
> GI Shoes
> GI Hard Tack
> GI Blues
> GI Love You
> GI Do
> GI Hope you love me too.

(Sound off:)

RON: Attention!

JOHN:

>You had a good home but you left—your right
>You had a good home but you left—your right
>Sound off: 1, 2
>Sound off: 3, 4
>Bring it on down
>1, 2, 3, 4
>1, 2, 3, 4.

(The Company sings "Brother to Brother":)

KIM:

>Now that you've gone away
>The sunlit days don't seem as warm as they used to be
>Since you're not here with me
>What once was clear now seems all lost in a mystery.

(Nancy and Kenneth echo Kim:)

>Brother, are you safe and well?
>There's so much to tell
>I need me someone just to talk to
>Brother, won't you come home soon?
>No one else can cheer me
>No one else can chase away the gloom.

>Brother, why'd you go away?
>Brother, what's a hero?
>Leaving home makes no sense to me.
>Daddy said you had to go away.
>Tell me what you're fighting for.
>Brother, help me understand your wars!
>Brother, help me understand your wars!

>Stay safe, my brother
>Hurry home, my brothers
>There's someone here who needs you
>And loves you.

Brother, what's a hero?
And why do you have to go away to be one?

NANCY: When my son, Luke, graduated from high school, it
looked like there was no way for him to go on to college
like some boys was able to do. He'd been talking to them
recruiters that was always at the school, telling the boys
about all them military benefits. *(A guitar begins playing the
theme of "Vietnam")* Oh, he didn't want to wait, he wanted us
to sign for him so he could go on in.

His daddy wouldn't do it, and I didn't want to. But he was
getting into trouble pretty regular at the time, and he told
us that it looked like he could go off to the Service or go
off to jail. Well, his daddy said at least he'd be alive in jail,
and he still wouldn't sign. Luke kept at me and kept at me,
and he got into more and more trouble all the time. Finally,
I signed. *(The guitar music stops)* He had just turned eighteen
when he finished basic, and shipped out to Vietnam. He
ended up a machine gunner in the 8th Battalion Marines,
and was pretty much in constant combat for a year. We got
letters from him. Sometimes the handwriting was so big and
scrawled that he would only get about five words on a page.

(The guitar playing begins again.)

KENNETH: When I was in Nam I laid up on a ridge looking down
at this village. There was women, children, pigs, I felt like
I was home. I told the captain, "The only way we gonna
win this war is to kill every man, women and child in the
country."

(The guitar music stops.)

JOHN *(As Captain)*: Well, if that's the way they want it.

(The guitar music picks up again, playing the intro to "Vietnam":)

I went walking one morning
The devil took me by the hand

Said, "Come on let me show you 'round my little place
I call it Vietnam
Ain't so much to look at
Just a quaint little jungle land
Before I'm through
It'll mean the world to you
You won't forget Vietnam."

Vietnam, where the sweetest flower
Died on the vine
Vietnam, it'll steal your heart
Steal your mind.

Come, all you space-age children
You never gonna understand
If you want to see real living and dying
Come over to Vietnam.
Pride's the first thing to leave you
Your fear is the last thing to run
You can't see too well
Staring straight into hell
Down the barrel of a gun.

Mama, don't you know me
I'm the boy next door.
Can I come home,
Mama? Don't you know me
I'm the boy next door
Can I come home?

NANCY: That year my boy was in the war I lost forty pounds,
and my hair turned completely gray. Seemed like the time
would never pass. The days just stood still. It was like mothers all over this country was holding their breath . . . waiting.
    When he come home, I thanked God that he was safe and
that we could go back to being a family. But it wasn't long
'til I could see things was different—oh, he never missed a
family gathering, but he always come late and left early. And

when he got married, he never even told me about it until it was over and done. I tried everything I knowed to bring my family back together, but things was never the same after that.

JOHN: I was fighting in the Korean War when I found out about the lynching of Emmett Till in Money, Mississippi. *(An organ plays "We Shall Overcome")* The Korean people I knew couldn't understand why I was so upset about that one child being killed in Mississippi, when every month Korean children were dying by the hundreds. I tried to explain it, what it was.

After we fought all over the world in the name of freedom, then to have a fifteen-year-old boy to be lynched in the "land of the free and the home of the brave" was just too much. That's when I knew it was time for me to go home. I was fighting on the wrong side in the wrong war! *(The organ music fades out)*

RON: I had this buddy. We was both medics. We wadn't in the fighting like them Marine and Army guys. We picked up the pieces after the fighting was over. Day after day, the same thing, trying to save the pieces of what was left. Pretty soon you're looking for anything to talk about instead of that—and somebody to talk to.

One day I heard him say he was from Washington, DC. Most of my people had been forced to move out of the mountains back in the '50s looking for work. They ended up 'round northern Virginia. I told him about my people—and everything—and we started talking. He told me his family was from North Carolina, but he was raised in DC.

After that we just sorta started hanging out together. Both of us loved Muddy Waters. A lot of friendships been started on less than that. We was friends.

In April that year I got rotated back to the States. It was hard to explain, but somehow I kinda hated to leave. I remember thinking, I must be going crazy, not wanting to go home.

I went home on a thirty-day leave. But I swear to God, in a week, I couldn't stand it. I'd watch that television and see them pictures, and it was like I'd keep looking, trying to see myself. They didn't even remind me of me.

I ended up in Greenville, Mississippi, on temporary duty. My orders got screwed up, and three months later I was still there. Then I'll be damned if my buddy from Nam didn't show up. Oh man, we had a party! It was just like old times.

One night we decided we was gonna go into Greenville, but there was a big football game that night and town was deserted. Somehow or another we decided to go to a movie. I don't even remember what was playing. We got our tickets and went on in, got some popcorn and Pepsi, started to go in to the movie when this woman says, "Hey you can't go in there!" I said, "Excuse me?" "Now you know better than that. He can't go in there. He has to set up there." And she pointed to the stairs going up to the balcony. I said, "We're in the Service. Me and him is together, ma'am." She said, "I don't care." He never said nothing the whole time. Then he just turned around and walked out. I just stood there holding a box of popcorn and a Pepsi.

We got a cab back to the base. But it never was the same after that. *(Music starts for "The Only War That's Fair to Fight")* I ended up in Illinois. He went to California. I never saw him again.

(The Company sings "The Only War That's Fair to Fight":)

KENNETH:
The only war that's fair to fight is the

ALL:
War to end oppression.

KENNETH:
The only war that's fair to fight is the

ALL:
War to win your freedom.

KENNETH:

The only war that's fair to fight is the

ALL:

War you fight to win your human rights.

KENNETH:

The only war that's fair to fight is the

ALL:

War to end oppression.

(The Company sings "Tree of Life." Nancy repeats the song in harmony to Michael's melody.)

RON *(Begins the chorus)*:
Ain't you got a right
Ain't you got a right
Ain't you got a right
To the tree of life.

(The Company repeats the chorus.)

SHAWN:
You may be black
You may be white
Ain't you got a right
To the tree of life.

(The Company repeats the chorus.)

NANCY:
Gonna tell my brother
Gonna tell my sister
Ain't you got a right
To the tree of life.

(The Company repeats the chorus.)

KENNETH:

> You may be young, you may be old
> You may be hungry, you may be cold
> But ain't you got a right
> To the tree of life.

(The Company repeats the chorus two more times. The audience sings along.
> *Then the Company begins "What Did They Do?":)*

ALL *(Begin the chorus):*

> What did they do with what they took from you?
> What did they do with mine?
> No use complaining what they took from you
> They been stealing from us all a long time.

JOHN:

> Ancient red man chief stand looking in grief
> The damage done to Mother Earth
> Lots of blood been shed through the years,
> No pain can equal its worth.
> Can't measure the sorrow of the buffalo people
> Used to dwell from shore to shore
> When the pilgrims began it was the red man's land
> Before they were forced to go.
> Those that are left, land-lost few
> Forced onto reservations
> Trail of tears, battles lost and won
> Endless treaty manipulations
> Fighting in the courts
> They been using the system
> Organizing a plan
> Standing with their brothers and sisters
> Winning back their land.

KENNETH:

> A lot of black people all over the world
> Still fighting a terrible fight

345

Thinkin' 'bout the past but lookin' to the future
Beginning to see the light.
History has proven that it's unacceptable
To keep a people down
Pain and suffering all those years
Shackled and whipped to the ground.
Families disrupted, where is the justice?
Millions gone to slave-ship sea.
With faith intact they broke their backs
Three hundred years of labor for free.
Now the only request after giving their best
Was for forty acres and a mule
Asking and waiting and asking again
Still treated like a fool.
It's been a long time since 1865
Some changes are hard to see
But freedom for you and freedom for me
Everybody in equality!

(The Company repeats the chorus.)

RON:

For over a hundred years people in the mountains
Lived in peace and harmony
Helping one another, living on the land
They knowed what it meant to be free.
Then some men from the banks, church and government,
Men from the industry
Took a look at the mountains, put their heads together
Said with disbelief:
"There's something wrong with this picture here
And there's gonna be hell to pay
You need money to spend, credit cards and bills
To live the American Way!"
You can't buy my pride, you can't sell my hope
You can't steal my identity
And when the air we breathe is sold a breath at a time
Hillbillies will still be free!

NANCY, ADELLA AND KIM:

    Things have been bad for
    The women of the world
    Since the dawn of time began
    From the Garden of Eden
    To the streets at night
    They blame us for original sin.

KIM:

    Our bodies exploited for greedy gains
    A way to sell and promote
    We hear, "Relax and enjoy it, baby!"
    Regardless of what we want.

ADELLA:

    We want equal pay for equal work
    Respect for our right to choose.
    If I want to be a mother, a wife, or a lawyer
    We can do anything we want to do.

NANCY:

    The Earth is our Mother
    The only place that our children will know
    Let's save the land, give them a future
    A place where we all can grow.

NANCY, ADELLA AND KIM:

    Changes for me, mean changes for you
    Let's help each other all we can
    There's a job to be done
    A war to be won
    We don't need a gun or a man.

(The Company repeats the chorus.)

ADELLA:

    The forces of evil tryin' to keep us down
    Are getting stronger every day

Between Iran Contra and Desert Storm who knows
How much we gotta pay.
Millions and millions of Welfare dollars
Have been spent since '33
Won't equal what they stole from the savings and loan
But here's the real tragedy:

KIM:

We got our people on the streets

NANCY:

Crack in our schools

RON:

Children living with AIDS

ADELLA:

And our national debt going through the roof.

JOHN:

Lord help you if you tell them you're gay

ADELLA:

'Cause they'll try their best to take what's left
Hold on to your self pride

ALL:

'Cause greed is the villain, and whoever is a willing
Can join in the militant line.
Don't be upset if we seem to forget
And left out your personal beef
We're all sisters and brothers if we're doing unto others
We all share the grief
The battle's not easy, the path is rough and greasy
It's gonna take a little more time
It might take some effort
But you and me together
Can get to work 'til we find:

(The Company sings the chorus:)

> What did they do with what they took from you?
> What did they do with mine?
> No use complaining what they took from you
> They been stealing from us all a long time.

(A dance break: the audience joins the Company, dancing, until Ron cues all to sing:)

> Let's get it all back this time!!!!
> What did they do?
> Uh-huh, uh-huh.
> What did they do?
> Oh yeah!!!!

THE END

Promise of a Love Song

_____

Co-created by:
Junebug Productions
Pregones Theater
Roadside Theater

Co-written by:
John O'Neal
Ron Short

Adapted text by:
Rosalba Rolón

Promise of a Love Song *is dedicated to the next generation of ensemble artists working to create theater that builds community and serves the cause of social justice.*

PRODUCTION AND PERFORMANCE HISTORY

Promise of a Love Song was written by John O'Neal and Ron Short, with adapted text by Rosalba Rolón from "Silent Dancing" and "El Olvido," from *Silent Dancing: A Partial Remembrance of a Puerto Rican Childhood* by Judith Ortiz Cofer (Arte Público Press, Houston, 1990); and composed by Desmar Guevara; Donald Harrison, Jr.; Ricardo Pons and Ron Short.

It was directed by Steve Kent and Rosalba Rolón; and the musical direction was by Ricardo Pons. The set and lighting were designed by Douglas D. Smith, the costumes were designed by Theresa Holden, the dramaturg was Rosalba Rolón, the company manager was Nicole McClendon and the executive producer was Theresa Holden. The original cast was Kim Neal Cole, Adella Gautier, Donald Harrison, Jorge Merced, John O'Neal, Soldanela Rivera and Ron Short. The original musicians were Waldo Chávez; Desmar Guevara; Donald Harrison, Jr.; Ricardo Pons; Ricky Sebastian and Ron Short.

Lyrics: "Toda una Vida," by Oswaldo Farres, 1950s, Bourne Co, c/o Ms. Beebe Bourne, 5 West 37th Street, New York, NY 10018 (page 361); "La Ultima Copa," by Juan Andrés Caruso, music by Francisco Canaro, 1926 (page 395).

The collaborators were Dudley Cocke (Roadside Theater), Alvan Colón Lespier (Pregones Theater), Theresa Holden (Holden and Arts Associates) and Arnaldo López (Documenter).

In New Orleans: Ashé Cultural Arts Center and the Contemporary Arts Center. In Whitesburg, Kentucky, and Norton, Virginia: Appalshop and the University of Virginia's College at Wise. In New York: Hostos Center for the Arts and Culture.

Management was provided by Holden and Arts Associates in Austin, Texas.

Co-commissioners were Lied Center for the Performing Arts (Lincoln, Nebraska), Flynn Center for the Performing Arts (Burlington, Vermont) and Cincinnati Arts Association—Aronoff Center for the Arts.

Funding was provided by Association of Performing Arts Presenters Arts Partners Program, National Endowment for the Arts, the Knight Foundation, National Performance Network, New York State Council for the Arts, New York City Department of Cultural Affairs, Arts Council of New Orleans.

Promise of a Love Song is a production of The Exchange Project, an ongoing artistic exchange among Junebug Productions, Pregones Theater and Roadside Theater.

—*TRH*

Setting and Characters

There are six actors in this play. One woman and one man playing an Appalachian mother and son; one woman and one man
playing a Puerto Rican–American father and daughter; and one
woman and one man playing an African-American husband and
wife. There is a full band up stage; the band is made up of musicians from each of the cultures represented by the play, and
their music and instruments. One of the African-American men
in the band also comes into the play to portray the son of the
man and woman.

Appalachian family: MOTHER and BILLY
African-American family: NELSON, DONNA and DONALD, their son
Puerto Rican–American family: FATHER and ANGELA

There are three distinct playing areas: a rural Appalachian
house, a New York tenement and a New Orleans shotgun house.
Each area has a scrim and full curtain in front of it, which can be
opened and closed as needed. The scrim depicts the locale for
each playing area. Both the scrim and the curtain create various
effects, such as silhouettes and lighting patterns.

There is a fourth playing area for the band, which is set
upstage of the rest. There is a scrim, which can be opened or
closed (but no curtain). The band area is as significant as the
other three, as characters emerge from there to take on roles,
and as characters from the other three playing areas engage the
band throughout the piece.

Once the actors and musicians enter the stage, they remain for the entirety of the play, as the action moves seamlessly from one playing area to another. Lights, music and other effects determine the focus of the action.

Act One

———

Scene 1

All performers enter. A soft spot comes up on the bandstand. The musicians go to the bandstand and tune their instruments. Each male actor moves to his respective playing area: a rural Appalachian house, a New York tenement and a New Orleans shotgun house. As the banjo plays "Greenwood Sidee'o" softly, the actors in New York and New Orleans open their curtains. The rural Appalachia curtain remains closed.
    Lights fade.

Scene 2

The soft sound of cymbals fills the stage. The Company whispers:

COMPANY: Mother . . . madre . . .

    (An actor puts on an apron, slowly turning into Mother.
      Lights fade.)

Scene 3

Lights come up on Mother in the Appalachian house. Two other women, one in the New York house and one in the New Orleans house, look on and listen to Mother. She sings a verse of "Greenwood Sidee'o":

MOTHER *(Singing to the audience)*:
>There was a lady lived in York
>All alee and lonely.
>Fell in love with her father's clerk
>Down by the Greenwood sidee'o.
>She loved him up, she loved him down
>All alee and lonely.
>Loved him 'til he filled her arms
>Down by the Greenwood sidee'o.

Aunt Mary Holyfield, who was my doctor that brought me into this world, taught me that song. She brought many a young'un into this world, so I reckon somehow or other that song 'bout them poor little babies that never had a chance stuck with her. It stuck with me. I thought it was the saddest, most tragic story ever. *(Sings:)*

>She bent her back against an oak
>All alee and lonely.
>First it bent and then it broke
>Down by the Greenwood sidee'o.

When I was a young girl, I'd sing it and cry for her. Mommy didn't like me singin' it, said it wasn't proper in the first place and it caused me to be too melancholy in the second. And she said that come from having too much time to think.

(Lights fade.)

Scene 4

We hear "Donna's Paris Theme." Lights come up on the New Orleans shotgun house as Donna puts on a stole, swirls around and sings.

DONNA:

> The nighttime seemed as bright as day
> With all the lights on old Broadway
> I was overwhelmed the first time that I went there
> But New York's charms were swept away.
> When first I went to Paris
> The elegant way
> The Champs-Elysées
> Embraced the small café that lived there.

In '64 I won a scholarship to study law at the Sorbonne. Oh, what a time to be a student in Paris! I met many of the great black artists and intellectuals in exile—Richard Wright, Josephine Baker, Louis Armstrong *(Pause for trumpet's arpeggio)* and lots of others. *(Sits)* One evening, I was invited to participate in a salon that James Baldwin, "Jimmy," was hosting in his home. He was even more eloquent in real life than he was in print. He spoke of how "The Movement" had changed his life. He needed the relative freedom from American racism that he found in Europe in order to write. At the same time, as a "native son," he had to take part in the struggle for justice in America.

He also spoke of the passion of a young Movement leader in Louisiana named Nelson Hardiman. Like Baldwin, Hardiman was a brilliant high school dropout who Jimmy thought was cut from the same cloth as Malcolm X and Nelson Mandela.

("Donna's Paris Theme" ends. Background kalimba music begins as lights come up on Nelson. He is behind the New Orleans scrim, standing on a platform. The audience sees through the scrim and into the past. Donna is sitting in front of the scrim, in the present.)

NELSON (*Over background music; alive in his memory*): When I was a kid, every time the circus came to town, me and my best buddy would be the first ones there to help set up. If they paid us fifty cents, they'd pay the white kids a dollar but we didn't care. We'd have been there if they hadn't paid a penny. We wasn't just chasing a dream, we were learning things.

They'd use the elephants to do the heavy lifting. They'd hitch the elephant to the big poles that hold the tents up, then tell him to, "Pull!" A single elephant could raise a whole tent by himself. When they didn't need that elephant anymore they'd take him off to the side and tie him up to a little stake in the ground with a little rope. And the elephant would stay there! That elephant, who could lift a whole huge tent by himself, wouldn't pull a little stake up from the ground because he was afraid to be free!

DONNA: Baldwin's stories of the passionate young hero were magnetic to me.

(*Following a rhythmic beat, Nelson's voice fades as he delivers the following lines, emphasizing the word "fear" and fading the rest of the line, retreating, while Donna speaks over his fading voice.*)

NELSON: *Fear!* . . . keeps us from calling a spade a spade . . .
DONNA: He was so bold.
NELSON: *Fear!* . . . keeps us riding on the back of the bus!
DONNA: Fearless!
NELSON: If these white people were truly committed to the struggle for justice, they'd be fighting against racism in the white community. I tell them to take on the Klan, the White Citizens Councils, hell, let them take on their own mamas.
DONNA: He was willing to talk about white people out loud in public the way most of us would only whisper in private. It was so liberating.

(*Lights fade on Nelson. The kalimba music ends. "Donna's Paris Theme" resumes, bringing her back to the present.*)

I admit, I'd been tempted by the romantic challenge of living the lush life on the Left Bank of Paris among the *Afro literati*. But after that evening at Jimmy's house I knew. A seed had been planted in me that would become my life's work. I knew I had to go back home.

("Donna's Paris Theme" ends. Lights fade.)

Scene 5

Musicians play "Toda una Vida." Lights come up on the New York tenement house. Father sings two verses of "Toda una Vida" behind the scrim while Angela opens a trunk in front of it. She finds some letters. These letters are represented by several yards of paper rolled and tied with a red ribbon.

FATHER *(Sings)*:
>Toda una vida
>Estaría contigo
>No me importa en qué forma
>Ni cómo ni dónde
>Pero junto a ti.
>
>Toda una vida
>Te estaría esperando
>Te estaría adorando
>Como vivo mi vida
>Que la vivo por ti.

(A spotlight comes up on Angela.)

ANGELA *(Reading letters)*: Dear Granma, I don't know what Mami has told you about our new life in the States. Has she told you about our apartment? It is tiny, in a huge apartment building that had once housed Jewish families, they tell me. It has just been turned into a tenement by us. *(Pause)* Hey, it is almost 1960, Puerto Ricans have arrived! So here we are in el building. Papi's doing well, with his job in the Brooklyn Navy Shipyard and all.

(To the audience) My father. My father died a long time ago. *(We can see Father's shadow behind the scrim as Angela continues reading)* He says that with myself and my brother, the military was the only option away from the sugarcane fields in the island.

(She chooses another letter.)

FATHER AND ANGELA: Querido Hermano, Las cosas por acá están bien.

(Father's voice fades as Angela continues to read:)

ANGELA: Sé que que no querías que me enlistara en el Navy, pero no había otra opción fuera de las centrales de caña, y con una esposa y dos niños. Todavía estoy asignado al Brooklyn Shipyard. *(She chooses another letter)* I like it here I guess. But everything is gray, the streets, the building, even the coat that Papi bought for me. Anyway, I'll write again soon. —Your favorite granddaughter, Angela.

(The Band plays "El Recuerdo," which means remembrance, a bolero. Father comes in front of scrim and faces Angela. They move together as if dancing, looking sideways, at the outside world. Father stands on the trunk, and from his pocket he pulls out a very long strand of rolled red ribbon. He throws it over Angela's shoulder. She catches it and ties up her hair with one end of the ribbon as Father makes a tie from the other end. Then he throws the strand of letters over her shoulder, which she also catches. She reads them silently, as Father reads them out loud:)

FATHER: I continue to look for a larger apartment. Not that we are uncomfortable or anything, but I do want what's best for my family. The children are small for now, but they will need more space eventually. In the meantime, I have given strict orders to my wife to keep the doors locked, *(The bolero ends abruptly. Father looks sideways, as if looking out a window)* the noise down. Ourselves to ourselves.

("Greenwood Sidee'o" plays as the lights fade on the New York tenement and come up on the rural Appalachian house.)

Scene 6

Billy appears behind the Appalachian scrim. We hear banjo music, while the Band plays an overlapping Latin rhythm. The Latin rhythm drops out as Billy takes his place by Mother, who is sitting.

A follow spot comes up on Billy, shyly playing the notes to "Greenwood Sidee'o" on his banjo.

Father sits in the New York tenement house, writing letters; Nelson sits in the New Orleans shotgun house, reading.

MOTHER: Mommy was fifteen when she married my daddy. He was eighteen or nineteen. Had eight children all told. I was the fourth. Started out on a piece of land belonged to Daddy's daddy. I remember Mommy telling how she got water out of the head of the Pound River. It starts as a spring and gets bigger as it goes along.

(Pause. Billy and Mother's hands move together in a gesture that follows the flow of the water. Father and Nelson make subtle sounds of breathing, turning pages and handling paper.)

I was born on Big Branch in 1910. Growed up down there. Went to school at Osborne's Gap, finished up the seventh grade. *(Sings:)*

> She bent her back against a thorn
> All alee and lonely.
> There she had two wee babes born
> Down by the Greenwood sidee'o.

I married Wesley Mullins in 1926. I was sixteen years old.
I had my first baby in 1927. We named him Henry. In 1929
I had a baby girl. We named her Hetty. In 1931 I had another
little boy, and his name was Lewis James. In 1933 Billy was
born. *(Lights up on Angela; she stares out from the New York
tenement. "Greenwood Sidee'o" ends)* Then I had a daughter
in 1935, and her name was Lilly. In 1937 I had another little
boy, and his name was Clovis.

BILLY: Bud. *(The light on Angela fades)*

MOTHER: Bud—we called him Bud. I don't know what got into
us. In 1940 I had another girl. Her name was April. We ran
out of names and began using months. In 1944 we had
another baby. We named him Dwight David. *(Billy sits near
Mother)* Mommy had eight and I had eight. Ever' household
had about that many. Some had more. They didn't pay no
'tention to it, you just raised 'em and that was it. When we
first married, we lived all over the place. Last sixty years
though I've settled down some. My husband's gone now
these past thirty years and the children all married off and
left me, except Billy.

BILLY *(Sings)*:
> Can she bake a cherry pie,
> Billy Boy, Billy Boy?
> Can she bake a cherry pie,
> Charming Billy?

(He continues singing softly as Mother speaks:)

MOTHER: Billy was eleven when he started takin' fits. Then he
started in on that singin', the same thing over and over,
sometimes it didn't make any sense at all . . .

BILLY *(Sings)*:
> St. Luke, Mark and John
> Hold ol' Pete while I get on.

MOTHER: Over and over 'til he'd jist freeze and fall over and start
shakin' all over. They got worse and worse . . .

BILLY *(Sings, louder and louder)*:
> Billy Boy, Billy Boy.
> I'm a wise boy, but some boys
> Are silly.

MOTHER: Then he'd jist set fer a long time and stare out.

BILLY *(Getting up)*: This'n here don't remember. That'n says she does, so I guess she does. When it comes to it, if you can believe one, that's good. Them ain't got nothin' to do with it. Us ain't got nothin' to do with it. This'n and that'n, that's all they is.

MOTHER: He went to school 'til the seventh grade. He was always smart. But, the seizures got so bad and he got to where he hurt people. Pinch and hit, not cruel, I don't think, just like that singing, *(Billy sings softly)* not able to help it. And they said he couldn't go no more.

BILLY *(Overlapping slightly)*:
> Home, home on the range
> Where the deer and the antelope play
> Where seldom is heard a discouragin' word,
> A discouragin' word, discouragin' word.

Why, I asked that'n? Why?! The rest of 'em goes. That'n says this'n is goin' to a special school. So, we go.

(Lights fade on Mother and Billy and the rural Appalachian house.)

Scene 7

The Band plays "Sincerely Yours/Funkily Yours." Lights come up on Donna in the New Orleans shotgun house.

DONNA *(Takes briefcase and walks from behind the scrim to downstage)*: I had to fight against smile-in-your-face racists every step of the way, but I finished Yale Law with honors in 1968 and took a job with the NAACP Legal Defense Fund.

(Lights come up on Nelson behind the scrim.)

NELSON: I stand with Mrs. Fannie Lou Hamer, who was kicked off her job as a timekeeper on a Mississippi plantation because she had the gall to go register to vote. Her byword was, "I'm sick and tired of being sick and tired!"

DONNA: The papers always showed him in some angry pose, fist clenched above his head with his mouth stretched wide. Distorted. But the more the media tried to make us hate him, the more the people loved him.

NELSON: Brother Kwame Torre's right: "The black man's got no business going to fight the yellow man to defend a country that the white man stole from the red man in the first place." *("Sincerely Yours/Funkily Yours" ends)*

DONNA: But when he came out *for* armed struggle in South Africa and the PLO, and *against* Israel and the war in Vietnam, the white power structure decided he'd gone too far. Though he hadn't even been charged with anything, Hardiman was dragged from his bed in the dead of night, beaten and held for weeks at the notorious Angola State Prison. Reluctantly, the NAACP national office agreed that we should take the case.

NELSON: They put this headstrong young woman, fresh out of law school on my case. They said that's the best they could do.

DONNA: I did all my legal homework, but I couldn't get a judge to hear the case until I got national network news to cover James Baldwin speaking about the Hardiman affair at a rally in New York.

NELSON: As it turned out, it was the best they could do.

DONNA: The very next day they let Hardiman out on bond. The road was muddy and rough but we got there.

NELSON: When the guards came to get me out of my cell I didn't know if they intended to lynch me or cut me loose.

DONNA: I knew what he looked like. I'd seen him on TV and in the papers. But I was not prepared for what happened when he stepped into the room.

(Nelson comes downstage from behind the scrim. The Band plays a soft arrangement of "Sincerely Yours.")

366

NELSON *(Avoiding Donna's gaze)*: I felt the woman before I saw her.

DONNA: My heart began to pound. I felt faint. I wondered if the others noticed.

NELSON: What was this I was feeling?

DONNA: He acknowledged the group, then slowly he turned and he took me into a private place deep inside himself.

(They face each other.)

NELSON: When we looked at each other, I felt like she had seen me, I mean, really seen me. It was like she knew things about me before I had to say a word.

DONNA: On the backseat of the car, we sat together silently all the way back to New Orleans.

(They sit.)

NELSON: We went to my office. Worked late into the night.

DONNA: He went to the place where he'd been staying.

NELSON: I packed a few clean clothes.

DONNA: We went to my new apartment.

NELSON AND DONNA: We've been together ever since.

(They look at each other. They kiss. Lights fade on the New Orleans shotgun house as Donna hugs Nelson. She delivers a verse of "If I Could Promise You a Love Song":)

DONNA:

> If I could promise you a love song
> I'd take a meter soft and sweet and curve the words
> Until they meet the place your smile leaves off.
> I'd make a song that smiles the way you do . . .
> If I could promise you a love song.

("If I Could Promise You a Love Song" ends. Lights down on the New Orleans shotgun house.

Lights up on the New York tenement. A young Angela, with ponytails, lovingly teases Father, who is seated on the trunk, writing letters.

In Appalachia, Mother playfully tries a new vest on Billy.
All three playing areas are now illuminated by bright pools of
light.)

Scene 8

We hear the sound of a keyboard and congas. A young Angela dances
while she speaks. She is writing to her grandmother. Billy sits, cleaning
his banjo; Nelson writes.

ANGELA *(Reciting her letter)*: Dear Granma, Mark today's date as
my first spanking in the United States as a result of playing
tunes on the pipes in my room to see if there would be an
answer. *(Billy cleans the banjo and Nelson taps on his trunk, both
creating heat pipe sounds)* There are these pipes, you see, they
are called heater pipes. They bang and rattle, even as we
sleep. I'm kind of getting used to it, so when they bang we
just speak louder. *(The music builds as Angela dances. Then she
sits on the floor)* The hiss from the valve makes you feel like
someone else is in the room. I say that's the dragon sleeping
next to me. You know, it is curious to know that strangers
live under our floor and above our heads, and that our own
heater pipe goes through everyone's apartments. *(Music
stops)* I miss our house in Puerto Rico. —Your Angela.

*(The Band plays a bolero. Father walks downstage from behind the
scrim. Mother fixes Billy's vest. Behind the scrim, Angela caresses
her father's Navy uniform while he speaks downstage, in front of
the scrim.)*

FATHER: Dear Brother, I have learned some painful lessons about
prejudice while searching for the apartment. But I don't
want to tell anybody. Maybe someday. So many of us coming over . . . things are changing in these neighborhoods
and people are panicking over here. I went to look for an
apartment, put on my Navy uniform to look my best. *(Nelson
and Billy enter from behind the scrims and walk downstage, join-*

ing Father) This man looks at my name tag, points his finger at it and asks, "You Cuban?" "No," I answered, looking past the finger and into his angry eyes. "I'm Puerto Rican." *(Pause. Billy and Nelson react, each in their own world)* And the door closed. *(Billy and Nelson begin to retreat. Father looks at Angela)* I wonder what will happen in this neighborhood if more Puerto Ricans continue to come here. For now, we are keeping busy with a New Year's Eve party, since we can't go to Puerto Rico. We'll have a good crowd of friends, Uncle Germán, our cousins and the kids. Our nephew will introduce his eighteen-year-old girlfriend to the family. I'll let you know how that goes. She just arrived from Puerto Rico.

(Lights fade.)

Scene 9

The Band plays "Greenwood Sidee'o." Lights with Appalachian patterns are projected over all three scrims. Mother and Billy venture out of their Appalachian world and into the other playing areas: looking, discovering and wondering. He wears the vest; she is dressed up, in a hat and blazer. They stop upstage center, in front of the Band for a moment.

MOTHER *(Walking downstage center)*: Tell you the truth, this world is a big ball to me. I don't know how people ever got anywhere. I'd never been nowhere much less to a place like that university hospital, but from the time Billy was eleven 'til he was eighteen we went ever' three months. He had whooping cough and it affected his brain. They said they found a black streak in his brain from coughin' so hard, but they said they couldn't operate or he'd be in worser shape. If that was now, they'd do somethin', but it's too late. *(Angrily, Billy rushes off to his Appalachian home)* If he lives 'til fall, he'll be sixty-five.

(She observes Billy. Lights come up on Billy. He sings:)

BILLY:

> To market, to market to buy a fat hog
> Jiggety, jiggety, jiggety jog.

One of them said, "What's wrong with this'n?" Other'n said, "I don't know, some kind of fits. You know them hillbillies, probably married her uncle." I asked that'n if he was my pa or my uncle. She said, "Don't ask foolish questions!" At first it was fun to go, but I was glad when we quit.

MOTHER: They said there was nothin' more they could do. We could get his medicine from any doctor and I could give it to him.

(Mother takes off her hat and crosses behind the Appalachian scrim, forming a silhouette. Then lights rise on Mother. She sings a verse of "Greenwood Sidee'o":)

> Then she drew out her wee penknife
> All alee and lonely.
> There she took those wee babes' lives
> Down by the Greenwood sidee'o.

BILLY: I tried to go back to school, but that'n said no. She just wanted me to stay home and work.

MOTHER *(Enters and gives him a pot and spoon to batter)*: He'd slip off and they'd send one of the other children after me to come get him. *(Lights fade on her)*

BILLY *(Has been waiting for her to leave, then puts down the pot and spoon)*: At recess they played a game, the boys and girls together . . . housekeeping. I wanted to play housekeeping with my danged ol' sweetheart Serecea . . . but she didn't want to.

(Lights up on Mother; she gives Billy back the pot and spoon, indicating that he should continue to batter.)

MOTHER: He like to wore me out. Ever' day was a rasslin' match. Tryin' to raise seven others: cook, farm, can. One day, I'd been up 'fore daylight canning beans outside in a tub. Well, this woman from the health department come by to see about Billy, and I just didn't have time to talk to her. She said, "My God. You work like a brute!"

Lord, that flew all over me. I ain't no brute. A brute is a dumb animal that has to be drove to work. Nobody drove me. I worked hard for a reason, my own reasons. Me and Billy we ain't no mindless brutes. But one day, later on up in early winter, I was feeding the livestock, and I was plumb wore out. I was cold and so tired I like to have cried. All the sheep was laying down in a stall. They looked so warm and restful all laying there together, and I real careful laid down, curled up next to 'em and they let me. I slept for 'bout an hour. When I woke up I thought, Lord that woman was right, I've become a brute. When I went back up to the house, my husband said, "Where in the world have you been? You stink like sheep."

(Mother teases Billy. The light on her fades. Billy sings:)

BILLY:

    Baa, baa black sheep
    Have you any wool?
    Yes sir, yes sir
    Don't be cruel
    To a heart that's true.

(Angela is in the New York tenement, in silhouette, brushing her hair. The Band plays "Bus Ride.")

Serecea started goin' to that town school and they wouldn't let me ride the bus. All them other'ns rode the bus, why couldn't I? I told that'n I wanted to marry Serecea. That'n said, "I reckon not." So I decided to ask Serecea. I went down to where them Vanover children lived. They was a whole mess of them, and I got on the bus with 'em, and I found Serecea and I set next to her all the way to town, but I couldn't git up the nerve to ask her. So we set, not sayin' nothin' and ever'body starin' at us. And when we got to town she got off and I stayed to save her seat, so's I could ask her goin' home. But some of them come an said, "Git off!" "This'n'll jist set right here, thank ye." "Fine, just set there all day then." And I did. It was hard but I did. Then come time to go home and the policeman come and said, "Git off!" And I locked hold on the seat rail in front of me, and I held on and they beat my knuckles 'til they bled and I held on, and one of them said, "They'll raise a fuss 'bout us beatin' up a dummy. Let's jist take the seats out." And they did, and they carried me out. All of the others was lined up outside . . . and there was Serecea in front . . . and I said . . . "Well, hello danged ol' sweetheart . . ." (*The music turns discordant. Mother and Donna appear behind their scrims*) . . . and she slapped me . . . (*"Bus Ride" ends. All three women stand in silhouette, as if staring out a window*) . . . hard in the face. Everybody laughed. This'n did, too.

(*Billy fades from view. The women release the curtains—they close sharply.*

Lights change. New York patterns appear over the scrims. Silence. All curtains open.)

Scene 10

A teenage Angela peeks out from behind the scrim.

ANGELA: Dear Granma, You wouldn't recognize this neighborhood. (*A Musician plays the congas. She enters from behind the scrim and walks downstage center*) Remember when we first moved here and you came to visit? Well, now it is mainly a Puerto Rican neighborhood. It is as if the heart of the city map was being gradually colored in brown. Papi's obsession with getting us out of here is getting to me. He doesn't want us to have friends because "we'll be moving out soon." But it is heaven for Mami.

(The Band plays "Dear Granma." Angela dances all over the stage, in awe of her city's tall buildings and crowds of people. She sings:)

> Granma, let me tell you
> What it's like to live in New York.

Papi always wants us to do our grocery shopping at the supermarket when he comes home on weekend leaves, but Mami insists that she can cook only with products whose labels she can read, and so during the week I go with her to la bodega across the street from el building. Ah, and have I told you that the final "e" is not pronounced for Palmolive and Colgate the way we do it in Spanish? For years I believed that they were Puerto Rican products. Imagine my surprise at first hearing a commercial on television for Colg*ate* and Palmol*ive*. I have to run. Bye. —Your favorite, Angela.

(She sings. The rest of the Company sings the chorus and dances behind the scrims.)

> Granma, let me tell you
> What it's like to live in New York.

COMPANY:
> Granma, let me tell you
> What it's like to live in New York.

(The Company continues to sing this refrain. Father comes from behind the scrim, wearing his Navy uniform. He stands downstage center.)

> Granma, let me tell you
> What it's like to live in New York.

("Dear Granma" ends.
Father speaks while a now-adult Angela observes him, as if looking back into a memory.)

FATHER: I have devised a system of back-and-forth travel. Every time I am sent to Europe, you will go back to Puerto Rico with your grandmother. Upon my return to Brooklyn Shipyard, I will wire you, and you will come back.

(The Band plays "Strangers," an Appalachian ballad, on the violin. As Angela speaks, she stares at this uniformed "image" of her father. Then he turns around with military precision.)

ANGELA: My father was a man who rarely looked into mirrors. What was he afraid of seeing? My mother prefers to remember him as the golden boy she married. He was a sensitive man whose energies had to be entirely devoted to survival. And that is how many minds are wasted in the travails of immigrant life.

(Lights fade. The curtain is drawn.)

Scene 11

The Band plays "Sincerely Yours" with an African flair. Lights come up on Nelson and Donna behind the New Orleans shotgun house scrim. They are facing each other in silhouette. Nelson sings:

NELSON:
> If I could promise you a love song
> I'd cup my hands to catch the sound of clear running
>   water
> Bubbling through a bed of stone and pebble
> And bring it to the sunny place that you make laughing.
> I'd make a song that lights up the air the way your laugh-
>   ter does,
> If I could promise you a love song . . .

(It's African Liberation Day, 1971. There is a musical transition into the "African Liberation Day Theme." Donna opens the curtain on the New York tenement scrim. Nelson is concluding a speech in Shakespeare Park. A crowd behind the scrims cheers him on, fists up. Shadows of the crowd are reflected on the walls.)

We've got a right to be proud of what we've done on this African Liberation Day. We're over two thousand strong here today. Next year we need to double our numbers if we want "South Africa Free by '73." 1971 is not the end. 1971 is a new beginning. But the best way we can help our brothers and sisters in Africa is to win the fight for justice here at home.

So what if it's true that white folk are guilty of making slaves of us back in the day, and ripping off the riches of Africa with colonialism. We need to understand all that, but let's not get bogged down in bitterness and anger because the future is in our hands. We're the only ones who can make ourselves free. "South Africa Free by '73."

(Lights go out on the crowd behind the scrims. Lights come up on Nelson, now in the New Orleans shotgun house. Donna enters carrying two coats and hats.)

Look at that crowd, Didi! This is the best African Liberation Day ever.

DONNA: Come on in the church office over here. Here, you need to put this on. *(Gives him a trench coat, hat and sunglasses)*

NELSON *(Makes believe he is putting them on, joking)*: What's this stuff? This ain't no Mardi Gras.

DONNA *(Putting on her coat)*: Just put it on, please. The federal court rejected our appeal. They refused to set aside your conviction. If you stay here these "crackers" will throw the book at you. So as your legal counsel I say you better get the hell out of here.

NELSON: We got people out there from every major black organization inside of two hundred miles . . . if I leave now the whole thing could fall apart.

DONNA: Any movement that depends on one man is no better than a one-man army.

NELSON: Where do you think I ought to go?

DONNA: We've got options. First stop is in Mexico. Then Cuba, Algeria, China. Here are passports, money, everything we'll need's in the car.

NELSON: They'd know you were involved. You'd lose your license to practice law.

DONNA: Attorney-client privilege, not to mention that they'd have to prove that I did something illegal. But that's all moot anyway. I'm going with you.

NELSON: Is this still my lawyer talking?

DONNA: No. It's the mother of your unborn child.

NELSON: The mother of my . . . Didi. You *gros com sa?* You don't mean I'm pregnant?

DONNA: No, fool. *I'm* pregnant.

NELSON: I'm gonna—hey, Rev! Somebody! I'm—we're going to have a baby! Come here, woman. We definitely got something to celebrate now.

DONNA: We'll have plenty of time to celebrate when we get to Mexico. Hurry up. Get changed.

NELSON: Didi . . . I can't do that. *(Takes off the sunglasses and hat)*

DONNA: You don't understand the urgency of the problem here.

NELSON: Don't ever tell me what I don't understand! Do you hear me? *(Pause)* What would I do in Cuba or Algeria or China? Or Africa 'far as that's concerned?

DONNA: What will you do in jail for the next thirty years?

NELSON: The same thing that Mandela's doing on Robbins Island, standing on principle.

DONNA: And what about me?

NELSON: You would not want a man who compromises on principle.

DONNA: What about our child?

NELSON: We'll love the child, Didi. That's what we'll do. And we'll teach the kid to love our people and to love the struggle for justice.

DONNA: You'll be in jail at best. What kind of father can you be sitting in jail?

NELSON *(Embracing her)*: I've got the best lawyer in the world. If they get me in jail, she won't let me stay in jail any longer than I have to, will you, baby? Come on, baby, let's go tell the people we going to have a new soldier for the revolution!

(The "African Liberation Day Theme" ends. Lights fade.)

Scene 12

Lights come up on the rural Appalachian house. Mother is dusting the furniture with a rag. Donna is sitting in front of the New Orleans shot-gun house scrim, rocking a baby, with a dim glow of light.

MOTHER: 'Bout the time Billy thought he was growed up, he wanted to go out on his own. Whenever he'd see his brothers and sisters goin' off, it was hard on him. He never saw the difference between him and them. I tried my best to explain it, but I don't understand either. *(She sits. Pause)* There are some things in this life we are not meant to understand. You don't have to understand ever'thing for it to be so and have a place in this world. Maybe that's what God is . . . under-standing. *(She comes from behind the scrim and walks down-stage)* One of my daughter-in-laws was here one time and I had 'bout a six-foot black snakeskin layin' out on the walk. I told her I found it under the house where I keep my taters. "Lord, have mercy, you mean there's a six-foot black snake living under your house? I would not stay here one minute. How can you live knowing that?" Ever'thing don't exist for my use and purpose. Some things have meaning beyond my knowing 'bout it. That snake's one of 'em. But I admit, if I run up on him, he's liable end up dead, 'cause I reckon they's things about me that snake don't understand either. *(She returns to behind the scrim. Lights fade on her and Donna)*

(Lights up on Billy singing:)

BILLY:
> Dim lights, thick smoke
> And loud, loud music.
> You'll never make a wife
> To a home-lovin' man.

There was one of them women in town and she had big breasts that she showed half of 'em and I was there one day gettin' a hot dog and a Grapette and she bent over and I pinched her on the breast and she screamed real loud and a man run up and this'n hit him in the pit of the stomach with my balled-up fist and he got this funny look on his face, and fell over. And this'n started laughing and the woman was screaming and this'n pinched the other'n and she slapped me and I grabbed her an squeezed her real tight 'til her breasts popped out . . . *(Lights up on Mother, who stares at him)* . . . and everybody was hollerin' and this'n felt so good . . .

(The Band plays an instrumental bolero. Billy picks up his banjo and hugs it as though he is dancing with it. As he swings around he sees Mother, who has continued to watch him. He realizes she has heard him and he moves to the background shyly.)

MOTHER: They told me if he come back, they had no course but to put him in jail. The doctor said his body was changin' and all they could do was change his medicine and maybe it would help, but ever'body but me was afraid of him. *(She sings:)*

> She rubbed the knife against her shoe
> All alee and lonely.
> The more she rubbed the redder it grew
> Down by the Greenwood sidee'o.

(She sits.)

The longest I've ever been away from him was three weeks when my oldest girl got real sick and I had to go stay with her. He whipped all his brothers. The girls left and stayed with family. Rocked my husband for half a day, kept him penned up in the barn. When I come home Wes said, "Next time we're jist gonna burn the place down and come with you."

(Lights come up on Billy, standing, clutching his banjo, singing softly:)

BILLY:
>Yes, I've been around the world,
>But I never found no girl.
>I'm a wise boy, but some boys are silly.

MOTHER: Some boys are just silly.

(Lights fade on them. Lights rise on Donna, who is seated in front of the New Orleans shotgun house scrim, holding the baby. A jail pattern is projected over the scrim. Nelson is behind the scrim, in "jail," reading a book.)

DONNA: Some boys are just silly. *(Sings:)*
>Hush little baby
>Don't you cry
>You know your daddy's bound to die
>All our trials will soon be over.

(Lights fade. Lights rise on Father behind the New York tenement scrim. Angela walks from behind the scrim to downstage. She watches her father, as if into a memory.)

FATHER: Estoy tratando de que nos asimilemos lo mejor posible. Acabo de comprar y cargar un arbol de Navidad cinco pisos hasta nuestro apartamento y ustedes son los únicos en el building que reciben regalos de Navidad y de Día de Reyes. Además tenemos el mayor de los lujos . . . nuestro propio televisor. Hey, ya estamos en los '60s. *(A Musician plays the chords of "Middle America" from behind the rural Appalachian house scrim)* We are one of the first families in the barrio to have a television set. And it keeps you kids inside the house. Compared to our neighbors in el building, we are rich. The Navy check is better than a factory check. The only thing is . . . I still can't buy a place away from the barrio. My greatest wish.

(A Musician enters, playing the guitar.)

ANGELA: His greatest wish was Mami's greatest fear . . . to live away from the barrio! The TV did help to keep us quiet inside the apartment. I loved the family series. My favorite was *Bachelor Father*, where the father treats his adopted teenage daughter like a princess because he is rich and has a Chinese houseboy to do everything for him. Then there was *Father Knows Best* and *Leave It to Beaver*. It was like a map of Middle America. *(Walks to trunk and stands on it)*

(Lights fade.)

Scene 13

Spotlight on a Musician. He sings:

MUSICIAN:
  The lives we live
  Are paid for by our children.
  The dreams we dream
  Slowly fade away.
  Still, we dance each dance
  Like it was the first time,
  But the fiddler's waiting
  And he has to be paid.
  Deep in the heart
  Of Middle America
  There's a two-for-one sale,
  A midnight madness jubilee.
  You can get it all here,
  Love, hope and happiness.
  It's all for sale,
  Satisfaction not guaranteed.

(Lights come up on the New Orleans house. The Musician walks over to Donna, who sits holding the baby as she sings:)

DONNA:

> There are some things
> We can never understand,
> How a man loves a woman
> And a woman loves a man.
> Are angels real?
> Does God really have a plan?
> How can some people live
> And never seem to give a damn?

DONNA AND MUSICIAN:

> Deep in the heart
> Of Middle America
> There's a two-for-one sale,
> A midnight madness jubilee.
> You can get it all here,
> Love, hope and happiness.
> It's all for sale,
> Satisfaction not guaranteed.

(Lights come up on the New York tenement. Father is singing. The Musician walks over and joins him.)

FATHER AND MUSICIAN:

> This is not my home,
> I'm a stranger here.
> Wherever I travel,
> I carry my home there.
> This is not my voice,
> No one listens anymore.
> Deep in my heart I hear
> A song from the other shore.

ALL:

> Deep in the heart
> Of Middle America
> There's a two-for-one sale,
> A midnight madness jubilee.

You can get it all here,
Love, hope and happiness.
It's all for sale,
Satisfaction not guaranteed.

(Blackout.)

Act Two

Scene 1

The playing area curtains are closed. There is a banjo placed on the trunk in front of the rural Appalachian house scrim. There are folded letters placed on the trunk in front of the New York tenement house scrim. And there is an open horn case placed on the trunk in front of the New Orleans shotgun house scrim. A spotlight rises on an Appalachian Musician. He plays an Irish drum. He freezes. Spotlight fades. A spotlight rises on a Puerto Rican Musician as he plays the congas in front of the New York tenement scrim. He freezes. Spotlight fades. A spotlight rises on an African-American Musician as he plays a tambourine in front of the New Orleans shotgun house scrim. He freezes. Spotlight fades. A spotlight rises on a drummer in the Band as he plays a trap set. A keyboardist and bass player join in and play the "Act Two Overture." As the musical number reaches its peak, the Company members enter and take their places behind their respective scrims. The Band plays "Mardi Grasly Yours." Donna sings over the music:

DONNA *(In silhouette behind the scrim)*:
> If I could promise you a love song
> I'd take the time to count the ways that love makes music,
> I'd take the days and stretch them out before your very
> feet,
> I'd take the nights' soft velvet sheets
> To wrap your dreams in,
> If I could promise you a love song.

(The music cross-fades from "Mardi Grasly Yours" to "Meters Groove."

Donna and Nelson enter between two scrims, dancing. The other actors dance in silhouette behind their scrims. Donna and Nelson are guests of honor at the Nubian Knights Ball, at which it has just been announced that they will be King and Queen of Nubian Knights for the next Carnival. Their son, Donald, and his Band are playing for the Ball.

"Meters Groove" ends. Lights rise to a bright glow on the New Orleans shotgun house. Donna and Nelson acknowledge the presence and greetings of the others throughout the scene.)

NELSON *(Wearing a fake smile)*: I don't know why in the hell I let you convince me to be the King of a reactionary Mardi Gras club like this.

DONNA *(Also smiling)*: It would have been rude to refuse the honor of having been elected King and Queen.

NELSON *(To a person at the ball)*: Hey, thanks, brother man! Thanks for your support.

DONNA: If the All African People's Coalition really wants to impact electoral politics, these are some of the key people you'll have to deal with. Maybe they won't be with you, but you definitely don't want them working against you.

DONALD *(Emerging from the Band area)*: Hey, Mom. *(Kissing her)* Hey, Pops. *(Dapping him)* They're really putting on the dog for y'all tonight.

NELSON: Hold up. The brother wants a picture of the royal family. *(They pose for a picture)*

DONNA: You're sounding really good tonight, too, son.

NELSON *(To photographer)*: Thank you, brother.

DONALD: Aw, you're just prejudiced, Mom. Everybody knows you're my number one fan.

DONNA: And proud of it too!

NELSON: Your music is fine, everybody loves it. So why you got to go to a music school? You ought to study something substantial, like math or science or history. Something that will help you be a better leader for our struggle.

DONNA: Nelson! This is neither the time nor the place.

NELSON: It's always the time for struggle. It's always the place. No one is free—

DONNA AND DONALD *(Teasing)*: until all are free!

DONNA: For heaven's sake, Nelson, this is a party and we're the guests of honor.

NELSON: Which makes it all the more important for us to stay focused. His generation's got a lifetime of struggle in front of them. Music is nice, but no revolution was ever won on the bandstand.

DONNA: Our music is the essence of our struggle. When our language, our social structures, our artifacts and our gods were destroyed, all we were able to hang onto was our music.

DONALD: Mom's right, Daddy. Black music is one of the greatest contributions anybody ever made to world culture. I'll tell you what, without music there wouldn't be much of a movement either.

DONNA: Precisely! So if you think the Jazz Academy College will help you develop your talent, son, go right ahead.

NELSON: It's not just a question of how to develop our talents. How will our talent work for us? We'd be irresponsible as parents in the struggle—

DONNA: "Irresponsible parents"? Now you stop right there, Mr. Nelson "Mandela" Hardiman. Don't you dare to raise that issue with me. Where were you when I was pregnant? In jail. Where were you during the first ten years of his life? In jail! *(Donald goes back to the bandstand)* Then when I finally got you out of jail did you stay home to help? No. You were running all over the place fighting for the so-called "revolution," while I was raising our child and making a living for our family. The only time you worried about being a parent was when there was a photo op for the happy family.

NELSON: That was a low blow, Donna.

DONNA: Donald! Where did he go?

NELSON: He had to get back to work. *(Donna walks away, retreating behind the scrim of the New Orleans home. Nelson focuses on the guests)* A constant struggle, yeah . . . a strong black woman . . . a constant struggle, brother. Good to see you, man. *(To Donna)* Didi! Donna! *(Exits behind the New Orleans scrim)*

(Nelson and Donna stand behind the scrim, arguing, in silhouette. From the bandstand, Donald sings "How Can You Say You Love Me":)

DONALD:

How can you say you love me, when you never treat me right?

How can you say you love me, when you never treat me right?

I always give you what you want, but when it's my turn it's a fight.

My mama then told me, "Son, love can be a rocky road."

My mama she then told me, "Son, love can be a rocky road."

Just when you give your heart sometimes love will turn so cold.

The only question left is whether I'll pack my bags and leave.

The only question left is whether I'll pack my bags and leave.

If you won't treat me right, said I'm moving down the line.

(Lights fade on the Band and the New Orleans shotgun house.)

Scene 2

Lights rise on the New York tenement. Father looks through the letters.
He begins to read one:

FATHER: My Dearest Brother, You are going to miss a great
New York's Eve party. On Saturday the whole family will
walk downtown to shop at the big department stores on
Broadway. I admit that it's easier to go shopping in el barrio,
where your face does not turn a clerk to stone. Where our
money is as green as anyone else's. I'll buy a dark suit for the
occasion. It's going to be a big celebration, and everyone is
excited because my wife's brother has bought a movie camera, which he will be trying out that night. I wish you were
here with us. Better yet, I wish we were in Puerto Rico, with
you. —Your dearest brother.

(The Band plays "Toda una Vida" as Father and Angela dress up
for the party. Father wears a suit with a vest and a hat. Angela, her
hair tied into a ponytail with a red ribbon, wears a scarf around
her hips and a white, faux fur stole. "Toda una Vida" ends. They
both sit on the trunk.)

ANGELA: We have a home movie of this party. Several times
my mother and I have watched it together. It is grainy and
short. And it is in color. The only complete scene in color
I can recall from those years. The movie opens with a sweep
of the living room.

(Movie music. Spotlights flicker, creating a "movie effect."
   As Angela continues, Mother becomes visible behind the rural
Appalachian scrim, rocking in silhouette. Angela comes from
behind the scrim and walks downstage. Father stands on the trunk
and pulls out a roll of red ribbons. He throws the ribbon toward
Angela. She catches the ribbon and then lets it drop to the floor.
Then he throws a second one, and so on . . .)

It is typical immigrant Puerto Rican decor for the time: the sofa and chairs are upholstered in bright colors, covered in transparent plastic. The linoleum on the floor is light blue. There are dime-sized indentations all over it, victim of the spike heels.

(Caught up in her story, she describes the flickering silent movie and lives it all at once. Father stands in front of the trunk, with gestures of handshakes and smiles.)

The room is full of people dressed in mainly two colors: dark suits for the men, red dresses for the women. We were dressed up like child models in the Sears catalog. My brother in a miniature man's suit and bow tie, and I in black patent leather shoes and a frilly dress with several layers of crinolines underneath. The women in red sitting on the couch are my mother and my eighteen-year-old cousin. My cousin has grown up in Paterson and is in her last year of high school. She doesn't have a trace of "la mancha," the mark of the new immigrant. She is wearing a tight, red-sequined cocktail dress. *(She and Father sit on the trunk)* Her brown hair has been lightened with peroxide around the bangs and she is holding a cigarette very expertly between her fingers.

(Silhouette of Mother fades.)

FATHER *(Walking downstage)*: She can pass for an American anywhere—at least for Italian, anyway. Her life is going to be different. She has an American boyfriend. He is older and has a car. If she marries him, even her name will be American. *(Returns to the trunk and sits next to Angela)*

ANGELA: For years I've had dreams and nightmares in the form of this home movie. Familiar faces pushing themselves forward into my mind. Like this old woman whose mouth becomes a cavernous black hole I fall into. And as I fall I can feel her laughter.

(The Band plays "Old Woman" as Angela becomes the old woman of her nightmares. They walk downstage close together, in the same rhythm, speaking simultaneously:)

FATHER AND ANGELA:

> Your cousin is pregnant by that man
> She's been sneaking around with.
> Would I lie to you?
> I was not invited to this party,
> But I came anyway.
> Your cousin was growing a *gringuito* in her belly
> She put something long and
> Pointy into her pretty self.
> Hmmm?
> And they probably flushed it down
> The toilet.
> The father does not want that baby.
> He is growing real children,
> With a wife who is
> A natural blond.
> And guess where your cousin will end?
> Hmmm?
> She'll be sent to a small town
> In Puerto Rico.
> A real change in scenery.
> La Gringa, they'll call her over there.
> Ha, ha, ha.
> La Gringa is what she always wanted to be!

(The nightmare ends. Lights fade.)

Scene 3

A soft light comes up on the Band. Donald, now a successful musician, steps downstage playing "Serenade." A spotlight comes up on him.

He crosses to the Appalachian house where a soft glow illuminates Mother and Billy exchanging gifts. She gives him an orange. He gives her a red ribbon for her hair.

391

Lights fade as Donald crosses to the New York tenement, where lights come up on Father and Angela. She is sitting on the trunk, where Father places a small package of old letters tied with red ribbon. He leaves. Donald continues to play for Angela.

Lights fade, then come up on the New Orleans shotgun house, where Donald now plays. Nelson and Donna sit together. "Serenade" ends. The spotlight on Donald fades.

It is Christmas 1998.

DONNA: Donald! This makes my holiday complete! You're supposed to be on tour with the band.

DONALD: I am, but I arranged a layover so I could see you guys for a couple of hours. Where've you been? I thought I was going to miss you.

DONNA: We were with Cousin Maudine and her family, celebrating Kwanzaa. She's got the sweetest little grandchild.

NELSON: Hey, it's great that you're here. I'm doing a fundraiser on "Creativity Night." You can be our guest star.

DONALD: I'm really sorry, Pops. I've got to split tonight. I'm headlining a benefit on New Year's Eve for the South African Children's Fund.

NELSON: Oh, I see.

DONNA: That's wonderful, dear.

DONALD: Yeah, yeah. Yo, dig. There're a couple of things I want to drop on y'all. This is for you, Pops. *(Hands him an envelope)*

NELSON: What's this?

DONALD: Go on. Open it.

NELSON: What in the world . . . ?

DONALD: You know my latest album, *Star Crossed Lovers*, it went platinum last week. That's practically unheard of in jazz, so I'm doing all right. So, Pops, considering how hard you've worked all your life to keep the All African People's deal afloat, I told my agent to sign the royalties from this album over to you. That's your first payment.

NELSON: I don't know what to say.

DONNA: "Thanks," is what people normally say in a situation like this.

NELSON: Thanks, son. *(They embrace)*

DONALD: I thought it would let a little pressure off you, Mom. *(Kisses Donna)* The other thing I wanted you guys to know is that I'm planning to get married.

(The Band plays a soft conga and bass rhythm.)

DONNA: Oh, baby, that's wonderful!

NELSON: Who is the lucky girl?

DONNA: Do we know her?

DONALD: Nah, I don't think so. Here's her picture. I met her in New York. She hasn't come down here yet. She's dying to find out about New Orleans though.

DONNA *(Looking at the picture)*: Donald, you're not serious about this, are you?

NELSON: What's wrong?

DONNA: What's wrong?!

DONALD: There it is!

DONNA: This is a white girl! That's what's wrong!

DONALD: She's not white.

DONNA: Natural blond and baby blue. If she's not white you have a real serious problem 'cause "creole wannabes" are worse than "real white folk."

NELSON: Let's try to get a handle on the big picture here.

DONNA: Nelson, you take your handle and stick it where the sun won't shine. I didn't struggle through life to raise what I thought was a strong, intelligent black man to have him run off with some no-count white girl.

NELSON: Donna . . .

DONALD: She's not white, Mom. She's Puerto Rican.

(The conga-bass rhythm ends.)

DONNA: That makes a whole lot of difference, huh!

NELSON: The African cultural influence is very strong in Puerto Rican culture. They have a whole different take on race. I have some very strong comrades in The Movement . . .

DONNA: This is not about some abstract movement. This is about my son. And I don't want half-white grandchildren not knowing what they are or who they are.

NELSON: It's not a question of skin color, Donna, it's a question of consciousness. Does she understand the relationship between class, race and the struggle for justice? What does she think about—

DONALD: She thinks I love her! And I think she loves me. And that wraps it. This is my life. I'm not just the focus of your arguments about politics. I'm flesh and blood and feelings. And I'm a horn player, a jazz man. That's all. *(Donna turns her back on Nelson and Donald)* Look, I love you guys, but I got to go. I'll let you know when the wedding is. I guess we'll have to do it in New York. If you think you can handle it, you'll be welcome. I won't bring her down here 'til I feel like you'll be comfortable with her.

(Donald moves to leave, but Nelson makes a pleading gesture for him to come closer to his mother. Donald gives her a quick kiss. She does not respond. He exits.)

DONNA: Where did I go wrong? Lord knows I did the best I could do. I needed more help from you.

NELSON: You sound like it's all over. We're not done yet. *(Comes closer, tries to embrace her softly)*

DONNA: Aren't we?

(Lights fade.)

Scene 4

Lights rise on the rural Appalachian house. Mother and Billy are arguing.

BILLY *(Chasing Mother around, agitated)*: You think them's not this'n don't you. This'n couldn't be that or know 'bout this or understand that . . . why not? Why can't I be anybody? I got no job, no children, no wife, house, no past, no future. *(Mother leaves the house, crossing upstage to face the Band)* If this'n is whatever you think I am, then why can't I be whatever I think I am. Why can't this'n? *(Lights fade on Billy. Mother remains with the Band)*

(Lights rise on the New York tenement house. Father is singing "La Ultima Copa," a cappella:)

FATHER:

Eche, amigo, no más; écheme y llene,
Hasta al borde la copa de champán
Que esta noche de farra y alegría
El dolor que hay de mi alma quiero ahogar.
Es la última farra de mi vida,
De mi vida, muchachos, que se va,
Mejor dicho que se ha ido tras de aquella,
Que no supo mi amor nunca apreciar.

(He continues to sing as a spotlight rises on Mother. She sings "Greenwood Sidee'o," a cappella, overlapping with Father.)

MOTHER:

Then she returned to her father's hall
All alee and lonely.
Saw two babes a-playing at ball
Down by the Greenwood sidee'o.
O babes, O babes if you were mine
All alee and lonely.
I'd dress you up in scarlet fine
Down by the Greenwood sidee'o.

Besides the Lord, it is this land that has been the most comfort to me. And it is Billy who has helped me to stay here. The only time my husband ever spoke directly to me in forty-four years, to tell me to do somethin', was to buy this land when we got the chance. Land is about raising family, generation after generation; not just its coal, timber, ground for one generation to use up. You don't say I'll be a mother 'til this child goes off on its own, then I won't be its mother.

It ain't no short-term thing . . . I'll live here on this land 'til
I don't need it no more, then I'll jist stop caring for it?

FATHER: Dear Brother, It was a great party after all. Lots of food,
pasteles, gandules, and the rice with the real *sofrito* you sent up
from the island. We can never find *sofrito* here. Maybe someday we'll sell the stuff ourselves. Oh, there was lots of rum,
lots of Palo Viejo, lots of domino . . . the more we played
and drank, the more we cried. I didn't cry, nor drink. But
you know, at midnight some people were reminded of the
island by the smells in the kitchen, you know . . . Oh, and
the music. We played Daniel Santos, Felipe Rodríguez . . .
(Sings:)

> Eche, amigo, no más; écheme y llene,
> Hasta al borde la copa de champán
> Que esta noche de farra y alegría
> El dolor que hay de mi alma quiero ahogar.

*(Father hums as the Band starts to play "Sincerely Yours." Lights
on the New York tenement fade.*

*Nelson and Donna appear behind the New Orleans shotgun
house scrim, in silhouette.)*

NELSON AND DONNA *(Sing)*:
> But such songs of love belong to men
> Who seek the simple end of pleasure.
> Though pleasure's sweet
> Lovers still are meat and bone
> Don't live alone
> And, like water drops, have histories.

(Lights fade.)

Scene 5

Three pools of light illuminate the scrims. As if in a silent movie, Billy is sitting, playing banjo for Mother, though it cannot be heard. Mother dances.

Father dances downstage of the New York tenement scrim.

Donna and Nelson dance downstage of the New Orleans shotgun house scrim. All dance in slow motion.

Angela dances slowly downstage, then stands.

ANGELA: The five-minute home movie ends with people dancing in a circle. My uncle, the creative filmmaker, must have asked them to do that so that they could file past him. Since you can't justify the absurd movements, people appear frantic, their faces embarrassingly intense. There is no music in my dream. I hear the dead and the forgotten speak; a conga line that keeps moving silently past me. It is comical and sad to watch silent dancing. *(Pause)* Move back, Uncle, give the dancers room to move. Soon it will be midnight.

(Lights on Angela quickly fade. Lights then fade on the others, dancing slowly.)

Scene 6

Lights come up on the rural Appalachian house, where Billy is now playing loudly and Mother is dancing excitedly.

MOTHER *(Out of breath)*: I got eight children, twenty-seven grandchildren, fifteen great-grandchildren, and nineteen-and-a-half acres to divide among 'em. Now they ain't gonna get much if that's how they look at it. But as a whole, it's still as important as when we come here, maybe more so. There's something to be said for looking at life as a whole thing, at looking at this world as a whole thing. You take the hard things and the good things and you make a life out of 'em. Billy taught me that.

I count ever' day a blessing that I can get up and fix him something to eat. He's been a great comfort to me. He's never been a burden. I know somebody else won't understand me saying that, but he's here no matter whatever else happens. He's here for me. I'm eighty-eight year old, though it don't seem that long somehow. 'Bout ever'body I growed up with is gone. My husband, Mommy, Daddy, brothers, sisters, friends, all gone. The hardest part is having nobody to share your memories with. Somebody who knows what you know without you having to explain it to 'em. My children are all living, but they're sprangled out like a bean vine all over this here country. 'Cept Billy. Somebody said one time, "I don't see why you don't put him in a home, so one time in your life you'd be free." Without Billy, I'd be jist another ol' woman. Without Billy, they'd a' moved me from here long ago. Free? Well I don't want to be free! Free of love?

BILLY *(Sings)*:
> There was a lady lived in York
> Billy Boy, Billy Boy.

(Mother comes close to Billy. He embraces her softly.)

This'n here don't remember. That'n says she does, and I guess she does. When it comes to it, if you can believe one, that's good. Them ain't got nothin' to do with it. Us ain't got nothin' to do with it. This'n and that'n, that's all they is.

BILLY AND MOTHER *(Sing)*:
> She loved him up, she loved him down
> All alee and lonely.
> Loved him 'til he filled her heart
> Down by the Greenwood sidee'o.

(Mother rests her head on Billy's shoulder. Lights fade on the rural Appalachian house.
> *Silhouettes and patterns come up on all three scrims: Billy and Mother face each other, joining hands; Father and Angela face each*

other, with her standing at a distance; Donna and Nelson stand side by side.)

DONNA AND NELSON *(Sing)*:
> The price of peace is charged in blood
> And this a time for struggle,
> When love songs made of fluffy stuff turn dry and brittle
> Blow away.
> What good's a parasol in heavy rain?
> A dainty cake to starving masses?
> Did crazed Nero stain his place in time
> With Love's lyric?
> All light unweighted things
> Like feathers, flutter in the wind.

(Lights fade.)

Scene 7

Father is dressed in white behind the New York tenement scrim. Angela sits on the trunk, her back to the audience, looking at her father.

FATHER: It is a dangerous thing to forget the climate of your birthplace, to choke out the voices of dead relatives when in dreams they call you by your secret name. It is dangerous to use weapons and sharp instruments you are not familiar with. *(Slowly takes off his white hat and suit)* It is dangerous to disdain the plaster saints before which your mother kneels, praying with embarrassing fervor, that you survive in the place you have chosen to live. *(Lights fade on Father)*

ANGELA: Jesús, María y José. To forget is a dangerous thing.

(Nelson comes from behind the New Orleans scrim and crosses to Angela. She gets up and joins him. They address the audience:)

NELSON: Read these living words.

ANGELA: Love the lives these words are made of.

NELSON: Know these lives to be your own,

ANGELA: And then, you'll know a love song.

ANGELA AND NELSON *(Sing)*:
> Made of sweat and bread and blood.
> You sing the tune you know I would
> If I could promise you a love song.

(Lights rise on a Musician, who enters playing guitar.)

ALL *(Sing)*:
> If you were me
> And I was you,
> Would I still do
> The things I do?
> Would you still say
> The words you say?
>
> Would we feel joy?
> Would we feel pain?
> Would every day
> Still start the same,
> A hope and a prayer
> For a love that's true?
> If you were me
> And I was you.
>
> There is no cure,
> No magic pill
> That can change
> Every ill.
> But . . . maybe
> If we could see
> What it's like
> To be you and me.

If you were me
And I was you
Would I be black,
Would you be blue,
To see what life
Put me through?
What would you do?

Would I hide my face
In shame
Every time I heard my name?
Could we both
Stand up proud and true?
If you were me,
And I was you.

If you were me,
And I was you?

(The Company walks toward the audience as it sings the last two verses. The Band plays the "Finale" as the Company takes a bow. Then they break the line to dance with each other; they dance as they exit, leaving the Band to play until the song ends.)

THE END

Crossing the Broken Bridge

Co-created and written by:
John O'Neal, Junebug Productions
Naomi Newman, A Traveling Jewish Theatre
Steve Kent, Director

Production and Performance History

Crossing the Broken Bridge was created and written by John O'Neal, Naomi Newman and Steve Kent. It was directed by Steve Kent. The lighting design was by Kate Mattson and the lighting direction was by David Welle. The two leading roles were performed by Naomi Newman and John O'Neal.

The play was a collaboration between and co-production of Junebug Productions of New Orleans, LA, and A Traveling Jewish Theatre of San Francisco, CA. Three co-commissioners helped to bring the play to life: Helena Presents, Helena, MT; Scottsdale Cultural Council, Scottsdale, AZ; and the University of Colorado, Office of Cultural Programs, Boulder, CO. The play premiered in 1991 in San Francisco, CA.

Crossing the Broken Bridge has been performed in the hometown of the two writers: New Orleans, LA, and San Francisco, CA. It has also been performed in Little Rock, AR; Scottsdale, AZ; Santa Cruz, Los Angeles, Davis, CA; Boulder, CO; Hartford, CT; Washington, DC; Miami, FL; Decorah, IA; Carbondale, Galesburg, IL; Kokomo, IN; Louisville, KY; Keene, Lewiston, ME; Detroit, MI; Collegeville, MN; Kansas City, MO; Helena, Missoula, MT; Omaha, NE; Manchester, NH; Trenton, NJ; Cooperstown, Rochester, Buffalo, Brooklyn, NY; Cincinnati, Dayton, OH; Portland, OR; University Park, Philadelphia, PA; Chattanooga, TN; San Antonio, TX; Reston, VA; Burlington, VT; Pullman, Olympia, WA.

—*TRH*

SETTING AND CHARACTERS

There are two actors in this play. One African-American man and one Jewish woman. In the original play, those two actors, Naomi Newman and John O'Neal, played themselves and introduced themselves with their own names. Throughout the play, they told many stories of their cultures and of the conflict between them. In the storytelling, each actor often portrayed other characters.

The stage is set with four chairs: two are placed at extreme stage left, one downstage, one upstage; two are placed at extreme stage right, one downstage, one upstage. A sheet is casually folded on each of the downstage chairs. A large tambourine-type drum is propped against the back of the chair at upstage right.

Act One

Naomi and John enter.

NAOMI *(To the audience)*: Good evening. This is John.

JOHN: And this is Naomi. We're very happy to be with you this evening.

> *(Using differing volumes in their voices and exaggerated dialects, they "test" if the audience can hear them when "they talk like this." This exaggerated exchange is meant to establish stereotypes and to raise awareness of how we perceive people simply from their voices and dialects.)*

NAOMI: We'd just like to check the acoustics in the room. *(To the audience)* Can you hear me when I talk like this?

JOHN *(To the audience)*: Can you hear me when I talk like this?

NAOMI *(To the audience)*: Can you hear me when I talk like this? *(To John)* Wait a minute, it's my turn, stop pushing. I'm a human being too. Get out of my way.

3 JOHN O'NEAL

JOHN: Can you hear me when I talk like this? "Yessum, hee, hee, hee, yessum. Excuse me, I'm sorry. Hee, hee, hee. Can you hear me now, suh? . . . ma'am?"

NAOMI: Can you hear me when I talk like this? "Listen, baby, don't get upset, we're going to make the deal. Your people will talk to my people. So what if you gotta show a little skin, you've got plenty of it. Trust me, trust me."

JOHN: Can you hear me when I talk like this? *(Singing)* "Swanee, how I love ya— What's that, sir? Oh. Then how about:" *(Singing)* "Summerti— What's that? Something with more of 'that special Negro quality' . . . Okay. A spiritual . . . Dance?! Sure, I can move . . . What you want, you know I've got it!"

NAOMI: Can you hear me when I talk like this? "The pound of flesh, which I demand of him, is dearly bought: 'tis mine and I will have it."

JOHN: Can you hear me when I talk like this? "It's time to share your love with God. Don't bring no tinkling change! I want to hear the sweet soft flutter of greenback-dollar bills."

NAOMI: Can you hear me when I talk like this? "I far prefer a Sauvignon to a Chardonnay. Remember that great wine in Province? I think it was a white Bordeaux. I know I kept the label. It was heaven."

JOHN: Can you hear me when I talk like this? "I don't like white people at all but I can't stand a Jew. 'Least with a cracker you know where you stand."

NAOMI: Can you hear me when I talk like this? "I've had it! You can't work with them. They hate everyone—Arabs, Koreans, Jews. They can't get ahead and are pissed-off at everyone who can."

JOHN: Can you hear me when I talk like this? *(As a homeless man)* Hey . . . you—

NAOMI *(To herself)*: Just pretend you didn't hear him.

JOHN: Lady, Can you spare eighty cents?

NAOMI: I'm sorry. I don't have any change.

JOHN: I only need eighty cents to get into the mission.

NAOMI: I said I have no change. Didn't you hear me?!

JOHN: Eighty cents! Do you hear me?

408

NAOMI: If you don't leave me alone, I'm going to have to call the police. POLICE, POLICE!

JOHN AND NAOMI: CAN YOU HEAR ME?

NAOMI: Boy, collaborations are trials of the soul.

JOHN: This is how it goes.

NAOMI: John, do you know how little time we have?

JOHN: Stop worrying about time, we'll do it. But first we have to agree on our mission statement.

NAOMI: No, no more mission-statement stuff. We're trying to create a theater piece, not a political party. Anyhow, we've got one. We spent a whole week writing one last year.

JOHN: Uh-uh. We've got three: yours, our director Steve's and mine.

NAOMI: What! We agreed it was a three-part statement.

JOHN: Naomi, you think we agreed when I'm still thinking about it.

NAOMI: Well I don't want to think about it any longer. I want us to get up on our feet and work . . . improvise . . . do something active.

JOHN: "If you don't know where you're going, any road will take you there."

NAOMI: What the hell is that suppose to mean? I've never done a mission statement for this kind of work. How can you know ahead of time what it's going to be? The work itself will tell you.

JOHN: You see.

NAOMI: What, what?

JOHN: We're coming from two entirely different places. We've got to get on the same beam.

NAOMI: Beam-shmeam. You just said it. We don't agree. That's what the piece is about; we don't agree and we're still working it out together. There's your mission statement.

JOHN: For what purpose?

NAOMI: To create a theater piece.

JOHN: Who's our primary audience? What do we want to happen as a result?

NAOMI: Enough. There's no time for this quibbling.

JOHN: It will take as long as it takes to get it right.

NAOMI: That's great! Twelve years from now we're going to have a gorgeous mission statement and not know what we're doing. Do you want to get up on the stage and act a mission statement? We're running out of time. *(John starts breathing)* What are you doing?

JOHN: Centering.

NAOMI: How long is that going to take?

JOHN: My grandfather told me, "Son, don't be in such a rush. At the end of the road is the grave. And it will be there no matter how long it takes you to get to it."

NAOMI: My grandmother always said, "Hurry up! Grab a hold of every minute. If you don't, by the time you get the hang of what it is to be alive—you're dead."

(They throw their hands up in the air.

A music jam begins. Upstage, Naomi plays lead "air" guitar with a scat line. She segues into "Hava Nagila." Downstage, John supports her with an "air" bass line.)

JOHN: If my grandmother told me once, she told me a thousand times: "You're just as good as anybody, baby, and don't you forget it!"

NAOMI: Oy. The sound of the shofar blowing: "Tekiah. Shevarim. Teruah."

(They meet upstage center, then slowly move downstage together.)

JOHN *(Simultaneously with Naomi)*: Funky fried fish, fried chicken, mashed potatoes, smothered liver and onions, collard greens, corn bread, boiled cabbage, barbecue, potato salad, cole slaw, bread-and-butter pickles, white soup-beans, black-eyed peas, okra and tomatoes, gumbo, rib tips, and rice with gravy all over it.

NAOMI *(Simultaneously with John)*: Corned beef, pastrami, chopped liver, chicken soup with matzo balls or kneidlach, smoked fish, gefilte fish, lox and bagels, potato salad, cole slaw, dill pickles, knishes, blintzes, stuffed cabbage! And whatever you got—a little sour cream on top—it wouldn't hurt.

(John walks past Naomi, crossing to the upstage-right chair. Naomi remains downstage.)

When I was a little girl growing up in Detroit, I thought the whole world was Jewish. My parents and all their friends were immigrants. We spoke Yiddish, we sang Yiddish songs . . . But, when I was in the third grade, we moved to a little town outside of Detroit where there were only a handful of Jews. One day, I'm walking home from school and this boy jumps in front of me, "You're not an American."

"Uh . . . yes, yes, I am, I am too!"

"No, you're not. You can't be. You're a Jew!"

I didn't have the heart to tell my parents, they were so proud of being Americans . . . But from that time on, I never really was sure I was "an American."

(John stands on the upstage-right chair and sings "My Country 'Tis of Thee." Naomi picks up the song. John moves off the chair and walks downstage during the following speech.)

JOHN: I must have been in the fifth grade when Daddy did something that made me real proud. He made a speech on the radio for National Negro History Week! All I can remember now is that he quoted Thomas Jefferson, "We hold these truths to be self evident that all men are created equal and endowed by their creator with certain unalienable rights, among these life, liberty and the pursuit of happiness." Then Daddy paused and said, "But the great Virginian held slaves." Soon after that speech, the head of the local NAACP had a cross burned on the front yard. He quickly packed up and left town. I wonder if any crosses are headed in our direction?

NAOMI: Oy! It's too much, life is too hard. Wait a minute, now what did my mother always say, "Take the big problems and make small ones out of them; take the small problems, make tiny ones; and from the tiny ones make nothing."

JOHN: "You're just as good as anybody, baby. And don't you forget it!"

411

(During the following, John moves the chairs into a diagonal line angled from downstage right to upstage left with a gap at center stage. Naomi uses the sheet from the downstage right chair to cover it again.)

NAOMI: I was raised as a socialist kid but I still had white privilege. The only black people I knew were the maids, who worked for us so that my mother could work ten hours a day with my father in their furniture store. We called them "mother's helpers." We ate dinner together, we did the dishes together—except my father.

My parents sometimes referred to them as "schwartzas." When my sister and I confronted them, they absolutely insisted it was not a pejorative word and they would never use the word "nigger." Oh yes, there were the fellows that drove the truck and loaded and unloaded the furniture.

These people were at the foundation of our world and yet we never entered theirs, and as a child I didn't even wonder about it, I thought it was natural.

JOHN *(Singing "It's All Right")*:
> . . . But you've got soul,
> And everybody knows that it's all right
> Yeah, it's all right . . .

(Naomi sings "Nice Work if You Can Get It" under John:)

NAOMI *(Singing)*: "The man who only lives for making money / Lives a life that isn't necessarily sunny . . . / Holding hands at midnight / 'Neath a starry sky / Nice work if you can get it / And you can get it if you try . . ."

JOHN: Dancing in the living room to doo-wop love songs and soft blue lights, or red lights, or next to no lights at all; grinding on a dime and giving nine cents change.

NAOMI *(Imitating her father)*: "Would it kill you if you dated a Jewish man just once, just for the novelty of it?"

JOHN: By the time we got old enough to be interested in sex, the white kids in the neighborhood stopped coming down to our house to play. We never had gone to theirs.

(John continues singing "It's All Right" under Naomi.)

NAOMI: When we got to be teenagers, my parents started worrying. One time my sister was invited to a birthday party in a bar. That was too much *goyim naches,* for my parents to handle. We moved back to Detroit!

JOHN: The rules of segregation were becoming clear. *(Singing "Black, Brown and White":)*

> Well if you're white,
> You're all right
> And if you're brown,
> Stick around.
> But if you're black,
> Oh, Brother, get back, get back, get back.

The only Jew that I knew of was Dr. Weinberg. He still kept a segregated waiting room, but he would treat colored people.

At church *(Naomi begins singing "Let My People Go"),* there were lots of stories about the righteous rage of the oppressed and exploited "Children of Israel." There was Daniel in the lions' den and Joshua at the battle of Jericho . . . Their heroes were almost as great as our own. Because of these things I didn't expect Jews to be as bad as other white people. *(He sings "Let My People Go" under Naomi)*

NAOMI: Every Passover, year after year, we are reminded that we were slaves in Egypt, and how we were freed from bondage. I still get chills at the seder when we hold up the matzo and say, "This is the bread of affliction your ancestors ate in Egypt. May all who are hungry come and eat. May all who are in need come and share this Passover." *(She continues the song under John)*

JOHN: I hated going to church on First Sundays! We had time for testifying, altar call, and the Lord's supper. All the time I'd be wondering, "How come God's got to be a white man?" I always wondered how come he's got to be a *man.*

NAOMI: We never talked about God. We celebrated most of the Jewish holidays at home in a secular way. On Saturday, instead of going to synagogue, we went to Litman's People's Yiddish Theatre. It's interesting; the household heroes that I remember best were Joe Louis, Paul Robeson and Marian Anderson. Still Kate Smith was my parents' favorite singer. I think they thought she was the singing Statue of Liberty. *(She sings "God Bless America" under John)*

JOHN: My daddy and a bunch of other young black men were waiting for the troop train that was to take them to the city for their physicals. One of them said, "Let's go over to that café and get some coffee, maybe wait in there."

The waiter told them, "Y'all can get it to go, but you can't drink it in here."

"But we're about to be drafted into Service, and it's freezing cold out there."

"I don't care. You won't drink it in here, and that's all there is to it!"

As they went back out into the bitter cold—without coffee—Daddy thought, "I'm good enough to go fight against the Nazis, and maybe die for this country, but I'm not good enough to sit down and drink a cup of coffee right here in my own hometown."

(John sings "America the Beautiful," overlapping Naomi's "God Bless America." Then John segues into "White Christmas" under Naomi.)

NAOMI: Damn it, one more Christmas carol and I'm going to puke. These are not my Holy Days. When my kids miss school for Rosh Hashanah and Yom Kippur they're marked absent. If there's a secular school in Christian America, I'm the Pope's mother!

JOHN: We take more shit than anybody! Anybody else in the world would have been done with this shit a long time ago.

NAOMI: We are survivors. Over the years, civilizations: they come, they go, but the Jews are still here.

JOHN: We can get by. This depression ain't gonna bother us because we ain't never had nothing to begin with. We know how to do without.

NAOMI: We know how to make something out of nothing. We take nothing, we put it in the ground, and something will come up.

JOHN: "If I ever get my hands on a dollar again, I'm gonna hold on to it 'til the eagle grins." *(Does an Arsenio Hall dog-pound hand motion)* I'm so broke I can't even change my mind.

NAOMI: I only wish we had as much power as they say we do. Believe me, if we controlled the banks and the media, it would be a fairer and much funnier world. (Ba-da-boom!)

So this little Jewish lady goes all the way to India, waits two years to see the guru. Finally it's time. She gets in line with thousands of devotees. She gets up to the guru and they say to her, "You can only say three words, three words."

"Don't worry, that's fine," she answers. So she bends down, she puts down her flowers. She puts down her fruit. She kisses the guru's feet. Then she looks up at the guru and says, "Sheldon, come home!"

(As a talk-show host) Well, that's fascinating. Please, tell us more about your unusual religious persuasion.

JOHN *(As a Baptist rabbi)*: I was ordained at the Baptist ministry, but I am also a practicing rabbi. You may say that I am a Baptist rabbi, a "Babbi," so to speak.

Now we have a problem: blacks and Jews are at each other's throats. We simply must get the Baptists to see the Jewish side of things, and the Jews have to see the Baptist side of things.

NAOMI: And which side are you on, sir?

JOHN: Some of my friends are Baptists, and some of my friends are Jews, and me, well, I'm for my friends. See there's no such thing as a problem without a solution—so, you see, if there's no solution, there's obviously no problem.

(Naomi assumes a steering-wheel stance.)

There are two towns on the Potomac in one place. Washington, DC, is where they run the government of the U.S. of A. But eighty percent of the people there live in a place called "Chocolate City." "People who go to Washington, DC, to do business with the United States of America seldom see "Chocolate City" or even know that it exists.

NAOMI: When I find myself in these neighborhoods I have to roll up my windows and lock my doors. I can't help it, I get scared. They're just *so* violent.

(John plays out the images that Naomi creates, using the chairs and drum to illustrate parts of her story.

He grabs the drum from behind the chair and raises it like a rising moon.)

JOHN: There's blood on the moon tonight. Somebody's bound to leave this world soon.

NAOMI: I dreamed that I was building a house in a large desolate lot where there was no sign of anything green growing. But the house was coming out peculiarly like a prison with hard lines, cement blocks and a ridiculously tall tower.

(John lowers the drum.)

Nonetheless I was giving a party to celebrate its construction. Everything was going haywire. The waiters were serving the food before the guests arrived. The menu was a mess. Everything was out of my control. I noticed a group of rabbis sitting together, talking and praying, oblivious to what was going on. Then I look up, and in the distance I see an army of men with gas masks and guns. They are spraying lethal pesticides and defoliants. I can't understand what they are trying to kill in this barren landscape. Then I realize they are bearing down on us. I run to the rabbi for help, but I can't get them to hear me. Alone, I run toward the army, screaming for them to stop. They keep coming. In the dream I know that I alone will not be able to stop them, only to slow them down a little, but I continue charging at them, screaming as loud as I can, "Go back, go back, you can't do this. No, no, you can't do this . . ."

(By this time, John has brought two chairs downstage center, stacking them. Naomi throws the sheet over the stacked chairs to make a podium. The other two chairs have been arranged as seats for speakers.)

JOHN *(As black academic)*: My esteemed colleagues . . . I've been asked to respond to the question: "Why is there so much tension between African-Americans and Jews?" The first thing you have to understand is that people always decide what they are going to do based on their own self-interests. That's the first law of nature: Look Out for Number One.

The second thing you have to understand is what has happened since the Second World War. During that time—due perhaps to the fact that anti-Semitism in the United States is not so bad as it is in Europe—the majority of the Jews in America have become a middle- to upper-middle-income population.

At the same time this has been happening, what happened to the African-Americans? Through Affirmative Action, a small percentage have been able to move into some of those middle-income jobs. But the sad fact is that the majority of black people are worse off now than they were before. The gap between black and white people is growing.

The average black person feels abandoned by folk once thought of as friends and allies, so now they are pissed off. I mean pissed at everybody. It really doesn't have all that much to do with Jews—*per se.*

But don't even mention Israel, no, no, no, no, no! One little country of about five million. Israel!—dominated by Europeans. Israel!—a country that was plopped down in the middle of Palestine. Israel!—a country that has always supported white South Africa. Israel!—gets three times more in trade and aid from the United States than the four hundred millions of people in the whole of black Africa. You damn right—people are mad and it's bound to get worse before it gets better.

NAOMI *(As Jewish academic)*: Ladies and gentlemen, I was hoping that the dialog at this conference would go in a different

direction. It's time we faced some difficult facts. I see that
I am forced to speak about the unspeakable. The problem
we have now is that African-Americans are taking their legitimate anger, and we know it is legitimate, and misdirect-
ing it at another oppressed people. Anti-Semitism is running wild in the African-American community. And who's
cracking the whip? Some of their leaders and teachers. We
are hearing from them, our traditional allies, the same vile
stereotypes that come from the far right, the neo-Nazis and
the Klan. They are singing the old "blame the Jew" tune,
this time with a new black beat.

Now we are blamed for the slave trade, for apartheid,
and for black poverty in America. Why even my learned col-
league insists on presenting Jews as monolithically affluent.
As if there were no working-class Jews. As if there were not
thousands of Jews—mostly women and old people—who
are living below the poverty line.

Now let us take a look at what is happening on campuses in
the United States today. Can you believe that there are edu-
cated African-Americans who are saying that the Protocols
of the Elders of Zion have validity. Why the Protocols of the
Elders of Zion was the basis of Hitler's "Mein Kampf." This
fictitious document claims to prove that the twelve tribes of
Israel gathered together in a cemetery with the devil and
devised a plan for Jews to overtake and rule the world. Now
how can anybody in their right mind believe such ridiculous
nonsense. And what are we Jews, and our children on campuses, supposed to do with this brand of racism?

And now for the most painful part of all. Look what
they've done to the idea of "Zionism." It's an outrage. I'll
tell you what Zionism means to me and to thousands of Jews
around the world. It means survival. Survival! It means a
place Jews can escape to, can come home to, when our time
is running out in whatever country. Like now in Ethiopia
or Russia. I know it has become exceedingly unfashionable,
especially in radical circles, but I stand here before you
today and say, "I am a Zionist. I may disagree with some of
the policies of the Israeli government. I believe that there

must be a Palestinian state—along with an Israeli one—and I am a Zionist. That doesn't make me a racist. That doesn't make me an imperialist. And by God it doesn't make me a Nazi."

(Both actors sit, glaring at each other. They cross to opposing sides of the podium, then lift the sheet to form a screen, which they stand behind. Dude pokes his head around the stage-right side of the screen, Urbie from around the stage-left side.)

JOHN *(As Dude)*: Every time you sit down to study our history, every time, without fail, you are going to find the Jew.

NAOMI *(As Urbie)*: Where, I'd love to read it. Because in no history book I have read have I found a Jew. You see, the Jew is never identified as a Jew, but as a Pole, an Armenian, a Frenchman.

JOHN *(As Dude)*: See there! You can't even get your thesis on the floor—

NAOMI *(As Urbie)*: I was putting my thesis on the floor—

JOHN *(As Dude)*: I was talking and you interrupted me!

NAOMI *(As Urbie)*: I interrupted you? Oh my God, a woman interrupted a man! Quick, someone out there, dial 911!

JOHN *(As Dude)*: Before I can get my thesis on the floor, she thinks, she's going to think— Well go ahead already!

(Urbie doesn't say anything.)

You got Bernal, Zinn, Meier, Herskovitz, Aptheker, all Jews. Engels, the Jew? Marx, the Jew—

NAOMI *(As Urbie)*: Freud.

JOHN *(As Dude)*: The Jew! Wait a minute, I'm talking about African and African-American history—

NAOMI *(As Urbie)*: I thought we were naming famous Jews.

JOHN *(As Dude)*: What about the great black scholars: Woodson, Johnson, Du Bois, Diop, Van Sertima? They think they know more about you than you know about yourself.

NAOMI *(As Urbie)*: Scholarship is part of the Jewish tradition. I'm not ashamed of that. And I would love to know when it became a crime for Jews to take an interest in African-American history?

JOHN *(As Dude)*: I'll give you a little bit of credit for that.

NAOMI *(As Urbie)*: How much? *(Dude gestures with thumb and second finger)* That's not very much.

JOHN *(As Dude)*: There're some Jews who will study 'til their eyes fall out; they will study and they will teach. They will tell you who you are. The Jew is trying to be the author of your history.

NAOMI *(As Urbie)*: If these books had not been written, what would we know?

JOHN *(As Dude)*: What do you know when everything you think you know about African-American history comes from books written by a bunch of Europeans—all the way back to Herodotus? You talking about what you can find in those books. I'm talking *primary sources.*

NAOMI *(As Urbie)*: Great, I'd love to know it—lead me to the "primary source."

JOHN *(As Dude)*: I am trying to talk about the African *man!* The African man is the original man.

NAOMI *(As Urbie)*: You've got to be kidding! The first human being was a woman. They call her "Lucy" —that's a woman.

JOHN *(As Dude)*: I guess you're going to claim she was a Jew too.

NAOMI *(As Urbie)*: Well, maybe, but we'll never know, because all the history we think we know was written by men, about men.

JOHN *(As Dude)*: Regardless, we do know she's an African.

NAOMI *(As Urbie)*: Yes. *She* was.

JOHN *(As Dude)*: She's always got to have the last word.

NAOMI *(As Urbie)*: No, you do.

(John lets go of the sheet.)

JOHN: My people did not "choose" to come to this country bound in chains. My people did not choose to raise the wealth of the western world on their backs as slaves. Most people don't know the glory of ancient Africa, the land which gave birth to all humankind. Most people don't know the inhuman horror of the Middle Passage and slavery, trade in human flesh for selfish gain.

(John sits.)

NAOMI*(As an African woman)*:
      My people, they be Dogon people.
      We African people.
      Africa, the place where I come from,
      By the white-top hill by the dum-dum tree.
      I come from that place.

      When they caught my people
      And carried us in chains to the sea
      And things were not so good, I cry.
      But I get used to it.

      When they fed us to the belly of the big ship
      And lock us down in chains
      My mother cried out
      And I cried harder still
      But I get used to it.

      When Belly of the Beast that bested the sea
      Growed slick with shit and puke
      And stink from people dead already
      And my mother growed sick and died
      And they would not let small, small me
      Go be by my mother
      To her long sleep in the sea.
      I cried.
      But, time, he go go so.
      I get used to it.

      On the day that he was born,
      I try to kill my man-child.
      I never want him to know this life to be a slave.
      But I was not so strong.
      I cannot make his breathing go
      The child, he keep on living.
      I get use to living too.

I can no more make my mouth know the language of my
   mother,
The language of my mother's people.
I can no more make my eye know how she look.
I can no more make my ear know how she speak.
I cannot cry.
I will not die.
I am used to this living.

If you make it so you can live and that you do,
You, you get used to it too.
If you do not, you will die.

JOHN *(Singing)*:
   Hush, little baby, don't you cry
   You know your daddy was born to die.

*(Naomi gathers the sheet at her ankles, slowly transforming herself
into a little lamb for "Ziamele.")*

   My trials. Lord, soon be over.

NAOMI AND JOHN *(Singing)*:
   Too late, my brother.
   Too late, but never mind,
   All my trials, Lord, soon be over.

   If religion was a thing that money could buy,
   Then the rich would live and the poor would die
   All my trials, Lord, soon be over.

*(Naomi begins singing "Ziamele" at counterpoint to John, who qui-
etly translates under her:)*

NAOMI:
   Unter Yiddeleh's vigeleh,
   Shteht a klor veiss tzigeleh.
   Dos Yiddeleh is geforen handlen.

Dos vet zein dein bafruf.
Roshenkehs mit mandlen.
Yiddeleh vet altz handlen.
Sholf zhe Yiddeleh, shof.

JOHN:

Under my little Jew's cradle,
Stands a pure white little lamb.
The little lamb went to market.
That will be your destiny.
Raisins and almonds.
My little Jew will have to handle everything.
Sleep ay little one, sleep.

(As a young Jewish boy) During World War II there was a sadness hovering around our lives that was personal yet seemed to come from far away. I would walk into the room and my mother would quickly wipe away tears. My father hardly sang at all anymore. The mailbox was at the center of the mystery. "Edith, anything today?"

"No, Yankel, not a word, nothing from anybody."

The story that perplexed me the most was about this man with a funny name, Ziegelbaum, who escaped from Poland, came to London, and there threw himself from a tall building to his death in order make the world pay attention to what was happening in the camps. I couldn't get it, I thought camps were where children went in the summer to have fun.

First our bundles were thrown into the cattle cars and the small children placed on top of the pile. Then seventy-five to a hundred people were pushed into each car and a few loaves of bread tossed in with them. Finally, two buckets, one filled with water and one left empty for excrement, were put into each wagon. Then the door was locked and barred from the outside. We traveled like that for three days and nights.

There was hardly any air to breathe inside the cattle car. Two of the four tiny windows were boarded up, the other two covered with barbed wire, crisscrossed. It was almost impossible to move, but somehow I managed to climb over to where my mother was and stayed there, pressed against her body, during the awful three-day journey. The feeling of her body during those last hours of her life has always stayed with me.

When we arrived in Auschwitz we were numb and dazed. We climbed off the cattle cars to the shrill commands of the SS. We did not yet know what the four black smoking chimneys in the distance meant, nor did we know the reason for our being forced into two groups.

My little sister, Judith, had her arms twined with mine and those of my older sister, Nanny. Quickly I motioned her over to where my mother and grandmother stood. Later, we learned that the older people and little children had been taken straight to the gas chambers.

(Naomi sings "Ziamele." And, again, John translates. The song ends.)

JOHN: First they came for the homosexuals, and I didn't speak up because I was not a homosexual.
NAOMI: Then they came for the communists, and I didn't speak up because I wasn't a communist.
JOHN: Then they came for the Jews, and I didn't speak up because I wasn't a Jew.
NAOMI: Then they came for the trade unions, and I didn't speak up because I wasn't a trade unionist.
JOHN: Then they came for the Catholics, and I didn't speak up because I was a Protestant.
NAOMI AND JOHN: Then they came for me.
And by that time no one was left to speak.

(They look at each other.
Intermission.)

Act Two

NAOMI *(As Rifke)*: They tell you "silence is golden." Feh! You know what silence is? Dangerous. "Don't say it." "Bite your tongue." "Mum's the word." Not me. I say: "Say it!" Waggle your tongue so the whole world can see. To quote Plato—a man who didn't keep his mouth shut, and people are still talking about him—"I only think in discourse." So you see I got a Platonic nature: I discourse my way through life.

Sometimes I talk myself into a purple confusion. That's okay. I'm not looking for perfection, just a way to chew on what life is dishing up, and, as you well know, some of it is just indigestible. We don't want a piece from the same old rotten pie. So we talk, and talk, and talk, and talk, until we bake a brand-new, twelve-grain, unbleached, no-artificial-anything bread big enough for everyone. Then something nourishing can go down. You got it? I deconstruct life with my mouth. Well spoken, *gut gesagt.*

(John and Naomi slap high-five. Then they re-set the chairs, singing "Freedom Is a Constant Struggle":)

JOHN AND NAOMI *(Sing)*:

> They say that freedom is a constant struggle
> They say that freedom is a constant struggle
> They say that freedom is a constant struggle
> Oh Lord, we've struggled so long
> We must be free, we must be free . . .

(They finish singing. John sits.)

JOHN *(As Larry, a Jewish Civil Rights worker)*: When I worked in The Civil Rights Movement in southwest Georgia I stayed in the home of a woman named Mrs. Annie Raines. She had a good-sized farm and for many years was the main midwife for everyone in the county, white as well as black. Everyone called her "Mama Dolly."

NAOMI *(As Mama Dolly, an African-American woman)*: I been living right here in Lee County since the day I was born and, the good Lord willing, that will be ninety-seven years on the twenty-sixth of July next, the good Lord willing, yes indeed. So I was already an old woman when the first Jew I ever knew to live in this county got here. The first time he come here he sat right there in the same chair you sitting in right now, yes, he did. To tell you the truth he looked like an ordinary white man to me. If you was to look at him I'll wager that you couldn't tell the difference between him and a white man neither.

When Reverend Wells come over here to ask me if I would take one or two Freedom Riders, who were coming in here to do voter-registration work, I really didn't know they had any Jews to speak of besides the ones you find in the Bible. Reverend Wells brought him in here, and I told him straight to his face, I wasn't expecting no *white* Freedom Riders.

JOHN *(As Larry)*: I'm not white, I'm Jewish.

NAOMI *(As Mama Dolly)*: It don't make a dime's worth of difference to me. 'Far as I'm concerned, you the first white person to set foot on my land since 1937. When the High Sheriff wants to see me, he puts a letter in my mailbox.

JOHN *(As Larry)*: What keeps the white people from coming out here?

NAOMI *(As Mama Dolly)*: That twelve-gauge, double-barreled shotgun. I got another one by the back door and a thirty beside my bed and I cleans and oil them *all* every Saturday night.

JOHN *(As Larry)*: But I thought this was a nonviolent movement.

NAOMI *(As Mama Dolly)*: That's right, son, and we aim to keep it that way.

(To the audience) Well, baby, Larry was to stay here for most of a year. I don't know that he did all that much good work, but some good things did come from him being here, though it was sometimes a sure 'nough struggle. I never could get it straight what it was he meant by saying he was a Jew. For an instance, the first morning he was here, trying to be hospitable, I got up early and made a big breakfast: biscuits and gravy, ham and eggs, home-fried potatoes, apply butter, fresh apply juice, fresh milk form the cow, everything. He picked at the food for a while, but I could see that he wasn't going to eat it, so I asked him, "What's wrong, Larry, you don't like soul food?"

JOHN *(As Larry)*: It looks like most everything is cooked in lard and it's against the Jewish religion to eat pork.

NAOMI *(As Mama Dolly, to the audience)*: We settled that right quick. I told him that if he was going to have special rules 'bout what he could and could not eat, he was going to have to do his own cooking. It took him a while to get the knack of it, but he got to be a right good cook before he left here.

Being he was so religious, I invited him to go to church with me that first Sunday he was here. The way he started jumping around, I thought he was going to get happy himself when the Young People's Gospel Choir was singing "Satisfied with Jesus." But then when the sermon got hot and Reverend Wells shifted into high gear, Larry looked like he thought the man had gone crazy or something. Then when Doreen McCalister got happy and started shouting, I just knew that Larry was set to buck and run. When we got home from church that day, he had a million questions. So I finally asked him, "What do they do at your church?"

JOHN *(As Larry)*: First of all, they call a Jewish church a "syn-agogue," and I'm not all that religious myself, so I really haven't been to synagogue that often—

NAOMI *(As Mama Dolly)*: So what did you mean by saying eating pork is against your religion, if you ain't got no religion for it to be against?

JOHN *(As Larry)*: Well, what I mean is that . . . well, being Jewish is a way of life.

NAOMI *(As Mama Dolly)*: You mean if I was to join the Jewish church, would I be Jewish?

JOHN *(As Larry)*: Yes, we have converts, like Sammy Davis, Jr., he's a Jewish convert.

NAOMI *(As Mama Dolly)*: Yes, un-huh, the poor thing. So being Jewish is kinda like being Baptist, huh?

JOHN *(As Larry)*: Yeah, I'd say so . . .

NAOMI *(As Mama Dolly)*: So I guess they have white Jews and black Jews and all different kinds of Jews, huh?

JOHN *(As Larry)*: That's certainly true.

NAOMI *(As Mama Dolly)*: Well, Larry, I still can't say that I under-stand how you figure that you ain't white. You could join the New Zion Baptist Church, but it sure would not make you colored. It seems to me that as long as you got black you going to have white. It don't matter how many differ-ent brands of white folks you got in some other country, they all get white when they come to America, that's just the way it is.

(Naomi and John sing "Wade in the Water":)

JOHN AND NAOMI *(Sing)*:
    Wade in the water
    Wade in the water, children
    Wade in the water
    God's gonna trouble the water . . .

(They finish singing. John raises the sheet, and, again, he pokes his head around one side while Naomi speaks to him and us from the other side.)

JOHN *(As Dude)*: You can't trust a Jew. They'll turn white on you in a minute.

NAOMI *(As Urbie)*: You people show no appreciation at all. You seem to forget our history together. We stood with you throughout the Civil Rights struggle. We marched with you. We died with you. What about Goodman and Schwerner?

JOHN *(As Dude)*: What about James Chaney? Remember him? Hundreds of blacks were beaten and killed, and all "you people" can think about is two Jews.

NAOMI *(As Urbie)*: Come on now. Let's get a touch of reality here. Jews made up two-thirds of the white Freedom Fighters, one-half of the Mississippi Volunteers, we gave three-quarters of the money and we're only three percent of the American population. That is not just two little Jews.

JOHN *(As Dude)*: They didn't come to Mississippi because they were Jews. They came because they were liberals and radicals.

NAOMI *(As Urbie)*: Well, for lots of Jews being radical and liberal comes from, and is, our religion.

JOHN *(As Dude)*: Looks like your religion is losing a lot of its practitioners here lately. Where are they now?

NAOMI *(As Urbie)*: That's great! First you kick us out of The Movement with all that Black Power stuff, and then you accuse us of abandoning you. That is really tricky.

JOHN *(As Dude)*: You're ducking the issue, baby, I'm asking where are they now?

NAOMI *(As Urbie)*: I'm answering. Some went where you told them to, back to work in their own communities. And some went into peace, ecology and other progressive movements.

JOHN *(As Dude)*: All of them?

NAOMI *(As Urbie)*: All right, all right, some did, mostly men. But what's the use, it's always the same: "If it's good, it's not you; if it's bad, it's the Jew."

(John drops the sheet.)

JOHN *(As Dude)*: We got a problem, brothers and sisters; I mean to tell you *we* have got a problem. The rich white folks think the poor white folk are fools. They tell them that the Jews are bad because they think they're the "chosen people," that they're "Christ killers," but that Jesus Christ was okay because he was the Jew that got killed.

Black folks? They try to make us out to be an aggravating bunch of monkeys that would probably be all right if the Jews would leave us alone.

See, nobody, red or yellow, brown or white, none of them think about us at all until we become a problem to them: we want a job, we want welfare, we want to buy stuff on credit but don't want to pay the bill. They want to walk down the street in peace and can't, 'cause we standing around with our attitudes hanging out. They want a nice clean neighborhood and can't have it 'cause we trying to move in, and when we move in they move out.

We want an education, we want Affirmative Action, we want a loan, we want a business, we want, we want out of jail, we want an abortion, we want free health care, we want equity, we want justice, we want, we want, we want! And ain't nobody thinking about us except as a problem to them.

Well, my brothers and sisters, I guess, we going to have to start thinking about ourselves.

NAOMI: John, there's a story I need to tell:

My theater company was having a promotional film made. When the shooting was over the director said, "Now I turn the footage over to my brilliant editor." A few weeks later we went to the studio to see a rough cut. When we got there, a small black man let us in. I was appropriately friendly and polite, but I didn't pay much attention. Then the director came out, put his arm around the black man and said, "This is the brilliant editor I was telling you about, he knows who you are, and he's been working on your faces for weeks. Come on; let's see the rough cut."

It was hard to look at the film. It was harder to look at the editor. But, most of all, it was hard to look at myself. They say that self-awareness is bad news. Me a racist? No way! Except I just couldn't imagine that the brilliant editor would have black skin.

JOHN: Boy have I got one for you:

Do you remember the festival we made at Cornell? I was working on this festival at Cornell University. One day Sally, a teacher who I would have cast to play the comic-strip character Blondie, stopped me to complain about how much trouble she was having, trying to work out a particular agreement with Naomi. In a hurry to get on to where I was going, I said, "You know how it is when you're dealing with a pushy Jewish woman."

Sally's jaw dropped and her rhythm changed. "Well! As one 'pushy Jewish woman to another . . .' I don't remember the rest of what she said, but if she had not challenged my prejudice, I probably wouldn't remember saying what I'd said either.

(They sing "If I Am Not for Myself":)

JOHN AND NAOMI *(Sing)*:
> If I am not for myself, who will be for me?
> If I am not for others, what am I?
> And if not now, when?

(Both simultaneously): Pardon me. Would you mind moving over a little bit. I don't like to trouble you, but if you would just move over a teeny-weeny bit. I know you can. I know you wouldn't want to stand in the way of growth, love and connection. I mean there's as much room over there as there is right here. Over there you wouldn't be blocking anybody. So just budget a little. Come on now, I know we can do this together. I'm not asking you to do it alone. I'm just asking you to move a little bit—with good will. I don't want you to do it against your will. It's gotta be what you want. If you would just understand that what I want is what you want, you would GET THE HELL OUT OF THE WAY!

(John picks up the drum and plays a rhythm underneath:)

JOHN: Yoruba, Bambatala, Ibo, Hausa, Ashanti, Mende, Bakongo, Ga, Malinke, Fante, Twi, Susu, Fulani, Wolof, Mandingo,

431

Bale, Bete, Senufo, Dioula, Ibibio, Dida, Fon, Somba, Bariba, Mina, Dendi, Akan, Bassa, Songhai, Zulu . . .

NAOMI *(Singing)*: HASHI VENU HA SHEM, Eylecha v'nashuva chadesh yamenu.

(John puts down the drum.
Naomi and John sing "Motherless Child":)

JOHN AND NAOMI *(Sing)*:
    Sometimes I feel like a motherless child . . .
    Sometimes I feel like a motherless child . . .
    Long way from my home.

(They finish singing.)

JOHN:
    Do you smell smoke?
    If you don't, it's not
    Because a tenement isn't burning—
    Down the street, in Derry, Beirut or San Salvador.
    Did you just hear a scream?
    If you didn't, it's not
    Because a woman wasn't raped.
    Since I asked if you smelled smoke . . .

NAOMI: Oh God, this street is deserted. Where is everybody? I'm not going to call a cab to get from the library to get to my house.

JOHN: Let's see . . . the summation of the variables indicating the relation between the mean and the norm . . .

NAOMI: What's he doing over there? Just keep going. I'm not going to cross the street.

JOHN: . . . divided by the total number of units in the sample equals . . .

NAOMI: Mustn't act afraid. He's so big.

JOHN: I hope Mike's at home and that he's still got those notes. He had to have a whole lot of help to pass this class. I wonder who's paying his rent . . .

NAOMI: What are you supposed to do? Put your fingers together and poke them in the eyes with your nails . . . ?

JOHN: I know he can't afford to live in this kind of neighborhood on his own. He's got more loans than I do. His folks don't have money.

NAOMI: If he wants my money I'll just give it to him. What if it's not my money he wants.

JOHN: Where's that address? 365 . . . Maybe that lady knows. Say, miss—

NAOMI: He's coming at me.

JOHN: Oh shit! This babe is spooked. I forgot where the hell I was.

NAOMI: For once in your lifetime don't panic. Scream. That's what you're supposed to do.

JOHN: How am I going to get out of this?

NAOMI: Scream, not like you're afraid, but fierce. Come on, make a sound. No, no . . . Don't touch me, stay away.

JOHN: Excuse me, ma'am, do you know where 365 Pratt Drive is?

NAOMI AND JOHN: No! NO! NO! NOOO!

(John runs.)

JOHN: Miz Schwartz, Miz Schwartz, are you in there? The whole block's on fire. Open your back door! I'm trapped!

NAOMI: Go away. I've got nothing left to steal.

JOHN: Nobody wants your junk. I'm trying to get out of here.

NAOMI: I'm telling you: leave me alone. I don't open middle of the night for anybody.

JOHN: I'm your neighbor from upstairs. There's a riot going on. You don't smell the smoke?

NAOMI: Hoodlums, all hoodlums.

JOHN: The whole place is on fire!

NAOMI: What? Another pogrom? The Nazis again?

JOHN: Open the door for God's sake!

NAOMI: God! He doesn't care.

JOHN: Please! Just open the damned door.

NAOMI: So go through the alley. Who's stopping you?

JOHN: It's too dangerous. The fire's closing in. We could both get out your front door.

NAOMI: Out my front door, in this riot, the hoodlums will kill me.

JOHN: We can get to my car. It's right down the street.

NAOMI: They . . . you . . . I don't know you.

JOHN: I'm Ruth Kingston's son. You used to fix our clothes. Up in there.

NAOMI: Forty years fixing up in this place. For what? Leave me alone.

JOHN: Ruth Kingston. Y'all used to cook together. You came to the funeral.

NAOMI: Ruth Kingston? Oh, Ruthie . . .

JOHN: You played cards.

NAOMI: She never let me win . . . ten lifetimes ago.

JOHN: Open up! This is crazy.

NAOMI (*Looking up*): Ribono Shel Olami! Now you make me my neighbor's keeper?

JOHN: You're going to make me risk my life and you're going to die in there.

NAOMI: Arthur. Artie, wait. I'm coming. I'll open. Enough. Dayenu. Enough.

(*John beats the drum to a crescendo as they exit the burning building.*)

JOHN: We have one more story.

NAOMI: So this woman dies and enters into the after-life world. She looks around. It's a banquet. Tables running over with food. Every kind you could imagine. Such abundance, such smiles, such deliciousness. "Not bad," she thinks, "maybe I can stop cooking for a change." She comes closer. She's about to join the party. Then she sees all these people in front of this feast, and they look miserable. Their faces tortured, worse than like those in the subway. "What's going on here?" She can't believe it. Nobody is eating. She looks closer yet, and she sees that they can't get the food into their mouths because, tied to their arms, are these long forks and spoons—

JOHN: The story works better if you use long chopsticks.

NAOMI: "Chopsticks"? What do you mean "chopsticks"?

JOHN: The story works better with chopsticks.

NAOMI: How do you know?

JOHN: I've heard the story.

NAOMI: What do you mean you've "heard the story," I just started the story.

JOHN: It's the same setup.

NAOMI: So what happens, let me see if it's the same story.

JOHN: Well, this guy—

NAOMI: "Guy"? "Guy"? It's a woman. If it's not a woman it's not the same story.

JOHN: Okay. So this woman walks over to St. Peter—

NAOMI: Vos var a "St. Peter"? It's the angel Raziel!

JOHN: Maybe it's a different story.

NAOMI: I won't be a stickler for detail, go ahead.

JOHN: This woman goes up to St. Peter and says, "What kind of place is this? Where am I?" And he says, "Lady, this is hell. If you don't recognize it, you must be in the wrong place. What's your name?"

NAOMI: "Chana Leah Bat Miriam."

JOHN: What are you talking about?

NAOMI: Her name, her name. I'm telling you her name. Try and say it: "Chana, Chana, Chaa . . ." Can you do it? It's back of the throat.

JOHN: In my story her name is Hannah, all right? "Hannah," she says. "My husband's name is Thomas and I have three kids: Jessie, Beulah and Ida Mae."

NAOMI: Motel, Rochel, Dovidel.

JOHN: "Oh," says St. Peter. "You're in the wrong place, darling. There's been a terrible mistake. You're supposed to be in Heaven. Come on." He takes her by the hand, leads her down this long corridor—

NAOMI: Right around the corner. In my tradition, Heaven and Hell are a lot closer together.

JOHN: Somehow I can believe that. He opens this door and there she sees the same banquet hall, the same tables, the same food the same chopsticks—

NAOMI: Forks and spoons—

JOHN: Same people, same clothes—

NAOMI: What do you know—it is the same story.

JOHN: But this time . . .

NAOMI: But this time . . .

NAOMI AND JOHN: They were feeding each other.

(John sings "I'm Gonna Sit at the Welcome Table"; Naomi sings "Hiney Matov":)

JOHN *(Sings)*:

    I'm gonna sit at the welcome table,

    I'm gonna sit at the welcome table,

    One of these days, Hallelujah!

    I'm gonna sit at the welcome table,

    I'm gonna sit at the welcome table,

    One of these days!

NAOMI *(Sings)*:

    Hiney matov u' manayim

    Shevet amim gam yachad.

(They finish their songs.)

THE END

Contributor Biographies

JUNEBUG PRODUCTIONS

Junebug Productions is a professional African-American arts organization located in New Orleans, LA. Its mission is to create and support artistic works that question and confront inequitable conditions that have historically impacted the African-American community. Through interrogation, we challenge ourselves and those aligned with the organization to make greater and deeper contributions toward a just society. Junebug Productions takes its name from a folk character, Junebug Jabbo Jones, who is a central figure in five company-created plays. This character comes from a long line of African storytellers. His ancestors include Aesop, African oral historians and modern street-corner poets. He is present whenever oppressed people take stock of their situation and begin to consider how to change things.

In the post-segregation era, Junebug Productions remains conscious of those bloody, difficult integration struggles that have now created a new set of equally challenging conditions.

A vital legacy of The Movement is the recognition that the greatest subsidies required for the development of culture usually come from the artists themselves. Therefore, Junebug Productions has evolved a working style based on collaboration among creative artists, managers and community organizations who share a commitment to similar goals and a desire to maximize scarce resources. Junebug Productions carries ten plays in its repertoire, three of them intercultural collaborations, and has toured these plays throughout the U.S. and internationally for more than thirty years.

JOHN O'NEAL, Junebug's Founder and Artistic Director for more than thirty years, co-founded the Free Southern Theater in 1963 as a cultural arm of The Southern Civil Rights Movement. For Free Southern Theater, O'Neal worked as a field director for the Student Nonviolent Coordinating Committee and worked as a national field program director with the Committee for Racial Justice. He has written eighteen plays, including his Junebug Jabbo Jones cycle of plays; a musical-comedy; poetry and essays. He has performed throughout the U.S. and around the world. He is the recipient of the Award of Merit from the Association of Performing Arts Presenters, the United States Artists Award, and a Ford Foundation Award.

In 2013, John O'Neal retired as the Artistic Director of Junebug Productions, but the company still carries on its work and mission in New Orleans.

THERESA RIPLEY HOLDEN is a theater artist, professor, performing arts manager and organizer. She is the Co-Director of Holden & Arts Associates, a management company; and the Director of the Artist and Community Connection (ACC), both based in Austin, TX. ACC, a not-for-profit organization, offers consulting services to diverse organizations and specializes in building equitable partnerships. Theresa also served as Managing Director of Junebug Productions and produced many of John O'Neal's plays. She also partnered with John O'Neal on his Color Line Project, a multi-year project held in numerous cities in the U.S. For more than twenty years, Theresa has planned, produced and consulted on numerous community-based projects around the U.S. She has served on many boards and funding panels across the U.S. She teaches theater courses on creating theater from stories in diverse communities. She presently teaches the Emerging Leadership Institute for Arts Presenters, which she has done for the past ten years. Theresa and John received the Leadership for a Changing World Award from the Ford Foundation.

STEVE KENT is a director and dramaturg, who has worked with John O'Neal for more than thirty years, collaborating with O'Neal on major productions with A Traveling Jewish Theatre and Roadside Theater. He has directed at the Croatian National Theatre, Manhattan Theatre Club, Mark Taper Forum, Illusion Theatre and 7 Stages. He has worked with the Urban Bush Women, and adapted *TEXTS* by Samuel Beckett with Joseph Chaikin at The Public Theater in New York and in Paris and London. Steve conducted workshops and rituals in Greece, based on the Eleusinian Mysteries, with Deena Metzger. He founded LA's Company and Provisional Theaters. He is a three-time LA Drama Critics Circle Award–winner. He is Director of Theatre at the University of La Verne in Southern California.

MICHAEL KECK's music has accompanied productions at Oregon Shakespeare Festival, Milwaukee Rep, Alliance Theatre, Indiana Rep, Seattle Rep, the Guthrie, Syracuse Stage, Arena Stage, Cincinnati Playhouse, and many others. His international music credits include the Market Theatre Johannesburg South Africa, National Theatre of Croatia–Zagreb, the Barbican Theatre Centre, and Bristol Old Vic. His acting credits include the McCarter Theatre, Berkeley Rep, Portland Center Stage, the Alliance Theatre, and various theaters in New York, where he currently resides. Temple University Press and Alta Mira Press have published excerpts from his solo performance piece *Voices in the Rain*. Michael received three Barrymore Award nominations for his work in Philadelphia. He is the recipient of the Theatre Bay Area TEC Design Excellence Award. He has served as a panelist for the National Endowment for the Arts, the New York State Council on the Arts, and Meet the Composer. He is a member of AEA, SAG-AFTRA, ASCAP, PEN and the Dramatists Guild. Michael composed music for, and performed in, *Ain't No Use in Going Home, Jodie's Got Your Gal and Gone* and *Junebug/Jack*. He composed the music for *Like Poison Ivy*.

ROADSIDE THEATER

In the rural mountains of Appalachia in 1975, a group of musicians and storytellers began experimenting with raucous versions of the centuries-old Jack tales they had grown up hearing. With no theatrical sets, costumes, or pretense of separation between the listener and the teller, performances were staged anywhere the actors hung their coats—in community centers, school rooms, church halls, and hunting clubs.

In 1977, the company took its newest play—a docudrama of two murders and the coming of its region's first coal boom—to Manhattan, where it received extensive national press. Roadside next wrote and toured a cycle of plays that presented a radically different version of Appalachia's history than the one published under the auspices of the absentee national and international energy corporations that continued to dominate the region's economic and political life. These dramas became the first collection of indigenous Appalachian plays and traveled across the country to forty-three states and Europe. In all, Roadside has created sixty plays, including a series of bilingual intercultural musicals with other national ensembles; dramas with traditional (folk) artists; and recently an experimental play with scores of historical reenactors.

Roadside is part of Appalshop, the award-winning multimedia arts and humanities institution which will turn fifty years old in 2020. Appalshop's staff and board of directors believe that the world is immeasurably enriched when people and their local cultures discover and tell their own stories and experience the stories of others.

DUDLEY COCKE is Roadside Theater's Artistic Director. He co-directed and co-authored the 2015 Off-Broadway Appalachian–

Puerto Rican musical *Betsy!* His essays about the role of art in a democracy have been widely published, and he is a recipient of the Heinz Award for Arts and Humanities.

DONNA PORTERFIELD is Roadside Theater's Managing Director. She has scripted three company plays and continues to be instrumental in the creation and teaching of the theater's community cultural-development residency model that enables communities to discover and perform their own stories.

RON SHORT is a playwright, composer and performer who grew up steeped in the Appalachian music and storytelling traditions of his family and community. He has scripted and composed music for fifteen Roadside musical plays and performed in all of the company's repertory.

PREGONES THEATER

In 1979, in Manhattan, a group of Puerto Rican artists wished to create a touring play that would take them into neighborhoods where most Puerto Ricans lived and worked. Out of this first production they created their ensemble and gave it a name: "Pregones," the Spanish word for "the chants of the street vendors." Today, Pregones Theater runs a 130-seat theater center in the South Bronx. To date it has produced more than sixty new plays and presented more than three hundred visiting artists from around the world. Pregones is home to a growing network of Latino actors, musicians, writers, directors, dancers and designers from diverse ethnic backgrounds. Pregones mines connections between theater and popular culture to create plays with a dynamic visual and musical character. The members of Pregones believe in developing lasting forms of audience participation among the least solvent communities.

In its first thirty-seven years, Pregones has performed and/ or worked in more than five hundred U.S. cities, thirty-seven states and eleven countries. Premieres include: *The Harlem Hellfighters on a Latin Beat, The Red Rose, Aloha Boricua, Game Over* and

Betsy! Though Pregones Theater is deeply rooted in its neighborhood in the South Bronx, the ensemble frequently partners with other communities, and has created partnerships and new works with other companies, such as Roadside Theater and Junebug Productions in the U.S., and with companies in Belgium and the Slovak Republic. Works resulting from these collaborations are: *Promise of a Love Song, Betsy!* and *Brides.*

In its institutional boldest move to date, Pregones has merged with Puerto Rican Traveling Theater, the Off-Broadway theater, founded by theater icon Miriam Colón in 1967, which is a leading force in the creation of a Latino theater scene in New York City. Working to deepen its impact as "Two Great Stages, One Great Theater," "Pregones + Puerto Rican Traveling Theater" continues to link art and community with a broad range of opportunities for its artists and its audience.

ROSALBA ROLÓN is Artistic Director of the merged Pregones Theater + Puerto Rican Traveling Theater, with venues in the Bronx and Manhattan. Rosalba co-founded Pregones in 1979. She is a performer, director and dramaturg. She favors the art of stage adaptations in an ensemble setting, collectively creating a broad range of original music-theater productions. Her credits include *The Red Rose, The Harlem Hellfighters on a Latin Beat, Hey Yo!* and *Dancing in My Cockroach Killers,* among others. Her collaborations include *Betsy!,* with Roadside Theater (KY), and *Brides,* with theaters in Belgium and the Slovak Republic. Rosalba received a 2015 TEER Pioneer Award by the National Black Theatre. She is a 2008 United States Artists Fellow. With Pregones, she has toured to more than five hundred cities in the U.S. and eighteen countries. Rosalba is a board member of both the National Association of Latino Arts and Cultures, and of United States Artists. She is a faculty member of both the Leadership Institutes of NALAC and ELI/Arts Presenters.

A TRAVELING JEWISH THEATRE

ATJT was founded in 1978 in Los Angeles by Corey Fischer, Albert Greenberg and Naomi Newman, who shared a desire to create works of theater from Jewish culture, history and imagination that would be accessible to audiences of all backgrounds. Until it closed in May 2012, ATJT created and presented scores of original works inspired by sources that ranged from the legends of the Hasidim to the reclamation of women's wisdom; from the role of storytelling in human experience to the politics of the Middle East; from the history of immigration to African-American/Jewish relations. ATJT searched for living images and narratives that celebrate our differences in ways that connect rather than separate people, and recognized that theater can be an instrument of healing for communities and cultures. ATJT toured throughout the U.S., Europe and the Middle East. It was recognized with awards from the Kennedy Center Fund for New American Plays, the Foundation for Jewish Culture and the National Endowment for the Arts. ATJT was one of a handful of founding members of the Network of Ensemble Theatres, the national support organization that has grown to include more than 160 member companies.

During its last ten years, ATJT created, among other projects, a collaboration with Israeli, Palestinian, American-Jewish and American-Egyptian performer/writers (*Blood Relative*); two modern adaptations of books from the Old Testament; a number of collaborations with the Word for Word Theatre Company; a reimagined *Death of a Salesman*; two solos by Newman; and an original play by Fischer, based on the history of The Group Theatre.

When the company realized that the changes in the nation's economy, which decimated support for the arts in the U.S., would make it impossible for ATJT to continue creating collaborative, ensemble theater, it chose to close rather than abandon its mission. Its company members: Fischer, Newman, Aaron Davidman and Sara Schwartz Geller all remain active theater makers.

NAOMI NEWMAN co-founded A Traveling Jewish Theatre in 1978. For more than three decades with ATJT, Naomi worked as director, playwright and performer, winning awards in each field. During that time, she developed four solo plays, an adaptation of the Biblical text Song of Songs and collaborated with Corey Fischer and Albert Greenberg on seven of ATJT's seminal works, including *Berlin, Jerusalem and the Moon*, published in TCG's *Ensemble Works: An Anthology*.

For her contributions to the cultural life in the Bay Area, Naomi has received a Tikkun Award, a Mill Valley Creative Achievement Award, and Theatre Bay Area's Community Leadership Award. A book containing an oral history of her life and career is now part of the Legacy Collection of The San Francisco Performing Arts Museum.

Although ATJT has closed its doors, Naomi remains active in the Bay Area as an individual theater artist. She continues to perform her solo, *Becoming Grace*, based on the writing of Grace Paley. Six of her short plays have been staged and, as dramaturg and director, she works with performer-writers on the development of new work.

Naomi's writing has appeared in: *Being Bodies*; *Callings*; *The Feminine Face of God*; *The Living Workplace*; *The Performer's Guide to the Collaborative Process*; *Uncoiling the Snake: Ancient Patterns in Contemporary Women's Lives*; *The Spiritual Art of Being Organized*; *Persimmon Tree Magazine* (online Spring 2008); *Exchanging Voices: A Collaborative Approach to Family Therapy* and *The Quotable Woman: The First 5000 Years*.